E-FINANCIAL STRATEGIES FOR SUSTAINABLE DEVELOPMENT

A Handbook for Promoting Financial Inclusion and Ending Poverty (SDG 1)

Electronic Commerce Management for Business

E-FINANCIAL STRATEGIES FOR SUSTAINABLE DEVELOPMENT

A Handbook for Promoting Financial Inclusion and Ending Poverty (SDG 1)

Ernesto D. R. Santibanez Gonzalez, PhD

Rajeev Sijariya, PhD

Vikas Garg, PhD

Editors

APPLE ACADEMIC PRESS

First edition published 2026

Apple Academic Press Inc.
1265 Goldenrod Circle, NE,
Palm Bay, FL 32905 USA

760 Laurentian Drive, Unit 19,
Burlington, ON L7N 0A4, Canada

CRC Press
2385 NW Executive Center Drive,
Suite 320, Boca Raton FL 33431

4 Park Square, Milton Park,
Abingdon, Oxon, OX14 4RN, UK

Library and Archives Canada Cataloguing in Publication

CIP data on file with Canada Library and Archives

Library of Congress Cataloging-in-Publication Data

CIP data on file with US Library of Congress

ISBN: 978-1-779640-94-9 (hbk)
ISBN: 978-1-779640-95-6 (ebk)
DOI: 10.1201/9781779640956

About the Book Series Electronic Commerce Management for Business

Editors-in-Chief:

Dr. Vikas Garg
Symbiosis Institute of Business Management, Noida,
Symbiosis International (Deemed University), Pune, India

Dr. Richa Goel
Symbiosis Centre for Management Studies, Noida,
Symbiosis International (Deemed University), Pune, India

Electronic trading, typically called e-commerce, involves procurement and distribution of electronic systems and other digital networks of goods or services. E-commerce stands for electronic commerce and concerns the electronic medium trade in goods and services. As the Internet grew, the volume of online trade has increased significantly. B2B, B2C, C2C, and related resources help to build online technology for future customer needs and markets. E-commerce has revolutionized industry, disrupted trade with the Internet, and created an e-commerce market for customers and enterprises through the electronic communications system.

The advances in internet and web-based technology have steadily eroded boundaries between traditional economies and the new online economy, including the amount of corporate money. The growth in e-commerce is enormous. Another explanation for this is the low cost of the PC and the rising use of the Internet. The corporate community is rapidly conscious of the possibilities provided by e-commerce.

This series mainly aims to discuss the role of e-commerce in today's business. It further highlights some critical issues in e-commerce, suggestions, and future strategies for e-commerce in years to come.

Topics of Books in the Series:

The primary endeavor of this series is to introduce and explore contemporary research developments in a variety of rapidly growing research areas. The volumes will deal with the following topics but not limited to:

- E-Business and Mobile Commerce
- Big Data Analytics
- Business and Data Analytics
- Implications of Technological Disruption
- Technology and the War for Talent
- Impact of New Technologies on Business
- Artificial Intelligence and Its Impact on Business
- Managing Global Competitiveness Using Technology
- Impact of New Technology on Global Labor Markets
- Blockchain in International Business
- IoT and Smart Cities
- IoT Strategies and Business models
- Industrial Internet of Things (IoT)
- AR (Augmented Reality) in Product Design and Manufacturing
- AR (Augmented Reality) and Training
- Use of AR (Augmented Reality) in Sales and Marketing
- Smart Manufacturing
- Cryptocurrency
- Strategies of Emerging Countries in the Era of New Technology
- The Roadmap to Thriving in the New Skills Economy
- Future of Mobile Apps
- Social Media – A Powerful Tool
- Big Data Powers Organizations
- Integration of Technology in HR Practices
- Skillset for Industry 4.0
- Managing Virtual Teams and Environments for Innovation
- Innovation in Business
- Effects of Shifts in Globalization on Emerging Economies
- Smart Global Supply Chain Management
- Corporate Governance in the New Global Technology-Driven Economy
- Business Intelligence Tools & Applications
- Cyber Defense & Information Technology
- Cloud Computing
- Data & Intelligent System Modelling
- Digital Marketing & Internet Marketing
- Smart Connected Products
- Impact of Technology on Financial Decisions
- Finance and Risk Management for Using New Technology

- Digital Transformation and Financial Services
- Banking services in the digital era
- Virtual Reality
- Robotics and Its Use in Business
- Industry 4.0 and Labor Issues

The series aims to serve as a valuable resource for researchers, academicians, and industry professionals and undergraduate, postgraduate, doctoral students in electronic commerce, Internet marketing, business innovation, digitization, technology in product design, management, and more.

Features of the volumes under this series will explore recent trends, model extensions, developments, solutions to real-time problems, and case studies.

BOOKS IN THE SERIES

Applications of Artificial Intelligence in Business and Finance 5.0
Editors: Richa Goel, PhD, Vikas Garg, PhD, and Michela Floris, PhD

Blockchain Technology: Unlocking the Value of 3Ts in Business World
Editors: Richa Chauhan, PhD, and Vidhi Kaul, PhD

Entrepreneurship and Sustainable Business Development
Editors: Ruchi Khandelwal, PhD, Deepa Kapoor, PhD, Nidhi Gupta, PhD, and Neha Gupta, PhD

The Role of Smart Technology and Industry 4.0 in Shaping Smart Cities
Editors: Vinay Kandpal, PhD, Manoj Kumar Nallapaneni, PhD, and Deep Chandra, PhD

Fintech and Blockchain Technology in Financial Markets
Editors: Neha Puri, PhD, Anjali Munde, PhD, and Emilia Alayerdov, PhD

E-Financial Strategies for Sustainable Development: A Handbook for Promoting Financial Inclusion and Ending Poverty (SDG 1)
Editors: Ernesto D. R. Santibanez Gonzalez, PhD, Rajeev Sijaria, PhD, and Vikas Garg, PhD

Green Finance and Sustainable Development Goals
Editors: Vikas Garg, PhD, Krishnendu Ghosh, PhD, and Ronita Ram, PhD

Industry 5.0: Innovation and Adoption for Sustainability
Editors: Tilottama Singh, PhD, Pradeep Suri , PhD, and
Zulkarin Jahangir, PhD

Global Sustainable Development: Integration of Digital and Human-Centric Pathways
Editors: Kavita Indapurkar, PhD, Neeru Sidana, PhD, and
Iqbal Thonse Hawaldar, PhD

About the Editors

Ernesto D. R. Santibanez Gonzalez, PhD
Professor and Executive Director CES 4.0, Faculty of Engineering, University of Talca, Chile and Research Professsor, ViceRectoria de Investigaciòn e Innovaciòn, University Arturo Prat, Chile.

Ernesto D. R. Santibanez Gonzalez, PhD, is currently, supervising and co-supervising graduate students in Brazil, Chile, and China. He leads the Circular Economy and Sustainability 4.0 Initiative (CES4.0), is a member of the Board of Directors (Counsellor) – National Forestry Society of Chile (SNF), and has developed more than 80 research, innovation, and consulting projects providing solutions to real problems in different countries around the world in industrial sectors such as energy, retail, mining, agri-food, forestry, logistics, and oil and gas. During the last five years, he has published more than 50 papers in top-tier journals. He has held visiting appointments at several universities in Brazil, China, and the United Kingdom—the most recent, before the COVID-19 pandemic, was at the London Business School.

His passion is to address and solve problems at the interface of climate change and sustainability that arise in many different fields, such as supply chain, energy efficiency, low-carbon economy, carbon capture and storage, smart city, smart manufacturing, sustainable and resilient supply chain, and sustainable operations management. The current research of Dr. Santibañez-Gonzalez is characterized by integrating mathematical models, big data, blockchain, and internet technology to understand, model, and provide practical solutions to companies and organizations that need to address climate change and sustainability problems. His experience in industrial engineering, operations management, and operations research, combined with a PhD in Production Engineering from the Federal University of Rio de Janeiro (UFRJ) in a joint program with the London School of Economics and Political Science (LSE), gives him a strong understanding of how to integrate information technology with quantitative methods to solve real-life problems.

He served as Associate Editor (AE) of Journal of Cleaner Production (Elsevier), Journal of Intelligent Manufacturing (Springer), and serving as AE for Modern Supply Chain Research and Applications (Emerald, new journal), International Journal of Big Data Mining for Global Warming, and Heliyon Business and Economics (Elsevier). He is also Editor-in-Chief of *Sustainable Operations and Computers*, a new journal sponsored by the Chinese Academy of Sciences and Elsevier. He has been the Managing Guest Editor of several special issues in top-tier journals, including *European Journal of Operational Research, Journal of Cleaner Production, International Journal of Production Research, Sustainability,* and Guest Editor for special issues in journals such as *International Journal of Production Economics, Computers and Industrial Engineering, and Science of the Total Environment.* He has also served as Regional Editor for the *International Journal of Physical Distribution and Logistics Management* (Emerald).

Rajeev Sijariya, PhD

Former Dean and Professor, Atal Bihari Vajpayee School of Management and Entrepreneurship, Jawaharlal Nehru University (JNU), India

Rajeev Sijariya, PhD, is currently associated with Jawaharlal Nehru University (JNU) as a Professor at the Atal Bihari Vajpayee School of Management and Entrepreneurship (ABVSME), India, where he also serves as the International Students Advisor. Earlier, he was Chairperson of the Special Centre for E-Learning (SCEL). He has vast teaching and corporate experience spanning over 24 years. He was nominated by the President of India to the National Institutes of Technology, the Indian Institute of Engineering Science and Technology, and Banaras Hindu University, Varanasi. He has received various awards and project grants, guided many PhD students, and published numerous research papers. He is an author, researcher, academician, thinker, motivator, orator, corporate trainer, and social activist. He holds an MSc (Physics–Electronics), MBA, and PhD in Management.

Vikas Garg, PhD
Associate Professor, Symbiosis Institute of Business Management, Noida, Symbiosis International (Deemed University), Pune, India

Vikas Garg, PhD, is an Associate Professor of Management at the Symbiosis Institute of Business Management, Noida, Symbiosis International (Deemed University), Pune, India. He has more than 20 years of experience, with over 10 PhD scholars under his guidance. He has published numerous research papers in various Scopus- and ABDC-indexed international and national journals. He is currently serving as Associate Editor of the *Journal of Sustainable Finance and Investment* (indexed in WoS and Scopus). He is also the Book Series Editor with Taylor & Francis for three book series: *Technology Innovations: Strategies for Business Sustainability and Growth; Emerging Trends in Technology in Management and Commerce; and Electronic Commerce Management for Business.* He has been actively working on new innovative ideas in the fields of patents and copyrights. He has served as the lead organizer for various international conferences, workshops, and case study competitions, including those affiliated with IEEE. He has received several national and international awards for his contributions as an academician, researcher, and employee.

Contents

Contributors

Tri Dev Acharya
University of North Dakota, United States

Mumtaz Alam
Fiji National University, Raipur, Chhattisgarh, India

Naushad Alam
Dhofar University, Salalah, Oman

Rashi Baliyan
Noida International University, Greater Noida, Uttar Pradesh, India

Deepak Deshmukh
Star Union Dai-Ichi Life Insurance, Mumbai, Maharashtra, India

Shikha Dubey
VBS Purvanchal University, Jaunpur, Uttar Pradesh, India

Ajay Dwivedi
Department of Financial Studies, VBS Purvanchal University, Jaunpur, India

Gayathri
Vivekanand Mahavidyalaya, Raipur, Chhattisgarh, India

Nidhi Goenka
Kalinga University, Raipur, Chhattisgarh, India

Tanishka Gupta
Jagannath International Management School (JIMS), Vasant Kunj, New Delhi, India

Mohsina Hayat
Bachelor of Management Studies, School of Commerce, Jain University, Bangalore, Karnataka, India

Chhavi Jain
Sharda University, Greater Noida, Uttar Pradesh, India

Sunaina Kanojia
Department of Commerce, Faculty of Commerce and Business, Delhi School of Economics, University of Delhi, Delhi, India

Shashi Kant
Department of Management, College of Business and Economics, Bule Hora University, Bule Hora, Oromia Region, Ethiopia

Pooja Kaushik
Galgotias College of Engineering and Technology, Greater Noida, Uttar Pradesh, India

Ruby Khan
Department of Accounting and Finance, College of Business, Jazan University, Jazan, Jazan Province, Kingdom of Saudi Arabia

Anmol Khatri
Alumnus, Prestige Institute of Management and Research, Gwalior, Madhya Pradesh, India

Santosh Kumar
Sharda University, Greater Noida, Uttar Pradesh, India

Sachin Mishra
PNB JEWRI MEERUT, Meerut, India

Navita Nathani
Amity Business School, Amity University, Madhya Pradesh, India

Pushpa Negi
Department of Finance, New Delhi Institute of Management, New Delhi, India

Vaishali Patil
Department of Finance, Prin. L. N. Welingkar Institute of Management Development and Research (PGDM), Mumbai, Maharashtra, India

Bijayananda Patnaik
National Institute of Technology (NIT) Raipur, Chhattisgarh, India

Deepti Patnaik
Kalinga University, Naya Raipur, Chhattisgarh, India

Mrinal Phalle
Department of Finance, Prin. L. N. Welingkar Institute of Management Development and Research (PGDM), Mumbai, Maharashtra, India

Neha Puri
Amity College of Commerce and Finance (ACCF), Amity University, Noida, Uttar Pradesh, India

Kiran Rohira
Department of Management, Prestige Institute of Management and Research, Gwalior, Madhya Pradesh, India

Swami Prasad Saxena
Department of Applied Business Economics, Dayalbagh Educational Institute (Deemed to be University), Dayalbagh, Agra, Uttar Pradesh, India

Rajeev Sijariya
Atal Bihari Vajpayee School of Management and Entrepreneurship (ABVSME), Jawaharlal Nehru University, New Delhi, India

Amandeep Singh
Sri Guru Tegh Bahadur Khalsa College, University of Delhi, Delhi, India

Amit Kumar Singh
Department of Commerce, Faculty of Commerce and Business, Delhi School of Economics, University of Delhi, Delhi, India

Sonam Singh
Department of Applied Business Economics, Dayalbagh Educational Institute (Deemed to be University), Dayalbagh, Agra, Uttar Pradesh, India

Yashi Singh
Department of Financial Studies, VBS Purvanchal University, Jaunpur, India

Raj Kumar Teotia
H. R. Institute of Science and Technology, Ghaziabad, Uttar Pradesh, India

Seema Tewari
School of Law, Delhi NCR Campus, Christ University, Ghaziabad, Uttar Pradesh, India

Shobhit Wadhwa
F. C. Manning School of Business, Acadia University, Wolfville, Nova Scotia, Canada

Bhavna Yadav
Department of Applied Business Economics,
Dayalbagh Educational Institute (Deemed to be University), Dayalbagh, Agra, Uttar Pradesh, India

Om Prakash Yadav
School of Business Management, Noida International University, Greater Noida, Uttar Pradesh, India

Abbreviations

AI	artificial intelligence
APT	Arbitrage Pricing Theory
CSR	Corporate Social Responsibility
DeFi	decentralized finance
DFI	digital financial inclusion
ESG	environmental, social, and governance
EUR/USD	Euro versus US Dollar
FA	financial attitude
FAW	financial awareness
FK	financial knowledge
FL	financial literacy
FS	financial socialization
IEA	International Energy Agency
ISM	interpretive structural modeling
LP	level partitioning
MFI	microfinance institution
MFO	microfinance finance organization
ML	machine learning
NFT	non-fungible token
NLP	natural language processing
RBI	Reserve Bank of India
RBV	resource-based view
SDG	Sustainable Development Goals
SHG	self-help group
SLR	systematic literature review
SSIM	structural self-interaction matrix

Acknowledgments

First and foremost, we express our profound gratitude to Almighty God. Throughout the creation of this book, we have been reminded of the divine gift of writing bestowed upon us. Your guidance and our faith in You empowered us to pursue our passion and realize our dreams. We extend our heartfelt thanks to our family members for their unwavering support during the demanding journey of completing this book. Their steadfast encouragement has been a cornerstone for us.

The editors wish to acknowledge the invaluable contributions of all individuals involved in this project, particularly the authors and reviewers who played a critical role in the review process. Without their dedication, this book would not have come to fruition. We are deeply grateful to each author for their contributions and to the chapter authors for their expertise and time. Additionally, we appreciate the reviewers' significant efforts to enhance the quality, coherence, and presentation of the chapters. Many of the authors also served as referees, and we highly value their dual roles.

We owe a tremendous debt of gratitude to those who provided detailed and constructive feedback on various chapters, prompting us to clarify concepts, delve deeper into insightful work, and elucidate the rationales behind specific recommendations. Our thanks also go to the many individuals who have guided us in mastering both the art and science of networking over the years.

—Editors

Foreword

E-financial strategies refer to the use of digital financial tools and technologies to promote financial inclusion and eradicate poverty. These strategies leverage advancements in technology, particularly the internet and mobile devices, to provide affordable and accessible financial services to underserved and marginalized populations.

Financial inclusion is a key component of the Sustainable Development Goals (SDGs) established by the United Nations, specifically SDG 1: No Poverty. SDG 1 aims to end poverty in all its forms by 2030, including eradicating extreme poverty, reducing the proportion of people living in poverty, and implementing social protection systems for the vulnerable.

E-financial strategies play a vital role in achieving SDG 1 by addressing the barriers that prevent individuals and communities from accessing formal financial services. Lack of access to financial services—such as bank accounts, credit, insurance, and savings—can perpetuate poverty by limiting economic opportunities and financial security. By leveraging digital technologies, e-financial strategies aim to overcome these barriers and empower individuals and communities to participate in the formal financial system.

Academics, students, professionals, and individuals across various fields can enhance and broaden their knowledge through the basic trends and activities presented in this book. It serves as a valuable guide both intellectual and practical work, emphasizing the need to rethink and assess the future implications of innovation management. I am delighted to write this foreword, as the editors have dedicated considerable effort to delivering an excellent solution and innovation. Each chapter in this book was chosen based on a rigorous peer review process conducted by experts in the field.

Preface

In an era characterized by rapid technological advancements and evolving financial landscapes, the pursuit of sustainable development has taken on a new dimension. The global community is increasingly recognizing the pivotal role of financial inclusion in eradicating poverty and fostering economic growth. The United Nations' Sustainable Development Goal 1 (SDG 1)—to end poverty in all its forms everywhere—serves as a clarion call for innovative solutions that can bridge the gap between the marginalized and the mainstream economy.

This book, *E-Financial Strategies for Sustainable Development: A Handbook for Promoting Financial Inclusion and Ending Poverty (SDG 1)*, aims to be a comprehensive guide for policymakers, financial institutions, development practitioners, and stakeholders who are committed to leveraging electronic financial strategies to achieve sustainable development. It explores the intersection of technology and finance, offering insights into how digital tools can be harnessed to promote financial inclusion and drive poverty alleviation efforts.

The journey of financial inclusion is multifaceted, involving the integration of digital payment systems, mobile banking, FinTech innovations, and inclusive financial policies. Each chapter of this book delves into these components, providing a thorough analysis of their potential to transform the economic landscape. From the implementation of mobile money services in remote areas to the creation of digital credit platforms that cater to the underserved, the strategies discussed herein are both practical and scalable.

A significant portion of this handbook is dedicated to case studies and best practices from around the world. These examples not only highlight success stories but also the challenges encountered along the way, offering valuable lessons for replication and adaptation in different contexts. By presenting a global perspective, this book underscores the universality of the need for financial inclusion while acknowledging the uniqueness of regional challenges.

The importance of collaboration and partnership is a recurring theme throughout this book. Achieving SDG 1 requires concerted efforts from governments, the private sector, non-governmental organizations, and international bodies. This handbook serves as a call to action, encouraging all stakeholders to work together in creating an inclusive financial ecosystem that leaves no one behind.

We are at a critical juncture where technology can be a powerful enabler of social change. However, the digital divide remains a significant barrier to inclusive growth. This book addresses these concerns by proposing strategies that not only leverage technology but also ensure its accessibility to the most vulnerable populations.

As you embark on this exploration of e-financial strategies, we hope you find the insights and recommendations within these pages both enlightening and actionable. Let this handbook be a catalyst for your efforts in promoting financial inclusion and making strides toward ending poverty. Together, we can turn the promise of digital finance into a reality for all.

Chapter 1 explores the money provided by public, commercial, and international organizations to assist programs and projects targeted at reducing the effects of climate change and preparing for its impact, which is referred to as "climate finance." Like many other countries, India is dealing with various climate-related complications, such as increasing temperatures, shifting weather patterns, water shortages, and heightened risks from these challenges. India requires climate financing to support its efforts to mitigate these problems and adapt to them. The current study examines the relative predominance of climate finance barriers using the ISM approach integrated with FMICMAC.

Chapter 2 emphasizes the importance of continued development in both AI and sustainability to address the complex challenges facing the investment community. A call to action is presented for stakeholders in the investment community to embrace the opportunities provided by AI and sustainability, collaborate on industry standards and best practices, and prioritize diversity, equity, and inclusion in AI development and implementation. Overall, smart sustainability offers a transformative approach to investment monitoring, aligning financial objectives with environmental and social goals to create a more sustainable and inclusive future.

Chapter 3 explores the emergence of the digital financial revolution, marking a pivotal moment in global economics, transcending conventional banking norms to empower individuals and communities through cutting-edge e-financial strategies. This study delves into the transformative capabilities of digital financial tools, emphasizing their role in fostering inclusivity and economic empowerment. Leveraging the pervasive reach of digital connectivity, e-financial strategies redefine financial interactions, presenting accessible solutions that surpass geographical limitations. At its essence, this revolution addresses the pressing issue of financial exclusion by extending services to unbanked and underbanked populations, thus fueling economic progress and disrupting the cycle of poverty.

Chapter 4 establishes the relationship between green initiatives and climate change, with a mediating variable identified as carbon drifts/carbon trading. The components of green initiatives for the purposes of this research include green financing, legislative frameworks, capacity building, awareness, and innovative tools. The study is based on a survey method in which 200 respondents were interviewed regarding their perceived awareness and knowledge about financial instruments and how their investments can affect climate change. The findings revealed that only awareness and climate change share a significant relationship with carbon drift as a mediating variable, while the remaining independent variables either have no significant impact or have a negative impact on climate change.

Chapter 5 explores the dynamic convergence of technology and financial inclusion. Technological advancements have become increasingly important in tackling the persistent issue of delivering financial services to underserved populations. This chapter examines how technological innovations—including digital payment platforms, mobile banking, blockchain, and FinTech solutions—have transformed financial access for underprivileged individuals. By conducting a thorough assessment of case studies and analyses, this study clarifies how new technologies are breaking down barriers, empowering individuals and enterprises, and promoting economic inclusion. Furthermore, the chapter examines the consequences of these changes and emphasizes the significance of ensuring that technological progress in financial services is fair, comprehensive, and enduring.

Chapter 6 explores the transformative potential of e-financial strategies in empowering women entrepreneurship in India. As digital technologies continue to reshape the business landscape, this review investigates the specific ways in which electronic financial tools and platforms can address challenges faced by women entrepreneurs—fostering financial inclusion, enhancing access to capital, and promoting economic independence. By synthesizing existing literature and case studies, the article provides a comprehensive overview of the current state of e-financial strategies in

India and their impact on women-led businesses. The findings underscore the importance of tailoring e-financial solutions to address gender-specific barriers and highlight the need for policy interventions and collaborative efforts from various stakeholders to create an enabling environment for women entrepreneurs to thrive.

Chapter 7 explores how microfinance has become a powerful instrument for eradicating poverty. Because microfinance is a dynamic field with no one-size-fits-all solution, many delivery strategies have developed over time. This study examines the growth of microfinance programs and the challenges faced by microfinance providers in applying e-financial techniques in rural areas. The development of microfinance has also been hampered by factors such as low financial literacy and a lack of digital infrastructure for related services and products. This study concludes that, in order to enable the sustainable expansion of microfinance for financial inclusion, microfinance providers should prioritize improving digital financial literacy among their clientele.

Chapter 8 explores how financial literacy plays a crucial role in shaping individuals' financial behavior and overall financial well-being. This article aims to measure the level of financial literacy—including digital financial literacy—and the financial behavior of people. The study employed a mixed-methods approach, combining published data with information collected through a survey of individuals. The analysis of information gathered on respondents' attitudes, perceptions, and knowledge related to financial issues provides mixed results, clearly indicating a lack of financial literacy among the population. The study proposes a framework to promote financial literacy and financial inclusion in India and offers a roadmap for future research in the field.

Chapter 9 aims to identify the optimal level of investment by analyzing the risk–return trade-off in diverse markets. It explores the intricacies of financial systems, highlighting the unique characteristics of each market and their implications for portfolio management. The chapter discusses the significance of artificial intelligence (AI) tools in navigating complex markets. By processing large volumes of data and recognizing patterns, AI tools can greatly improve decision-making in portfolio management. They offer predictive insights, automate routine tasks, and enhance risk management. This chapter utilizes AI tools in conjunction with conventional quantitative techniques and financial models to determine the most advantageous investment strategy. It considers variables such as market volatility, diversification benefits, and investor risk tolerance. The chapter offers valuable perspectives for investors aiming to optimize returns while mitigating risk in today's intricate and dynamic financial environment.

Chapter 10 explores the act of saving, a vital aspect of personal finance, which allows individuals to allocate income for future necessities such as consumption, investment, or emergencies. The process of saving can be particularly daunting for young adults transitioning from adolescence to adulthood. This study investigates the complex relationship between various factors and saving behavior among Indian university students, who encounter unique financial challenges amid India's rapid socioeconomic changes. The paper begins with a literature review, followed by an in-depth methodology section, then presents the results, discusses them, and concludes with recommendations. This research significantly contributes to our understanding of saving behavior among Indian university students and suggests strategies to boost financial literacy—ultimately paving the way for a more financially secure future for this demographic.

Chapter 11 explores green bonds, which are certificates of indebtedness that allocate funds to investments in sustainable development, infrastructure, energy-saving devices, and conservation efforts. Since their inception in the early 2000s, the market has experienced exponential growth, driven by governments, multilateral institutions, corporations, and financial intermediaries. Governments create enabling environments through policy frameworks and regulatory incentives, while multilateral institutions provide technical assistance and certification standards. Corporations fund sustainability initiatives that align with corporate social responsibility objectives, while financial intermediaries facilitate the issuance and distribution of sustainable instruments. Green bonds can convert investments into eco-friendly endeavors, fostering a low-carbon, resilient, and inclusive economy by reducing carbon emissions.

Chapter 12 explores the field of "financial literacy and SDGs." Research has advanced significantly as countries place greater emphasis on financial education and skill development. This study provides an overview of existing research, trends, and future directions. The efficacy of financial literacy, its impact on economic growth, and its ability to promote sustainable practices have been widely studied. Prospective areas of research include advancing financial competencies and evaluating their influence on income distribution, assessing international cooperation initiatives, promoting environmentally friendly technologies, and designating green tax proceeds for environmental efforts. The continually expanding body of research offers critical guidance for decision-makers committed to enhancing financial literacy and achieving the Sustainable Development Goals (SDGs).

Chapter 13 explores that there has been considerable debate over whether new-age FinTech can replace traditional banking. This study unearths the intellectual structure of research in the domain of artificial intelligence (AI) and its role in shaping the future of FinTech and banking worldwide. Furthermore, it attempts to identify imminent research gaps in the literature, highlighting the risks and challenges associated with using AI in FinTech and banking. The literature assessing the use of artificial intelligence in the finance sector remains both limited and narrow in scope. The findings suggest that FinTech has significantly transformed the delivery of financial services, enabling banks to innovate, invest in technology, and adopt a customer-centric strategy. Future research is needed to quantify the risks associated with AI and machine learning (ML) in relation to data security and privacy, unemployment, ethical concerns, regulatory risks, and threats to financial stability.

Chapter 14 examines strategies for improving financial literacy to empower marginalized and vulnerable groups in achieving financial inclusion and reducing poverty. Financial education and services are often inaccessible to these populations, despite the fact that financial literacy is essential for individuals to successfully navigate complex financial systems. A number of strategies are discussed to address these issues, including targeted educational campaigns, innovative technologies, and community-based initiatives. The chapter emphasizes the importance of inclusion and culturally sensitive approaches that consider the specific needs and contexts of different communities. It also highlights the role of financial institutions, nonprofit organizations, and government policies in fostering an environment that supports financial inclusion and empowerment. The role of technology in financial inclusion, along with the challenges and opportunities associated with digital literacy, is also highlighted.

CHAPTER 1

Unraveling the Complex Web of Climate Finance Barriers in India: An Integrated ISM and Fuzzy MICMAC Analysis

SHIKHA DUBEY,[1,*] YASHI SINGH,[1] AJAY DWIVEDI,[2] SACHIN MISHRA,[3] and TRI DEV ACHARYA[4]

[1]*VBS Purvanchal University, Jaunpur, Uttar Pradesh, India*

[2]*Department of Financial Studies, VBS Purvanchal University, Jaunpur, India*

[3]*PNB JEWRI MEERUT, Meerut, India*

[4]*University of North Dakota, United States*

*Corresponding author

ABSTRACT

Climate finance refers to the funding provided by public, commercial, and international bodies to support programs and projects aimed at mitigating the impacts of climate change and enhancing adaptation measures. In India, a country grappling with intensifying heatwaves, unpredictable weather, water scarcity, and other climate-related challenges, climate finance plays a crucial role in enabling mitigation and preparedness efforts. This study investigates the relative significance of barriers to climate finance using the Interpretive Structural Modeling (ISM) approach integrated with FMICMAC analysis. The findings highlight that the absence of long-term funding is the most critical barrier to accessing climate finance in India,

E-Financial Strategies for Sustainable Development: A Handbook for Promoting Financial Inclusion and Ending Poverty (SDG 1). Ernesto D. R. Santibanez Gonzalez, Rajeev Sijariya, and Vikas Garg (Eds.)

DOI: 10.1201/9781779640956-1

whereas high transaction costs are comparatively less significant. These insights emphasize the importance of understanding the financial requirements of developing nations and the strategic mobilization of financial resources. They also serve as a foundation for future research into the climate finance ecosystem and related governance mechanisms.

1.1 INTRODUCTION

The most dramatic and strange problem our generation faces right now is climate change. Suppose the current rate of 0.2°C per decade continues! The Earth will warm up by 15°C by 2050! According to the Special Report of the Intergovernmental Panel on Climate Change, as compared with pre-industrial times, the Earth has heated up by 1.0°C (IPCC, 2018). In their report, the IPCC notes that a request was made in 2018 by the UNFCCC Parties for a special exploration into the implications of 1.5°C global warming over pre-industrial levels and associated global greenhouse gas emissions. This proposal was introduced in response to the convening of the UN Framework Convention on Climate Change's 21st Conference of Parties endorsing the Paris Agreement. Part II of the UNFCCC is also included. Well-known scholars and authorities on climate change have declared a climate emergency on Earth and suggested immediate action (Lenton, 2020).

"Climate finance" describes the funds raised locally, nationally, or internationally from public, private, and alternative financing sources to support adaptation and mitigation projects aimed at addressing climate change. This acknowledges the wide variations in the amount of climate change that each country contributes to and the level of preparedness for halting it and lessening its impacts. As significant investments are necessary to notably reduce emissions, climate funding is essential for mitigation. Due to the substantial financial resources they require, climate financing is just as important for adaptation as it is for mitigating the negative outcomes and adapting to a changing climate.

The UNFCCC Standing Committee on Finance offers the most formal definition of climate financing currently in use. The goals of climate finance are to decrease greenhouse gas emissions, enhance greenhouse gas relief, and minimize the vulnerability of biological and human systems to the adverse impacts of climate change. According to this definition, climate funding is the flow of money to any projects, strategies, or programs that strive to address climate change on a global scale, across all economic sectors, for both adaptation and mitigation.

According to some estimates, between rich and developing nations, holdings as vast as USD 359 billion could be mobilized each year to help combat climate change (Buchner et al., 2013). According to Jianchun Fang (2019), the bulk of the prevailing economy, climate change, and natural disasters negatively impact the economy. Based on a quantitative exploration of the impact of natural disasters on economic growth in these regions, Ethiopia, Malawi, Central America, and the Caribbean could experience a 1% GDP loss due to droughts and floods (Ali, 2014). It is suggested that the global economy could lose up to 5% of its value entirely due to climate change if nothing is done.

Extreme weather events like droughts and floods are believed to have the potential to reduce poverty in areas with low food security, diminish assets, cause asset depreciation, and slow down the pace of economic growth. It is proposed that developing countries are the only ones where disasters negatively impact economic growth (Mafira, 2023). Only in developing countries does a 1°C rise in annual temperature result in a 1.4% drop in per capita GDP. It is argued that natural disasters have little impact on GDP per capita, even though they result in significant welfare losses (Urfi Khan, 2012). Investigating the impacts of natural disasters on G20 countries advances the study of climate change, the scope and consequences of natural disasters, and natural capital as the foundation of sustainable development. Additionally, this research provides insightful information regarding how nations might utilize natural capital to promote long-term sustainable development.

Sustainable finance is more expensive than conventional financial products, financing climate ventures is still perceived as risky, and expertise is scarce in this field (Mafira, 2023). The G20 Sustainable Finance Working Group is considering multiple resolutions to tackle these long-standing challenges. There is also talk about bridging the climate finance gap and expanding mixed finance. Put into operation digital technology, draft statutes with incentives, and build gap-derisking establishments to keep transaction expenses low (Mafira, 2023).

In the year 2012, the International Energy Agency (IEA) approximated an 80% chance of meeting the 2°C aim if non-energy CO_2 emissions and other GHGs were also reduced. This suggests a total of USD 140 trillion in investments would be needed by all rich and developing nations by the year 2050 (IEA, 2012). According to the research, poor nations will have to provide between USD 140 and USD 300 billion in 2030 and between USD 280 and USD 500 billion yearly by 2050 for adaptation, based on various emission scenarios. This is because the money needed for adaptation is reliant on the speed and efficiency of global mitigation efforts.

1.2 RESEARCH METHODOLOGY

The current study makes use of secondary data sources, identifies barriers to climate finance access in India through a review of the literature, and uses the ISM methodology with integrated FMICMAC to examine the barriers in climate finance accessibility in India that were identified as well as illustrated in the investigation's flowchart.

1.3 BARRIERS TO CLIMATE FINANCE ACCESSIBILITY IN INDIA

Accessing climate funding can be difficult due to many hurdles that prevent cash from flowing to projects and activities focused on mitigating and adapting to climate change (Panda, 2016). The following are some of the primary challenges that the literature review identified:

1.3.1 LOW ACCESS TO FINANCE

Many organizations, especially in developing nations, encounter difficulties in obtaining climate finance because of a lack of financial resources and their inability to satisfy the demanding criteria set forth by funding institutions.

1.3.2 HIGH RISK PERCEPTION

Due to the uncertainty surrounding the effects of climate change and the long-term nature of such projects (Dennis Tirpak, 2014), climate-related projects are frequently viewed as high-risk investments. This impression may put off prospective investors (Panda, 2016).

1.3.3 INSUFFICIENT PROJECT READINESS

Climate-related projects may not have the requisite planning, technical capability, or documentation to meet the funding agencies' requirements, which makes them unattractive to investors (Ghosal, 2021; Ravi, 2018).

1.3.4 HIGH TRANSACTION COSTS

Particularly for smaller projects or organizations, the expenses involved with applying for, negotiating, and disbursing climate money can be substantial. Potential beneficiaries may be put off by these expenses (Ghosal, 2021).

1.3.5 SHORTAGE OF LOCAL EXPERTISE

Local knowledge in managing sustainable projects and climate finance is lacking in many areas (Chandni Singh, 2021). The creation and execution of initiatives qualified for climate finance may be hampered by this lack (Soeder, 2020).

1.3.6 A MISMATCH BETWEEN INVESTMENT AND NEEDS

An area or community's unique requirements and objectives may not always be met by climate finance, resulting in an ineffective distribution of resources (Dennis Tirpak, 2014).

1.3.7 LACK OF TRANSPARENCY AND ACCOUNTABILITY

Issues with transparency in the distribution and application of climate funding may cause stakeholders to lose faith in one another. Accountability issues can result in poor management and financial abuse (Dennis Tirpak, 2014; Vanderheiden, 2015).

1.3.8 USE OF FOSSIL FUELS

It's possible that some initiatives and sectors will continue to heavily rely on fossil fuels, which fuel climate change (Nico Bauer, 2016). By supporting initiatives that maintain this reliance, climate finance objectives may be compromised (Soeder, 2020).

1.3.9 LACK OF LONG-TERM FUNDING

Long-term solutions are needed to combat climate change, yet money for such initiatives frequently comes in short funding cycles. Over time, this may impede the growth and sustainability of climate initiatives (Schalatek, 2012).

For the efficient mobilization of climate financing and the achievement of global climate targets, these obstacles must be removed (Urfi Khan, 2012). These issues can be resolved, and the funding flow for climate-related programs facilitated by strategies like capacity building, risk mitigation techniques, better project planning, and increased transparency (Ali, 2014).

1.4 INTERPRETIVE STRUCTURAL MODELING (ISM): OVERVIEW

The lack of long-term funding, low access to financing, high risk perception, inadequate project readiness, lack of local expertise, mismatch between investment and needs, lack of transparency and accountability, use of fossil fuels, and high transaction costs are just a few of the challenges associated with climate finance.

As such, it becomes imperative to employ any instrument that could aid in comprehending and addressing these difficulties (Shankar Chandramowli, 2011). ISM offers a clear view of the system and the components that researchers are examining, as well as an organized, directed framework for difficult problems (Nagendra Sohani, 2012). Basically, ISM is the systematic application of graph theory, which was first proposed by Warfield and briefly reviewed by Malone (Anukul Mandal, 1994). ISM's many appealing qualities make it appropriate for use in the current study, which will be covered in the following manner (Figure 1.1).

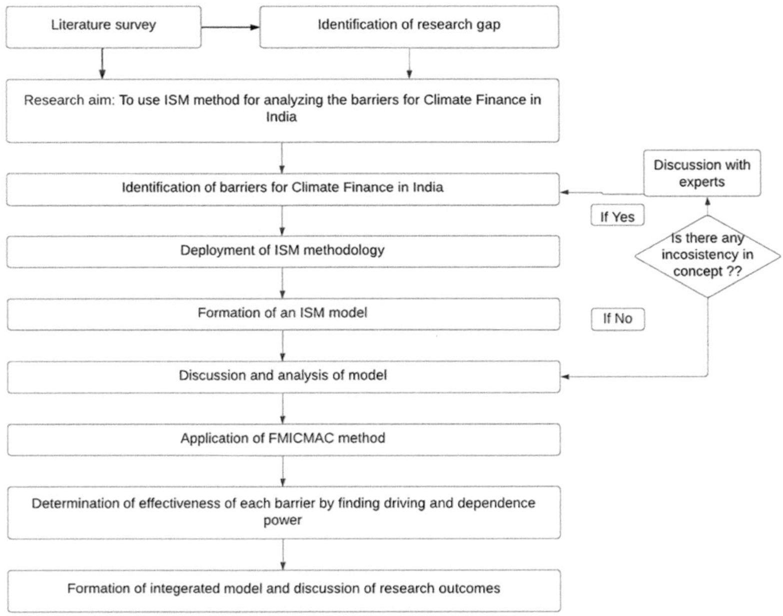

FIGURE 1.1 Flowchart of proposed research work.

- By utilizing the knowledge and real-world experience of experts, it deconstructs a complicated system into a number of simpler parts and produces an understandable model. (Sanjay Kumar, 13).
- This approach allows orders to be enforced on complicated elements (Anukul Mandal, 1994).
- The ISM technique has also been employed by researchers and deputed organizations from a variety of fields, including the National Aeronautics and Space Administration (NASA), to find solutions to complicated problems (Ali, 2014; Sanjay Kumar, 13).
- Transitive interactions and relationships between the variables (or elements) of a system have been widely studied using ISM (Shankar Chandramowli, 2011). The obstacles to climate finance in India are considered in the current study.
- ISM assigns a rating to the elements and functions without having any prior knowledge of the system's history (Anukul Mandal, 1994).

Given that this approach uses group judgment to identify every variable and how they relate to one another, it is interpretive in nature. Finding linkages between the barriers would help to clarify the picture much more accurately than considering each piece separately, especially for complicated challenges like the one under examination.

1.4.1 INTERPRETIVE STRUCTURAL MODELING (ISM) DEVELOPMENTAL STEPS

First, the different obstacles to climate financing implementation in India are noted. Second, a pairwise comparison of the variables results in the preparation of an organized self-interaction matrix. Creating the first reachability matrix by changing the symbols to binary values is the third step. The concept of transitivity, which holds that if L is related to M and M is related to N, then there is definitely a relationship between L and N, is then applied to build the final reachability matrix. The fourth process involves leveling the resulting matrix, and the fifth step generates a directed graph. Ultimately, the ISM model is ready. Figure 1.2 shows the ISM method's step-by-step methodology.

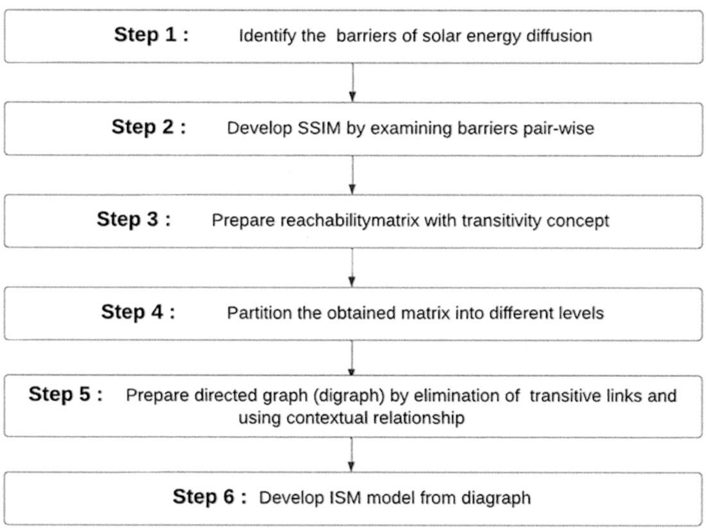

FIGURE 1.2 Steps involved in ISM method.

Source: Modified from Md. Fahim Ansari a (2013).

1.4.2 FORMATION OF THE STRUCTURAL SELF-INTERACTION MATRIX

The numerous barriers to climate finance in India have been contextually analyzed through a review of the literature and expert perspectives.

To determine the contextual link, the expert panel conducted pairwise comparisons. The four symbols listed below are utilized to produce SSIM.

- V indicates that variable i facilitates the achievement of variable j,
- A indicates that reaching variable i is made possible by variable j,
- X indicates that variables i and j support one another, whereas
- Indicates that there is no relationship between the two.

Table 1.1 depicts the developed SSIM based on the contextual relationships among the variables.

TABLE 1.1 Structural Self-Interaction Matrix (SSIM) for Barriers in Attaining Climate Finance in India

Variables	**1**	**2**	**3**	**4**	**5**	**6**	**7**	**8**	**9**	**10**
Climate Finance		A	A	A	A	A	A	A	A	A
Low Access to Finance			A	X	A	X	O	A	O	V
High Risk Perception				O	O	O	X	O	O	V
Insufficient project readiness					O	O	O	O	O	O
High Transaction Costs						O	O	O	O	V
Shortage of Local Expertise							O	X	X	O
Mismatch between Investment and Needs								A	O	V
Lack of Transparency and Accountability									O	V
Use of fossil Fuels										O
Lack of Long-Term Funding										

1.4.3 FORMATION OF REACHABILITY MATRIX

Using specific rules, the binary integers "0" and "1" can be substituted for the symbols V, A, X, and O in order to convert the SSIM produced in Section 1.4.3 into the initial reachability matrix. The rules used to create the initial reachability matrix are as follows:

- When V is present in the SSIM, the reachability matrix should use "1" in the (i, j) entry and "0" in the (j, i) entry.
- When A is present in SSIM, the reachability matrix should use '0' for the (i, j) entry and '1' for the (j, i) entry.
- When X is present in SSIM, the reachability matrix should use '1' for both the (i, j) and (j,i) entries.
- When O is present in SSIM, the reachability matrix should use '0' for both the (i, j) and (j,i) entries.

Table 1.2 shows the initial reachability matrix obtained for the Barriers to Climate Finance Accessibility in India.

TABLE 1.2 Reachability Matrix (RM) of Barriers to Climate Finance Accessibility in India

Variables	1	2	3	4	5	6	7	8	9	10	Driving Power
Climate Finance	1	0	0	0	0	0	0	0	0	0	1
Low Access to Finance	1	1	0	1	0	1	0	0	0	1	5
High Risk Perception	1	1	1	0	0	0	1	0	0	1	5
Insufficient project readiness	1	1	0	1	0	0	0	0	0	0	3
High Transaction Costs	1	1	0	0	1	0	0	0	0	1	4
Shortage of Local Expertise	1	1	0	0	0	1	0	1	1	0	5
Mismatch between Investment and Needs	1	0	1	0	0	0	1	0	0	1	4
Lack of Transparency and Accountability	1	1	0	0	0	1	1	1	0	1	6
Use of fossil Fuels	1	0	0	0	0	1	0	0	1	0	3
Lack of Long-Term Funding	1	0	0	0	0	0	0	0	0	1	2
Dependence Power	10	6	2	2	1	4	3	2	2	6	

After applying the transitivity concept—which was previously discussed in section 1.4.3—Table 1.3 displays the final reachability matrix that was created. Lastly, the final reachability matrix is used to calculate driving and dependence power.

TABLE 1.3 Final Reachability Matrix (FRM) of Barriers to Climate Finance in India

Variables	1	2	3	4	5	6	7	8	9	10	Driving Power
Climate Finance	1	0	0	0	0	0	0	0	0	0	1
Low Access to Finance	1	1	1*	1	0	1	1*	1*	1*	1	9
High Risk Perception	1	1	1	1*	0	1*	1	1*	1*	1	9
Insufficient project readiness	1	1	1*	1	0	1*	1*	1*	1*	1*	9
High Transaction Costs	1	1	1*	1*	1	1*	1*	1*	1*	1	10
Shortage of Local Expertise	1	1	1*	1*	0	1	1*	1	1	1*	9
Mismatch between Investment and Needs	1	1*	1	1*	0	1*	1	1*	1*	1	9
Lack of Transparency and Accountability	1	1	1*	1*	0	1	1	1	1*	1	9
Use of fossil Fuels	1	1*	1*	1*	0	1	1*	1*	1	1*	9
Lack of Long-Term Funding	1	0	0	0	0	0	0	0	0	1	2
Dependence Power	10	8	8	8	1	8	8	8	8	9	

1.4.4 LEVELS PARTITIONING

Using level partitioning (LP), each barrier's prominence is determined. The reachability set and antecedent set are now obtained using the reachability matrix. The reachability set consists of the variable and a group of variables that it influences. The variable plus the collection of variables that affect it make up the antecedent set. For every variable, the various sets are obtained, such as the reachability, antecedent, and intersection sets (Ali, 2014). According to the ISM model, the barrier that first achieves the same reachability and intersection set is categorized as level 1. In this instance, barrier 1 is given level 1, which is displayed in Tables 1.4 and 1.5.

TABLE 1.4 Level Partitioning (LP)

Elements (Mi)	Reachability Set R (Mi)	Antecedent Set A (Ni)	Intersection Set R (Mi)∩A(Ni)	Level
1	1	1, 2, 3, 4, 5, 6, 7, 8, 9, 10	1	1
2	2, 3, 4, 6, 7, 8, 9	2, 3, 4, 5, 6, 7, 8, 9	2, 3, 4, 6, 7, 8, 9	3
3	2, 3, 4, 6, 7, 8, 9	2, 3, 4, 5, 6, 7, 8, 9	2, 3, 4, 6, 7, 8, 9	3
4	2, 3, 4, 6, 7, 8, 9	2, 3, 4, 5, 6, 7, 8, 9	2, 3, 4, 6, 7, 8, 9	3
5	5	5	5	4
6	2, 3, 4, 6, 7, 8, 9	2, 3, 4, 5, 6, 7, 8, 9	2, 3, 4, 6, 7, 8, 9	3
7	2, 3, 4, 6, 7, 8, 9	2, 3, 4, 5, 6, 7, 8, 9	2, 3, 4, 6, 7, 8, 9	3
8	2, 3, 4, 6, 7, 8, 9	2, 3, 4, 5, 6, 7, 8, 9	2, 3, 4, 6, 7, 8, 9	3
9	2, 3, 4, 6, 7, 8, 9	2, 3, 4, 5, 6, 7, 8, 9	2, 3, 4, 6, 7, 8, 9	3
10	10	2, 3, 4, 5, 6, 7, 8, 9, 10	10	2

TABLE 1.5 Level Partitioning Iterations

Elements (Mi)	Reachability Set R (Mi)	Antecedent Set A (Ni)	Intersection Set R (Mi)∩A(Ni)	Level
1	1	1, 2, 3, 4, 5, 6, 7, 8, 9, 10	1	1
2	1, 2, 3, 4, 6, 7, 8, 9, 10	2, 3, 4, 5, 6, 7, 8, 9	2, 3, 4, 6, 7, 8, 9	
3	1, 2, 3, 4, 6, 7, 8, 9, 10	2, 3, 4, 5, 6, 7, 8, 9	2, 3, 4, 6, 7, 8, 9	
4	1, 2, 3, 4, 6, 7, 8, 9, 10	2, 3, 4, 5, 6, 7, 8, 9	2, 3, 4, 6, 7, 8, 9	
5	1, 2, 3, 4, 5, 6, 7, 8, 9, 10	5	5	
6	1, 2, 3, 4, 6, 7, 8, 9, 10	2, 3, 4, 5, 6, 7, 8, 9	2, 3, 4, 6, 7, 8, 9	
7	1, 2, 3, 4, 6, 7, 8, 9, 10	2, 3, 4, 5, 6, 7, 8, 9	2, 3, 4, 6, 7, 8, 9	
8	1, 2, 3, 4, 6, 7, 8, 9, 10	2, 3, 4, 5, 6, 7, 8, 9	2, 3, 4, 6, 7, 8, 9	
9	1, 2, 3, 4, 6, 7, 8, 9, 10	2, 3, 4, 5, 6, 7, 8, 9	2, 3, 4, 6, 7, 8, 9	
10	1, 10	2, 3, 4, 5, 6, 7, 8, 9, 10	10	
1 2 3 4				

1.4.5 INTERPRETIVE STRUCTURAL MODELING (ISM) MODEL DEVELOPMENT

Barriers such as a lack of long-term funding lie as the topmost barrier to climate finance accessibility in India, whereas high transaction costs are identified as the bottommost variable that is least significant. These levels are displayed in Figure 1.3 of the ISM model.

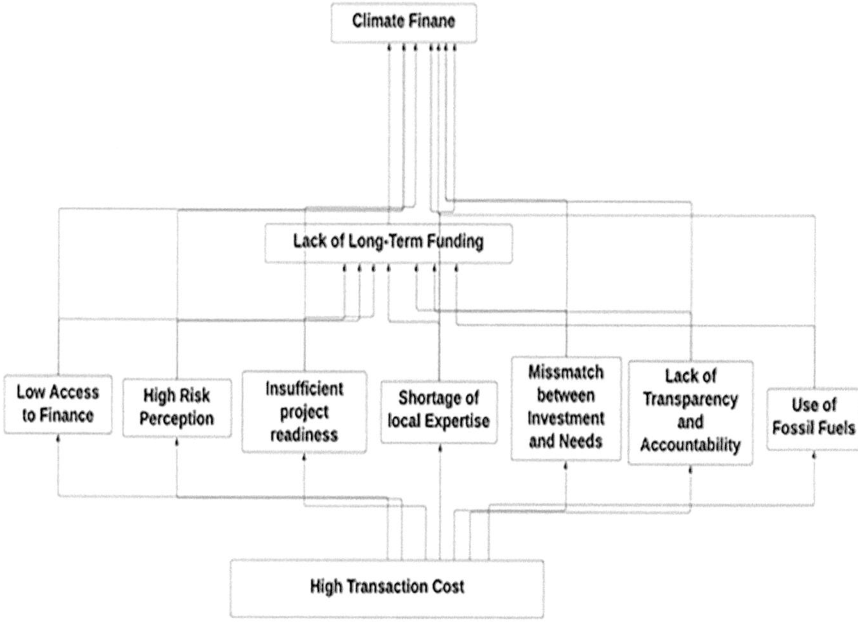

FIGURE 1.3 ISM model of barriers to climate finance accessibility in India.

1.4.6 BARRIER CLASSIFICATION: MICMAC ANALYSIS

By means of MICMAC analysis, the obstacles have been classified. MICMAC is essentially a categorization tool that uses cross-impact matrix multiplication. MICMAC analysis is done based on the identified driving and dependence powers. Barriers can be divided into four categories using MICMAC analysis: connecting, autonomous, independent, and dependent barriers. Figure 1.4 displays the results of the MICMAC analysis for India's barriers to climate finance accessibility.

MICMAC

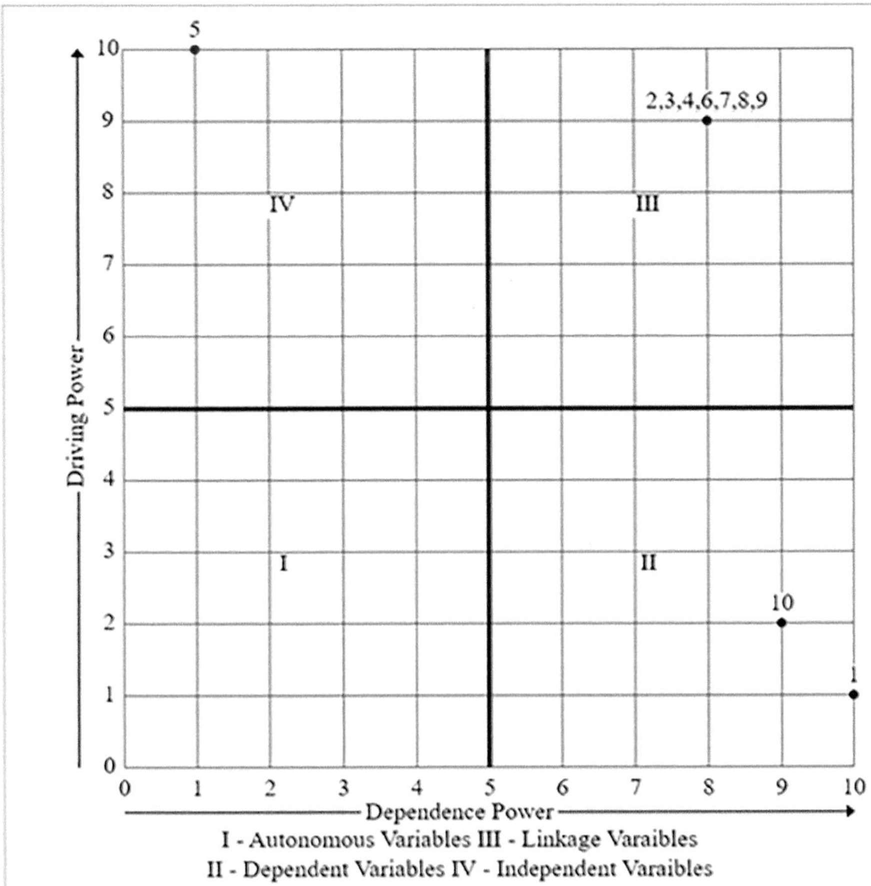

FIGURE 1.4 Depicts MICMAC analysis for barriers to climate finance accessibility in India.

1.5 SUGGESTED MEASURES TO MITIGATE BARRIERS TO CLIMATE FINANCE ACCESSIBILITY IN INDIA

For India to combat climate change and meet sustainable development goals (SDG), barriers to accessing climate finance must be reduced. The flow of climate money to projects and initiatives in the nation is hampered by a number of obstacles. Here are some ideas for how to get around these obstacles:

1.5.1 STRENGTHENING REGULATORY AND POLICY FRAMEWORKS

To give investors and project developers certainty and predictability, legislation and regulations pertaining to climate finance should be improved and streamlined. Create a specific regulatory agency or authority to supervise climate financing efforts and guarantee adherence to global norms.

1.5.2 CAPACITY BUILDING AND AWARENESS

To improve their comprehension of climate finance methods and requirements, invest in programs that expand the capacity of government officials, financial institutions, and project developers. Inform stakeholders about the sources of climate finance that are available and how to obtain them.

1.5.3 RISK MITIGATION INSTRUMENTS

To entice private sector involvement in climate projects, develop and promote the usage of risk mitigation tools like insurance and guarantees. To assist lenders and investors in assessing and managing climate-related risks, develop a framework for climate risk assessment.

1.5.4 FINANCIAL INNOVATION

Introduce green bonds, climate-focused investment funds, and other financial products that can mobilize climate money to encourage financial innovation. Encourage financial institutions and banks to create green lending services and products.

1.5.5 PUBLIC-PRIVATE PARTNERSHIPS (PPPS)

Encourage public-private partnerships (PPPs) between the two sectors to pool resources and expertise for climate projects. Encourage the commercial sector to participate in climate projects by offering incentives and subsidies.

1.5.6 DATA AND TRANSPARENCY

Enhance data collection and reporting processes to monitor the movements and results of climate funding. Ensure that the distribution and use of climate financing is transparent and accountable.

1.5.7 LOCAL CAPACITY AND LOCALIZATION

Promote the localization of climate money by aiding neighborhood projects and neighborhood groups. Encourage decentralized finance (DeFi) strategies that give local players more authority in attempts to adapt to and withstand climate change.

1.5.8 SIMPLIFIED ACCESS PROCEDURES

Reduce administrative constraints on project developers by streamlining and simplifying the application and approval processes for climate finance. Create specialized help desks for climate finance to guide applicants through the procedure.

1.5.9 CROSS-SECTOR INTEGRATION

To increase the resilience of diverse development initiatives, such as infrastructure, agriculture, and energy, cross-sector coordination and integration of climate considerations are encouraged.

1.5.10 INTERNATIONAL COOPERATION

Participate in international alliances and partnerships to obtain climate money from international funds and organizations. Encourage the equitable and fair allocation of climate finance among developing nations.

1.5.11 MONITORING AND EVALUATION

Put in place reliable monitoring and evaluation systems to determine how investments in climate financing are performing and to make the required corrections for ongoing progress.

1.5.12 CLIMATE REPORTING AND DISCLOSURE

Mandating financial disclosures connected to climate change for businesses and financial institutions will increase openness and promote investment in projects that are climate-resilient.

1.5.13 GREEN STANDARDS AND CERTIFICATION

To guarantee that funded projects follow environmentally friendly practices, create and implement green standards and certification procedures.

1.5.14 COMMUNITY ENGAGEMENT

Participate in the decision-making process for climate finance projects with your community to make sure that your needs and concerns are taken into account.

By removing these obstacles and putting these policies in place, India may more easily obtain climate funding and hasten the transition to a low-carbon and climate-resilient economy. Additionally, it will support international efforts to address climate change.

1.6 CONCLUSION

The fragmentation and disagreement of the climate finance framework, which favours developing countries, is evident as the need for climate funding increases globally. States must allocate resources across a wide range of channels to a wide range of mitigation and adaptation projects in order to address a subject as complicated and resource-intensive as climate change. However, the financial regime is growing without a clear purpose or a well-defined policy for maximizing the leverage of the several diverse components towards a shared aim, rather than avoiding unfavorable competition and needless duplication. Additionally, it is crucial that investments made by the public and commercial sectors do not unduly complicate matters by funding projects with high emissions and poor adaptation (Ali, 2014). A wide variety of disputed estimates result from regime applicants' disagreements regarding how climate finance should be well-defined and planned, notwithstanding an increase in the amount of capital branded as climate finance. (Falconer, 2014; Paul Bodnar, 2015).

It is imperative that all governments and stakeholders comprehend the financial needs of emerging nations and the potential means of mobilizing these financial resources. Resources should be distributed in a way that balances adaptation and mitigation. Building on these results, future studies can analyze the climate finance system and other climate governance subsystems in greater detail. Systems that oversee forestry or adaptation, for instance, are comparable to other governance frameworks, most notably those that oversee development assistance. Subsequent investigations should look into the manner in which developing countries' and institutions' sustained endorsement of fossil fuel production and use impacts or is impacted by the dispersion of climate money.

KEYWORDS

- **climate change**
- **climate finance**
- **climate funding**
- **climate risk**
- **economic efficiency**
- **level partitioning**
- **long-term solutions**
- **mobilization effectiveness**

REFERENCES

Ali, R. D. (2014). Identification of flexible manufacturing system dimensions and their interrelationship using total interpretive structural modelling and fuzzy MICMAC analysis. *Global Journal of Flexible Systems Management*, *15*, 131–143.

Anukul Mandal, S. D. (1994). Vendor selection using interpretive structural modelling (ISM). *International Journal of Operations & Production Management*.

Chandni Singh, M. M. (2021). Climate change adaptation in Indian cities: A review of existing actions and spaces for triple wins.

Dennis Tirpak, L. B. B. (2014). *Italian Journal of International Affairs*.

Falconer, A. D. (2014). What is climate finance? Definitions to improve tracking and scale up of climate finance.

Ghosal, M. G. (2021). Climate change vulnerability of rural households in flood-prone areas of Himalayan foothills, West Bengal, India.

Jianchun Fang, C. K. (2019). Natural disasters, climate change, and their impact on inclusive wealth in G20 countries. *Environmental Science and Pollution Research*, *26*, 1455–1463.

Mafira, T. (2023). G20 and sustainable climate finance: Experiences from the Indonesian presidency. In *Bridging the Climate Finance Gap* (pp. 82–88).

Md. Fahim Ansari, A., & Kumar, R. (2013). Analysis of barriers to implement solar power installations in India using interpretive structural modeling technique. *Renewable and Sustainable Energy Reviews*, *27*, 163–174.

Nagendra Sohani, N. S. (2012). Developing interpretive structural model for quality framework in higher education: Indian context. *Journal of Engineering, Science and Management Education*, *5*, 495–501.

Nico Bauer, I. M. (2016). Global fossil energy markets and climate change mitigation–An analysis with REMIND. *Climatic Change*.

Panda, A. (2016). Exploring climate change perceptions, rainfall trends and perceived barriers to adaptation in a drought-affected region in India.

Paul Bodnar, J. B. (2013). Mobilizing international climate finance: Lessons from the fast-start finance period–Research reports and studies.

Paul Bodnar, J. B. (2015). What counts: Tools to help define and understand progress towards the $100 billion climate finance commitment–Working and discussion papers; toolkits.

Ravi S. Prashad, R. S. (2018). Implementing climate change adaptation: Lessons from India's National Adaptation Fund on Climate Change (NAFCC).

Sanjay Kumar, S. L. (2013). Customer involvement in greening the supply chain: An interpretive structural modeling methodology. *Journal of Industrial Engineering International*.

Schalatek, L. (2012). Democratizing climate finance governance and the public funding of climate action. *Democratization*.

Shankar Chandramowli, M. T. (2011). Analysis of barriers to development in landfill communities using interpretive structural modeling. *Habitat International*, *35*(1), 246–253.

Smita Nakhooda, & Charlene Watson, O. A. (2015). The global climate finance architecture.

Soeder, D. J. (2020). Fossil Fuels and Climate Change. In *Fracking and the Environment*.

Timothy M. Lenton, J. R. (2020). Climate tipping points–Too risky to bet against: The growing threat of abrupt and irreversible climate changes must compel political and economic action on emissions. *Nature*.

UNFCCC. (n.d.). Introduction to climate finance. United Nations Climate Change: https://unfccc.int/topics/introduction-to-climate-finance (accessed on 7th July 2025).

Urfi Khan, A. H. (2012). Smart organizations: Modelling of enablers using ISM. *International Journal of Intelligent Enterprise*, *1*(3/4), 248–252.

Vanderheiden, S. (2015). Justice and climate finance: Differentiating responsibility in the Green Climate Fund. *Italian Journal of International Affairs, 50*(1).

CHAPTER 2

Smart Sustainability: Harnessing AI for Investment Monitoring

DEEPTI PATNAIK[1,*] and BIJAYANANDA PATNAIK[2]

[1]*Kalinga University, Naya Raipur, Chhattisgarh, India*

[2]*National Institute of Technology (NIT) Raipur, Chhattisgarh, India*

*Corresponding author

ABSTRACT

Smart sustainability represents a paradigm shift in investment monitoring, leveraging artificial intelligence (AI) to integrate environmental, social, and governance (ESG) considerations into investment strategies. This chapter explores the intersection of AI and sustainability, highlighting the potential of AI-driven investment monitoring to enhance decision-making, improve efficiency, and mitigate risks. Key findings include the importance of addressing bias and ensuring transparency in AI models, the role of emerging technologies such as blockchain and IoT in sustainable investment monitoring, and the potential impact of AI on future investment strategies. Furthermore, the chapter emphasizes the importance of continued development in both AI and sustainability to address the complex challenges facing the investment community. A call to action is presented for stakeholders in the investment community to embrace the opportunities presented by AI and sustainability, collaborate on industry standards and best practices, and prioritize diversity, equity, and inclusion in AI development and implementation. Overall, smart sustainability offers a transformative approach to investment monitoring, aligning financial objectives with environmental and social goals to create a more sustainable and inclusive future.

E-Financial Strategies for Sustainable Development: A Handbook for Promoting Financial Inclusion and Ending Poverty (SDG 1). Ernesto D. R. Santibanez Gonzalez, Rajeev Sijariya, and Vikas Garg (Eds.)

DOI: 10.1201/9781779640956-2

2.1 INTRODUCTION

In today's rapidly evolving world, the concept of sustainability has taken center stage, driven by pressing environmental concerns and the need for responsible stewardship of resources. However, as we confront the challenges of climate change, resource depletion, and population growth, traditional approaches to sustainability are no longer sufficient. Enter the era of Smart Sustainability, a paradigm that leverages cutting-edge technology, particularly artificial intelligence (AI), to revolutionize how we address environmental issues (IPCC, 2018). This essay explores the essence of Smart Sustainability, its significance in modern society, the role of sustainable investments, and the transformative potential of AI in advancing environmental stewardship.

Smart sustainability transcends the conventional notions of environmental conservation by integrating technology-driven solutions into every aspect of sustainable practices. At its core, smart sustainability emphasizes the synergistic relationship between intelligent systems and ecological responsibility. This approach encompasses a broad spectrum of innovations, including IoT (Internet of Things) devices, renewable energy technologies, data analytics, and AI-driven decision-making processes. By harnessing the power of interconnected technologies, Smart Sustainability aims to optimize resource utilization, reduce waste, and mitigate environmental impact across various domains, such as energy, transportation, agriculture, and urban development.

Sustainable investments are pivotal in spearheading the transition towards Smart Sustainability. As awareness of environmental and social concerns grows, investors are placing greater emphasis on companies exhibiting robust commitments to sustainability. Sustainable investments span various financial instruments, encompassing green bonds, socially responsible mutual funds, and impact investing strategies. These investments not only yield financial returns but also drive positive environmental and social impacts. By channeling capital into environmentally responsible ventures and firms, sustainable investments stimulate innovation, advocate sustainable business models, and cultivate long-term resilience in addressing environmental challenges (Morgan Stanley Institute for Sustainable Investing, 2020).

AI stands as a base in the quest for smart sustainability, offering transformative capabilities to address complex environmental issues effectively.

AI-powered technologies enable both organizations and governments to scrutinize immense data volumes, discern patterns, and enhance decision-making across various sectors. In the realm of environmental conservation, AI enables predictive modeling for climate change, facilitates precision agriculture techniques, optimizes energy distribution networks, and enhances resource management strategies. Through machine learning algorithms, AI systems persistently acquire knowledge and adjust, resulting in improved resource allocation, minimized environmental impact, and heightened resilience to environmental disturbances (World Economic Forum, 2019).

One compelling example of AI's role in advancing sustainability lies in energy management systems. Traditional energy grids often struggle to balance supply and demand efficiently, leading to inefficiencies, grid instability, and increased greenhouse gas emissions. However, AI-enabled energy management solutions offer a promising alternative. By leveraging real-time data analytics and predictive algorithms, these systems optimize energy production, storage, and distribution, thus maximizing renewable energy utilization and minimizing reliance on fossil fuels. For instance, AI algorithms can forecast energy demand patterns, dynamically adjust power generation from renewable sources, and optimize energy storage systems for peak efficiency. As a result, AI-powered energy management not only reduces carbon emissions but also enhances grid reliability and affordability, paving the way for a more sustainable energy future (Arbab-Zavar et al., 2020).

Smart sustainability represents a paradigm shift in how we approach environmental conservation, leveraging technology and innovation to address pressing ecological challenges. Sustainable investments drive the transition towards environmentally responsible practices, while AI serves as a powerful enabler, providing the analytical tools and insights needed to optimize resource management and mitigate environmental impact. As we navigate the complexities of the 21st century, embracing smart sustainability offers a pathway towards a more resilient, equitable, and sustainable future for generations to come.

2.2 INVESTMENT MONITORING

In the dynamic landscape of financial markets, investment monitoring serves as a fundamental cornerstone for both investors and fund managers.

It empowers them to oversee portfolio performance, assess risks, and make informed decisions. Historically, investment monitoring leaned on manual methods, periodic reports, and basic analytics. Yet, with the rise of sophisticated technologies, notably AI, the landscape of investment monitoring is experiencing a profound shift.

Traditional methods of investment monitoring have long been characterized by manual processes and reliance on historical data. These methods typically involve periodic reporting, where investors receive updates on the performance of their portfolios at predefined intervals, such as monthly or quarterly. Additionally, fundamental analysis plays a crucial role, focusing on assessing the financial health, growth prospects, and market position of individual companies or assets (Yeo and Jacob, 2020). Technical analysis, conversely, relies on historical price and volume data to discern trends and patterns in asset prices.

Although traditional approaches have shown some effectiveness, they are intrinsically constrained by multiple factors. Firstly, manual procedures consume time and are susceptible to errors, resulting in decision-making delays and potential inaccuracies in portfolio evaluation. Secondly, dependence solely on historical data might neglect emerging trends, market shifts, and unforeseen events that could affect investment outcomes. Furthermore, traditional methods frequently lack the scalability and flexibility needed to respond to swiftly changing market circumstances, leaving investors susceptible to missed opportunities and increased risks.

The challenges and limitations of traditional investment monitoring methods are manifold. One of the primary challenges is the incapacity to process and analyze extensive volumes of data in real-time. As financial markets become increasingly complex and interconnected, the volume and velocity of data generated pose significant challenges for manual analysis (Yeo and Jacob, 2020). Furthermore, traditional methods may struggle to identify and quantify risks accurately, particularly in volatile market conditions or during periods of economic uncertainty.

Another limitation of traditional investment monitoring is the lack of predictive capabilities. Historical data can provide valuable insights into past performance but may not necessarily forecast future trends or market movements (Choi and Youngjae, 2019). As a result, investors may miss opportunities or fail to mitigate risks effectively.

Moreover, traditional methods often suffer from cognitive biases and subjective judgments, which can cloud decision-making and lead to suboptimal outcomes. Human analysts may be influenced by emotions, personal beliefs, or cognitive heuristics, resulting in biased assessments and investment decisions (Yeo and Jacob, 2020).

The rise of AI-based solutions heralds a paradigm shift in investment monitoring, presenting unmatched capabilities in data processing, analysis, and decision-making. AI encompasses various technologies such as machine learning (ML), natural language processing (NLP), and deep learning, empowering computers to learn from data, discern patterns, and make predictions without explicit programming (Choi and Youngjae, 2019).

A significant benefit of AI-driven solutions lies in their capacity to manage vast amounts of data instantaneously. Utilizing ML algorithms, they can dissect diverse datasets, such as market prices, news articles, social media sentiment, and macroeconomic indicators, to extract actionable insights and pinpoint investment prospects or risks (Vargas and Luis, 2018). By managing information at scale, AI-driven solutions empower investors to make more informed decisions and promptly adapt to evolving market conditions.

Furthermore, AI-based solutions offer predictive capabilities that transcend traditional methods. ML models can forecast asset prices, identify market trends, and anticipate shifts in investor sentiment, enabling proactive risk management and portfolio optimization. Additionally, AI algorithms can detect anomalies and outliers in data, alerting investors to potential threats or opportunities that may have been overlooked using conventional methods.

Moreover, AI-driven solutions alleviate cognitive biases and subjective judgments inherent in human decision-making. Through their reliance on data-driven analysis and statistical models, AI algorithms offer impartial insights and recommendations, thereby diminishing the influence of emotional biases and elevating the caliber of investment choices (Vargas and Luis, 2018).

By incorporating AI-based risk models, portfolio managers can identify and quantify risks more accurately, including tail risks and systemic threats that traditional methods may overlook (Vargas and Luis, 2018). Furthermore, AI algorithms can optimize portfolio diversification, asset selection, and risk-adjusted returns, leading to superior performance and resilience in volatile market conditions.

The foundations of investment monitoring are undergoing a profound transformation with the integration of AI-based solutions. Traditional methods, characterized by manual processes and historical analysis, are giving way to data-driven, predictive approaches enabled by AI technologies. By harnessing the power of AI, investors and fund managers can overcome the limitations of traditional methods, enhance decision-making, and unlock new opportunities for alpha generation and risk management (Yeo and Jacob, 2020). As AI continues to evolve, its role in investment monitoring will become increasingly indispensable, reshaping the future of finance and empowering investors to navigate complex market dynamics with confidence and agility (Choi and Youngjae, 2019).

2.3 ARTIFICIAL INTELLIGENCE FOR SUSTAINABLE INVESTMENT MONITORING

The monitoring of sustainable investments has grown in significance for investors aiming to align their portfolios with ESG standards. AI technologies provide robust instruments for analyzing extensive datasets, recognizing patterns, and making well-founded investment choices. The utilization of AI in investment analysis, with a particular emphasis on ML for evaluating environmental and social impacts, alongside predictive analytics for risk management in sustainable investing, is essential. AI has transformed investment analysis through enhanced data processing, pattern recognition, and decision-making capabilities. Specifically within sustainable investing, AI technologies are pivotal in scrutinizing ESG data to assess the sustainability performance of companies and sectors.

For example, NLP algorithms can extract insights from various textual sources like corporate sustainability reports, news articles, and social media posts. Through the analysis of this unstructured data, investors can acquire deeper insights into companies' ESG practices and their potential influence on financial performance (Hess et al., 2020).

ML techniques offer powerful tools for assessing the environmental and social impact of investment portfolios. Supervised learning algorithms can classify companies based on their ESG performance, allowing investors to identify leaders and laggards in sustainability practices. For example, Support Vector Machines (SVM) and Random Forest classifiers have been used to classify companies into different ESG categories based on their reported metrics (Huang et al., 2018).

Unsupervised learning techniques like clustering and dimensionality reduction can categorize companies with comparable ESG attributes, offering insights into portfolio diversification and risk exposure. Through clustering companies according to their ESG profiles, investors can pinpoint potential risks and opportunities linked with various sectors or regions (Ghosh et al., 2019).

Sentiment analysis, another application of ML, can assess public perceptions and attitudes towards companies' sustainability efforts. Through the analysis of news articles, social media posts, and other textual sources, sentiment analysis algorithms can evaluate the general sentiment toward a company's ESG performance and reputation. Positive sentiment may indicate strong public support for sustainable practices, while negative sentiment could signal potential reputational risks (Bhaskar et al., 2021).

Predictive analytics is essential for managing risks in sustainable investing. AI-powered predictive models can forecast ESG risks, allowing investors to proactively manage their portfolios and mitigate potential losses. For example, time series forecasting models, such as Autoregressive Integrated Moving Average (ARIMA) and Long Short-Term Memory (LSTM) networks, can predict future trends in ESG metrics based on historical data (Sinha et al., 2020).

Additionally, ML algorithms can identify patterns and anomalies in ESG data that may signal emerging risks or opportunities. For instance, anomaly detection algorithms, such as Isolation Forest and One-Class SVM, can identify unusual patterns in ESG metrics that deviate from historical norms. These anomalies could indicate environmental incidents, social controversies, or governance issues that may impact a company's financial performance (Srivastava et al., 2020).

Furthermore, risk factor models, such as the Fama-French model adapted for ESG factors, can quantify the impact of ESG risks on investment returns. By incorporating ESG factors into traditional risk models, investors can better understand the sources of risk in their portfolios and adjust their investment strategies accordingly (Carhart, 2015).

Utilizing AI in sustainable investment monitoring presents considerable prospects for investors to incorporate ESG factors into their decision-making paradigms comprehensively. Leveraging ML methodologies for evaluating environmental and social impacts allows investors to pinpoint sustainable investment prospects, evaluate risks, and fine-tune their portfolios for sustained performance over the long haul. Moreover, predictive analytics empowers investors to foresee forthcoming trends, detect nascent risks, and preemptively administer their portfolios to meet their sustainability objectives. As AI technologies advance, their role in sculpting the trajectory of sustainable investing will only become more pivotal.

2.4 SUSTAINABLE INVESTMENT MODELS

Sustainable investing has garnered substantial attention as investors progressively acknowledge the significance of ESG considerations in their decision-making frameworks. The development of AI models tailored for sustainable investments concentrates on the integration of ESG factors and showcases the successful investment models driven by AI. Through the utilization of AI technologies, investors can augment their capacity to discern sustainable investment prospects, mitigate risks, and fulfill both financial and non-financial goals.

Designing AI models for sustainable investments requires careful consideration of various factors, including data selection, feature engineering, model architecture, and evaluation metrics. These elements are crucial for ensuring the effectiveness and reliability of AI-driven investment strategies.

1. **Data Selection:** The foundation of AI models lies in the quality and relevance of the data used for training and analysis. In the context of sustainable investments, relevant data sources may include financial databases, ESG ratings agencies, corporate sustainability reports, satellite imagery, and social media sentiment analysis. It is essential to select data sources that provide comprehensive coverage of ESG factors across companies and sectors.

2. **Feature Engineering:** Feature engineering encompasses the process of converting raw data into meaningful input features that encapsulate the underlying connections between ESG factors and financial performance. Techniques such as text embedding for NLP-based analysis, image processing for satellite imagery, and network analysis for social media data can help extract relevant features for AI models. Feature engineering is crucial for ensuring that AI models can effectively capture the complexities of ESG integration.

3. **Model Architecture:** Selecting the right model architecture hinges on the analysis's goals and data attributes. Various AI models can be utilized, ranging from regression and classification models to clustering algorithms and sophisticated deep learning structures like recurrent neural networks (RNNs) and convolutional neural networks (CNNs). Choosing an appropriate model architecture is crucial for capturing the intricate connections between ESG factors and financial performance effectively.

4. **Evaluation Metrics:** Evaluation metrics are essential for assessing the performance and effectiveness of AI models in sustainable investments. These metrics may include traditional financial performance measures, such as risk-adjusted returns, the Sharpe ratio, and alpha, as well as ESG-specific metrics, such as ESG scores, carbon footprint, and social impact indicators. By evaluating AI models against these metrics, investors can gauge their ability to generate alpha while promoting sustainability objectives. Integrating ESG factors into investment models necessitates a comprehensive strategy that acknowledges the interconnectedness of ESG aspects. Environmental considerations encompass carbon emissions, energy efficiency, water usage, and biodiversity conservation. Social factors encompass labor practices, human rights, diversity and inclusion, and community engagement. Governance factors comprise board diversity, executive compensation, shareholder rights, and ethical business practices. AI models can analyze and quantify these ESG factors, providing investors with actionable insights into companies' sustainability performance and risk exposure. For example, ML algorithms can predict future trends in environmental metrics, identify social controversies or governance scandals, and assess the overall sustainability profile of companies and sectors. Several case studies demonstrate the effectiveness of AI-driven investment models in incorporating ESG factors and generating positive financial and sustainable outcomes.

5. **Satellite Imagery Analysis for Deforestation Monitoring:** One case study involves the application of ML algorithms to analyze satellite imagery for monitoring deforestation and land use changes. By analyzing satellite imagery data, AI models can

identify deforestation hotspots, assess the impact on biodiversity, and inform investment decisions in forestry and agriculture sectors (Buhr et al., 2020). One compelling case study delves into the utilization of NLP algorithms for sentiment analysis, specifically examining corporate sustainability reports and news articles. Through the analysis of textual data, AI models adeptly gauge public sentiment regarding companies' sustainability endeavors, discern emerging ESG trends, and evaluate reputational risks. This insightful information equips investors to make well-informed decisions, enabling them to navigate and mitigate risks associated with negative publicity or controversies (Othman et al., 2020). In addition, AI-driven risk models have been innovatively crafted to evaluate the influence of ESG factors on investment returns and portfolio performance. By integrating ESG metrics into traditional risk models, AI algorithms can pinpoint companies or sectors vulnerable to high ESG risk exposure, facilitating adjustments in portfolio allocations as deemed necessary. This proactive risk management approach empowers investors to minimize losses and optimize long-term returns (Kharoufeh et al., 2022).

Constructing sustainable investment models that harness AI for ESG integration presents remarkable opportunities for investors to harmonize their portfolios with sustainability goals while concurrently achieving favorable financial outcomes. By meticulously designing AI models, incorporating pertinent ESG factors, and leveraging advanced analytical methodologies, investors gain actionable insights into companies' sustainability performance, facilitating informed investment decisions. Case studies underscore the efficacy of AI-driven investment models in tackling intricate challenges and fostering positive outcomes within the realm of sustainable investing.

2.5 CONNECTING SUSTAINABILITY AND CORPORATE SOCIAL RESPONSIBILITY (CSR) WITH SUSTAINABLE INVESTMENT

Sustainability and CSR are deeply intertwined concepts that are pivotal in shaping sustainable investment strategies (Carroll, 1999). Sustainable investment entails deploying capital into companies, organizations, or projects with the dual objective of generating financial returns while fostering positive ESG outcomes (Eccles and Serafeim, 2013). The practices of sustainability and CSR within companies exert significant influence on their appeal to sustainable investors and their long-term financial performance.

1. **Alignment of Values:** Sustainable investors frequently adhere to values that prioritize environmental conservation, social equity, and ethical business practices (Clarkson et al., 2011). Firms showcasing a strong dedication to sustainability and CSR are often aligned with these values, making them appealing investment prospects. Through integrating ESG criteria into their investment strategies, sustainable investors can support companies that mirror their commitment to responsible business conduct, thereby fostering favorable social and environmental impacts (Dyllick and Hockerts, 2002).
2. **Risk Mitigation:** Sustainability and CSR practices can function as indicators of long-term resilience and risk management within companies (Freeman et al., 2010). Companies that prioritize sustainability tend to proactively address environmental risks, such as climate change impacts or resource scarcity, thereby reducing their exposure to regulatory, reputational, and operational risks (Lee, 2008). Similarly, companies investing in CSR initiatives, such as community development programs or employee welfare initiatives, may bolster their social license to operate and mitigate potential social risks (Porter and Kramer, 2011). Sustainable investors acknowledge the significance of risk mitigation in preserving investment value over the long term, favoring companies with robust sustainability and CSR performance (GRI, 2016).
3. **Innovation and Competitive Advantage:** Sustainability and CSR can catalyze innovation and cultivate cultures of continuous improvement within companies (Hart and Milstein, 2003). Companies investing in sustainable practices often pioneer innovative solutions to environmental challenges, leading to cost savings and operational efficiencies (Shrivastava, 1995). Likewise, CSR initiatives prioritizing stakeholder engagement and social impact can augment companies' reputation, brand loyalty, and market competitiveness (Porter and Kramer, 2002). Sustainable investors recognize the potential for innovation and competitive advantage

associated with sustainability and CSR, making them more inclined to invest in companies demonstrating leadership in these domains (Bansal and Roth, 2000).

4. **Stakeholder Engagement and Transparency:** Sustainability and CSR necessitate companies to engage with a diverse array of stakeholders, including investors, employees, customers, communities, and regulators (Matten and Crane, 2005). Companies prioritizing stakeholder engagement and transparency are better positioned to build trust and credibility with investors, fostering enduring relationships founded on mutual respect and accountability (Donaldson and Preston, 1995). By disclosing ESG performance data and engaging stakeholders, companies can enhance their reputation and underscore their commitment to responsible business practices (Gray et al., 1997). Sustainable investors value transparency and stakeholder engagement as indicators of corporate integrity, making them more likely to invest in companies exhibiting these characteristics (Stiglitz et al., 2010).
5. **Long-Term Value Creation:** Ultimately, sustainability and CSR are pivotal in the creation of long-term value for companies and investors alike (Elkington, 1997). Companies integrating sustainability into their core strategies are better positioned to adapt to evolving market trends, regulatory requirements, and stakeholder expectations, enhancing their resilience and sustainability over the long term (Henderson, 2001). Sustainable investors recognize the importance of investing in companies prioritizing long-term value creation, thus more likely to allocate capital to companies with robust sustainability and CSR performance (Hawken et al., 1999).

Sustainability and Corporate Social Responsibility (CSR) play crucial roles in guiding sustainable investment choices, impacting how appealing companies are to investors, managing risks, fostering innovation and competitive edge, engaging stakeholders transparently, and creating long-term value (Ioannou and Serafeim, 2017). Companies that prioritize sustainability and CSR frequently draw investments from sustainable investors and attain favorable financial and non-financial results. By incorporating sustainability and CSR into sustainable investment strategies, companies align their business objectives with the principles of responsible and ethical investing, thereby contributing to a more sustainable and inclusive global economy (Figure 2.1).

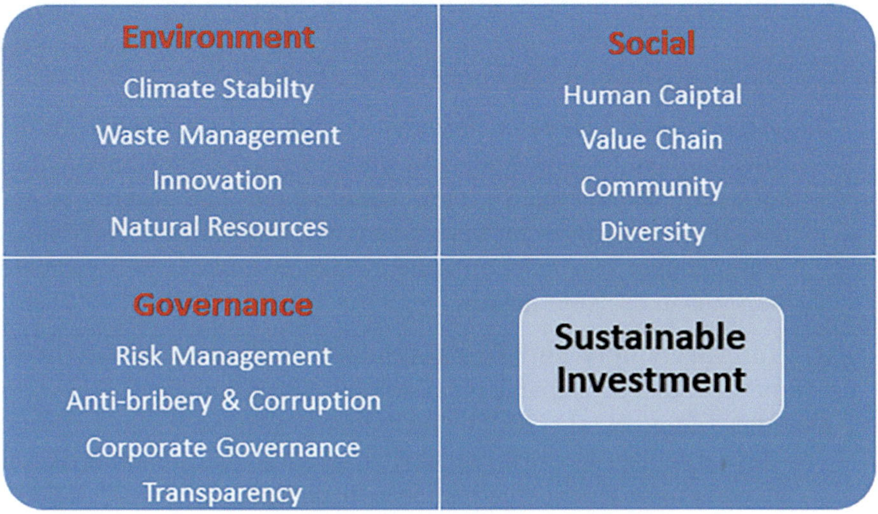

FIGURE 2.1 Figure showing the ESG in sustainable investment.

2.6 ETHICAL CONSIDERATIONS AND TRANSPARENCY IN AI-BASED INVESTMENT MONITORING

As AI becomes increasingly integrated into investment decision-making processes, ethical considerations and transparency are paramount to ensure fairness, accountability, and trustworthiness. AI-based investment monitoring holds great promise for enhancing portfolio management, risk assessment, and decision support. However, it also presents ethical challenges related to bias, fairness, and transparency. This chapter explores the importance of addressing bias and ensuring fairness in AI models, the necessity of transparency in investment decision-making, and the ethical frameworks guiding AI-based investment monitoring.

2.6.1 ADDRESSING BIAS AND FAIRNESS IN AI MODELS

Bias in AI models can perpetuate and exacerbate existing inequalities, leading to unfair outcomes and societal harm. To mitigate bias and ensure fairness in AI models, several strategies can be employed:

1. **Data Bias Mitigation:** AI models rely on data for training and decision-making, making it crucial to identify and address biases in the data (Zeng et al., 2021). This involves carefully selecting diverse and representative datasets, conducting bias audits, and implementing data preprocessing techniques such as data augmentation and bias correction algorithms.
2. **Algorithmic Fairness:** Fairness metrics and constraints can be incorporated into AI models to ensure equitable outcomes across different demographic groups (Buolamwini and Gebru, 2018). Techniques such as fairness-aware ML and fairness constraints optimization can help mitigate disparate impacts and promote fairness in decision-making.
3. **Interpretability and Explainability:** Making AI models interpretable and explainable is essential for identifying and addressing bias (Zeng et al., 2021). Techniques such as model-agnostic interpretation methods, causal inference, and counterfactual explanations enable stakeholders to understand how AI models make decisions and detect instances of bias or discrimination.

2.6.2 ENSURING TRANSPARENCY IN INVESTMENT DECISION-MAKING

Transparency is essential for fostering trust, accountability, and informed decision-making in investment management. In the context of AI-based investment monitoring, transparency can be achieved through:

1. **Explainable AI (XAI):** XAI techniques enable investors to understand the rationale behind AI-driven investment recommendations and predictions (Zeng et al., 2021). By providing transparent explanations of model outputs, XAI enhances trust and confidence in AI models and enables stakeholders to validate and interpret model decisions.
2. **Open Data and Open Source:** Making investment data and AI algorithms publicly accessible promotes transparency and fosters collaboration and peer review (FINRA, 2021). Open data initiatives, such as financial disclosure platforms and ESG data repositories, enable investors to access relevant information and assess the integrity and reliability of investment models.

3. **Regulatory Compliance:** Regulatory frameworks are pivotal in fostering transparency and accountability within investment decision-making processes (SEC, 2021). Mandates like the European Union's General Data Protection Regulation (GDPR) enforce transparency and data privacy measures, bolstering investor trust and fortifying market integrity.

2.6.3 ETHICAL FRAMEWORKS FOR AI-BASED INVESTMENT MONITORING

Ethical frameworks provide guidance and principles for responsible and ethical AI-based investment monitoring. Some key ethical considerations include:

1. **Fairness and Equity:** Ethical AI models should prioritize fairness and equity by ensuring that investment decisions do not discriminate against individuals or groups based on protected characteristics such as race, gender, or socioeconomic status.
2. **Privacy and Data Protection:** Ethical AI-based investment monitoring should respect individuals' privacy rights and adhere to data protection regulations (European Commission, 2018). Investors must obtain informed consent for data collection and use and implement robust security measures to protect sensitive information.
3. **Accountability and Governance:** Ethical AI frameworks emphasize accountability and governance mechanisms to ensure transparency, accountability, and oversight throughout the AI lifecycle (SEC, 2021). This includes establishing clear lines of responsibility, conducting regular audits, and providing avenues for recourse and redress in case of AI-related harm.

Ethical considerations and transparency are essential pillars of AI-based investment monitoring, ensuring fairness, accountability, and trustworthiness in decision-making processes. By addressing bias and fairness in AI models, ensuring transparency in investment decision-making, and adhering to ethical frameworks, investors can harness the transformative potential of AI while upholding ethical principles and promoting societal welfare.

2.7 IMPLEMENTATION AND ADOPTION OF AI-BASED INVESTMENT MONITORING

The implementation and adoption of AI in investment monitoring represent a significant paradigm shift in the financial industry. AI technologies offer the potential to enhance decision-making processes, improve portfolio management, and mitigate risks. However, the successful integration of AI into investment practices requires overcoming various barriers and challenges. Also strategies for integrating AI into investment practices, overcoming barriers to adoption, and real-world examples of AI-based investment monitoring platforms are explored.

The integration of AI in investment monitoring entails incorporating advanced algorithms, ML techniques, and big data analytics into current investment procedures. AI technologies excel in analyzing large datasets, detecting patterns, and providing actionable insights to aid investment decisions. Embracing AI-based investment monitoring platforms can yield numerous advantages, such as:

1. **Enhanced Decision-Making:** AI algorithms can process and analyze complex datasets, enabling investors to make more informed and data-driven decisions (Garcia and Vayanos, 2020). By leveraging AI-driven insights, investors can identify investment opportunities, assess risks, and optimize portfolio performance.

2. **Improved Efficiency:** AI-based investment monitoring platforms can automate repetitive tasks, streamline workflows, and enhance operational efficiency (Lo, 2020). By automating data collection, analysis, and reporting processes, AI technologies can free up human resources to focus on higher-value activities such as strategy development and client engagement.

3. **Risk Mitigation:** AI algorithms can detect and mitigate investment risks more effectively than traditional methods (Elliott et al., 2020). By analyzing market trends, sentiment analysis, and macroeconomic indicators, AI-based systems can identify potential risks and provide early warnings to investors, enabling them to adjust their investment strategies accordingly.

2.7.1 OVERCOMING BARRIERS TO ADOPTION

Despite the potential benefits, the adoption of AI in investment monitoring encounters several barriers and challenges. These hurdles include:

1. **Data Quality and Availability:** The success of AI-based investment monitoring relies on the availability of high-quality and relevant data (Chen et al., 2020). However, accessing and integrating diverse datasets from disparate sources can be challenging, particularly in the financial industry where data privacy and regulatory compliance are paramount.
2. **Lack of Trust and Understanding:** Many investors and financial professionals may be hesitant to adopt AI-based investment monitoring due to a lack of trust in AI algorithms and a limited understanding of how they work (Barberis et al., 2018). Overcoming these trust and perception issues requires education, transparency, and demonstration of the value proposition of AI technologies.
3. **Regulatory and Compliance Concerns:** Regulatory requirements and compliance standards pose significant challenges to the adoption of AI in investment monitoring (Liu et al., 2021). Financial regulators closely scrutinize AI-based systems to ensure transparency, fairness, and compliance with existing regulations such as the General Data Protection Regulation (GDPR) and the Securities and Exchange Commission (SEC) guidelines.

2.7.2 STRATEGIES FOR INTEGRATING AI INTO INVESTMENT PRACTICES

To overcome these barriers and facilitate the adoption of AI-based investment monitoring, several strategies can be employed:

1. **Data Governance and Management:** Establishing robust data governance frameworks and data management processes is critical to ensuring the quality, integrity, and security of investment data (Chen et al., 2020). This includes data standardization, data lineage tracking, and data quality assurance procedures to enhance data reliability and consistency.

2. **Education and Training:** Providing education and training programs on AI technologies and their applications in investment monitoring can help increase awareness, build trust, and enhance the skills of financial professionals (Barberis et al., 2018). Training programs should cover topics such as ML, data analytics, and AI ethics to empower professionals to leverage AI effectively.
3. **Collaboration and Partnerships:** Collaboration between financial institutions, technology vendors, and regulatory authorities can facilitate the development and adoption of AI-based investment monitoring platforms (Liu et al., 2021). By fostering partnerships, sharing best practices, and collaborating on research and development initiatives, stakeholders can accelerate the adoption of AI technologies and address common challenges collectively.

2.7.3 REAL-WORLD EXAMPLES OF AI-BASED INVESTMENT MONITORING PLATFORMS

Several real-world examples demonstrate the successful implementation and adoption of AI-based investment monitoring platforms:

1. **BlackRock Aladdin:** BlackRock's Aladdin platform is a comprehensive investment management system that leverages AI and ML to analyze investment risks, optimize portfolios, and support decision-making (BlackRock, 2021). Aladdin combines advanced analytics, risk modeling, and portfolio optimization capabilities to help investors manage their investments more effectively.
2. **QuantConnect:** QuantConnect is an open-source algorithmic trading platform that provides access to historical market data, back testing tools, and AI-driven trading strategies (QuantConnect, 2021). The platform allows users to develop, test, and deploy AI-based trading algorithms across different asset classes and markets.
3. **Wealthfront:** Wealthfront is a robo-advisor platform that uses AI and ML to provide personalized investment advice and portfolio management services (Wealthfront, 2021). The platform analyzes clients' financial goals, risk tolerance, and investment preferences to recommend customized investment strategies and allocate assets efficiently.

The implementation and adoption of AI-based investment monitoring offer significant opportunities to enhance decision-making, improve efficiency, and mitigate risks in the financial industry. By overcoming barriers to adoption, such as data quality, trust, and regulatory concerns, and leveraging strategies for integrating AI into investment practices, stakeholders can realize the full potential of AI technologies. Real-world examples of AI-based investment monitoring platforms demonstrate the feasibility and effectiveness of AI-driven approaches in transforming investment management and delivering value to investors.

2.8 FUTURE TRENDS AND OPPORTUNITIES IN SUSTAINABLE INVESTMENT MONITORING

With sustainability increasingly central in the investment domain, the role of technology, particularly AI, is primed to substantially extend its reach in sustainable investment monitoring. This chapter explores future trends and opportunities in sustainable investment monitoring, focusing on emerging technologies, the potential impact of AI on investment strategies, and opportunities for innovation and collaboration.

2.8.1 EMERGING TECHNOLOGIES IN SUSTAINABLE INVESTMENT MONITORING

1. **Blockchain Technology:** Blockchain technology has the potential to revolutionize sustainable investment monitoring by providing transparent, immutable, and auditable records of transactions and asset ownership (Bashir et al., 2021). By leveraging blockchain-based platforms, investors can track the provenance of assets, verify ESG credentials, and ensure compliance with sustainable investment criteria.
2. **Internet of Things (IoT):** IoT devices, such as sensors and smart meters, facilitate real-time monitoring of ESG metrics at the asset level (Fraczek et al., 2020). IoT data offers valuable insights into energy consumption, carbon emissions, supply chain transparency, and various other ESG factors, empowering investors to make better-informed investment choices.

3. **Big Data Analytics:** Big data analytics techniques, including ML and predictive analytics, enable investors to analyze large and complex datasets to identify trends, patterns, and anomalies (Abubakar et al., 2021). By integrating big data analytics into sustainable investment monitoring, investors can uncover hidden insights, assess risks, and optimize portfolio performance.

2.8.2 POTENTIAL IMPACT OF AI ON FUTURE INVESTMENT STRATEGIES

1. **Enhanced Decision-Making:** AI-driven investment strategies can enhance decision-making by providing real-time insights, predictive analytics, and personalized recommendations (Karam et al., 2020). AI algorithms can analyze vast amounts of data, identify market trends, and predict investment opportunities, enabling investors to make more informed and timely decisions.
2. **Risk Management:** AI technologies can improve risk management by detecting and mitigating investment risks more effectively than traditional methods (Haque et al., 2021). AI algorithms can analyze market data, sentiment analysis, and macroeconomic indicators to identify potential risks and provide early warnings to investors, enabling them to adjust their investment strategies accordingly.

AI can streamline the integration of ESG factors into investment strategies through ESG data analytics, impact assessment tools, and sustainability scoring models (Dong et al., 2021). By harnessing AI-powered ESG analysis, investors can pinpoint sustainable investment prospects, evaluate ESG risks, and align their portfolios with their sustainability goals.

2.8.3 OPPORTUNITIES FOR INNOVATION AND COLLABORATION

1. **Cross-Sector Collaboration:** Collaboration between financial institutions, technology providers, ESG rating agencies, and regulatory authorities can foster innovation and accelerate the

development and adoption of AI-driven sustainable investment monitoring solutions (Haque et al., 2021). By sharing data, expertise, and best practices, stakeholders can overcome common challenges and unlock new opportunities for sustainable investment.

2. **Integration of Multiple Data Sources:** Incorporating data from various origins, such as financial records, ESG metrics, satellite imagery, and social media feeds, can offer a holistic perspective on investment prospects and hazards (Dong et al., 2021). Through the utilization of diverse datasets and advanced analytical methods, investors can delve into market intricacies, spot emerging patterns, and enhance the quality of their investment choices.
3. **Innovative Financial Instruments:** Innovations in financial instruments, such as green bonds, sustainability-linked loans, and impact investing funds, can support sustainable investment objectives and promote collaboration between investors and issuers (Karam et al., 2020). By developing innovative financial products that align with ESG goals, investors can mobilize capital towards sustainable projects and drive positive social and environmental impact.

The future of sustainable investment monitoring lies at the intersection of technology, innovation, and collaboration. Emerging technologies such as blockchain, IoT, and big data analytics offer new opportunities to integrate ESG considerations into investment strategies and enhance decision-making processes. AI-driven investment strategies have the potential to revolutionize investment management by providing real-time insights, predictive analytics, and personalized recommendations. Opportunities for innovation and collaboration abound, with cross-sector partnerships, data integration, and financial instrument innovation driving sustainable investment forward.

2.9 CONCLUSION AND FUTURE WORK

The intersection of AI and sustainability presents immense opportunities for the investment community to drive positive ESG outcomes while achieving financial returns. This chapter has highlighted key findings regarding the integration of AI into sustainable investment monitoring, emphasizing the importance of continued development in both AI and sustainability.

Throughout this discussion, we have explored the role of AI in investment monitoring, including its potential to enhance decision-making, improve efficiency, and mitigate risks. We have also examined emerging technologies such as blockchain, IoT, and big data analytics, which offer new avenues for integrating ESG considerations into investment strategies. Furthermore, we have discussed the potential impact of AI on future investment strategies, including its ability to facilitate ESG integration, enhance risk management, and drive innovation in financial instruments.

As we look towards the future, it is clear that continued development in both AI and sustainability will be critical to addressing the complex challenges facing the investment community. AI technologies are rapidly evolving, offering new capabilities such as explainable AI (XAI), reinforcement learning, and NLP that can further enhance sustainable investment monitoring. Similarly, advancements in sustainability science, data collection methods, and impact measurement frameworks are essential for improving the accuracy, reliability, and comparability of ESG data.

In light of these findings, there is a pressing need for stakeholders in the investment community to take action and embrace the opportunities presented by AI and sustainability. This includes asset managers, institutional investors, wealth advisors, and financial regulators collaborating to develop industry standards, best practices, and regulatory frameworks that promote transparency, accountability, and responsible investment practices. It also entails fostering a culture of innovation, experimentation, and knowledge sharing within the investment community to drive continuous improvement in sustainable investment strategies.

Additionally, stakeholders must prioritize diversity, equity, and inclusion (DEI) in AI development and deployment to guarantee that AI technologies serve all stakeholders and do not perpetuate existing disparities. This entails tackling bias in AI algorithms, fostering diversity within AI teams, and actively involving diverse stakeholders to comprehend their requirements and preferences.

Lastly, the journey towards a sustainable future requires collective action, collaboration, and commitment from all stakeholders in the investment community. By harnessing the power of AI and sustainability, we can create investment strategies that deliver both financial returns and positive societal impact, paving the way for a more sustainable and inclusive future for generations to come.

KEYWORDS

- **ai algorithms**
- **artificial intelligence**
- **big data analytics**
- **diversity, equity, and inclusion**
- **financial instruments**
- **natural language processing**
- **quantconnect**
- **satellite imagery**
- **sustainability-linked loans**

REFERENCES

Abubakar, S., Ginting, M. S., Khare, A., & Tan, K. (2021). Big data analytics in the financial sector: Challenges, opportunities, and future directions. *Journal of Big Data*, *8*(1), 1–23.

Arbab-Zavar, B., et al. (2020). Machine learning in energy systems: Forecasting, optimization, and control. *Renewable and Sustainable Energy Reviews*, *135*, 1–14.

Bansal, P., & Roth, K. (2000). Why companies go green: A model of ecological responsiveness. *Academy of Management Journal*, *43*(4), 717–736.

Barberis, N., Greenwood, R., Jin, L., & Shleifer, A. (2018). Extrapolation and bubbles. *Journal of Financial Economics*, *129*(2), 203–227.

Bashir, M. A., Ramzan, N., & Yasin, M. M. (2021). Sustainable supply chain management using blockchain technology: A review and research agenda. *Sustainability*, *13*(8), 4332.

Bhaskar, A., et al. (2021). ESG sentiment analysis: A natural language processing approach.

BlackRock. (2021). Aladdin. https://www.blackrock.com/aladdin (accessed on 7th July 2025).

Buhr, S., et al. (2020). Using deep learning to quantify carbon emissions from satellite imagery.

Buolamwini, J., & Gebru, T. (2018). Gender shades: Intersectional accuracy disparities in commercial gender classification. *Proceedings of the 1st Conference on Fairness, Accountability and Transparency*, 81–91.

Carhart, M. M. (1997). On persistence in mutual fund performance. *The Journal of Finance*, *52*(1), 57–82.

Carroll, A. B. (1999). Corporate social responsibility: Evolution of a definitional construct. *Business & Society*, *38*(3), 268–295.

Chen, Y., Fang, Y., Zhang, C., & Zhang, Z. (2020). Big data and artificial intelligence in investment research and management: new platforms, capabilities, and challenges. *Pacific-Basin Finance Journal*, *62*, 101352.

Choi, Y., et al. (2019). Deep learning in finance: A review. *Journal of Financial Data Science*, *1*(1), 1–33.

Clarkson, M. B. E., Li, Y., Richardson, G. D., & Vasvari, F. P. (2011). Does it really pay to be green? Determinants and consequences of proactive environmental strategies. *Journal of Accounting and Public Policy*, *30*(2), 122–144.

Dong, Y., Chen, J., Xie, L., & Li, X. (2021). The integration of ESG factors into portfolio management: A machine learning approach. *Sustainability*, *13*(9), 5208.

Dyllick, T., & Hockerts, K. (2002). Beyond the business case for corporate sustainability. *Business Strategy and the Environment*, *11*(2), 130–141.

Eccles, R. G., & Serafeim, G. (2013). The performance frontier: Innovating for a sustainable strategy. *Harvard Business Review*, *91*(5), 50–60.

Elkington, J. (1997). *Cannibals with Forks: The Triple Bottom Line of 21st Century business*. Capstone.

Elliott, M., Garg, A., & Ren, Y. (2020). Quantitative investment in hedge funds: An empirical investigation of performance, risk, and market integration. *Journal of Banking & Finance*, *112*, 105274.

European Commission. (2018). General Data Protection Regulation (GDPR). https://gdpr.eu/ (accessed on 7th July 2025).

Financial Industry Regulatory Authority (FINRA). (2021). AI in finance. https://www.finra.org/investors/insights/ai-finance (accessed on 7th July 2025).

Fraczek, S., Lenza, P., & Marinelli, M. (2020). Internet of Things (IoT) and big data in supply chain management: A systematic literature review. *Computers in Industry*, *125*, 103294.

Freeman, R. E., Harrison, J. S., Wicks, A. C., Parmar, B. L., & De Colle, S. (2010). *Stakeholder Theory: The State of the Art*. Cambridge University Press.

Garcia, D., & Vayanos, D. (2020). The intertemporal capital asset pricing model. *Journal of Financial Economics*, *138*(1), 74–103.

Ghosh, S., et al. (2019). Machine learning applications in ESG investment strategies.

Gray, R., Kouhy, R., & Lavers, S. (1995). Corporate social and environmental reporting: A review of the literature and a longitudinal study of UK disclosure. *Accounting, Auditing & Accountability Journal*, *8*(2), 47–77.

GRI. (2016). *GRI Sustainability Reporting Standards*. Global Reporting Initiative.

Haque, M., Saqib, N. A., Farooq, M. S., & Muzamil, S. (2021). Artificial intelligence and its applications in financial markets: A comprehensive review. *Journal of King Saud University-Computer and Information Sciences*, *33*(1), 84–94.

Hart, S. L., & Milstein, M. B. (2003). Creating sustainable value. *Academy of Management Perspectives*, *17*(2), 56–67.

Hawken, P., Lovins, A., & Lovins, L. H. (1999). *Natural Capitalism: Creating the Next Industrial Revolution*. Little, Brown & Company.

Henderson, R. (2001). The role of the corporation in society: An alternative view and opportunities for future research. *Journal of Management Studies*, *38*(8), 1183–1219.

Hess, D. B., et al. (2020). Using natural language processing to measure firm environmental performance.

Huang, E. Y., et al. (2018). Using machine learning to enhance ESG investing.
Intergovernmental Panel on Climate Change. (2018). *IPCC Special Report on Global Warming of 1.5°C*.
Investopedia. (n.d.). Investment monitoring definition. https://www.investopedia.com/terms/i/investment-monitoring.asp (accessed on 7th July 2025).
Ioannou, I., & Serafeim, G. (2017). The consequences of mandatory corporate sustainability reporting: Evidence from four countries. *Harvard Business School Working Paper*, (17–024).
Karam, A., Badr, G., & Sayed, S. M. (2020). The role of artificial intelligence in shaping future financial markets: A review. *Journal of Accounting, Auditing & Finance*, *35*(4), 659–683.
Kharoufeh, M. A., et al. (2022). AI-driven ESG investment models: Opportunities and challenges.
Lee, K. H. (2008). Opportunities for green marketing: Young consumers. *Marketing Intelligence & Planning*, *26*(6), 573–586.
Liu, B., Li, Y., Chen, J., & Liu, X. (2021). A survey on AI in fintech: Impacts, applications, challenges, and solutions. *Information Fusion*, *75*, 62–85.
Lo, A. W. (2020). The adaptive markets hypothesis: Market efficiency from an evolutionary perspective. *Journal of Portfolio Management*, *46*(4), 22–34.
Matten, D., & Crane, A. (2005). Corporate citizenship: Toward an extended theoretical conceptualization. *Academy of Management Review*, *30*(1), 166–179.
Morgan Stanley Institute for Sustainable Investing. (2020). Sustainable investing: Establishing long-term value and performance.
Othman, N., et al. (2020). Natural language processing for sentiment analysis in ESG investing.
Porter, M. E., & Kramer, M. R. (2002). The competitive advantage of corporate philanthropy. *Harvard Business Review*, *80*(12), 56–68.
Porter, M. E., & Kramer, M. R. (2011). Creating shared value. *Harvard Business Review*, *89*(1/2), 62–77.
QuantConnect. (2021). About QuantConnect. https://www.quantconnect.com/about (accessed on 7th July 2025).
SEC. (2021). Division of Corporation Finance: CF Disclosure Guidance: Topic No. 9–Cybersecurity. https://www.sec.gov/corpfin/cf-disclosure-guidance-topic-9 (accessed on 7th July 2025).
Shrivastava, P. (1995). The role of corporations in achieving ecological sustainability. *Academy of Management Review*, *20*(4), 936–960.
Sinha, R., et al. (2020). Environmental, social and governance (ESG) factors: Predictive ability in the US stock market.
Srivastava, S., et al. (2020). Anomaly detection in ESG data: A machine learning approach.
Stiglitz, J. E., Sen, A., & Fitoussi, J. P. (2010). *Report by the Commission on the Measurement of Economic Performance and Social Progress*. Commission on the Measurement of Economic Performance and Social Progress.
Vargas, J. L., et al. (2018). A survey of predictive modeling for algorithmic trading. *Journal of Big Data*, *5*(1), 1–30.
Wealthfront. (2021). How Wealthfront works. https://www.wealthfront.com/how-it-works (accessed on 7th July 2025).

World Economic Forum. (2019). *Harnessing Artificial Intelligence for the Earth: 10 frontier technologies for sustainable development.*

Yeo, J., et al. (2020). Artificial intelligence and machine learning in financial services. *Deloitte Insights.*

Zeng, S., Shi, Y., Wu, S., & Rui, Y. (2021). A survey on explainable artificial intelligence (XAI) in finance. *Frontiers in Artificial Intelligence*, *4*, 615971.

CHAPTER 3

Digital Financial Revolution: Empowering Lives Through E-Financial Strategies

RAJEEV SIJARIYA,[1] OM PRAKASH YADAV,[2] RAJ KUMAR TEOTIA,[3] and RASHI BALIYAN[4]

[1]*Atal Bihari Vajpayee School of Management and Entrepreneurship (ABVSME), Jawaharlal Nehru University, New Delhi, India*

[2]*School of Business Management, Noida International University, Greater Noida, Uttar Pradesh, India*

[3]*H. R. Institute of Science and Technology, Ghaziabad, Uttar Pradesh, India*

[4]*Noida International University, Greater Noida, Uttar Pradesh, India*

*Corresponding author

ABSTRACT

The emergence of the Digital Financial Revolution marks a pivotal moment in global economics, transcending conventional banking norms to empower individuals and communities through cutting-edge E-Financial Strategies. This study delves into the transformative capabilities of digital financial tools, emphasizing their role in fostering inclusivity and economic empowerment. Leveraging the pervasive reach of digital connectivity, E-Financial Strategies redefine financial interactions, presenting accessible solutions that surpass geographical limitations. At its essence, this revolution addresses the pressing issue of financial exclusion by extending services to unbanked and underbanked populations, thus fueling economic progress

E-Financial Strategies for Sustainable Development: A Handbook for Promoting Financial Inclusion and Ending Poverty (SDG 1). Ernesto D. R. Santibanez Gonzalez, Rajeev Sijariya, and Vikas Garg (Eds.)

DOI: 10.1201/9781779640956-3

and disrupting the cycle of poverty (Dewi,2020). E-Financial Strategies encompass a wide array of digital tools, spanning from mobile banking applications to blockchain technology, all of which streamline financial processes and democratize wealth management. These strategies not only revolutionize the mechanics of financial transactions but also democratize access to financial services, empowering individuals to make informed decisions regardless of their prior financial acumen. Through real-life case studies ranging from rural to urban environments, we witness firsthand the tangible impact of E-Financial Strategies, illustrating their pivotal role as lifelines in underserved communities and catalysts for innovation within fintech ecosystems. Nevertheless, this paradigm shift presents its own set of challenges. Issues such as digital literacy, cybersecurity, and regulatory frameworks must be addressed to ensure the sustainable and inclusive growth of the digital financial landscape. By confronting these challenges head-on, stakeholders can lay the groundwork for a future where digital financial strategies serve as transformative agents, fostering a more inclusive and empowered global economy (Benamati,2019).

3.1 INTRODUCTION

As we embark on a journey into the heart of the Digital Financial Revolution, it becomes evident that this seismic shift in the financial landscape is not confined to the realm of banking and transactions alone. Instead, it represents a profound reconfiguration of the very essence of financial interactions, striving to dismantle barriers and empower lives in unprecedented ways (Binomoli,2007). The ubiquity of digital connectivity forms the backbone of this revolution, offering a gateway to financial services that transcend geographical constraints. E-Financial Strategies, as the driving force behind this evolution, encapsulate a diverse array of digital tools and methodologies designed to streamline financial processes and enhance accessibility. From the convenience of mobile banking applications to the revolutionary potential of blockchain technology, these strategies not only redefine the mechanics of financial transactions but also hold the promise of inclusivity. At the core of the Digital Financial Revolution is the pursuit of financial inclusion (Dewi,2020). Traditional banking systems, with their reliance on physical infrastructure and stringent requirements, often left vast segments of the population marginalized. E-Financial Strategies, by leveraging digital platforms, have the transformative potential to extend the reach of financial services to the unbanked and underbanked populations (Dholakia,2004). This inclusivity is not just a matter of convenience; it is a powerful tool for breaking the cycle of poverty and catalyzing economic development. Moreover, the Digital Financial Revolution reshapes the dynamics of wealth management. E-Financial Strategies empower individuals to navigate the complexities of personal finance, providing them with tools for budgeting, investment, and asset management. Through intuitive interfaces and algorithmic insights, individuals can make informed decisions, irrespective of their prior financial expertise (Dholakia,2004). This democratization of wealth management is a cornerstone of the revolution, ensuring that financial empowerment becomes a universal right rather than a privilege (Flood,2020).

As we delve deeper into this discourse, we will explore case studies that illustrate the tangible impact of E-Financial Strategies on diverse communities. From rural areas where mobile banking has become a lifeline to urban centers witnessing the rise of fintech startups, the revolution is unfolding in myriad ways. We will also confront the challenges that accompany this transformation, such as issues of digital literacy, cybersecurity, and regulatory frameworks. In essence, the Digital Financial Revolution, driven by E-Financial Strategies, transcends the mere digitization of money; it is a reimagining of financial ecosystems, with the potential to uplift individuals, communities, and entire economies. This exploration seeks not only to understand the present landscape but also to chart the course for a future where digital financial strategies are not just tools but transformative agents, fostering a more inclusive and empowered global economy (Donner,2008). "Digital Financial Revolution: Empowering Lives through E-Financial Strategies" explores the transformative impact of digital financial strategies on individuals' lives and broader societal inclusion. In an era dominated by technological advancements, the financial landscape is witnessing a revolution characterized by the integration of electronic means into traditional financial services. This chapter delves into the multifaceted dimensions of this revolution, examining how E-Financial Strategies serve as catalysts for empowerment and inclusivity. The discussion encompasses various aspects, including the accessibility of financial services through digital platforms, the democratization of wealth management, and the role of E-Financial Strategies in fostering financial literacy (Flood,2020). The abstract highlights the potential of digital financial tools to reach previously underserved populations, breaking down barriers that hindered financial inclusion (Tabuena,2021). Moreover, the abstract explores real-life examples and case studies showcasing the positive outcomes of E-Financial Strategies, illustrating how these innovations have not only improved financial access but also empowered individuals to take control of their economic destinies. The abstract concludes by emphasizing the ongoing shift towards a more inclusive and empowered society, driven by the ongoing Digital Financial Revolution and the strategic implementation of E-Financial Strategies (Gupta,2017).

3.1.1 DEFINING FINANCIAL INCLUSION

Financial inclusion is a concept that goes beyond merely having a bank account. It encapsulates the idea of providing affordable and accessible financial services to all segments of society, including the unbanked and underbanked populations (Flood,2019). Historically, barriers such as geographical distance, lack of infrastructure, and financial illiteracy have excluded a significant portion of the global population from the formal financial system. Financial inclusion has transcended mere economic policy to become a global imperative, reflecting a collective commitment to empower individuals across all strata of society (eMarketer 2019). As the world undergoes a paradigm shift in the way financial services are accessed and utilized, the evolution of financial inclusion emerges as a beacon of hope, promising to dismantle barriers, bridge gaps, and unlock the economic potential of billions. This chapter embarks on a journey through the uncharted waters of this evolution, exploring its historical roots, contemporary strategies, and the transformative impact on individuals and communities (Flood, 2020).

3.1.2 THE RISE OF E-FINANCIAL STRATEGIES

E-financial strategies encompass a diverse array of digital tools and platforms that leverage technology to bring financial services to the fingertips of those who were once excluded. From mobile banking and digital wallets to online banking platforms, these strategies are reshaping the financial landscape, breaking down traditional barriers, and creating opportunities for financial inclusion on an unprecedented scale (Kaushik,2016).

- **Section 1: Mobile Banking and Payments**

  1. **The Pervasiveness of Mobile Phones:** The widespread adoption of mobile phones, even in the most remote corners of the

globe, has paved the way for mobile banking and payment solutions (Donner,2008). Mobile money platforms have emerged as powerful tools for financial inclusion, enabling individuals to conduct transactions securely without the need for a traditional bank account (Kotler,2013).

2. **Empowering the Unbanked:** Mobile banking not only provides a convenient way to conduct financial transactions but also empowers the unbanked by giving them control over their finances. Case studies from regions where mobile banking has made significant strides demonstrate the transformative impact on individuals and communities (Flood,2020).

➢ **Section 2: Digital Wallets**

1. **Storing, Managing, and Transferring Funds Digitally:** Digital wallets have become synonymous with the ease of managing and transferring funds electronically. These wallets, accessible through smartphones, offer a user-friendly interface for individuals who may not have access to traditional banking infrastructure (Rathore,2017).

   i. **Digital Storage of Funds:** The chapter begins by delving into the concept of storing funds digitally, emphasizing the departure from physical cash and traditional banking methods. Digital wallets, online banking platforms, and emerging technologies like blockchain are discussed as innovative solutions that provide secure and convenient alternatives for individuals to store their financial assets. The advantages of accessibility, real-time monitoring, and the integration of multiple accounts within digital storage systems are highlighted (Ibrahim,2018).

   ii. **Efficient Fund Management:** The digital era has given rise to sophisticated tools and platforms that empower users to manage their funds with unprecedented efficiency. This section explores how individuals can leverage financial apps, budgeting software, and robo-advisors to gain insights into their spending patterns, set financial goals, and make informed investment decisions. The integration of artificial intelligence and ML in financial management applications is also discussed as a means to enhance personal finance strategies.

iii. **Seamless Digital Transfers:** The chapter then shifts focus to the evolution of digital fund transfers, dissecting how technology has streamlined the process of moving money between individuals and accounts. Mobile banking applications, peer-to-peer payment platforms, and the global reach of digital currency transactions are explored. The convenience of instant transfers, reduced transaction costs, and the elimination of geographical barriers are emphasized as key advantages of digital fund transfers.

iv. **Cryptocurrencies and the Future Landscape:** An integral part of the digital finance revolution is the emergence of cryptocurrencies. This section delves into how digital currencies, led by the pioneering Bitcoin, are reshaping the way funds are stored, managed, and transferred. The decentralized nature of blockchain technology, the potential for borderless transactions, and the evolving regulatory landscape surrounding cryptocurrencies are discussed as influential factors in the future of digital finance.

v. **Security Measures in the Digital Realm:** Given the increased reliance on digital platforms for financial transactions, security becomes a paramount concern. The chapter explores the various security measures embedded in digital financial systems, such as encryption technologies, multi-factor authentication, and biometric verification. The importance of user education in promoting secure digital financial practices is also underscored.

vi. **Challenges and Ethical Considerations:** While digital finance brings a plethora of benefits, it is not without challenges. This section discusses issues such as cybersecurity threats, data privacy concerns, and the ethical considerations associated with the use of advanced technologies in financial transactions. Striking a balance between innovation and responsible practices becomes a crucial aspect of navigating the digital financial landscape.

2. **Inclusion beyond Borders:** Digital wallets transcend geographical boundaries, allowing for cross-border transactions without the need for traditional banking intermediaries. This aspect of e-financial strategies opens up new possibilities for global financial inclusion and economic participation. This chapter explores the profound impact of inclusion on a worldwide scale, emphasizing the importance of diversity, equality, and a collaborative approach to fostering a more inclusive global society (Saura,2019).

   i. **Cultural Diversity: A Mosaic of Perspectives:**

      - Cultural inclusion recognizes and values the diversity of traditions, languages, and perspectives worldwide.
      - Understanding and appreciating cultural differences contribute to a richer global tapestry, fostering mutual respect and collaboration.

   ii. **Global Workplace Inclusion: Breaking Down Barriers:**

      - Inclusive workplaces embrace diversity in terms of nationality, ethnicity, and background.
      - Organizations benefit from a global talent pool, diverse perspectives, and a more innovative and adaptable workforce (Rathore,2017).

   iii. **Gender Inclusion: Empowering Women Everywhere:**

      - Gender inclusion addresses disparities and empowers women worldwide.
      - Promoting gender equality not only benefits individuals but also contributes to economic development and social progress.

   iv. **Educational Inclusion: Bridging the Knowledge Divide:**

      - Inclusive education focuses on providing equal learning opportunities for students globally.
      - Technology plays a crucial role in bridging educational gaps and ensuring access to quality learning resources beyond borders.

v. **Inclusive Technology: Bridging the Digital Divide:**

- Technological inclusion aims to bridge the digital divide, ensuring equitable access to digital resources globally.
- Initiatives such as affordable internet connectivity and accessible technology empower individuals across borders.

vi. **Financial Inclusion: Empowering Economies Worldwide:**

- Financial inclusion initiatives aim to provide access to banking and financial services globally.
- Closing financial gaps contributes to poverty reduction and stimulates economic growth in diverse regions.

vii. **Environmental Inclusion: A Unified Approach to Sustainability:**

- Environmental inclusion emphasizes collective responsibility for sustainable practices.
- Global cooperation is essential to address climate change, protect biodiversity, and ensure a harmonious relationship with the planet.

viii. **Healthcare Inclusion: Ensuring Well-being for All:**

- Inclusive healthcare initiatives prioritize equal access to medical resources and services.
- Global health efforts, collaborative research, and equitable vaccine distribution exemplify inclusive approaches to healthcare.

ix. **Human Rights: A Universal Commitment:**

- Human rights inclusion transcends borders, advocating for the dignity and rights of individuals worldwide.
- Collective efforts are essential to address human rights violations and promote a just and inclusive global society.

x. **Social Media and Global Connection: Breaking Isolation:**

- Social media platforms create virtual spaces for global connection and inclusivity (Saura,2019).

- Digital communities enable individuals to share experiences, ideas, and support beyond geographical constraints.

➢ **Section 3: Online Banking Platforms**

1. **Access to a Range of Financial Services:** Online banking platforms provide a comprehensive suite of financial services, from account management to loan applications. The digital nature of these platforms eliminates the need for physical proximity to a bank, making financial services accessible to individuals in remote areas. The transformative impact of providing individuals with access to diverse financial services examines how this access fosters financial inclusion, economic growth, and overall well-being (Kotler,2013).

   i. **Breaking Down Barriers: Financial Inclusion for All:**

   - Access to a range of financial services is synonymous with financial inclusion, breaking down traditional barriers that once excluded vast segments of the population.
   - From banking and credit to insurance and investment options, inclusive financial services empower individuals to participate fully in the economic landscape (Noromor,2020).

   ii. **Banking Beyond Boundaries: The Rise of Digital Banking:**

   - Digital banking has emerged as a powerful force in expanding access to financial services, transcending geographical limitations.
   - Online banking, mobile apps, and digital wallets provide individuals with the ability to manage their finances conveniently, irrespective of their location.

   iii. **Microfinance: Empowering Entrepreneurs at the Grassroots:**

   - Microfinance institutions play a pivotal role in extending financial services to small entrepreneurs and those in underserved communities.

- Access to microloans empowers individuals to start or expand small businesses, contributing to local economic development.

iv. Mobile Money: Revolutionizing Transactions:

- Mobile money services have revolutionized financial transactions, particularly in regions with limited access to traditional banking infrastructure.
- Easy, secure, and instant transfers via mobile devices empower individuals to send and receive money, fostering financial connectivity.

v. Investment Opportunities for All: Robo-Advisors and Financial Inclusion:

- Robo-advisors leverage technology to provide automated, cost-effective investment advice to a broader audience.
- Access to investment opportunities, once reserved for a select few, is democratized through robo-advisory services, enabling individuals to grow their wealth.

vi. Insurance for Risk Mitigation: Protecting Livelihoods:

- Access to insurance services is a crucial aspect of comprehensive financial inclusion.
- Insurance products provide a safety net, mitigating risks associated with health, property, and unforeseen events, ensuring financial stability for individuals and families.

vii. Government Initiatives: Driving Inclusive Financial Policies:

- Governments play a vital role in driving inclusive financial policies that ensure a range of services is accessible to all citizens.
- Direct benefit transfers, financial literacy programs, and supportive regulatory frameworks contribute to an inclusive financial ecosystem (Kotler,1969).

viii. Educational Finance: Investing in Knowledge and Skills:

- Access to financial services extends beyond transactions, encompassing educational finance.
- Loans and financial aid for education empower individuals to invest in knowledge and skills, breaking the cycle of limited opportunities (Kotler.,2017).

ix. Sustainable Finance: Aligning Financial Services with Environmental Goals:

- The concept of sustainable finance involves aligning financial services with environmental and social goals.
- Access to sustainable finance options supports environmentally conscious individuals and businesses, contributing to global efforts for a more sustainable future (Ibrahim ,2018).

x. Empowering Future Generations: Youth Financial Inclusion:

- Fostering financial inclusion for the youth is pivotal for building economically empowered future generations.
- Access to educational finance, youth-friendly banking services, and financial literacy programs set the stage for lifelong financial resilience.

2. **Overcoming Traditional Banking Constraints:** The traditional banking model often involves high operational costs, resulting in services that are unaffordable for many. E-financial strategies, being inherently digital, reduce these overheads, making financial services more affordable and thus encouraging wider adoption. This chapter explores how emerging technologies and progressive financial strategies are breaking free from conventional constraints, offering a glimpse into a future where banking transcends traditional boundaries (Kotler,1969).

i. **Digital Banking: Liberating Financial Access:**

- Digital banking has emerged as a liberating force, freeing individuals from the constraints of physical branches and rigid banking hours.
- With the advent of online platforms and mobile apps, customers can now access banking services anytime, anywhere, fostering unparalleled convenience.

ii. **Decentralized Finance (DeFi): Redefining Banking Structures:**

- Decentralized Finance, or DeFi, is disrupting traditional banking by leveraging blockchain technology to create a decentralized financial system.
- Through smart contracts and blockchain, DeFi eliminates the need for intermediaries, providing users with direct and inclusive access to financial services (Suginraj,2017).

iii. **Open Banking: Fostering Collaboration and Innovation:**

- Open banking initiatives break down the silos of traditional financial institutions, fostering collaboration between banks and third-party providers.
- By opening up access to financial data and services, open banking encourages innovation, competition, and a more customer-centric approach (Statista, 262966).

iv. **Neobanks: Agility Beyond the Brick-and-Mortar:**

- Neobanks, born in the digital age, operate without physical branches, allowing them to prioritize agility and innovation.
- These digital-only banks leverage technology to provide users with seamless, user-friendly experiences, challenging the conventions of traditional banking.

v. **Mobile-First Approach: Banking in the Palm of Your Hand:**

- A mobile-first approach is revolutionizing banking by prioritizing the user experience on smartphones.

- Mobile banking applications offer a range of services, from account management to financial planning, putting the power of banking directly into users' hands (Gupta,2017).

vi. AI and Machine Learning: Personalizing Financial Experiences:

- Artificial Intelligence (AI) and Machine Learning (ML) algorithms are transforming traditional banking by personalizing services based on user behavior and preferences.
- From customized financial advice to fraud detection, these technologies enhance the overall customer experience.

vii. Cryptocurrencies: Beyond Traditional Currency Systems:

- Cryptocurrencies, led by Bitcoin and Ethereum, challenge traditional currency systems by operating on decentralized blockchain networks.
- The rise of digital currencies introduces new possibilities for borderless transactions and financial inclusion, transcending the limitations of traditional banking.

viii. Biometric Security: Enhancing Trust and Safety:

- Overcoming security concerns associated with traditional banking, biometric authentication methods such as fingerprint and facial recognition enhance trust and safety in digital transactions.
- Biometric security measures provide users with a seamless yet highly secure banking experience.

ix. Financial Inclusion Initiatives: Bridging Gaps Globally:

- Financial inclusion initiatives leverage technology to reach unbanked and underbanked populations globally.
- From mobile money solutions to innovative lending platforms, these initiatives aim to bridge gaps and empower individuals who were traditionally excluded from formal banking systems.

x. **Regulatory Adaptation: Navigating a New Banking Landscape:**

- Regulatory bodies are adapting to the changing financial landscape by creating frameworks that accommodate innovative financial technologies.
- Regulatory support for financial innovation is essential to foster a balanced environment that encourages progress while ensuring consumer protection.

➢ **Section 4: Overcoming Barriers to Financial Inclusion**

1. **Geographic Accessibility:** One of the primary barriers to financial inclusion has been geographic distance. E-Financial strategies, especially those based on mobile and online platforms, transcend these physical barriers, reaching individuals in remote and underserved areas.

2. **Affordability and Cost-Effectiveness:** Traditional banking services often come with high transaction costs, making them unaffordable for many. E-Financial strategies address this by leveraging digital platforms that are inherently more cost-effective, making financial services more accessible to a broader population.

3. **Financial Literacy:** Digital interfaces accompanying E-Financial strategies can be powerful tools for financial education. By simplifying complex financial concepts, these interfaces empower individuals to make informed decisions regarding their financial well-being. Efforts to promote financial literacy can enhance the effectiveness of E-Financial strategies in promoting inclusion.

➢ **Section 5: Case Studies and Success Stories**

1. **M-Pesa in Kenya:** M-Pesa, an innovative mobile money service, has etched its place in the financial landscape of Kenya, redefining how transactions are conducted and bringing financial inclusion to the forefront. This chapter explores the transformative journey of M-Pesa, its origins, impact, and the pivotal role it plays in shaping Kenya's

financial ecosystem. The success story of M-Pesa, Kenya's mobile money platform, is a testament to the transformative impact of e-financial strategies. By providing a convenient and secure way for individuals to transact digitally, M-Pesa has significantly increased financial inclusion in Kenya.

2. **India's Aadhaar Enabled Payment System (AEPS):** It stands as a pioneering initiative in the realm of financial inclusion, leveraging technology to bridge gaps and empower the unbanked population. This chapter delves into the intricacies of AEPS, exploring its origins, functionalities, impact, and the role it plays in revolutionizing financial services for millions across the nation (Suginraj,2017).

   i. **The Aadhaar Foundation: A Biometric Revolution:**
      - The Aadhaar initiative, launched in 2009, laid the groundwork for AEPS by providing a unique 12-digit identification number linked to biometric data for every Indian resident.
      - With over a billion Aadhaar registrations, the foundation was laid for an inclusive and secure digital identification system.

   ii. **Understanding AEPS: A Biometrically Secured Payment Gateway:**
      - AEPS leverages the Aadhaar infrastructure to enable secure and biometrically authenticated financial transactions.
      - Users can access banking services, including cash withdrawals, balance inquiries, and fund transfers, using their Aadhaar number and fingerprint authentication.

   iii. **Inclusive Banking for the Unbanked:**
      - AEPS targets the unbanked and underbanked population, allowing them to access basic financial services without the need for traditional bank accounts.
      - Rural and remote areas benefit significantly as AEPS brings banking services closer to individuals who

were historically excluded from the formal financial system.

iv. Fingerprint Authentication: The Key to Financial Inclusion:

- Fingerprint authentication ensures the security and uniqueness of transactions, reducing the risk of fraud.
- This biometric approach enhances financial inclusion by providing a secure and accessible means for individuals who may not be familiar with traditional banking methods.

v. Cashless Transactions: A Paradigm Shift:

- AEPS facilitates cashless transactions, reducing reliance on physical currency and enhancing financial literacy.
- Users can make payments and access various financial services without the need for physical cards or extensive paperwork.

vi. Government Initiatives and AEPS: Direct Benefit Transfers (DBT):

- The Indian government leverages AEPS for Direct Benefit Transfer (DBT) programs, ensuring that subsidies and welfare payments reach beneficiaries directly.
- AEPS plays a pivotal role in streamlining the distribution of social welfare benefits, reducing leakages, and enhancing efficiency.

vii. AEPS in Rural India: Transformative Impact:

- In rural areas, where banking infrastructure is limited, AEPS serves as a lifeline, empowering communities with access to financial services.
- The system supports agricultural transactions, government payouts, and various financial activities crucial for rural development.

viii. Challenges and Innovations: Evolving the AEPS Landscape:

- While AEPS has achieved remarkable success, challenges such as connectivity issues and technological awareness persist.
- Continuous innovations, including the integration of AEPS with mobile banking and digital wallets, contribute to overcoming these challenges and expanding its reach.

ix. Security Measures: Ensuring Trust in Digital Transactions:

- The Aadhaar infrastructure incorporates robust security measures to safeguard user data and transactions.
- Multi-layered authentication protocols and encryption technologies contribute to building trust in AEPS transactions.

x. Future Prospects: AEPS in the Digital India Vision:

- AEPS aligns with the Digital India vision, fostering a digitally empowered society and a knowledge economy.
- Future prospects include broader integration with emerging technologies, enhanced services, and a deeper penetration into remote areas.

➢ Section 6: Regulatory Framework and Security

1. The Need for a Robust Regulatory Framework:

As E-Financial strategies gain prominence, it becomes crucial to establish a regulatory framework that ensures the security and privacy of users. Governments and regulatory bodies play a pivotal role in creating an environment that fosters trust in digital financial transactions (Murthy, 2016).

2. Collaborative Efforts for Security

Collaboration between governments, regulatory bodies, and industry stakeholders is essential to address security concerns associated with E-Financial strategies. Establishing standards for data protection, encryption, and user authentication is paramount to build and maintain trust in digital financial services (Murthy, 2016).

- **Section 7: The Future of E-Financial Strategies**

1. **Blockchain and Cryptocurrencies:** The advent of blockchain technology and cryptocurrencies introduces new possibilities for financial inclusion. By providing decentralized and secure financial solutions, these technologies have the potential to reach individuals who were previously excluded from traditional banking systems. The intricacies of blockchain technology and cryptocurrencies, their origins, functionalities, and the transformative impact they have on the financial sector (Murthy, 2016).

   i. **Blockchain Unveiled: The Foundation of Decentralization:**

   - Blockchain, the underlying technology behind cryptocurrencies, is a decentralized and distributed ledger that records transactions across a network of computers.
   - The immutable and transparent nature of blockchain ensures trust in transactions, eliminating the need for centralized intermediaries (Kaushik, 2016).

   ii. **Cryptocurrencies: Digital Currencies in a Decentralized World:**

   - Cryptocurrencies are digital or virtual currencies that utilize cryptographic techniques for secure financial transactions.
   - Bitcoin, introduced in 2009, was the first decentralized cryptocurrency, paving the way for a myriad of alternative digital currencies.

   iii. **Decentralized Finance (DeFi): Redefining Financial Services:**

   - Decentralized Finance, or DeFi, leverages blockchain to recreate traditional financial services in a decentralized manner.

- DeFi applications include lending, borrowing, trading, and yield farming, providing users with a permissionless and open financial ecosystem.

iv. Smart Contracts: Executing Trust in Code:

- Smart contracts are self-executing contracts with the terms directly written into code on the blockchain.
- These contracts automate and enforce agreements, reducing the need for intermediaries and enhancing the efficiency of transactions.

v. Bitcoin: Digital Gold and Store of Value:

- Bitcoin, often referred to as digital gold, is a decentralized and finite cryptocurrency that serves as a store of value.
- Its decentralized nature, capped supply, and scarcity contribute to its appeal as a hedge against inflation and traditional economic uncertainties.

vi. Ethereum and the Era of Programmable Money:

- Ethereum introduced the concept of programmable money, enabling the creation of decentralized applications (DApps) and smart contracts.
- Ethereum's versatility has catalyzed the development of a diverse range of decentralized projects beyond simple currency use cases.

vii. Challenges and Scalability: Navigating the Roadblocks:

- Blockchain and cryptocurrencies face challenges, including scalability concerns, energy consumption debates, and regulatory uncertainties.
- Ongoing research and development efforts aim to address these challenges and enhance the scalability and sustainability of blockchain networks (Kharandoo, 2017).

vii. **Initial Coin Offerings (ICOs) and Tokenization: Democratizing Funding:**

- ICOs enabled startups to raise capital by issuing tokens on blockchain networks, democratizing funding opportunities.
- Tokenization extends beyond fundraising, representing ownership of assets like real estate, art, and even individual pieces of companies.

ix. **Central Bank Digital Currencies (CBDCs): A Paradigm Shift in Traditional Finance:**

- Central banks worldwide are exploring the creation of CBDCs, digital versions of national currencies, on blockchain technology.
- CBDCs aim to modernize the financial system, enhance payment efficiency, and maintain control over monetary policy.

x. **The Future of Finance: Integration and Innovation:**

- The future of finance holds the promise of continued integration of blockchain and cryptocurrencies into traditional systems.
- Innovations such as non-fungible tokens (NFTs), cross-border payment solutions, and blockchain-based identity verification are poised to transform various facets of the financial sector.

2. **Artificial Intelligence and Machine Learning:** The integration of artificial intelligence (AI) and machine learning (ML) into E-Financial strategies can enhance the personalization and efficiency of financial services. These technologies can analyze user behavior, predict financial needs, and offer tailored solutions, further promoting financial inclusion (Tabuena, 2021).

   - **Potential Benefits of Financial Inclusion:** The process of providing access to a wide range of financial services to individuals and businesses has numerous potential benefits.

Here are some key points highlighting the advantages of financial inclusion:

i. **Poverty Reduction:**

- Financial inclusion can empower individuals and communities economically, helping to lift them out of poverty.
- Access to financial services allows people to save, invest, and build assets, breaking the cycle of poverty.

ii. **Economic Growth:**

- By broadening access to financial resources, financial inclusion stimulates economic activity and fosters overall economic growth.
- Small and medium-sized enterprises (SMEs) gain the necessary capital to expand, creating jobs and contributing to economic development.

iii. **Entrepreneurship and Innovation:**

- Increased access to credit enables entrepreneurs to start or expand businesses, fostering innovation and job creation.
- Financial inclusion provides a platform for individuals to turn their ideas into viable businesses.

iv. **Risk Mitigation and Resilience:**

- Financially included individuals can better manage risks through insurance and savings products, increasing resilience against unexpected events.
- Insurance products can provide a safety net during emergencies, preventing financial setbacks.

v. **Education and Healthcare:**

- Financial inclusion facilitates access to funds for education, allowing individuals to invest in their skills and knowledge.
- Improved access to healthcare financing ensures that individuals can afford necessary medical treatments.

vi. Gender Equality:

- Financial inclusion can empower women by giving them control over their finances and access to credit.
- Women's participation in the formal financial sector can contribute to narrowing gender gaps in economic opportunities.

vii. Financial Stability:

- A more inclusive financial system contributes to overall financial stability by reducing the reliance on informal and unregulated financial channels.
- Diverse participation in the financial sector enhances the resilience of the financial system.

viii. Social Welfare Distribution:

- Government assistance and social welfare programs can be more efficiently distributed through digital financial channels, reaching beneficiaries directly.
- Financial inclusion helps in promoting inclusive growth by ensuring that the benefits of development programs reach all segments of society.

ix. Digital Transformation:

- Financial inclusion often involves the adoption of digital financial services, contributing to the overall digital transformation of economies.
- Digital financial tools promote efficiency, transparency, and cost-effectiveness in financial transactions.

x. Improved Financial Literacy:

- Financial inclusion initiatives often include educational components, improving financial literacy and empowering individuals to make informed financial decisions.
- Increased understanding of financial concepts enhances the effectiveness of financial services.

xi. **Reduced Income Inequality:**

- Financial inclusion can contribute to reducing income inequality by providing marginalized groups with opportunities to build wealth and access financial resources.
- It promotes a more equitable distribution of economic benefits.

xii. **Government Revenue Collection:** Inclusive financial systems facilitate more efficient tax collection, contributing to government revenue and supporting public services.

xiii. **Global Economic Integration:** Financially included individuals and businesses are better positioned to participate in the global economy, fostering international trade and economic integration.

xiv. **Community Development:** Financially empowered communities are better equipped to invest in local development projects, such as infrastructure, education, and healthcare facilities.

xv. **Social Inclusion:** Financial inclusion can contribute to social inclusion by providing marginalized groups with the means to participate in economic activities and social life.

3.2 CONCLUSION

In conclusion, E-Financial strategies represent a revolutionary force in the pursuit of global financial inclusion. From mobile banking to digital wallets and online platforms, these strategies leverage technology to break down traditional barriers and provide access to financial services for the unbanked and underbanked. The success stories of M-Pesa in Kenya and India's AEPS showcase the real-world impact of E-Financial strategies in transforming lives and promoting economic inclusion. As we look to the future, the continued evolution of E-Financial strategies, coupled with advancements in blockchain, cryptocurrencies, AI, and ML, holds the promise of even greater financial inclusion. However, it is crucial to address regulatory challenges and security concerns to ensure the sustainability and trustworthiness of these digital financial ecosystems. Policymakers, financial institutions, and technology providers must collaborate to harness the full potential of E-Financial strategies. By doing so, we can create a more inclusive and equitable financial landscape, where individuals, regardless of their geographical location or socio-economic status, can participate fully in the global economy. The journey towards financial inclusion through E-Financial strategies is not just a technological evolution; it is a transformative force that has the power to uplift communities and reshape the future of finance.

KEYWORDS

- **digital connectivity**
- **digital financial revolution**
- **digital literacy**
- **economic empowerment**
- **e-financial strategies**
- **financial literacy**
- **inclusive growth**

REFERENCES

Benamati, J. S., & Serva, M. A. (2007). Trust and distrust in online banking: Their role in developing countries. *Information Technology for Development*, *13*(2), 161–175.

Dewi, N. P. R. C. (2020). Digital marketing strategy on travel tourism businesses in marketing 4.0 era. *International Research Journal of Management, IT and Social Sciences*, *7*(3), 58–64.

Dholakia, N., & Kshetri, N. (2004). Internet commerce as a solution to the global digital divide: Selected cases of e-development. In S. Krishna & S. Madon (Eds.), *The digital challenge: Information technology in the development context* (pp. 237–250). Ashgate Publishing.

Donner, J. (2008). Research approaches to Internet use in the developing world: A review of the literature. *The Information Society*, *24*(3), 140–159.

eMarketer. (2019). *India Time Spent with Media 2019*. https://www.emarketer.com/content/india-time-spent-with-media-2019 (accessed on 7th July 2025).

Flood, E. C. (2020). Ecommerce decelerates amid global retail contraction but remains a bright spot. *Global Ecommerce 2020*.

Gupta, Seema. (2017). *Digital Marketing*. McGraw Hill Education (India) Private Limited.

Ibrahim, S. S., & Ganeshbabu, P. (2018). A study on the impact of social media marketing trends on digital marketing. *Shanlax International Journal of Management*, *6*(1), 120–125.

Kaushik, R. (2016). Digital marketing in Indian context. *International Journal of Computational Engineering and Management*, *19*(2), 12–17. http://ijcem.org/papers032016/ijcem_032016_03.pdf (accessed on 7th July 2025).

Kharandoo, G. (2017). Digital marketing in India–Its scope, growth and development. *International Journal of Management, IT & Engineering*, *7*(5), 289–296. https://papers.ssrn.com/sol3/papers.cfm?abstract_id=3635922 (accessed on 7th July 2025).

Kotler, P., & Keller, K. J. (2013). *Marketing Management*. Pearson Education Ltd.

Kotler, P., & Levi, S. J. (1969). Broadening the concept of marketing. Pearson Education Ltd.

Murthy, S. (2016). Always keep your customers close and your loyalist closer. *The Economic Times*. https://articles.economictimes.indiatimes.com/collections/digital-marketing (accessed on 7th July 2025).

Noromor, R. (2020). The digital marketing landscape in the Philippines. *Emerge Digital Agency*.

Rathore, A., Singh, M., Pant, M., & Sharma, C. (2017). Emerging trends in digital marketing in India. *International Conference on Innovative Research in Science, Technology and Management*, 107–115. http://data.conferenceworld.in/MIMT/P107-115.pdf (accessed on 7th July 2025).

Saura, J. R., Palos-Sanchez, P. R., & Correia, M. B. (2019). Digital marketing strategies based on the e-business model: Literature review and future directions. In *Organizational Transformation and Managing Innovation in the Fourth Industrial Revolution* (pp. 86–103).

Statista. (n.d.). *Number of Internet Users in Selected Countries*. https://www.statista.com/statistics/262966/number-of-internet-users-in-selected-countries/ (accessed on 7th July 2025).

Suginraj, M. (2017). Growth of online marketing in India–A study. *International Journal of Research in Management & Business Studies (IJRMBS)*, *4*(3), 9–14. https://ijrmbs.com/vol4issue3SPL1/suginraj.pdf (accessed on 7th July 2025).

Tabuena, A. C., Hilario, Y. M. C., & Buenaflor, M. P. (2021). Overview and exemplar components of the research methodology on the research writing process for senior high school students. *International Journal of Trend in Scientific Research and Development*, *5*(3), 117–126.

Zhang, G., Dubinsky, A. J., & Tan, Y. (2011). Impact of blogs on sales revenue: Test of a network model. *International Journal of Virtual Communities and Social Networking (IJVCSN)*, *3*(2), 60–74.

CHAPTER 4

Shaping Tomorrow: Understanding Youth Perspectives on Climate Change

NAVITA NATHANI,[1] KIRAN ROHIRA,[2] PUSHPA NEGI,[3] and ANMOL KHATRI[4]

[1]*Amity Business School, Amity University, Madhya Pradesh, India*

[2]*Department of Management, Prestige Institute of Management and Research, Gwalior, Madhya Pradesh, India*

[3]*Department of Finance, New Delhi Institute of Management, New Delhi, India*

[4]*Alumnus, Prestige Institute of Management and Research, Gwalior, Madhya Pradesh, India*

*Corresponding author

ABSTRACT

The research is undertaken to establish the relation between green initiatives and climate change, with a mediating variable named carbon drifts/carbon trading. The components of green initiatives for the purpose of our research are green financing, legislative framework, capacity building, awareness, and innovative tools. The research conducted is based on a survey method, wherein 200 respondents were interviewed based on their perceived awareness and knowledge about financial instruments and how their investments can affect climate change. Purposive sampling is used, and primary data collection is carried out through a standardized questionnaire. Furthermore, opinions on the intermediate factor, CO_2 trading, were gathered as a categorical distinction, differentiating between high and low

E-Financial Strategies for Sustainable Development: A Handbook for Promoting Financial Inclusion and Ending Poverty (SDG 1). Ernesto D. R. Santibanez Gonzalez, Rajeev Sijariya, and Vikas Garg (Eds.)

DOI: 10.1201/9781779640956-4

perceptions of carbon trading. Data is analyzed using ANCOVA to test the mediation effect. The study revealed that only awareness and climate change share a significant relationship with carbon drift as a mediating variable, while the rest of the independent variables have no significant impact or have a negative impact on climate change.

4.1 INTRODUCTION

Green financing is a powerful tool to fight against climate change and an emerging area worldwide. Despite this, as of late, green finance remains a complex subject. Green finance refers to monetary investments made solely to promote environmental protection. Green finance includes green asset funding, green loans, and green investments. The private sector can help support environmental projects that the government does not fund adequately.

To understand its significance, one must first recognize the harsh consequences of unchecked carbon emissions on the environment through the burning of fossil fuels for various industrial processes and energy production, which results in greenhouse gas emissions that further lead to global warming, ecological disruptions, rising sea levels, and so forth. Green finance can address these challenges by redirecting capital flow towards sustainable projects through various green investment options such as green bonds, loans, and funds. These projects use efficient technologies, renewable energy infrastructure, and more to combat carbon emissions at their source.

Moreover, green financing incentivizes businesses and industries to adopt sustainable practices. Companies are now able to recognize the increasing importance of environmental responsibility in securing financing and investor confidence. By incorporating eco-friendly operations, integrating energy-efficient technologies, and embracing sustainable supply chain practices, businesses can tap into green financing opportunities. This not only diminishes their environmental impact but also promotes a culture of sustainability across industries.

Environmental degradation is likely more pronounced in less fortunate nations, requiring significant green funding initiatives. Agricultural nation-state governments might create and implement policies that promote green finance. Green bonds are increasingly being used to provide long-term support for environmental projects.

Climate change calls for urgent preservation and remedial measures; it's an existential challenge today and has emerged as a global crisis with long-term consequences for our planet. Additionally, strategies to reduce carbon emissions by exploiting renewable energy have gained prominence. Governments and industries worldwide have been investing in clean energy technologies and incentivizing their adoption to curb greenhouse gas emissions. However, to achieve this mission, efforts and education at the individual level are of great importance, such as reducing energy consumption, minimizing waste, adopting eco-friendly lifestyles, and, more importantly, focusing on green investments that will not only earn financial returns but will also generate positive environmental and social impacts, ultimately resulting in long-term perceived value for an investor. This chapter, therefore, aims to study the perception of young minds towards climate change through the knowledge of green finance initiatives and investments.

4.2 THEORETICAL FRAMEWORK

According to the International Energy Agency (IEA), three-quarters of global greenhouse gas emissions originate from the energy sector. Further, research from the United Nations Environment Programme (UNEP) shows a significant increase in investments in renewable energy, offsetting carbon emissions associated with conventional energy sources. Moreover, studies conducted by the Climate Policy Initiative (CPI) highlight the substantial role of green bonds in financing climate-friendly projects. To reduce carbon footprints, these bonds have mobilized a large chunk of money towards projects aiming to reduce carbon footprints by contributing to funding and supporting clean energy transportation and efficiency programs.

It is evident that to foster sustainable innovation, many apex financial institutions like the European Investment Bank (EIB) and the Federal Reserve Bank are showcasing the ripple effect of green financing. Smart grid technologies, solar panel efficiency, and renewable storage solutions are accelerating the global transition towards a low-carbon economy.

By directing capital towards research and development in clean energy technologies, green financing stimulates innovation cycles. Research done by the World Bank emphasizes the importance of policy frameworks and regulatory mechanisms to unlock the full potential of green financing.

Additionally, there is a growing demand for sustainable investment options, as data from the Global Sustainable Investment Alliance (GSIA) indicates the increasing prominence of environmental, social, and governance (ESG) factors in investment choices, thereby prioritizing sustainability. While the role of government in capacity building and designing attractive environmental policy is crucial, there is an urgent need to create crystal-clear policies to safeguard investors and scale up green initiatives.

The present study used the PERMA theory to assess the financial well-being of the participants. Given by Dr. Seligman in 2011, the theory propounds a five-point method:

P – Positive Emotion, E – Engagement, R – Relationships, M – Meaning, and A – Accomplishment towards green investments.

As soon as this concept gains popularity, it will attract and engage more and more investors to think green and act green.

The theory coined by Svante Arrhenius on anthropogenic climate change first predicted that the surface temperature of the Earth can be altered by changes in CO_2 levels (1896). Further, Roger Revelle and H.E. Suess (1957) significantly contributed to it, highlighting human activities as the primary cause of the rapidly increasing global warming and climate change. Moreover, the Greenhouse Effect theory, pioneered by Joseph Fourier in 1824, posits that certain gases known as greenhouse gases lead to the rise in temperatures. To address this imminent threat, the government has taken various measures, such as the Paris Agreement of 2015, which stands as a landmark initiative.

The concept of green initiatives has evolved over time due to growing environmental concerns such as climate change, resource depletion, increasing CO_2 levels, and more. Additionally, people are now much more informed about the impact of anthropogenic activities on the environment, which entails the critical requirement for sustainable practices in various industries. Moreover, government policies and regulations have come into existence to address these issues. These policies also incentivized and mandated businesses to adopt green practices, encouraging the development of green initiatives. Furthermore, the mandate of CSR activities towards the environment and society by the government for corporates with a certain specific turnover limit, the response of the financial sector such as the issuance of green bonds, green loans, and green investment funds, and upcoming global initiatives and agreements, for instance, the

Paris Agreement, all together highlight the shift from traditional investment models towards modern or green investment models.

4.3 LITERATURE REVIEW

As climate change has become an important issue and to mitigate the same, financial institutions are offering green financing. However, the availability of green loans is still in question. According to the author, green loans are comparatively less risky and can be used by businesses to grow and minimize the default risk (Afridi et al., 2021). Also, to guarantee a smooth shift between the traditional and green economy and accelerate the process, robust policies on green finance initiatives can play a pivotal role. Backstrand et al. (2006) highlighted the global challenge of environmental change, considering it one of the most significant hurdles facing humanity. They assessed the effectiveness of green support following the 2015 Paris Agreement, acknowledging green financing as a crucial force in fostering long-term sustainable development and combating ecological threats.

Researchers who have conducted their research on green finance initiatives among Asian countries revealed that India and China did considerably well in developing and implementing policies and procedures for the same (Mumtaz et al., 2019). However, the effective monitoring and its direct or indirect impact on climate change or towards a green environment require a systematic analysis. In spite of green banking policies in existence, the improvement is limited, which may be because of inadequate green finance promotion (Rashid et al., 2018). Also, according to the author, it is very important to keep a check on whether green finance is being contributed to green projects or not, and corrective action must be taken by the government to bridge the gap.

As per the research conducted on the impact of green financing on carbon reduction for climate change mitigation, with the mediating role of energy efficiency, an envelope-based data package model was used, which evaluated the overall energy and efficiency factors in Asian countries, considering both favorable factors (GDP) and unfavorable outputs (CO_2 and SO_2), as well as energy consumption and non-energy inputs like labor and capital stock. The research findings suggest that there is considerable potential for enhancement of energy efficiency in various countries, ultimately resulting in reduced CO_2 emissions (Chang et al., 2021).

Moreover, there is a critical need to investigate the kind of interaction of green financing with renewable electricity sources and efficiency in both developed and developing countries (Liu et al., 2023). Effective execution of post-COVID-19 policies is seen as important for the effectiveness of green projects. The research projects that approximately 26 trillion dollars in green financing activities will be necessary by 2030 to amplify global energy efficiency. Adding to this, Chang et al. (2020) in their study highlight the importance of understanding the difference between green financing, carbon flows, and strategies for mitigating environmental change.

One of the research articles that emphasizes the importance of green finance to manage both financial and environmental concerns suggests that strategic guidance to stakeholders is the key to improving environmental control during emergency situations, especially those caused by fossil fuel by-products (Desalegn et al., 2022). Additionally, their research focused on examining the foundational concepts of carbon markets, acknowledging both successful strategies and implementation failures while emphasizing the emergence of assessments like the Clean Development Mechanism, which integrates evaluation frameworks for carbon credits. The main goal of comprehensive green development relates to achieving economic growth that offers more financial opportunities to a larger number of people, communities, or countries, while safeguarding vulnerable groups. It is emphasized that there's no specific minimum sample size required for effective analysis in these types of reviews. It is suggested that legal agreements could help to bridge the financial gaps that stem from discrepancies between financial and ecological strategies.

Discussion on the concept of carbon trading, a market-based strategy to reduce CO_2 emissions while enhancing both financial and environmental benefits, revealed that by December 31, 2021, the carbon market had exchanged 483 million tons of carbon, worth 8.622 billion yuan, supported by the improvements in China's fossil fuel by-product exchange system (NIE, Chen et al., 2021). Examining the interconnection among green finance, economic development, and environmental quality in 30 Chinese provinces and municipalities from 2010 to 2017, a study employs a green finance development index and various environmental indicators. Zhou et al. (2020) suggested that the positive impact of green finance on economic growth and its contribution to environmental improvement are noteworthy. Furthermore, the study highlights the influence of green finance on environmental quality at different levels of economic development, which plays a crucial role in fostering a harmonious relationship between economic progress and environmental well-being, in accordance with the theory of the environmental Kuznets curve.

Li et al. (2003) investigated the impact of green finance and natural resources on environmental sustainability in 11 countries from the period 2001–2008. The findings suggest that green financing plays a crucial role in significantly reducing carbon emissions, while natural resource rents have adverse effects on environmental sustainability. It also focuses on the need for implementing strategies to enhance such activities to achieve sustainability goals. Sadiq, Amayri et al. (2022) further discussed in their paper that governments all around the world are struggling with environmental challenges generated due to economic activities. The authors considered a timeline from 1995 to 2018 to check the impact of carbon footprints on green finance and renewable energy in South Asia. They assessed the long-term connections among these variables using Ordinary Least Squares (OLS) analysis. Results identified that green finance, clean energy, and green financial instability act as the major factors. Specifically, it highlighted the critical role of green bonds, greenhouse gas emissions reduction, and green economic development in fostering green finance and renewable energy production. Interestingly, the research also revealed a positive and substantial relationship between research and development expenditures and green finance development in South Asia. These findings suggest that investing in research and development could serve as a crucial pathway towards achieving a greener economy in South Asia, offering practical implications for policymakers and stakeholders striving for sustainable development in the region. In fact, they found that a 1% increase in research and development spending led to a decrease in environmental sustainability by 0.070% to 0.080%. An initiative on the Silk Road Economic Belt by Yang et al. (2021) emphasized how renewable and non-renewable energy sources, along with economic growth and investment, affect CO_2 emissions in countries involved in China's Silk Road. They analyzed data from 24 SREB (Silk Road Economic Belt) economies between 1995–2014 using a method called Autoregressive Distributed Lag (ARDL). The findings suggest that using more renewable energy and investing in capital significantly reduces CO_2 emissions in these countries over both short and long terms. A pattern called the Environmental Kuznets Curve was also found, showing that as economies grow, CO_2 emissions initially rise but then start to decrease.

4.4 RESEARCH GAP

The present research addresses an important and timely topic. As per the demographic dividend, India is one of the youngest countries in the world. The present young population is the future leader of tomorrow. Hence, it is significant to understand the young minds towards green investments, who are crucial stakeholders in addressing future sustainability. How do they perceive green finance? What is the role of the government in the legislative framework and in providing training? This research further considers the impact of educational initiatives in shaping attitudes towards climate change. The proposed research may contribute to the existing body of knowledge for a more nuanced understanding of how youth perceive and engage with climate change and green initiatives (Figure 4.1).

RESEARCH MODEL

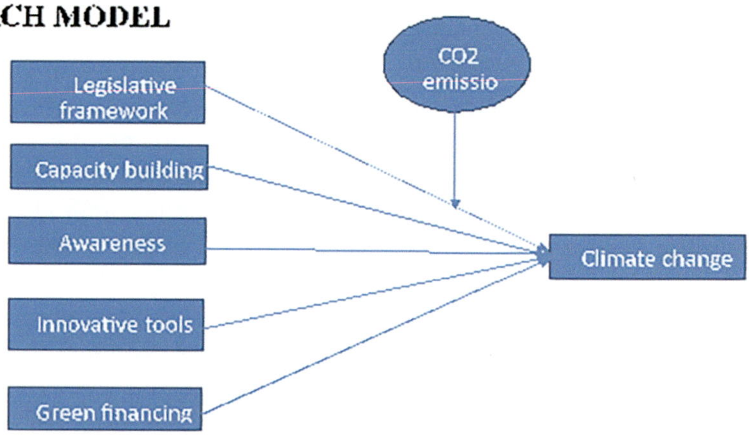

FIGURE 4.1 Model of the study.

4.4.1 *OBJECTIVES*

To establish the relationship between components of green initiatives such as green financing, legislative framework, capacity building, awareness, innovative tools on climate change with mediating variable carbon emission.

4.4.2 *HYPOTHESIS:*

- **H01.** Legislative framework is not affecting climate change with the mediating variable carbon emission.

- **H02.** Green financing does not impact on climate change with the mediating variable carbon drifts.
- **H03.** Capacity building does not impact climate change with the mediating variable carbon drifts.
- **H04.** There is no impact of awareness on climate change with the mediating variable carbon drifts.
- **H05.** There is no impact of innovative tools on climate change with the mediating variable carbon drifts.
- **H06.** CO_2 emission is not affecting climate change with the mediating variable carbon drifts.

4.5 RESEARCH METHODOLOGY

The research undertaken was a causal study, while a survey method was employed to collect data from respondents with knowledge about financial instruments and investments who studied a Sustainability course in their curriculum. For the sampling process, a non-probability purposive sampling technique was applied. Data collection relied on a standardized questionnaire developed by Dr. Marwan Mohamed Abu Orabi (2020), utilizing a Likert scale ranging from 1 to 5 agreement levels, where 1 indicated strong disagreement and 5 represented strong agreement. The questionnaire was distributed among 332 respondents, out of which we received 210 respondents with fully filled responses, and 10 were removed as outliers. In addition, perceptions related to the mediating variable, CO_2 emission, were collected as a categorical variable, distinguishing between high and low CO_2 emission perceptions. The reliability of data inputs is being assessed using Cronbach's reliability test to ensure that the measures accurately represent the intended variable and remain consistent upon repeated measurements (Table 4.1). All the variables considered for the study had Cronbach's alpha values greater than 7, and all the items asked in the questionnaire were reliable for conducting the study. The ANCOVA test was employed to analyze the effects of independent variables on the dependent variable, considering the mediating variable CO_2 trading (Figure 4.2).

4.5.1 RESULTS OF RELIABILITY TEST

TABLE 4.1 Reliability Statistics

Variables	Cronbach's Alpha	No. of Items
Green Finance	0.939	8
Legislative Framework	0.823	2
Capacity Building	0.881	5
Awareness	0.885	4
Invtool	0.887	4
Climate Change	0.725	3
Carbon Emission	0.887	3

The demographic variable "Gender" was assessed among the 200 participants in the study. The results, presented in Table 4.2, reveal that the sample comprises 125 individuals (62.5%) identified as "Male" and 75 individuals (37.5%) identified as "Female." These values represent the frequency and percentage distributions for each gender category. These findings provide an overview of the gender distribution within the study population. The descriptive statistics result is presented in Table 4.3.

4.6 DATA DISTRIBUTION

TABLE 4.2 Descriptive Statistics for Gender

		Frequency	Percent	Valid Percent	Cumulative Percent
Valid	1	125	62.5	62.5	62.5
2		75	37.5	37.5	100.0

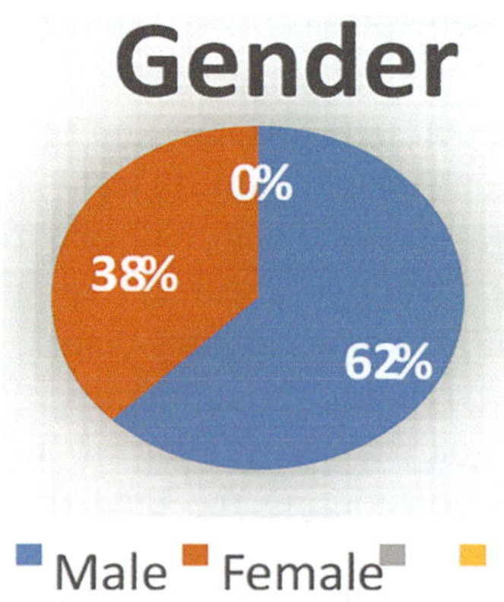

FIGURE 4.2 Showing percentage of females and males respondents.

TABLE 4.3 Descriptive Statistics

	N	Minimum	Maximum	Mean	Std. Deviation
Green Financing	200	5.00	25.00	16.2650	5.77073
Legislation Framework	200	6.00	30.00	19.7050	6.37031
Capacity Building	200	4.00	20.00	13.1250	4.10042
Awareness	200	4.00	20.00 20.00	12.6100	4.67946
Innovative Tools	200	4.00	15.00	13.1100	4.42672
Climate Change	200	3.00		9.2050	3.16910
CO_2 emission	200	3.00	15.00	8.6400	3.42770
Valid N (listwise)	200				

Table 4.3 presents descriptive statistics for various variables, including Green Financing, Legislation Framework, Capacity Building, Awareness, Innovative Tools, Climate Change, and CO_2 Trading. These statistics are based on a sample size of N = 200 for each variable. This provides insights into the central tendency and variability within the study.

- **Green Financing:** Respondents, on average, rated Green Financing at M = 16.27 out of 25 (SD = 5.77). Scores ranged from 5 to 25.
- **Legislation Framework:** The mean score for Legislation Framework was M = 19.71 out of 30 (SD = 6.37). Responses varied from 6 to 30. With the high mean value (19.71), the legislative framework seems to be a dominant factor among all.
- **Capacity Building:** Respondents, on average, gave a score of M = 13.13 out of 20 (SD = 4.10). Scores ranged from 4 to 20.
- **Awareness:** The mean score for Awareness was M = 12.61 out of 20 (SD = 4.68). Scores varied from 4 to 20.
- **Innovative Tools:** Respondents, on average, rated Innovative Tools at M = 13.11 out of 20 (SD = 4.43). Scores ranged from 4 to 20.
- **Climate Change:** The mean score for Climate Change was M = 9.21 out of 15 (SD = 3.17). Scores varied from 3 to 15.
- **CO2 Emission:** Respondents, on average, gave a score of M = 8.64 out of 15 (SD = 3.43) for CO_2 emission. Scores ranged from 3 to 15.

4.7 NORMALITY TEST

H0: The population from which the sample is drawn follows a normal distribution.

Based on the results of the Kolmogorov-Smirnov test for normality, p = [$p > 0.05$], which indicated that the data was normally distributed and there is no significant deviation, we fail to reject the null hypothesis (H0). Therefore, there is evidence to suggest that the data follows a normal distribution, supporting the acceptance of the null hypothesis.

Data analysis was undertaken using SPSS software to measure the effect of the legislative framework, green financing, awareness, innovative tools, and capacity building, with the mediating variable CO_2 trading on climate change. Analysis of Covariance (ANCOVA) was used. An examination for equality of variance across groups was conducted. With an insignificant F value of 0.715 and a P-value of 0.399, the test results suggest that the error variance of the dependent variable, climate change (CCTOT), can be regarded as equal across groups. The findings are summarized in Table 4.4, presenting the results of Levene's Test of Equality of Error Variances.

TABLE 4.4 Levene's Test of Equality of Error Variances[a]
Dependent Variable: CCTOT

F	df1	df2	Sig.
.715	1	198	.399

Tests the null hypothesis that the error variance of the dependent variable is equal across groups.

a. Design: Green financing + legislative framework + capacity building + awareness + innovative tools + CO_2 emission (mediating variable) (Table 4.5).

TABLE 4.5 Test of Between Subject Effects.

Dependent variable: CCTOT

Source	Type III Sum of Squares	df	Mean Square	F	Sig	Partial Eta Squared	Noncent. Parameter	Observed Powerb
Corrected Model	1033.624[a]	6	172.271	34.455	.000	.517	206.731	1.000
Intercept	116.259	1	116.259	23.252	.000	.108	23.252	.998
GFTOT	3.756	1	3.756	751	.387	.004	.751	.139

TABLE 4.5 *(Continued)*

Source	Type III Sum of Squares	df	Mean Square	F	Sig	Partial Eta Squared	Noncent. Parameter	Observed Powerb
LFTOT	11.457	1	11.457	2.292	.132	.012	2.292	.325
CBTOT	.142	1	.142	.028	.866	.000	.028	.053
AWTOT	19.574	1	19.574	3.915	.049	.020	3.915	.504
ITTOT	13.581	1	13.581	2.716	.101	.014	2.716	.375
C02TOT	43.193	1	43.193	8.639	.004	.043	8.639	.833
Error	964.971	193	5.000					
Total	18945.000	200						
Corrected Total	1998.595	1	199					

The parameter estimates indicate that the mean square value is 3.756, p = .751, and the F value is .387, which shows an insignificant relationship between green financing and climate change; hence, H01 is not rejected. For the legislative framework, the mean square was 11.457, while the F value is 2.292, p = .132, and for capacity building, the F value is .028, p = .866, which depict no significant relationship, and H02 and H03 were also rejected. Furthermore, a significant relationship was found among awareness, with an F value of 3.915, p = .049; innovative tools, with an F value of 2.716, p = 0.101; and CO_2 emission, with an F value of 8.639 and p value of .004.

4.8 FINDINGS

Research findings are as follows:

- **F1:** There is an insignificant impact of the legislative framework on climate change with the mediating variable carbon drifts.
- **F2:** There is an insignificant impact of green financing on climate change with the mediating variable carbon drifts.
- **F3:** There is an insignificant impact of capacity building on climate change with the mediating variable carbon drifts.
- **F4:** There is a significant impact of awareness on climate change with the mediating variable carbon drifts.

- **F5:** There is a significant impact of innovative tools on climate change with the mediating variable carbon drifts.
- **F6:** There is a significant negative impact of CO_2 emissions on climate change with the mediating variable carbon drifts.

4.9 DISCUSSION

The present study aimed to understand the youth's perception of climate change. The results showed that the young generation is aware of the threats of climate change and innovative tools that may be used to mitigate the effects of CO_2 emissions. However, at the same time, youth perceive that there is an urgent need to enforce laws by the government and encourage people to invest in green funding through regular training programs to strengthen the capacity building of the nation. Even with strong laws, sometimes they aren't enforced well, which weakens their impact on climate change. Monitoring and consequences for not following these laws can be lacking. Additionally, the money going into green projects might not be enough to tackle climate change adequately. Moreover, efforts to build skills and knowledge about climate change are often local and might be unable to reach globally.

There is a significant impact of innovative tools on climate change, as the creation and application of cutting-edge technologies, including solar, wind, geothermal, and advanced biofuels, can be crucial in lowering greenhouse gas emissions. These technologies help in the transition to a low-carbon energy system by offering sustainable substitutes for fossil fuels. Here lies a potential contradiction, while we've noted the youth's positive outlook regarding the impact of innovative tools on climate change due to their awareness, there seems to be a weak relation between capacity-building efforts, training initiatives, and climate change. This discrepancy could stem from their limited knowledge about the existence of these tools or perhaps a lack of detailed understanding regarding the benefits these technologies offer.

There is a negative impact of CO_2 emissions on climate change. Trading carbon dioxide emissions might not be properly monitored by governments. This can lead to fraud and manipulation in the market, making the whole system less effective in reducing emissions. There is a pressing requirement for consciousness among people regarding issues related to global warming and climate change to think in the direction of adopting sustainable practices. Heuristics or mind mapping techniques can be employed for the youth in such a way that they are able to think beyond their emotions, greediness, and personal returns because they represent our future investors who are responsible for the sustainability of the planet. The practice can also broaden their perspectives beyond just seeking high returns on investment and control their emotions by incorporating a mindful allocation of funds, including green projects as an important avenue to be considered while drafting their formula plans, encouraging a balanced approach in their investment strategies, resulting in a more sustainable future.

4.10 SUGGESTIONS AND IMPLICATIONS

According to the perceived value of our youth, their awareness about the issue and usage of innovative tools can significantly impact climate change, and this may be based on their own learnings, attitudes, surroundings, and knowledge. However, other variables such as green financing, legislative frameworks, and capacity building are not notably acknowledged in their perspective. The study recommends government intervention and policy formulation considering all these factors. The framework should be designed in such a way that it encourages investors to consider green financing as their primary investment avenue. Additionally, robust capacity building and training should be provided for younger generations to comprehend and engage in climate-conscious investing.

Also, to get funding for eco-friendly projects, policymakers, financial institutions, investors, and individuals are urged to prioritize and support green financing as an essential tool for building a more sustainable and resilient future as a result of the study's findings and recommendations. However, it is crucial to understand the challenges and restrictions associated with it. The full realization of its potential may be hampered by financial and commercial restrictions, technological and infrastructural limitations, and regulatory and policy issues. Strengthening regulatory frameworks, promoting public-private partnerships, and fostering innovation and R&D by governments, financial institutions, and stakeholders is required to overcome these obstacles. Academicians are recommended to emphasize the significance of integrating green investment into financial planning and basic financial literacy curricula. A further suggestion for researchers is to replicate this study, incorporating different variables within an alternative context. An important takeaway from our study for general investors is the potential motivation and encouragement to engage in green projects utilizing innovative tools for investment.

4.11 CONCLUSION

Out of all the green initiatives, some of the variables were significant with climate change while others were not related, which requires our prime attention. The overall study concludes that a lot of collective efforts by people, government, financial institutions, and other stakeholders are still required to build a sustainable environment and shift the trend towards a low-carbon economy. Green funding can help reduce carbon and can fight climate change to a large extent. By using money smartly through investments, we can speed up the shift to a sustainable future. Policymakers, investors, and others can use this study's ideas to fight climate change better and make the world more environmentally friendly. Further research is needed to explore the long-term effects of green funding on climate and carbon change. In order to reduce climate change, the study examines how green money may affect carbon drift. The research examines the efficiency of green initiatives in lowering carbon emissions and its potential to support international efforts for climate change mitigation.

KEYWORDS

- **ANCOVA**
- **capacity building**
- **carbon drifts**
- **carbon trading**
- **climate change**
- **financial instruments**
- **green financing**
- **green initiatives**
- **innovative tools**
- **legislative framework**

REFERENCES

Afridi, F. E. A., Jan, S., Ayaz, B., & Irfan, M. (2021). Green finance incentives: An empirical study of the Pakistan banking sector. *Amazonia Investigate*, *10*(41), 169–176.

Afzal, A., Rasoulinezhad, E., & Malik, Z. (2022). Green finance and sustainable development in Europe. *Economic Research-Ekonomska Istraživanja*, *35*(1), 5150–5163.

Akomea-Frimpong, I., Adeabah, D., Ofosu, D., & Tenakwah, E. J. (2022). A review of studies on green finance of banks, research gaps and future directions. *Journal of Sustainable Finance & Investment*, *12*(4), 1241–1264.

Bäckstrand, K., Bernstein, S., Betsill, M. M., & Zondervan, R. (2012). Transforming governance and institutions for global sustainability: Key insights from the Earth System Governance Project. *Current Opinion in Environmental Sustainability*, *4*(1), 51–60.

Bhattacharyya, R. (2022). Green finance for energy transition, climate action and sustainable development: Overview of concepts, applications, implementation and challenges. *Green Finance*, *4*(1), 1–35.

Chang, L., Wang, J., Xiang, Z., & Liu, H. (2021). Impact of green financing on carbon drifts to mitigate climate change: Mediating role of energy efficiency. *Frontiers in Energy Research*, *9*, 785588.

Charles, G., & Philip, B. (2020). Green finance: Recent drifts, confrontation and prospect opportunities for sustainable development in India. *Mukt Shabd Journal*, *9*(4), 1854–1865.

Desalegn, G., & Tangl, A. (2022). Enhancing green finance for inclusive green growth: A systematic approach. *Sustainability*, *14*(12), 7416.

Jia, Q. (2023). The impact of green finance on the level of decarbonization of the economies: An analysis of the United States,' China's, and Russia's current agenda. *Business Strategy and the Environment*, *32*(1), 110–119.

Li, T., Umar, M., Mirza, N., & Yue, X. G. (2023). Green financing and resources utilization: A story of N-11 economies in the climate change era. *Economic Analysis and Policy*, *78*, 1174–1184. https://doi.org/10.1016/j.eap.2023.05.007 (accessed on 7th July 2025).

Li, X., Chen, L., & Lin, J. H. (2023). Borrowing-firm environmental impact on insurer green finance assessment: green loan subsidy, regulatory cap, and green technology. *Environmental Impact Assessment Review*, *99*, 107007.

Liu, Z., Xu, J., Wei, Y., Hatab, A. A., & Lan, J. (2021). Nexus between green financing, renewable energy generation, and energy efficiency: Empirical insights through DEA technique. *Environmental Science and Pollution Research*, 1–14.

Madaleno, M., Dogan, E., & Taskin, D. (2022). A step forward on sustainability: The nexus of environmental responsibility, green technology, clean energy and green finance. *Energy Economics*, *109*, 105945.

Mumtaz, M. Z., & Smith, Z. A. (2019). Green finance for sustainable development in Pakistan. *IPRI Journal*, *19*(2), 1–34.

Ozili, P. K. (2022). Green finance research around the world: A review of literature. *International Journal of Green Economics*, *16*(1), 56–75.

Rashid, M. H. U., & Uddin, M. M. (2018). Green financing for sustainability: Analysing the trends with challenges and prospects in the context of Bangladesh. *International*

Journal of Green Economics, *12*(3/4), 192–. https://doi.org/10.1504/IJGE.2018.097876 (accessed on 7th July 2025).

Revelle, R., & Suess, H. E. (1957). Carbon dioxide exchange between the atmosphere and ocean and the question of an increasing atmospheric CO_2 during past decades. *Tellus*, *9*, 18–27.

Sadiq, M., Amayri, M. A., Paramaiah, C., Mai, N. H., Ngo, T. Q., & Phan, T. T. H. (2022). How green finance and financial development promote green economic growth: Deployment of clean energy sources in South Asia. *Environmental Science and Pollution Research*, *29*(43), 65521–65534. https://doi.org/10.1007/s11356-022-19947-9 (accessed on 7th July 2025).

Sharma, G. D., Verma, M., Shahbaz, M., Gupta, M., & Chopra, R. (2022). Transitioning green finance from theory to practice for renewable energy development. *Renewable Energy*, *195*, 554565.

Sinha, A., Mishra, S., Sharif, A., & Yarovaya, L. (2021). Does green financing help to improve environmental & social responsibility? Designing SDG framework through advanced quantile modelling. *Journal of Environmental Management*, *292*, 112751.

Triki, R., Kahouli, B., Tissaoui, K., & Tlili, H. (2023). Assessing the link between environmental quality, green finance, health expenditure, renewable energy, and technology innovation. *Sustainability*, *15*(5), 4286.

Volz, U. (2018). Fostering green finance for sustainable development in Asia. *SSRN Electronic Journal*. https://doi.org/10.2139/ssrn.3198680 (accessed on 7th July 2025).

Wang, X., Zhao, H., & Bi, K. (2021). The measurement of green finance index and the development forecast of green finance in China. *Environmental and Ecological Statistics*, *28*, 263285.

Yang, Z., Abbas, Q., Hanif, I., Alharthi, M., Taghizadeh-Hesary, F., Aziz, B., & Mohsin, M. (2021). Short- and long-run influence of energy utilization and economic growth on carbon discharge in emerging SREB economies. *Renewable Energy*, *165*, 43–51. https://doi.org/10.1016/j.renene.2020.10.141 (accessed on 7th July 2025).

Zhou, X., Tang, X., & Zhang, R. (2020). Impact of green finance on economic development and environmental quality: A study based on provincial panel data from China. *Environmental Science and Pollution Research*, *27*, 19915–19932. https://doi.org/10.1007/s11356-020-08383-2 (accessed on 7th July 2025).

CHAPTER 5

Breaking Barriers: How Technology is Revolutionizing Access to Financial Services for the Underserved

CHHAVI JAIN,[1] SANTOSH KUMAR,[1] and NAUSHAD ALAM[2]

[1]*Sharda University, Greater Noida, Uttar Pradesh, India*

[2]*Dhofar University, Salalah, Oman*

*Corresponding author

ABSTRACT

This chapter explores the dynamic convergence of technology and financial inclusion. Technological advancements have become increasingly important in tackling the persistent issue of delivering financial services to underserved populations. This chapter examines how technological innovations, including mobile banking, digital payment platforms, blockchain, and fintech solutions, have transformed financial access for underprivileged people. By conducting a thorough assessment of case studies and analyses, this study clarifies how new technologies are breaking down barriers, empowering individuals and enterprises, and promoting economic inclusion. Furthermore, the chapter examines the consequences of these changes and emphasizes the significance of guaranteeing that technological progress in financial services is fair, comprehensive, and enduring.

5.1 INTRODUCTION

In the sphere of international finance, the notion of financial inclusivity has surfaced as a pivotal factor influencing both economic advancement and

E-Financial Strategies for Sustainable Development: A Handbook for Promoting Financial Inclusion and Ending Poverty (SDG 1). Ernesto D. R. Santibanez Gonzalez, Rajeev Sijariya, and Vikas Garg (Eds.)

DOI: 10.1201/9781779640956-5

societal development. Yet, despite significant strides in advancing financial services over the years, a substantial portion of the world's population remains excluded from formal banking systems. This exclusion primarily affects underserved and marginalized communities, perpetuating cycles of poverty, inequality, and economic disenfranchisement. However, amid these challenges, a beacon of hope has emerged—the transformative power of technology. In this introductory section, we set out on a quest to examine the transformative impact of technology on enhancing access to financial services for marginalized populations. This process involves breaking down barriers and facilitating increased economic inclusion and empowerment.

5.1.1 THE IMPERATIVE OF FINANCIAL INCLUSION

Financial inclusion, which encompasses the accessibility and utilization of formal financial services by every segment of society, is fundamental to fostering inclusive economic growth. This entails a variety of services such as savings accounts, credit options, insurance offerings, and payment systems, all crucial for enabling individuals and enterprises to engage effectively in the formal economic sphere. However, despite its importance, financial exclusion remains a pervasive issue, particularly among vulnerable and marginalized populations. Factors such as geographical remoteness, lack of documentation, limited financial literacy (FL), and institutional barriers contribute to this exclusion, trapping millions in a cycle of financial vulnerability and social marginalization.

5.1.2 THE ROLE OF TECHNOLOGY IN DRIVING INCLUSION

Against this backdrop of entrenched financial exclusion, technological innovation has emerged as a powerful catalyst for change. The financial terrain is undergoing a profound transformation, propelled by the widespread integration of mobile devices, the emergence of blockchain technology, and the proliferation of fintech innovations. These digital advancements are reconfiguring access to financial services, fostering inclusivity, and granting individuals and communities greater empowerment. Mobile banking, for example, has emerged as a game-changer, allowing individuals to conduct banking transactions, access credit, and make payments using their smartphones, bypassing the need for traditional brick-and-mortar banks. Similarly, digital payment platforms offer convenient and affordable alternatives to cash-based transactions, fostering greater financial inclusion and economic participation.

5.1.3 THE PROMISE OF FINTECH SOLUTIONS

Moreover, the ascent of fintech, an abbreviation for financial technology, marks the onset of a fresh epoch characterized by innovation and upheaval within the financial services sector. Fintech startups harness state-of-the-art technologies like artificial intelligence (AI), machine learning (ML), and big data analytics to craft inventive solutions tailored to the specific requirements of marginalized demographics. These solutions range from peer-to-peer lending platforms and microfinance apps to digital insurance services and blockchain-based remittance networks. By harnessing the power of technology, fintech firms are unlocking new pathways to financial inclusion, extending access to credit, insurance, and other vital services to those who were previously excluded.

Throughout this chapter, we will delve into a series of case studies and analyses that illuminate the transformative impact of technology on financial inclusion. We will explore real-world examples of mobile banking initiatives reaching remote communities in developing countries, fintech startups providing affordable credit to small businesses, and blockchain platforms revolutionizing cross-border remittances. Through these case studies, we will uncover the tangible benefits of technological innovation in breaking down barriers, empowering individuals and enterprises, and fostering inclusive economic growth.

5.1.4 ENSURING FAIRNESS AND SUSTAINABILITY

While we applaud the potential of technology to advance financial inclusion, it's imperative to recognize and tackle the potential risks and challenges that may arise during its implementation. Issues such as data privacy, cybersecurity, and algorithmic bias must be carefully managed to ensure that technological progress in financial services is fair, comprehensive, and enduring. Moreover, efforts to promote financial inclusion must be grounded in principles of sustainability, ensuring that interventions are equitable, environmentally responsible, and socially impactful in the long term.

This introduction sets the stage for a comprehensive exploration of how technology is revolutionizing access to financial services for the underserved, highlighting the opportunities, challenges, and implications of this transformative shift. By incorporating case studies, analyses, and theoretical perspectives, we aim to explore the intricacies of technological innovation and its impact on financial inclusion. Our objective is to foster a more inclusive and equitable financial ecosystem.

In summary, the convergence of technology and financial inclusion holds immense promise for transforming the lives of underserved populations around the world. Through mobile banking, digital payment platforms, blockchain, and fintech solutions, technology is breaking down barriers, expanding access to financial services, and catalyzing economic empowerment. However, realizing this promise requires concerted efforts from governments, financial institutions, technology firms, and civil society to ensure that technological progress is equitable, sustainable, and inclusive. As we navigate the complexities of this digital revolution, let us remain steadfast in our commitment to building a financial system that leaves no one behind.

5.2 LITERATURE REVIEW

In recent times, an increasing amount of scholarly work has examined how technology intersects with financial inclusion, highlighting the transformative capabilities of digital innovations in broadening access to financial services for marginalized communities. This review of literature seeks to offer a thorough examination of pivotal topics, perspectives, and discussions in this domain, drawing from various academic research, reports, and empirical investigations.

Ndung'u (2018) provided a case study of M-Pesa's success in revolutionizing financial inclusion in Kenya. Through innovations in mobile-based financial services and supportive policy reforms, Kenya has witnessed a remarkable increase in formal financial inclusion rates, signaling the transformative power of technology in driving financial development and stability. The success of M-Pesa underscores the importance of innovative solutions and collaborative efforts among regulators, governments, and financial institutions in fostering financial inclusion.

Moreover, the advent of digital currency and mobile technology presents opportunities to penetrate financial systems in underserved populations. Sapovadia (2018) sheds light on the transformative potential of digital currency and mobile technology in addressing financial exclusion. By significantly reducing the costs associated with small transactions and streamlining processes, these technologies offer an affordable and efficient alternative to conventional financial systems. Several developing nations, including India, Brazil, and Nigeria, have embraced mobile technology as a means to address financial exclusion, thereby facilitating enhanced financial inclusion.

Furthermore, financial technologies (fintech) have been proposed as a means to extend access to financial services in rural communities, particularly as physical bank branches dwindle. However, Friedline et al. (2020) highlighted a significant disparity in access, particularly among poor rural communities and rural communities of color, who often lack the high-speed internet connections necessary for fintech adoption. Their research underscores the phenomenon of digital redlining, wherein poor rural communities of color experience disproportionately low rates of fintech adoption. This digital divide perpetuates financial inequalities, with rural communities' increasing white population benefiting from higher rates of internet connectivity, even amidst high poverty levels.

Furthermore, financial technology, or FinTech, has emerged as a key driver of inclusive finance globally. Hasan et al. (2020) delve into China's FinTech landscape, highlighting both its advancements and the persistent regional disparities in inclusive development. Their research underscores the importance of addressing these disparities through targeted policy interventions and regulatory frameworks.

Utilizing authentic data and thorough analyses, their research provides valuable insights applicable to policymakers, researchers, and practitioners, with the objective of enhancing comprehension regarding the role of FinTech in advancing inclusive development.

Nigeria, a prominent player in West Africa with a population of approximately 202 million, boasts one of the largest youth populations globally, presenting a vast market for various services. However, despite its potential, Nigeria grapples with a low level of financial inclusion, particularly in areas where access to financial services such as banks is inadequate, leaving a significant portion of the population financially vulnerable. Wayne et al. (2020) illuminate the utilization of technology by Nigerian banks to enhance financial inclusion initiatives within the nation. Their study sought to contribute to discussions surrounding financial inclusion, vulnerability, and financial technology in an emerging economy, providing insights into approaches to address current disparities.

Meanwhile, Raj and Upadhyay (2020) delve into the technological revolution shaping India's financial landscape and the pivotal role that FinTech plays in accelerating financial inclusion. Their paper discusses regulatory initiatives aimed at fostering the FinTech movement, emphasizing the importance of collaboration between banks and FinTech firms to drive mutual growth and benefit. Additionally, the paper addresses concerns related to data confidentiality and customer protection while harnessing the benefits of FinTech, highlighting the role of RegTech and SupTech in mitigating potential risks.

Poverty reduction and income inequality pose persistent challenges across economies worldwide, particularly in developing nations. In response, digital financial services have emerged as a pivotal platform, offering significant opportunities to access financial resources across various domains. Agwu (2021) undertook an exploration to gauge the potential of technology in bridging the widening gap of financial exclusions. Their findings illuminated that many individuals and businesses excluded from formal financial institutions often gravitate towards the informal sector due to its personalized approach and deeper customer relationships. The informal sector, in contrast to traditional financial institutions, offers a more accessible and less bureaucratic avenue for financial services. Consequently, the paper advocated for a reevaluation by financial institution managers, urging them to integrate elements of informal sector practices to attract the unbanked and underbanked segments of the population.

On the other hand, Rauniyar et al. (2021) explored digital financial inclusion (DFI) and its relationship with FinTech innovation, illustrating how FinTech serves as a catalyst for digitalization and digitization, thereby enhancing DFI. Their study examined the interplay between FinTech, financial innovation, and DFI, presenting a conceptual framework that outlines the transition from traditional financial ecosystems to modern landscapes facilitated by DFI. By identifying critical gaps and opportunities, the research underscores the enduring significance of FinTech in shaping a robust financial and economic system in the digital era of Industry 4.0.

Dwivedi et al. (2022) highlighted the persistent challenge of financial inclusion facing the majority of the Indian population, particularly in rural and semi-urban areas. Amidst the backdrop of the COVID-19 pandemic, the paper investigated the role of technology-enabled financial services in addressing this challenge. Through an examination of governmental policies and the development of FinTech amid the pandemic, the research uncovers a substantial endeavor by the government to advance financial inclusion. This is exemplified by the establishment of 411 million banking accounts over a span of six years. Despite progress, the paper underscores the need for continued government support to motivate citizens to embrace innovative financial services for inclusive growth.

Asif et al. (2023) emphasized the growing prominence of FinTech businesses in India, driven by the government's commitment to expanding financial services to the underbanked population. Utilizing regression and correlation analysis alongside secondary data from the RBI, the research assessed the influence of FinTech and digital financial services on financial inclusion. Results indicated that FinTech enterprises significantly contributed to improving financial inclusion, notably among the middle class. These findings provide valuable guidance for policymakers aiming to achieve widespread inclusion in the formal financial sector.

In his study, Wanof (2023) emphasized the significance of financial access in nurturing an inclusive and sustainable economy, particularly for marginalized communities. Through a qualitative review of literature, the research investigated how digital technology advancements have enabled greater financial access for underserved demographics. By analyzing digital banking platforms, electronic payment systems, and alternative financing approaches, the study underscored the transformative role of digital innovation in overcoming conventional obstacles to financial inclusion, such as geographical limitations and operational expenses. Overall, the findings underscore the potential of digital technology to empower low-income individuals and contribute to building a more inclusive financial ecosystem.

Srivastava's study in 2024 aimed to unravel the intricate interplay between digital banking services, financial inclusion, and sustainable development in the Indian context, shedding light on the manifold implications of this convergence. The research paper delved into the significant role that digital banking services played in promoting financial inclusion and contributing to sustainable development in India. With a focus on the transformative impact of technology on the banking sector, the study examined how digital banking services had expanded access to financial products and services for previously underserved and unbanked populations. Furthermore, the paper explored how these advancements aligned with India's goals of achieving sustainable development and reducing socioeconomic disparities. By analyzing the challenges and opportunities associated with digital banking adoption, the research shed light on the potential for fostering inclusive economic growth and achieving long-term sustainability in the Indian context.

In their 2024 study, Renaldo et al. sought to enhance understanding of Indonesia's fintech sector, emphasizing fintech categories, key players, and the influence of market aggregators. With internet usage expanding to 67%, Indonesia became a prime environment for fintech development, bolstered by regulatory structures and government initiatives aimed at fostering the sector's growth. The study employed a multifaceted methodology, including literature reviews, case studies, stakeholder interviews, field research, statistical and SWOT analyses, user surveys, and continuity analysis. The study's insights aimed to offer a profound understanding of Indonesia's fintech evolution, serving as a foundation for shaping public policies, fostering business development, and optimizing internal investments in the digital era.

The persistent challenges of poverty and income inequality worldwide, particularly in developing nations, necessitate innovative solutions for financial inclusion. Digital financial services offer promising avenues to address these disparities, with technologies like mobile banking and fintech playing a pivotal role. However, equitable access to these services remains a challenge, especially in marginalized rural communities and among underbanked populations. Successful case studies from countries like Kenya and India demonstrate the transformative impact of technology-enabled financial services in driving inclusive growth. Moreover, regulatory frameworks and collaborative efforts between governments, financial institutions, and technology firms are essential to ensure widespread adoption and mitigate risks. Overall, digital financial services have the potential to significantly improve access to finance, empower underserved populations, and contribute to sustainable development globally.

5.3 DISCUSSION AND FINDINGS

This chapter illuminated the pivotal significance of digital financial services and financial technology (FinTech) in confronting the enduring obstacles of poverty and income disparity worldwide, particularly in developing regions. Research underscored technology's capacity to narrow the chasm of financial exclusion through the provision of accessible and effective financial services. Nevertheless, hurdles like the digital divide and regulatory issues must be tackled to guarantee fair access to these services. Success stories from countries like Kenya and India underscored the transformative impact of technology-enabled financial services in driving financial inclusion and sustainable development. Moreover, research on China's FinTech landscape and Indonesia's fintech industry provided insights into regional disparities and opportunities for growth. The findings emphasize the importance of continued government support, collaboration between stakeholders, and innovative approaches to foster inclusive economic growth and reduce socioeconomic disparities. Certainly, here are the key findings observed.

5.3.1 TECHNOLOGICAL ADVANCEMENTS AS CATALYSTS FOR CHANGE

The literature review emphasizes the crucial contribution of technology in advancing financial inclusion, providing a means to surmount conventional obstacles and extend the reach of financial services. Mobile banking, digital payment platforms, blockchain technology, and fintech solutions have emerged as potent instruments for reaching marginalized communities, facilitating smoother and more efficient financial transactions for both individuals and businesses. The findings suggest that these technological advancements hold immense promise for breaking down barriers and promoting economic empowerment among the underserved.

5.3.2 REAL-WORLD IMPACT AND CASE STUDIES

Through an examination of empirical evidence and case studies, we gain insights into the tangible impact of technological innovations on financial inclusion. Case studies of mobile banking initiatives, fintech startups, and blockchain platforms highlight success stories of reaching remote communities, providing access to credit, and facilitating cross-border remittances. These results highlight how technology holds the power to bring about transformative change, enabling inclusive growth and empowering individuals and businesses who were previously marginalized from formal financial systems.

5.3.3 POLICY AND REGULATORY CONSIDERATIONS

The study emphasizes the importance of supportive policy and regulatory frameworks in nurturing an enabling environment for technological innovation in financial services. Clear regulatory guidance, consumer protection measures, and collaborative approaches involving governments, financial institutions, and technology firms are crucial for driving the adoption and scaling of fintech solutions. Furthermore, the findings underscore the need for policymakers to address regulatory gaps and ensure that technological progress is equitable, sustainable, and inclusive.

5.3.4 ETHICAL AND SOCIAL IMPLICATIONS

Ethical considerations and social implications emerge as critical themes in the discussion, highlighting the need for responsible innovation and safeguards to protect consumers' rights. Concerns regarding data privacy, cybersecurity risks, algorithmic bias, and digital exclusion underscore the importance of ethical frameworks and equity-focused approaches in the development and deployment of fintech solutions. The results underscore the importance of tackling these challenges to guarantee that the advantages of financial inclusion are distributed fairly across society.

5.3.5 FUTURE DIRECTIONS AND RECOMMENDATIONS

Looking ahead, the study points to several areas for future research and action in advancing financial inclusion through technology. These include exploring innovative technologies such as AI and distributed ledger technology, assessing the long-term sustainability and scalability of fintech solutions, and examining the impact of socio-cultural factors on financial behavior (FB) and inclusion. Moreover, the findings underscore the importance of interdisciplinary approaches and stakeholder collaboration in driving meaningful progress towards inclusive and sustainable financial ecosystems.

In summary, this research highlights how technology holds the potential to transform access to financial services for underserved populations by overcoming barriers. By leveraging technological innovations, policymakers, practitioners, and stakeholders can unlock new pathways to financial inclusion, empower individuals and communities, and foster inclusive economic growth. However, realizing this vision requires concerted efforts to address regulatory challenges, ethical considerations, and social implications, ensuring that technological progress is equitable, sustainable, and enduring. Through collaborative action and interdisciplinary research, we can build a future where financial empowerment knows no bounds, and all individuals have the opportunity to thrive in the digital economy.

5.4 LIMITATIONS

While the study on how technology is revolutionizing access to financial services for the underserved offers valuable insights and findings, there are several limitations that warrant acknowledgment.

5.4.1 GEOGRAPHICAL SCOPE

The focus of the study may be limited to specific regions or countries where technological innovations in financial services are more prevalent. As a result, the results might not comprehensively reflect the varied experiences and obstacles encountered by underserved communities in different geographical regions.

5.4.2 DATA AVAILABILITY

The literature review and empirical evidence relied upon in the study may be limited by data availability and accessibility. Some regions or populations may have limited data on their financial inclusion status, making it challenging to draw comprehensive conclusions or generalize findings.

5.4.3 TECHNOLOGY ADOPTION

The study may not fully account for disparities in technology adoption rates among underserved populations. Factors such as digital literacy, access to internet connectivity, and smartphone ownership may vary significantly, influencing the effectiveness of technological solutions in promoting financial inclusion.

5.4.4 REGULATORY ENVIRONMENT

While the study acknowledges the importance of supportive policy and regulatory frameworks, it may not delve deeply into the complexities of regulatory environments across different jurisdictions. Variations in regulatory approaches and legal frameworks could impact the scalability and sustainability of fintech solutions for financial inclusion.

5.4.5 ETHICAL CONSIDERATIONS

The discussion of ethical implications and social consequences may be limited in scope, focusing primarily on broad ethical principles rather than specific ethical dilemmas faced by underserved populations. Further exploration of ethical challenges, such as data privacy, algorithmic bias, and digital exclusion, could enrich the analysis.

5.4.6 LONG-TERM IMPACT

The study may not fully capture the long-term impact of technological innovations on financial inclusion and economic empowerment. Understanding the sustainability of fintech solutions and their ability to address systemic barriers to financial access requires longitudinal research and ongoing monitoring.

5.4.7 INTERSECTIONAL PERSPECTIVES

The research might lack sufficient consideration of intersectional elements like gender, race, ethnicity, and socio-economic status, which intersect with access to technology and outcomes of financial inclusion. Integrating intersectional perspectives could offer a more nuanced comprehension of the obstacles encountered by marginalized groups.

5.4.8 *BIAS AND ASSUMPTIONS*

Like any research endeavor, the study may be subject to biases and assumptions inherent in the selection of literature, methodologies, and analytical frameworks. Acknowledging and mitigating potential biases is essential for ensuring the validity and reliability of the study's findings. By recognizing these limitations, future research can strive to address these gaps and complexities, fostering a more comprehensive understanding of how technology can truly break barriers and promote inclusive access to financial services for underserved populations.

5.5 SUGGESTIONS FOR FUTURE RESEARCH AND ACTION

The following suggestions are proposed for future research and action in advancing the agenda of breaking barriers through technology to revolutionize access to financial services for the underserved:

5.5.1 *BROADEN GEOGRAPHIC SCOPE*

Subsequent research endeavors should strive to broaden the geographic coverage of the study to include a diverse array of regions and nations, including those with restricted technological infrastructure and financial service accessibility. This expanded viewpoint will facilitate a more holistic comprehension of the obstacles and prospects for advancing financial inclusion on a global scale.

5.5.2 *ENHANCE DATA COLLECTION*

Efforts should be made to improve data collection and analysis methodologies, particularly in regions with limited data availability. Collaborative initiatives between researchers, policymakers, and financial institutions can facilitate the collection of accurate and reliable data on financial inclusion indicators, enabling more robust analyses and evidence-based policymaking.

5.5.3 INCORPORATE INTERSECTIONAL PERSPECTIVES

In upcoming research, it is imperative to employ an intersectional lens, taking into account the interplay between various factors such as gender, race, ethnicity, and socio-economic status in relation to technological access and outcomes of financial inclusion. By integrating intersectional perspectives, scholars can gain deeper insights into the specific hurdles encountered by marginalized groups and devise tailored strategies to meet their requirements.

5.5.4 LONGITUDINAL STUDIES

Longitudinal studies are needed to assess the long-term impact and sustainability of technological innovations on financial inclusion. By tracking changes in access, usage, and outcomes over time, researchers can identify trends, evaluate the effectiveness of interventions, and inform strategies for scaling successful initiatives.

5.5.5 POLICY AND REGULATORY ANALYSIS

Further research is needed to conduct in-depth analyses of policy and regulatory frameworks governing fintech and financial inclusion. Comparative studies across different jurisdictions can shed light on best practices, regulatory gaps, and areas for reform to ensure that regulatory environments are conducive to fostering inclusive and sustainable financial ecosystems.

5.5.6 ETHICAL CONSIDERATIONS AND SOCIAL IMPLICATIONS

Continued attention should be paid to ethical considerations and social implications arising from the adoption of technology in financial services. Future research should explore specific ethical dilemmas faced by underserved populations, such as data privacy, algorithmic bias, and digital exclusion, and develop frameworks for addressing these challenges in a fair and equitable manner.

5.5.7 COMMUNITY ENGAGEMENT AND STAKEHOLDER COLLABORATION

Collaboration between researchers, policymakers, financial institutions, technology firms, and civil society organizations is essential for driving meaningful progress towards financial inclusion. Future research should prioritize community engagement and stakeholder collaboration to ensure that interventions are informed by local needs, perspectives, and priorities.

5.5.8 CAPACITY BUILDING AND KNOWLEDGE SHARING

Efforts should be made to build capacity and facilitate knowledge sharing among stakeholders involved in promoting financial inclusion. Training programs, workshops, and online platforms can provide researchers, practitioners, and policymakers with the tools and resources needed to develop innovative solutions, implement effective policies, and advocate for inclusive financial systems.

By pursuing these suggestions, researchers, policymakers, and practitioners can advance the agenda of breaking barriers through technology to revolutionize access to financial services for the underserved. By embracing interdisciplinary approaches, collaborative partnerships, and a commitment to equity and inclusion, we can work towards building a future where everyone has the opportunity to participate fully in the financial ecosystem, regardless of their background or circumstances.

5.6 CONCLUSION

The journey through the realms of technology and financial inclusion has revealed a dynamic landscape shaped by innovation, challenges, and opportunities. From the abstract notions of breaking barriers to the concrete findings of empirical research, the exploration of how technology is revolutionizing access to financial services for the underserved has provided valuable insights and directions for future action.

The literature review illuminated the transformative potential of technology in driving financial inclusion, highlighting the role of mobile banking, digital payment platforms, blockchain technology, and fintech solutions in expanding access to financial services. Through case studies and analyses, we witnessed firsthand the real-world impact of these innovations, from reaching remote communities to empowering small businesses and facilitating cross-border transactions.

However, amidst the promise of technological progress, we must navigate a complex terrain fraught with challenges and limitations. Regulatory frameworks, ethical considerations, and data limitations underscored the need for careful stewardship and responsible innovation in the fintech space. The intersectional perspectives of gender, race, and socio-economic status reminded us of the importance of inclusive approaches that address the diverse needs of underserved populations.

Looking ahead, the path forward calls for collaborative action and interdisciplinary engagement. Future research must broaden its geographic scope, enhance data collection methodologies, and incorporate intersectional perspectives to deepen our understanding of financial inclusion dynamics. Policy and regulatory analysis, coupled with stakeholder collaboration and community engagement, will be instrumental in shaping inclusive and sustainable financial ecosystems.

In conclusion, the journey to break barriers and revolutionize access to financial services for the underserved is an ongoing endeavor—one that requires vision, perseverance, and a commitment to equity and inclusion. By harnessing the transformative power of technology and fostering collaborative partnerships, we can build a future where financial empowerment knows no bounds, and all individuals have the opportunity to thrive in the digital economy. Together, let us embark on this journey with hope, determination, and a shared vision of a more inclusive and equitable world.

KEYWORDS

- **blockchain**
- **digital payment platforms**
- **economic empowerment**
- **financial inclusion**
- **fintech solutions**
- **mobile banking**
- **sustainable development**
- **underserved populations**

REFERENCES

Agwu, M. E. (2021). Can technology bridge the gap between rural development and financial inclusions? *Technology Analysis & Strategic Management*, *33*(2), 123–133.

Asif, M., Khan, M. N., Tiwari, S., Wani, S. K., & Alam, F. (2023). The impact of fintech and digital financial services on financial inclusion in India. *Journal of Risk and Financial Management*, *16*(2), 122.

Dwivedi, R., Alrasheedi, M., Dwivedi, P., & Starešinić, B. (2022). Leveraging financial inclusion through technology-enabled services innovation: A case of economic development in India. *International Journal of E-Services and Mobile Applications (IJESMA)*, *14*(1), 1–13.

Friedline, T., Naraharisetti, S., & Weaver, A. (2020). Digital redlining: Poor rural communities' access to fintech and implications for financial inclusion. *Journal of Poverty*, *24*(5–6), 517–541.

Hasan, M. M., Yajuan, L., & Mahmud, A. (2020). Regional development of China's inclusive finance through financial technology. *SAGE Open*, *10*(1), 2158244019901252.

Ndung'u, N. (2018). The M-Pesa technological revolution for financial services in Kenya: A platform for financial inclusion. In *Handbook of Blockchain, Digital Finance, and Inclusion, Volume 1* (pp. 37–56). Academic Press.

Raj, B., & Upadhyay, V. (2020). Role of FinTech in accelerating financial inclusion in India. In *3rd International Conference on Economics and Finance organized by the Nepal Rastra Bank at Kathmandu, Nepal during February* (pp. 28–29).

Rauniyar, K., Rauniyar, K., & Sah, D. K. (2021). Role of FinTech and innovations for improvising digital financial inclusion. *International Journal of Innovative Science and Research Technology*, *6*(5), 1419–1424.

Renaldo, N., Junaedi, A. T., Musa, S., Wahid, N., & Cecilia, C. (2024). Mapping the financial technology industry in Indonesia. *Journal of Applied Business and Technology*, *5*(1), 61–66.

Sapovadia, V. (2018). Financial inclusion, digital currency, and mobile technology. In *Handbook of Blockchain, Digital Finance, and Inclusion, Volume 2* (pp. 361–385). Academic Press.

Srivastava, S. S. D. S. (2024). Exploring the role of digital banking services in advancing financial inclusion and sustainable development in India. *Ajasra*, *13*(2), 873–887.

Wanof, M. I. (2023). Digital technology innovation in improving financial access for low-income communities. *Technology and Society Perspectives (TACIT)*, *1*(1), 26–34.

Wayne, T., Soetan, T., Bajepade, G., & Mogaji, E. (2020). Technologies for financial inclusion in Nigeria. *Research Agenda Working Papers*, *2020*(4), 40–56.

CHAPTER 6

Empowering Her Enterprise: A Comprehensive Review of E-Financial Strategies Catalyzing Women Entrepreneurship in India

TANISHKA GUPTA*

Jagannath International Management School (JIMS), Vasant Kunj, New Delhi, India

*Corresponding author

ABSTRACT

Women entrepreneurship in India faces multifaceted challenges ranging from societal norms to economic barriers. This research article explores the transformative potential of E-financial strategies in empowering women entrepreneurship in India. As digital technologies continue to reshape the business landscape, this review investigates the specific ways in which electronic financial tools and platforms can address challenges faced by women entrepreneurs, fostering financial inclusion, enhancing access to capital, and promoting economic independence. By synthesizing existing literature and case studies, the article provides a comprehensive overview of the current state of E-financial strategies in India and their impact on women-led businesses. The findings underscore the importance of tailoring E-financial solutions to address gender-specific barriers and highlight the need for policy interventions and collaborative efforts from various stakeholders to create an enabling environment for women entrepreneurs to thrive. The chapter includes an introduction to the context of women entrepreneurship in India, followed by a literature

E-Financial Strategies for Sustainable Development: A Handbook for Promoting Financial Inclusion and Ending Poverty (SDG 1). Ernesto D. R. Santibanez Gonzalez, Rajeev Sijariya, and Vikas Garg (Eds.)

DOI: 10.1201/9781779640956-6

review highlighting the challenges faced by women entrepreneurs and the theoretical framework underpinning E-financial strategies. Subsequently, the methodology section outlines the systematic review process adopted. The findings section presents a synthesis of key insights from the literature review, followed by a discussion on the implications for policy and practice. Finally, the article concludes with recommendations for future research directions and interventions aimed at fostering the empowerment of women entrepreneurs through E-financial strategies in India.

6.1 INTRODUCTION TO WOMEN ENTREPRENEURSHIP IN INDIA

Entrepreneurship is a subset of the business regime, which is responsible for the establishment of organizations, no matter how big or small, that contribute significantly to the beneficial growth of the nation and its economy (Wennekers and Thurik, 1999). These are the highly skilled and knowledgeable individuals who can enter a firm to gain market share and make high-potential decisions, ultimately turning a profit (Markman et al., 2003). These days, the government also promotes entrepreneurship in an effort to improve economic conditions and end poverty by creating jobs (Vandenberg, 2006). Through initiatives like Startup India, MUDRA Yojana Scheme for Women, Annapurna Scheme, Stree Shakti Package for Women Entrepreneurs, Bharatiya Mahila Bank Business Loan, Mahila Udyami Nidhi Scheme, and so forth., the government and banks are offering financial help to women and youth.

The days of Indian culture, where women were expected to remain silent and not actively participate, are long gone. Instead, women were seen as subordinates, with men acting as the true boss. However, in the current situation, which is also the case in the 21st century, educated women are not willing to limit themselves; rather, they are gaining equal knowledge and standing on an equal footing in this society dominated by males (Wajcman, 2013). Despite the social barriers that women in India face, they nevertheless aspire to work, and there are many inspiring tales of successful female entrepreneurs. The proverb "There's a woman behind every successful man" has evolved as a result of women opening up important opportunities, such as entrepreneurship. We may have seen a large number of female professionals in the fields of engineering, medicine, law, and other areas. The majority of female entrepreneurs are often found in the kitchen, mostly preparing and selling goods like pappad, pickles, and powders (Patil et al., 2021).

In addition to the fact that the number of women entrepreneurs in India is drastically increasing, the government of India places a high value on this growth. Our central government has announced a number of programs aimed at assisting women and upholding the value placed on them. In addition, a number of non-governmental organizations are educating women about becoming entrepreneurs by collaborating with the government. As a result, women entrepreneurs may now expand their businesses from small to large-scale ventures.

A woman who is an entrepreneur is someone who is self-assured, inventive, and creative, who can work alone or with others to achieve financial independence. She also creates jobs for others by starting, building, and managing her business while maintaining a balance with her social, familial, and personal life. The rise of female entrepreneurs has been a fascinating story in the dynamic terrain of India's economic development, exhibiting fortitude, inventiveness, and revolutionary potential. Women in India are dismantling obstacles, dispelling myths, and securing their places in the entrepreneurial ecosystem—from big metropolises to rural hinterlands.

Indian women have historically demonstrated resourcefulness and an entrepreneurial spirit in a variety of fields, but frequently in the informal or conventional family business sectors (Kumar, 2016). However, in recent decades, there has been a noticeable increase in the official acknowledgment and empowerment of women in business. The 1990s' economic liberalization, along with progressive governmental efforts and sociological changes, created the foundation for promoting an atmosphere that was favorable to women entrepreneurs. The government's emphasis on inclusive growth, gender equality, and women's empowerment through programs like Mudra Yojana and the Stand-Up India initiative has encouraged women from a variety of socioeconomic backgrounds to pursue their entrepreneurial dreams.

The trajectory of women entrepreneurship in India is influenced by the complex interaction of cultural norms, gender dynamics, and economic inequities that characterize the country's socio-economic environment (Torri et al., 2014). Rural places provide a distinct mix of possibilities and difficulties compared to metropolitan centers, which provide access to markets, networks, and resources. Women entrepreneurs in rural India frequently struggle with social hurdles, lack of access to infrastructure, education, and capital. However, programs like the Self-Help Groups (SHGs) and the National Rural Livelihoods Mission (NRLM) have given rural women the ability to launch and grow businesses, promoting communal development and economic self-reliance.

Even with the advancements, cultural prejudices, patriarchal attitudes, and structural barriers to markets, capital, and technological access remain major obstacles for Indian women entrepreneurs (Pramanik et al., 2023). The persistent gender disparity in financing access continues to be a significant obstacle, making it difficult for female entrepreneurs to get venture capital, credit, and collateral. Furthermore, long-standing prejudices and cultural norms sometimes deter women from pursuing business endeavors, restricting their autonomy and reinforcing gender roles. Another major obstacle facing women is juggling entrepreneurial aspirations with family obligations; this requires creative problem-solving and strong support networks to successfully manage work-life integration (Couzy, 2012).

Despite the obstacles, Indian women entrepreneurs are using their resourcefulness, fortitude, and inventiveness to propel innovation, upend sectors of the economy, and have a positive social effect. Women-led businesses are using technology, branching out into new industries, and meeting gaps in the market. Examples of these include artisanal crafts, sustainable agriculture, and e-commerce startups and software companies. With women-led businesses promoting issues including women's empowerment, healthcare, education, and environmental sustainability, social entrepreneurship has become a powerful force for change. A thriving ecosystem of female-led innovation and entrepreneurship is being fostered via collaborative platforms, incubators, and accelerators specifically designed for female entrepreneurs. These spaces offer networking, capacity-building, and mentorship opportunities.

The burgeoning trend of female entrepreneurship in India bears significant ramifications for the advancement of socio-economic policies, portending a more comprehensive, just, and robust economy. Women-led businesses help to create jobs, reduce poverty, and strengthen communities in addition to increasing GDP (Niethammer, 2013). Through entrepreneurship, women's economic engagement and gender diversity open up new paths to wealth, encourage innovation, and boost competitiveness in the global marketplace (Veras, 2015). In addition, female entrepreneurs act as role models and change agents, encouraging the next generations of women to follow their goals and ambitions, breaking down barriers and changing the face of entrepreneurship in India.

6.2 METHODOLOGY

This study explores the transformational potential of E-financial techniques in empowering women entrepreneurs in India using a comprehensive literature review and synthesis methodology. The research technique utilized in this study presents a systematic approach to gathering, examining, and combining relevant case studies and current literature. First, a thorough examination of the literature was conducted, including books, reports, conference proceedings, and scholarly journals that were published between 2010 and 2022. To find relevant research, search terms like "women entrepreneurship," "E-financial strategies," "financial inclusion," "access to capital," and "India" were used. The focus was on choosing studies that shed light on the difficulties encountered by female entrepreneurs and the effectiveness of e-financial solutions in resolving these difficulties in the Indian setting. After pertinent literature was selected, a thorough analysis was conducted to extract the research's main conclusions, methodology, and theoretical frameworks. Subsequently, these results were thematically synthesized, arranging the information to clarify recurring themes, patterns, and gaps in the literature about the influence of E-financial methods on the empowerment of women entrepreneurs in India. Cross-referencing results from several studies was done at various points in the synthesis process in order to confirm new insights and pinpoint areas of agreement or disagreement. Furthermore, methodological rigor, results dependability, and relevance to the study issue were among the factors used to evaluate the quality of the chosen studies. The study was conducted in accordance with ethical criteria to guarantee accurate citation of sources, protection of intellectual property rights, and preservation of study participants' identity and confidentiality. All things considered, this systematic review and synthesis technique provides a strong foundation for examining the body of research on e-financial strategies and the empowerment of women entrepreneurs in India, offering insightful information for practice and policy.

6.3 A SYNTHESIS OF E- FINANCIAL STRATEGIES AND WOMEN ENTREPRENEURS

Stereotypes and restricted access to education provide serious obstacles for Indian women entrepreneurs (Adikaram et al., 2023). Persistent gender prejudices in Indian society frequently uphold conventional gender roles, confining women to the home and diminishing their potential for entrepreneurship (Tiwari, 2006). Women's entrepreneurial goals are further hampered by stereotypes that depict them as less competent or suitable for leadership positions in business, which deters them from pursuing endeavors outside of accepted standards (Ely et al., 2010).

These issues are made worse by a lack of access to high-quality education, especially in rural regions where socioeconomic constraints frequently limit girls' educational options (Chimombo, 2005). In addition to depriving women of the fundamental knowledge and skills required for entrepreneurship, this lack of access to education perpetuates cultural norms that place a higher value on marriage and family than on advancing one's professional life (Mudau et al., 2017). As a result, managing educational gaps and conquering preconceptions present a double challenge for female entrepreneurs (Elliot et al., 2021). This emphasizes the urgent need for comprehensive interventions to address these systemic difficulties and advance gender equality in entrepreneurship.

Through a thorough review of existing literature, the following table 6.1 has been compiled showcasing the various categories of e-financial strategies that are utilized by women entrepreneurs in their day-to-day business activities.

TABLE 6.1 E-Financial Strategies Employed by Women Entrepreneurs

S. No.	E-Financial Strategies	Description of E-Financial Strategies	References
1	Online Crowdfunding	Utilizing online platforms to raise funds from a large pool of individuals for business ventures or projects.	Groza et al. (2020); Kromidha et al. (2023); Wang et al. (2023)
2	E-Commerce Expansion	Leveraging online marketplaces or creating own e-commerce platforms to reach wider audiences and increase sales.	Hussin et al., (2017); Padmannavar (2011); Sultana and Akter (2021); Xu (2016)
3	Digital Marketing	Utilizing digital channels such as social media, email, and SEO to promote products or services leads to increased brand visibility and sales.	Bhagat et al., (2019); Sihotang et al., (2020); Srividhya et al., (2022)

TABLE 6.1 *(Continued)*

S. No.	E-Financial Strategies	Description of E-Financial Strategies	References
4	E-Business Networking	Engaging in online networking communities, forums, and groups to connect with other entrepreneurs, mentors, and potential collaborators fosters business growth and opportunities.	Escap (2006); Hossain and Tanjela (2018); Talib et al., (2019)
5	Virtual Financial Management	Utilizing online accounting software and virtual financial management services to track finances, manage expenses, and optimize cash flow enables better financial decision-making.	Kanapathipillai et al., (2021); Kassim (2023); Rajandran and K.V.R (2024)
6	Online Financial Education	Accessing online courses, webinars, and resources to enhance financial literacy, investment knowledge, and business management skills, empowering women entrepreneurs to make informed financial decisions.	Asandimitra et al. (2017); Baba et al. (2024); Genoviva et al. (2019); Hasan et al. (2023)
7	E-Procurement	Utilizing online platforms for procurement processes, including sourcing suppliers, negotiating contracts, and managing purchases, to streamline operations and reduce costs.	Kithatu-Kiwekete et al. (2020); Kiwikete et al. (2017); Tsuma et al. (2017)
8	E-Invoicing	Implementing electronic invoicing systems to automate billing processes, improve payment accuracy, and expedite cash flow enhances efficiency and reduces administrative burdens.	Eze et al., (2017); Lalangui (2022); Wu (2013)
9	Remote Workforce Management	Leveraging online tools and platforms for remote workforce management, including project management software, communication tools, and virtual collaboration platforms, to facilitate productivity and flexibility in operations.	Afsa et al. (2009); Afshan et al. (2021); Hawsawi (2023)
10	Online Business Loans	Accessing online lending platforms and financial institutions offering business loans tailored to women entrepreneurs, providing capital for growth, expansion, or working capital needs.	Karmakar et al. (2018); Rashid et al. (2019); RUSANDRY (2023); Umejiaku (2020)

Source: Author's own enumeration through literature.

Women entrepreneurs in India encounter several obstacles that are ingrained in the country's social, cultural, and economic structures (Tambunan, 2009). The prevalent gender prejudice and assumptions that enforce conventional gender roles and frequently confine women to the home rather than promoting their involvement in business are among the biggest obstacles (Bonvillain, 2020). A cultural barrier to entrepreneurship is created when family and societal expectations place a higher priority on marriage and raising children than on women's job goals (Rahman and Azam, 2012). Furthermore, because investors and financial institutions often prefer to work with male entrepreneurs, women often face prejudice and a lack of assistance when trying to obtain capital, which feeds the cycle of inequality (Nelson et al., 2009).

The difficulties experienced by women entrepreneurs in India are further compounded by the lack of access to education and skill-building opportunities (Goodrich et al., 2018). Even if the percentage of female literacy has increased, there is still a sizable gender disparity in educational achievement, especially in rural regions (Diprete, 2013). This difference makes it more difficult for women to get the information and abilities needed to launch and run successful enterprises. Their entrepreneurial path is further hampered by their restricted access to networking and mentorship possibilities, as they frequently lack role models and support systems to help them navigate the complexities of business growth (Emon et al., 2024).

For Indian women entrepreneurs, navigating the regulatory and legal landscape also poses significant obstacles (Mukherjee, 2018). Intuitive legal frameworks, opaque bureaucratic procedures, and a lack of knowledge on legal rights and obligations provide formidable obstacles to launching and growing a firm (Adekunle, 2024). Women business owners frequently find it difficult to follow regulations, which can be especially challenging for those in traditionally male-dominated fields or in unusual businesses (Yang et al., 2019). In addition, the lack of gender-responsive policies and programs makes matters worse for women, as they are frequently disregarded in government schemes and programs meant to encourage entrepreneurship.

In India, one of the main obstacles impeding women's entrepreneurship is their limited access to markets and technology (Koneru, 2017). Gender prejudices that are deeply ingrained in society make it difficult for women-owned enterprises to reach markets, and networking opportunities are few (Orser et al., 2021; Singh et al., 2021). Furthermore, women entrepreneurs suffer disproportionately from the digital divide, especially those from marginalized or rural areas where access to digital platforms and technology is necessary for company growth and expansion. Targeted measures that give women access to markets, technology, and digital literacy programs are necessary to narrow this gap (Bailey et al., 2021).

Furthermore, because they frequently juggle several jobs and responsibilities, women entrepreneurs in India have substantial challenges in maintaining a work-life balance (Mathew et al., 2011; Singh et al., 2023). Many women are forced to choose between their commitments to their families and their business goals due to the lack of accessible childcare options and support networks (Stone, 2007). To tackle this issue, comprehensive workplace policies that assist women in striking a balance between their personal and professional lives are needed. Examples of these policies include flexible work schedules, support for childcare, and family-friendly work environments.

India's female entrepreneurs confront a variety of obstacles, including ingrained gender stereotypes, restricted access to resources and education, market limitations, legislative hurdles, and problems juggling work and personal obligations (Sinha, 2005). To address these issues and create an environment that supports women's entrepreneurship and allows them to reach their full potential as agents of social change and economic growth, policymakers, financial institutions, civil society organizations, and the private sector must work together.

E-financial strategies are based on a theoretical framework that incorporates a number of information technology, finance, and economics concepts and principles (Ononiwu and Gerard, 2015). Fundamentally, e-finance strategies make use of digital platforms and technology to streamline financial procedures, improve decision-making, and enable effective resource allocation in the digital age (Xu, 2022). The Efficient Market Hypothesis (EMH), which holds that financial markets are efficient at reflecting all available information, is one important theoretical pillar (Degutis and Novickyte, 2014). This suggests that e-finance strategies should strive to quickly and successfully take advantage of informational advantages. Adding to this, Modern Portfolio Theory (MPT) places a strong emphasis on risk management and diversification, recommending that digital technologies be used by e-financial strategies to create diversified portfolios that are suited to each investor's risk tolerance and investment goals (House III, 1996).

Furthermore, behavioral finance sheds light on the ways in which human psychology and emotions impact financial decision-making, emphasizing how crucial it is to comprehend investor behavior while creating e-financial strategies (Gulati and Singh, 2024). E-financial solutions may be developed to reduce irrational behavior and enhance investment results in digital settings by using behavioral finance concepts like prospect theory and cognitive biases (Che Hassan, 2023). In addition, frameworks for evaluating asset pricing and risk-return relationships are provided by the Capital Asset Pricing Model (CAPM) and Arbitrage Pricing Theory (APT). These frameworks aid in the development of e-financial strategies that aim to maximize returns while effectively managing risks in digital asset management systems and online trading platforms.

Furthermore, ideas related to information technology (IT) and information systems (IS) are vital in forming e-financial strategies, especially when it comes to fintech innovation and digital transformation. The strategic significance of IT infrastructure, digital platforms, and data analytics skills in e-finance is emphasized by the Resource-Based View (RBV) and Dynamic Capabilities Theory. These factors drive organizational performance and competitive advantage. Additionally, the Diffusion of Innovations Theory and the Technology Acceptance Model (TAM) shed light on the factors that affect the success or failure of e-financial strategies in the digital ecosystem by describing how investors, financial institutions, and market participants adopt and diffuse e-financial technologies.

Moreover, considering the growing regulatory scrutiny and compliance demands in digital banking, the Regulatory Compliance framework is critical for e-financial initiatives (Tucker et al., 2019). In order to ensure transparency, accountability, and trust in digital financial transactions, compliance theories like Agency Theory and Stakeholder Theory are used to influence the creation of e-finance strategies that are in line with legal requirements, moral standards, and corporate governance procedures (Kumar, 2014). The creation of e-financial strategies that attempt to secure digital assets, fend off cyberattacks, and boost resilience in the face of technical interruptions and vulnerabilities is also guided by theories of cybersecurity and risk management.

To effectively use digital technologies for financial decision-making, portfolio management, market analysis, and risk mitigation, the theoretical framework supporting e-financial strategies integrates ideas from finance, economics, information technology, and regulatory compliance (Kamal, 2023). In order to generate value, encourage innovation, and advance financial inclusion in the digital economy, e-financial strategies can leverage the revolutionary potential of digital finance by utilizing theories such as MPT, EMH, Behavioral Finance, IT/IS theories, and Regulatory Compliance frameworks.

6.4 DISCUSSION AND CONCLUSION

Various obstacles encountered by women entrepreneurs in utilizing financial tools for their empowerment are mentioned below. The following table 6.2 highlights issues such as gender bias in lending, lack of collateral, limited financial literacy (FL), underrepresentation in venture capital, networking disparities, and family caregiving responsibilities. These challenges hinder women entrepreneurs' access to capital, mentorship, networking opportunities, and time allocation for business development, thus impeding their entrepreneurial empowerment and inhibiting business growth and success.

TABLE 6.2 Challenges and Impact on Women Entrepreneurs

Serial No.	Challenges Faced by Women Entrepreneurs	Description of Challenges	Impact on Entrepreneurial Empowerment
1	Gender Bias in Lending	Women entrepreneurs often face discrimination or bias in access to loans and financing, resulting in lower approval rates, higher interest rates, or less favorable terms compared to their male counterparts.	Limited access to capital hinders business growth, expansion, and innovation, impeding entrepreneurial empowerment.
2	Lack of Collateral	Traditional lending institutions may require collateral for loans, which women entrepreneurs may struggle to provide due to disparities in asset ownership or access to property rights, limiting their ability to secure financing.	Without collateral, women entrepreneurs may struggle to obtain loans, hindering investment in business ventures and inhibiting empowerment opportunities.
3	Limited Financial Literacy	Women entrepreneurs may face challenges in understanding financial concepts, managing finances effectively, and navigating complex financial tools and resources, leading to suboptimal financial decisions and strategies.	Lack of financial literacy inhibits women entrepreneurs' ability to leverage financial tools, plan for growth, and maximize profitability, constraining entrepreneurial empowerment.

TABLE 6.2 *(Continued)*

Serial No.	Challenges Faced by Women Entrepreneurs	Description of Challenges	Impact on Entrepreneurial Empowerment
4	Underrepresentation in Venture Capital	Women entrepreneurs encounter disparities in access to venture capital funding, as they are often underrepresented and face biases in investment decisions made by venture capitalists and angel investors.	Limited access to venture capital constrains women entrepreneurs' ability to scale their businesses, pursue high-growth opportunities, and achieve entrepreneurial empowerment on a larger scale.
5	Limited Networking Opportunities	Women entrepreneurs may have fewer networking opportunities, connections, and access to influential networks compared to men, resulting in limited access to mentorship, funding, partnerships, and resources.	Networking gaps restrict women entrepreneurs' access to critical resources, support systems, and opportunities for growth, hindering entrepreneurial empowerment and success.
6	Family and Caregiving Responsibilities	Balancing family and caregiving responsibilities with entrepreneurial pursuits can pose challenges for women entrepreneurs, affecting their ability to dedicate time, energy, and resources to business development and financial management.	Juggling multiple roles and responsibilities may limit women entrepreneurs' capacity to focus on business growth, pursue opportunities, and access financial tools, impeding entrepreneurial empowerment.

Source: Author's own enumeration through literature.

In the dynamic landscape of the 21st century, women entrepreneurs face multifaceted challenges ranging from gender biases to resource constraints. However, the emergence of e-financial strategies presents a promising avenue for overcoming these hurdles. By leveraging digital platforms and innovative financial technologies, women entrepreneurs can enhance their competitiveness and foster sustainable growth.

Firstly, e-financial tools offer women entrepreneurs greater access to capital. Crowdfunding platforms, peer-to-peer lending, and online microfinance services democratize funding opportunities, enabling women to secure necessary resources for their ventures irrespective of traditional banking barriers or discriminatory lending practices.

Secondly, e-financial solutions streamline operational efficiencies. Cloud-based accounting software and digital payment systems facilitate cost-effective financial management, enabling entrepreneurs to allocate resources strategically and optimize cash flow. Moreover, the automation of administrative tasks reduces time burdens, allowing women to focus on core business activities and innovation.

Thirdly, e-commerce platforms empower women entrepreneurs to expand market reach and diversify revenue streams. Online marketplaces and social media commerce facilitate direct consumer engagement and international trade, overcoming geographical limitations and traditional distribution channels.

Lastly, e-financial strategies foster networking and knowledge-sharing opportunities. Online communities and digital forums provide avenues for women entrepreneurs to connect, collaborate, and access mentorship and support networks, enriching their entrepreneurial journey with valuable insights and guidance. In essence, by embracing e-financial strategies, women entrepreneurs can surmount barriers, amplify their impact, and catalyze inclusive economic growth in the 21st-century digital economy.

KEYWORDS

- **digital transformation**
- **economic empowerment**
- **efficient market hypothesis**
- **e-financial solutions**
- **e-financial strategies**
- **financial inclusion**
- **knowledge-sharing**
- **portfolio management**
- **women entrepreneurship**

REFERENCES

Adekunle, D. T. A. (2024). Challenges associated with entrepreneurship, vocational education and self-employment in Nigeria.

Adikaram, A. S., & Razik, R. (2023). Femininity penalty: Challenges and barriers faced by STEM woman entrepreneurs in an emerging economy. *Journal of Entrepreneurship in Emerging Economies*, *15*(5), 1113–1138.

Afshan, G., Shahid, S., & Tunio, M. N. (2021). Learning experiences of women entrepreneurs amidst COVID-19. *International Journal of Gender and Entrepreneurship*, *13*(2), 162–186.

Afza, T., & Amir Rashid, M. (2009). Marginalized women social well-being through enterprise development: A glimpse of remote women status in Pakistan. *Journal of Chinese Entrepreneurship*, *1*(3), 248–267.

Asandimitra, N., & Kautsar, A. (2017). Financial self-efficacy on women entrepreneurs' success. *International Journal of Academic Research in Business and Social Sciences*, *7*(11), 293–300.

Baba, M. S., & Vali, S. M. (2024). A study on improving women entrepreneur through financial literacy. *EPRA International Journal of Economics, Business and Management Studies (EBMS)*, *11*(1), 85–90.

Bailey, L. E., & Nyabola, N. (2021). Digital equity as an enabling platform for equality and inclusion. *Pathfinders for Peaceful, Just, and Inclusive Societies / NYU Center on International Cooperation*. https://cic.nyu.edu/resources/digital-equity-as-an-enabling-platform-for-equality-and-inclusion (accessed on 7th July 2025).

Bhagat, R., & Sambargi, S. (2019). Evaluation of personal innovativeness and perceived expertise on digital marketing adoption by women entrepreneurs of micro and small enterprises. *International Journal of Research and Analytical Reviews (IJRAR)*, *6*(1), 338–351.

Bonvillain, N. (2020). *Women and Men: Cultural Constructs of Gender*. Rowman & Littlefield Publishers.

Chimombo, J. P. (2005). Issues in basic education in developing countries: An exploration of policy options for improved delivery. *Journal of International Cooperation in Education*, *8*(1), 129–152.

Couzy, M. (2012). Conflicting roles: Balancing family and professional life—A challenge for working women.

Degutis, A., & Novickytė, L. (2014). The efficient market hypothesis: A critical review of literature and methodology. *Ekonomika*, *93*(2), 7–23.

DiPrete, T. A., & Buchmann, C. (2013). *The Rise of Women: The Growing Gender Gap in Education and What it Means for American Schools*. Russell Sage Foundation.

Elliott, C., Mantler, J., & Huggins, J. (2021). Exploring the gendered entrepreneurial identity gap: Implications for entrepreneurship education. *International Journal of Gender and Entrepreneurship*, *13*(1), 50–74.

Ely, R. J., & Rhode, D. L. (2010). Women and leadership. In *Handbook of Leadership Theory and Practice* (pp. 377–410).

Emon, M. H., & Nipa, M. N. (2024). Exploring the gender dimension in entrepreneurship development: A systematic literature review in the context of Bangladesh. *Westcliff International Journal of Applied Research*, *8*(1), 34–49.

ESCAP, U. (2006). *Entrepreneurship and E-Business Development for Women*.

Eze, P., & Obikeze, C. O. (2017). The extent of utilization of e-marketing application by small and medium enterprises in South Eastern States of Nigeria. *Management Studies and Economic Systems*, *54*(5805), 1–10.

Genoveva, B. G., & Gaby, B. (2019). The influences of financial, entrepreneurial education, and social support towards women entrepreneur's performance. *JIMFE (Jurnal Ilmiah Manajemen Fakultas Ekonomi)*, *5*(2), 109–120.

Goodrich, C. G., Gurung, K., Rizal, P. A., & Silpakar, S. (2018). Reflections on policies for women small and medium entrepreneurs: Status, challenges and opportunities in the Hindu Kush Himalayas and the SAARC region. In *South Asian Women Development Forum*.

Groza, M. P., Groza, M. D., & Barral, L. M. (2020). Women backing women: The role of crowdfunding in empowering female consumer-investors and entrepreneurs. *Journal of Business Research*, *117*, 432–442.

Gulati, A., & Singh, S. (2024). Financial self-efficacy of consumers: A review and research agenda. *International Journal of Consumer Studies*, *48*(2), e13024.

Hasan, R., Ashfaq, M., Parveen, T., & Gunardi, A. (2023). Financial inclusion – Does digital financial literacy matter for women entrepreneurs? *International Journal of Social Economics*, *50*(8), 1085–1104.

Hawsawi, Z. (2023). Unpacking the dynamics of digital entrepreneurship: Managing work-family boundaries among women entrepreneurs. *Journal of Information Technology Management*, *15*(Special Issue), 202–235.

Hossain, T. (2018). Empowering women through e-business: A study on women entrepreneurs in Dhaka City. *Asian Business Review*, *8*(3), 21–160.

House III, P. J. (1996). *A Study to Evaluate Individual Attributes and Correlate These Qualities with Investment Means to Compose an Appropriate Portfolio Mix*.

Hussin, H. H., Jemari, M. A., Kasuma, J., Yacob, Y., & Panie, R. (2017). Factors influencing e-commerce adoption among Malay women entrepreneurs in Kuching Sarawak. *Journal of Borneo-Kalimantan*, *3*(1).

Kamal, C. N. P. (2023). Integrated cost accounting and investment analysis: Transformative insights for strategic decision-making and financial performance enhancement. *Indonesian Interdisciplinary Journal of Sharia Economics (IIJSE)*, *6*(3), 3342–3370.

Kanapathipillai, K., Narayanan, S., & Kumaran, S. (2021). Are women entrepreneurs' business performances influenced by financial resources? Empowering women entrepreneurs in Malaysia through financial resources post-COVID-19 pandemic. *European Journal of Management and Marketing Studies*, *7*(1).

Karmakar, A., Habib, S. N., & Ahmed, A. (2018). Socio-economic factors affecting the perception of women entrepreneurs towards bank loan: A study on Rajshahi City. *Asian Business Review*, *8*(3), 105–114.

Kassim, S. (2023). The empowering path: Exploring the mediating role of entrepreneurship in the relationship between financial management skills, group identity, and women's empowerment in rural areas.

Kithatu-Kiwekete, A., & Vyas-Doorgapersad, S. (2020). E-procurement within the City of Johannesburg Metropolitan Municipality, South Africa: A gendered perspective. *Trends in eBusiness and eGovernment*, *2020*, 43.

Kiwekete, A. K., & Doorgapersad, S. V. (2017). Gender-based e-procurement within the City of Johannesburg Metropolitan Municipality. *International Journal of eBusiness and eGovernment Studies*, *9*(1), 9–23.

Koneru, K. (2017). Women entrepreneurship in India—Problems and prospects. https://ssrn.com/abstract=3110340 (accessed on 7th July 2025).

Kromidha, E., Yadav, N., & Ilavarasan, P. V. (2023). Digital microfinance crowdfunding for disconnected women entrepreneurs in India. *International Journal of Entrepreneurship and Small Business*, *50*(4), 459–481.

Kumar, P. (2016). Indian women as entrepreneurs.
Kumar, R. (2014). *Strategies of Banks and Other Financial Institutions: Theories and Cases*. Elsevier.
Lalangui, M. A. R. (2022). Effects of electronic invoicing, micro-enterprise sector in the province of El Oro. *Education Development and, 2022*, 123.
Markman, G. D., & Baron, R. A. (2003). Person–entrepreneurship fit: Why some people are more successful as entrepreneurs than others. *Human Resource Management Review, 13*(2), 281–301.
Mathew, R. V., & Panchanatham, N. (2011). An exploratory study on the work-life balance of women entrepreneurs in South India. *Asian Academy of Management Journal, 16*(2), 77–95.
Mudau, T. J., & Obadire, O. S. (2017). The role of patriarchy in family settings and its implications to girls and women in South Africa. *Journal of Human Ecology, 58*(1–2), 67–72.
Mukherjee, S. (2018). Challenges to Indian micro small scale and medium enterprises in the era of globalization. *Journal of Global Entrepreneurship Research, 8*, 1–19.
Nelson, T., Maxfield, S., & Kolb, D. (2009). Women entrepreneurs and venture capital: Managing the shadow negotiation. *International Journal of Gender and Entrepreneurship, 1*(1), 57–76.
Niethammer, C. (2013). Women, entrepreneurship and the opportunity to promote development and business. *Brookings Blum Roundtable Policy Brief, 37*(1–10).
Ononiwu, C. G. (2015). Mechanisms for emergent usage of adaptive information systems: A critical realist case of e-financial systems in South Africa.
Orser, B., Liao, X., Riding, A. L., Duong, Q., & Catimel, J. (2021). Gender-responsive public procurement: Strategies to support women-owned enterprises. *Journal of Public Procurement, 21*(3), 260–284.
Padmannavar, S. S. (2011). A review on e-commerce empowering women's. *International Journal of Computer Science and Telecommunications, 2*(8), 74–78.
Pramanik, S., & Mitra, D. (2023). Women entrepreneurship over the last two decades: A study of trends and changes. In *Gender Equality from a Modern Perspective* (pp. 91–115). Apple Academic Press.
Rajandran, K. V. R. (2024). Financial management practices and the performance of women entrepreneur in Thiruvarur Taluk of Thiruvarur District, Tamilnadu. *Migration Letters, 21*(S6), 430–439.
Rashid, A. G., & Ejaz, L. (2019). Interest-free microcredit loans: Pakistani female entrepreneurs. *Journal of Islamic Marketing, 10*(3), 860–873.
Rehman, S., & Azam Roomi, M. (2012). Gender and work-life balance: A phenomenological study of women entrepreneurs in Pakistan. *Journal of Small Business and Enterprise Development, 19*(2), 209–228.
Rusandry, R. (2023). The effectiveness of providing business capital loans in developing women's entrepreneurial soul. *Journal of Entrepreneurial and Business Diversity, 1*(2), 137–142.
Sihotang, J., Puspokusumo, R. A. A. W., Sun, Y., & Munandar, D. (2020). Core competencies of women entrepreneur in building superior online business performance in Indonesia. *Management Science Letters, 10*(7), 1607–1612.

Singh, M. A., Tiwari, M. P., & Yadav, M. A. (2023). Balanced work-life: Female entrepreneurs. *International Journal of Research and Review Techniques*, *2*(1), 43–48.

Singh, S., & Dash, B. M. (2021). Gender discrimination in accessing finance by women-owned businesses: A review. *Journal of International Women's Studies*, *22*(9), 381–399.

Sinha, S. (2005). *Developing Women Entrepreneurs in South Asia: Issues, Initiatives and Experiences*.

Srividhya, K. M., & Paramasivam, J. (2022). A study on perception towards women entrepreneurship in digital marketing. *Journal of Positive School Psychology*, 9265–9271.

Stone, P. (2007). *Opting Out? Why Women Really Quiet Careers and Head Home*. University of California Press.

Sultana, F., & Akter, A. (2021). Women e-commerce: Perspective in Bangladesh. *Journal of Management, Economics, and Industrial Organization*, *5*(3), 1–13.

Talib, A., & Yusoff, M. N. (2019). Women entrepreneurship through e-business. *International Journal of Supply Chain Management*, *8*(1), 710–716.

Tambunan, T. (2009). Women entrepreneurship in Asian developing countries: Their development and main constraints. *Journal of Development and Agricultural Economics*, *1*(2), 27–40.

Tiwari, N. (2006). Changing gender identity and gender roles of emerging adults: A case study in Bhopal (Doctoral dissertation, Indian Institute of Technology, Bombay (India)).

Torri, M. C., & Martinez, A. (2014). Women's empowerment and micro-entrepreneurship in India: Constructing a new development paradigm? *Progress in Development Studies*, *14*(1), 31–48.

Tsuma, V. I., & Kanda, M. (2017). Factors affecting the adoption of e-procurement systems among international non-governmental organizations in Kenya. *International Journal of Academic Research in Accounting, Finance and Management Sciences*, *7*(2), 164–176.

Tucker, J. G., Stipano, D., Hall, K., Clegg, B., & Carral, A. (2019). Square peg meets round hole: Regulatory responses to challenges created by innovation in banking. *Business Lawyer*, *75*, 2491.

Umejiaku, R. I. (2020). Access to credit on the growth of women entrepreneurs in Jos, Plateau State: The influence of financial support services. *Innovation Journal of Social Sciences and Economic Review*, *2*(1), 24–34.

Vandenberg, P., & Creation, J. (2006). Poverty reduction through small enterprises. *SEED Working Paper*, *75*, 1–60.

Véras, E. Z. (2015). Female entrepreneurship: From women's empowerment to shared value creation. *Journal on Innovation and Sustainability RISUS*, *6*(2), 109–123.

Wajcman, J. (2013). *Managing Like a Man: Women and Men in Corporate Management*. John Wiley & Sons.

Wang, Y., Li, Y., Wu, J., Ling, L., & Long, D. (2023). Does digitalization sufficiently empower female entrepreneurs? Evidence from their online gender identities and crowdfunding performance. *Small Business Economics*, *61*(1), 325–348.

Wennekers, S., & Thurik, R. (1999). Linking entrepreneurship and economic growth. *Small Business Economics*, *13*, 27–56.

Wu, R. (2013). An overview of e-invoicing in China and the factors affecting individual's intention to B2C e-invoicing adoption.

Xu, Y. (2016). *From E-Commerce to She-Commerce: The Rise of She-Era? A Small-Scale Case Study on Female Entrepreneurs on Taobao in China*.

Xu, Y. (2022). The strategy of how to deeply integrate technology and finance in the internet environment. *Journal of Environmental and Public Health*, *2022*.

Yang, T., & del Carmen Triana, M. (2019). Set up to fail: Explaining when women-led businesses are more likely to fail. *Journal of Management*, *45*(3), 926–954.

CHAPTER 7

Rural Maharashtra: Microfinance Growth and Challenges for Microfinance Providers in Implementing e-Financial Strategies

MRINAL PHALLE,[1,*] DEEPAK DESHMUKH,[2] and VAISHALI PATIL[1]

[1]*Department of Finance, Prin. L. N. Welingkar Institute of Management Development and Research (PGDM), Mumbai, Maharashtra, India*

[2]*Star Union Dai-Ichi Life Insurance, Mumbai, Maharashtra, India*

*Corresponding author

ABSTRACT

Microfinance has emerged as an effective tool for poverty reduction. Due to the dynamic nature of microfinance and the absence of a one-size-fits-all approach, various delivery models have emerged over time. The study will look at the growth of microfinance programs and the challenges faced by microfinance providers in implementing e-financial strategies in rural areas of Maharashtra. The study utilized primary and secondary data sources, with a three-year period of data being analyzed for the years 2020, 2021, and 2022. Data was collected from 150 microfinance providers in the Raigad district of Maharashtra. Factor analysis and ANOVA were used to determine the challenges faced by microfinance providers in implementing e-financial strategies. The study suggests that microfinance providers in rural areas of Maharashtra face

E-Financial Strategies for Sustainable Development: A Handbook for Promoting Financial Inclusion and Ending Poverty (SDG 1). Ernesto D. R. Santibanez Gonzalez, Rajeev Sijariya, and Vikas Garg (Eds.)

DOI: 10.1201/9781779640956-7

challenges in selecting customers with a clear target because they lack clarity about the appropriate products and processes to meet their clients' needs. Furthermore, factors like financial literacy (FL) and the lack of digital infrastructure for microfinance products and services have been impeding the growth of microfinance. The research study concludes that microfinance providers should emphasize promoting digital FL among microfinance clients, enabling the sustainable growth of microfinance for financial inclusion.

7.1 INTRODUCTION

The rural sector plays a vital role in India's base production, given its heavy dependence on agriculture. However, many Indian families face restricted access to credit, leading to increased poverty among the poor. Microfinance emerges as a potent tool for delivering credit support and essential financial services to boost productivity and income generation. Moreover, it has the potential to raise the standard of living for both men and women by enabling self-employment and providing services like remittances and microinsurance. The effective operation of the Grameen Bank-Bangladesh model has piqued the interest of development economists worldwide in the concept of microfinance. In India, the microfinance movement gained momentum in the 1990s when various organizations and non-governmental entities recognized the potential of providing small loans, savings, and insurance products to the poor. These financial services aimed to empower individuals, particularly women, enabling them to start or expand small businesses, manage consumption during lean periods, and build assets. To promote financial inclusion and uplift the underprivileged population, the Indian government launched several credit-linked poverty alleviation programs. These initiatives, including the innovative SHGs, encourage women from similar socio-economic backgrounds to form SHGs. These SHGs foster regular savings among members, and the accumulated funds are used to provide microcredit within the group. Additionally, the SHGs are linked to commercial banks or regional rural banks, granting them access to formal credit for income-generating activities, small businesses, and livelihood initiatives.

Furthermore, the Government of India initiated the Microfinance Institution (MFI) / Microfinance Organization (MFO) – Bank Linkage program in the early 1990s. Officially launched in 1992, this collaborative effort between the government, commercial banks, and MFIs aims to promote financial inclusion and enhance access to credit for low-income individuals, particularly in rural areas. The linkage facilitates the outreach of microfinance services, improving financial inclusion for the underprivileged population, especially in rural and semi-urban areas. Self-Help Groups (SHGs) and Microfinance Providers, also known as Microfinance Institutions (MFIs), are two essential components of the microfinance ecosystem, playing crucial roles in promoting financial inclusion and empowering underprivileged communities. MFIs serve as intermediaries between financial markets and the economically marginalized population, extending formal financial services to those who lack access to traditional banks. They adopt various models to provide micro-credit, including group-based lending (often linked to SHGs), individual lending, and other innovative methods tailored to their clients' needs. To support these efforts, the Reserve Bank of India (RBI) has been actively involved in regulating and promoting the healthy growth of microfinance in the country. The RBI has issued guidelines to regulate the interest rates charged by MFIs, ensure fair practices, and promote transparency. The RBI's involvement has brought stability to the sector and improved the credibility of MFIs. Nevertheless, despite these efforts, the microfinance sector in India has faced significant challenges over the years. One of the most notable events was the Andhra Pradesh microfinance crisis in 2010, which shed light on the risks associated with aggressive lending practices and coercive recovery methods. This unfortunate situation resulted in a surge of borrower indebtedness and tragically led to suicides among some borrowers. In response, the Indian government and regulatory authorities took proactive measures to strengthen the regulatory framework and enhance consumer protection in the microfinance sector.

Fast forward to the recent COVID-19 pandemic, which presented an entirely new set of difficulties for microfinance providers in the country. As the pandemic took a toll on the economy, many borrowers found it increasingly challenging to repay their loans due to widespread job losses, reduced income, and disruptions to businesses. The pandemic exposed the vulnerabilities of the informal sector and the precarious financial situations faced by many microfinance clients. Nonetheless, microfinance in India has played a transformative role in the country's financial landscape.

It emerged as a response to the challenge of financial inclusion and poverty alleviation in a country with a significant population of low-income individuals and informal workers. As of March 2019, the SHG-BLP initiative achieved numerous milestones, encompassing approximately 1000 crore groups and serving 1250 crore households all over India. Additionally, around 50.77 crore SHGs had received loans worth Rs. 87,000 crores. The SHG Bank Linkage Program has experienced significant expansion and has progressed into a more sophisticated and developed system. However, despite these achievements, only 1.07 lakh of the 6.4 lakh villages, as per RBI Banking Statistics 2020, have developed banking services, leaving more than five lakh villages without them. Therefore, it is crucial to examine the expansion of microfinance under SHG-BLP and Microfinance Finance Institute (MFI)/Microfinance Finance Organization (MFO) Bank linkage and its effects on the development of the nation.

7.2 LITERATURE REVIEW

Microfinance serves as a pivotal tool for alleviating poverty, with SHGs constituting a vital aspect. These groups, as defined by Dwaraki et al. (1996), consist of unregistered associations of disadvantaged individuals who voluntarily pool funds for lending within their community, thus enabling access to capital. Additionally, Parker (2013) highlights the potential of microfinance, particularly in women-owned businesses, to drive poverty reduction in rural areas. Cross-sector partnerships, as proposed by Casselman and Sama (2013), present opportunities for leveraging the strengths of both for-profit and non-profit MFIs to enhance impact. However, despite the three-decade success story of microfinance programs, Sekhi (2007) notes persistent challenges in providing access to the working poor.

Addressing gender disparities, Santa Chaudhary (2014) suggests focusing on capacity building, awareness-raising, and education to empower women through microfinance initiatives. Despite the demonstrated efficacy of self-help and microfinance organizations in poverty reduction, challenges persist, including infrastructural limitations and product diversification issues. To advance microfinance in rural areas, cross-sector collaborations and educational initiatives are recommended. Nevertheless, Ikechukwu (2012) identifies various hurdles faced by microfinance banks, including institutional shortcomings, infrastructure deficits, and cultural barriers.

Nasir (2013) outlines additional challenges for MFIs, such as limited product diversity, small client bases, high interest rates, and liquidity shortages. Montgomery and Weiss (2011) and Mosley and Hulme (1998) stress the importance of offering tailored financial services and sustainable interest rates to cover operational costs. Research by Gutierrez and Serrano (2009) highlights the interplay between social and financial efficiency in microfinance operations. Furthermore, Chahine and Tannir (2010) demonstrate that MFIs with larger client bases tend to perform better financially, underscoring the significance of scale in enhancing overall effectiveness.

In the realm of digital financial inclusion (DFI), Al Khub (2021) investigates various factors including internet access, education levels, owner experience, firm size, socioeconomic status, manager age, and FL. The study advocates for the implementation of digital skills training programs to enhance financial inclusion, particularly in rural areas, and emphasizes the importance of improving digital infrastructure to promote accessibility to formal financial services. Similarly, Sharon Buteau's research (2021) underscores the necessity of closely monitoring policy implementation and developing tailored digital financial services to cater to the unique needs of vulnerable groups. Furthermore, enhancing digital literacy is highlighted as essential for ensuring the effective utilization of digital solutions for financial inclusion.

Kaur's study (2014) on the financial crisis in Andhra Pradesh sheds light on the challenges faced by MFIs, particularly their inability to recover operational costs, leading to unsustainability. The crash was attributed to the incompatibility of MFIs with the political system. Mahapatra and Dutta's study (2016) focuses on identifying determinants of microfinance sustainability, particularly the impact of loan balance on operational sustainability. This aspect is crucial for the effective functioning of MFIs.

While microfinance has emerged as a potent tool for empowering individuals and enabling them to enhance their personal abilities and voice against social exploitations, the microfinance sector in India faces challenges. A significant number of MFIs operate without proper regulation, charging high interest rates from poor borrowers. To address these challenges and ensure the sustainability of MFIs, Mahapatra and Dutta (2016) conducted a study analyzing factors such as loan balance per borrower, cost per borrower, and yield on gross loans. Their study recommended enhancing economies of scale to reduce the cost per borrower and increase efficiency. In a mixed survey methodology, Baland et al. (2008) found that the survival of microfinance programs was not time-dependent, but loan and savings sizes tended to grow over time. They also noted that group failures were often attributable to personal conflicts and leadership issues. Panda (2008) highlighted the positive impact of increased literacy in reducing social stigmas and traditional issues, leading to improved average personal income. Sahu's qualitative exploratory research (2015) discovered that longer membership in SHGs intensified women's economic and political empowerment, though it might not necessarily lead to social or political empowerment. Guha's field survey in West Bengal (2007) identified challenges such as low repayment by clients, stemming from factors like having more children/dependents in the family, double-dipping of loans, and poor income flow. Kumar and Sensarma's study (2017) revealed significant inefficiencies in the microfinance sector, with size and profitability impacting efficiency and aging leading to increased inefficiency. Mirpourian et al.'s empirical study (2016) reveals that borrowers' paying capacity tends to improve as they approach their loan limit, and self-motivation correlates positively with borrowers' repayment performance. Srinivasan (2011) highlights disparities in the impact of MFIs across different segments of society. Twaha and Rashid (2012) observe that aging and size negatively affect operational efficiency, while the number of clients has a positive influence on efficiency. In contrast, Narwal and Yadav (2014) emphasize the positive impact of size on profitability and outreach.

The relationship between Gross Domestic Product (GDP) and micro-credit to SHGs is evident in studies by Pati (2015) and Sharma and Puri (2013), underlining microfinance's role in promoting economic growth and financial inclusion. Mader (2014) and Copestake (2010) stress microfinance's significance in fostering financial inclusion and achieving positive social outcomes by facilitating market development and capital accumulation. Additionally, Mader (2013) highlights the importance of credit availability to MFIs in establishing robust credit relations. Swain and Wallentin (2017) note a special preference for microfinance in the southern parts of India, suggesting regional variations in implementation. This observation is supported by Laha and Kuri (2014), who find relatively better performance in women's empowerment in the southern part of India compared to other regions. However, Twaha and Rashid's empirical analysis (2012) indicates that outreach negatively impacts productivity, signaling the need to address specific challenges to enhance the effectiveness of microfinance programs. Pati (2015) identifies key variables affecting the sustainability and outreach of MFIs, including operating expenditure, capital structure, and asset quality, which significantly influence the success and impact of microfinance initiatives.

In addressing challenges faced by microfinance programs, this comprehensive study compiles data from various categories of microfinance providers representing different legal forms of MFIs, including societies, trusts, Sec-8 companies, NBFC-MFIs, and cooperatives. This study encompasses 27% of NBFC-MFIs, 28% of cooperatives, and 45% of commercial banks, addressing the research gap by analyzing differences in challenges faced by experienced microfinance providers implementing e-financial strategies compared to those with less operational experience.

7.2.1 OBJECTIVE OF STUDY AS FOLLOWS

1. To study growth of microfinance program under the SHG and MFI/MFO Bank Linkage Program
2. To identify challenges faced by microfinance providers in implementing e-financial strategies

7.3 METHODOLOGY

In the present study, the growth of the microfinance program has been analyzed under the SHG and MFI/MFO Bank Linkage Program based on secondary data. The Compound Annual Growth Rate (CAGR) was used to assess the growth of the microfinance program. The outreach parameters used for growth included the total number of SHGs linked, disbursement and outstanding amounts, and bank-wise disbursement under the SHG and MFI/MFO Bank Linkage Program. To comprehend the challenges encountered by microfinance providers and promote further outreach of microfinance programs in rural areas, primary data was gathered through surveys. The study involved 150 microfinance providers and 4 Small Finance Banks, encompassing approximately 96% of the microfinance sector in the Raigad district of Maharashtra. The sample was drawn using a stratified sampling method from all legal forms of MFIs, representing societies, trusts, Sec-8 companies, NBFC-MFIs, and cooperatives. It includes 27% of NBFC-MFIs, 28% of cooperatives, and 45% of commercial banks. After analyzing the growth of microfinance providers and before suggesting measures for improving the microfinance programs, factor analysis was used to determine the challenges faced by microfinance providers from the Raigad district of Maharashtra. The research included 15 variables to analyze the challenges faced by microfinance providers. The mean of the challenges faced by microfinance programs varied significantly between categories, as determined by the ANOVA. To ascertain whether there is any variation in the difficulties faced by microfinance providers according to age, the t-test has been utilized (Table 7.1).

7.3.1 HYPOTHESIS

The following hypotheses are tested for challenges faced by microfinance providers:

- **H0 1a:** There is no statistically significant difference in the mean values of challenges encountered by microfinance providers.
- **H1 1a:** There is a statistically significant difference in the mean values of challenges encountered by microfinance providers.
- **H0 2b:** There is no statistically significant difference in the mean values of challenges encountered by microfinance providers by age.
- **H1 2b:** There is a statistically significant difference in the mean values of challenges encountered by microfinance providers by age.

7.4 RESULT AND DISCUSSION

7.4.1 DEMOGRAPHIC DETAILS

TABLE 7.1 Descriptive Statistics of Sample

Demographic		N (%)
Gender		
	Male	46 (46%)
	Female	53 (53%)
	Undisclosed	1 (1%)
Work Experience (in Year)		
	Freshers	83 (83%)
	0–2	16 (15%)
	2–5	1 (1%)

Respondent gender distribution: Males 46%, Females 53%, Non-disclosed 1%. Majority were freshers (83%), followed by 0–2 years' experience (16%), and 2–5 years' experience (1%).

7.4.2 GROWTH OF MICROFINANCE PROGRAM

A compound annual growth rate (CAGR) was used to assess the growth of the microfinance program. Microfinance programs are implemented in two ways: SHG-BPL Program and MFI/MFO-Bank Linkage Program; thus, progress under both approaches is examined in the study using data from the years 2020, 2021, and 2022.

TABLE 7.2 Progress Under SHG-BLP Program (Number in lakh/Rs. in crore)

Outreach Parameter (As on 31 March of Year)	2019–2020	2020–2021	2021–2022	CAGR (%)
Total Number of SHGs Linked	102.43	112.23	118.93	5.10
Total Number of SHGs Linked (in Amt)	26152.05	37477.61	47240.48	21.79
Total Number of SHGs extended loans	31.46	28.87	33.98	2.60
Total Number of SHGs extended loans AMT	77659.35	58070.68	99729.22	8.69
Loans outstanding against SHGs	56.77	57.8	67.40	5.89
Loans outstanding against SHGs in amts	108075.07	103289.71	151051.30	11.81

Source: NABARD Microfinance Report 2020 and 2022.

Table 7.2 shows the total number of SHGs linked, increasing from 2019–20 to 2021–22 with a CAGR of 5.10%, where the total SHGs that extended loans and the amount indicated a drop in the year 2020–21 because of the COVID–19 pandemic. Even though loan outstanding against SHGs is increasing from the year 2019–20 to 2021–22, which indicates a negative sign for the outreach of the SHG BLP program, the amount of loan outstanding against SHGs increased from 108075.07 lakh crore to 151051.30 lakh crore within the period of 2019–20 to 2021–22.

Table 7.3 shows the progress of the MFI/MFO program. Loans disbursed by banks and FIs to MFIs and MFOs decreased in 2021–2022, indicating the challenges faced by MFIs and MFOs, such as a lack of funds to cater to their clients. Loans outstanding against MFIs and MFOs decreased in amount in 2020 and 2021 because of the COVID-19 pandemic. From tables 7.2 and 7.3, the outreach of the SHG-BLP program is higher than that of the MFIs/MFOs program, as MFIs/MFOs must overcome challenges such as a lack of funds, which prevents them from expanding into rural regions.

TABLE 7.3 Progress Under MFI/MFO-Bank Linkage (Number in lakh/Rs. in crore)

Outreach Parameter (As on 31 March of year)	2019–2020	2020–2021	2021–2022	CAGR (%)
Loans disbursed by banks/FIs to MFIs/ MFOs	20,744	28,601	24,686	5.97
Loans disbursed by banks/FIs to MFIs/ MFOs in Amts	20,875.97	15,322.33	26,567.02	8.37
Loans outstanding against MFIs/ MFOs	52,288	61,259	58,849	4.02
Loans outstanding against MFIs/ MFOs in Amts	29,896.67	24,494.04	38,806.35	9.08

Source: NABARD Microfinance Report 2020 and 2022.

7.4.3 CHALLENGES FACED BY MICROFINANCE PROVIDERS

Present study has applied factor analysis, including 15 variables, to analyze the challenges faced by microfinance providers in India. The mean of the challenges faced by microfinance programs varied significantly between categories, as determined by the ANOVA. To ascertain whether there is any variation in the difficulties faced by microfinance providers according to age, the t-test has been utilized.

As per Table 7.4, Cronbach's alpha for the factor yielded a value of 0.796, indicating the reliability of the variables used for the study. The present study used factor analysis to determine the challenges faced by microfinance providers operating in rural areas, where 15 variables are analyzed. By retaining only variables with Kaiser's criterion greater than one, we can see that factor 1 explains 24.459% of the variance, factor 2 explains 37.185%, factor 3 explains 46.224%, factor 4 explains 53.622%, factor 5 explains 60.813%, and factor 6 explains 67.618% of the variance, as shown in Table 7.4. Since only five of the initial eigenvalues are greater than 1, the number of variables has been cut from 15 to 6, as shown in Table 7.5.

TABLE 7.4 Reliability Statistics

Cronbach's Alpha	No. of Items
0.796	15

TABLE 7.5 Total Variance Explained

Component	Initial Eigenvalues			Extraction Sums of Squared Loadings			Rotation Sums of Squared Loadings		
	Total	% of Variance	Cumulative%	Total	% of Variance	Cumulative%	Total	% of Variance	Cumulative %
1	3.669	24.459	24.459	3.669	24.459	24.459	3.053	20.355	20.355
2	1.909	12.726	37.185	1.909	12.726	37.185	2.337	15.583	35.938
3	1.356	9.039	46.224	1.356	9.039	46.224	1.314	8.759	44.696
4	1.110	7.398	53.622	1.110	7.398	53.622	1.240	8.267	52.964
5	1.079	7.191	60.813	1.079	7.191	60.813	1.104	7.358	60.321
6	1.021	6.805	67.618	1.021	6.805	67.618	1.095	7.297	67.618
7	0.938	6.253	73.871						
8	0.805	5.368	79.239						
9	0.777	5.182	84.421						
10	0.684	4.562	88.982						
11	0.577	3.847	92.830						
12	0.531	3.542	96.372						
13	0.385	2.569	98.941						
14	0.094	0.627	99.567						
15	0.065	0.433	100.000						

Extraction Method: Principal Component Analysis.

Also, since the total squared sums of loadings after rotation are more than 60%, we can make the variables, and Table 7.5 shows that six factors have been found. After rotation, the first factor, "internal environment," explains 20.355% of the variation; the second factor, "lack of digital infrastructure," explains 35.938%; the third factor, "higher rate of interest," explains 44.696%; the fourth factor, "external environment," explains 52.964%; the fifth factor, "level of digital FL," explains 60.321%; and the sixth factor, "laws and regulations," explains 67.618%, as shown in Table 7.5 (Table 7.6).

TABLE 7.6 Rotated Component Matrix

	Component					
	1	**2**	**3**	**4**	**5**	**6**
Higher rate of interest	0.057	–0.197	0.799	0.060	0.085	0.100
No collateral securities	–0.894	–0.201	0.023	–0.099	–0.003	–0.070
MFIs lack of mechanism to assess credit needs of clients	–0.913	–0.041	0.062	0.126	–0.025	0.098
Lack of Digital Infrastructure	0.101	0.888	0.008	0.021	0.017	0.117
MFIs lack of adequate training facilities to staff	0.740	0.279	0.090	0.116	0.059	–0.100
Higher transaction cost	0.527	0.202	–0.010	–0.098	–0.290	–0.285
inadequate information about the present status of clients	0.464	0.375	0.437	0.062	0.233	0.026
Level of Digital Financial Literacy	0.015	0.120	0.049	–0.040	0.915	–0.097
Difficulty in reaching to clients	–0.142	–0.930	0.077	–0.039	–0.109	–0.034
Small & irregular cashflows of clients	0.024	0.144	0.466	0.604	–0.105	0.032
Multiple loans by clients	0.129	0.396	0.450	–0.153	–0.277	–0.326
Increased competition	–0.063	–0.108	–0.129	0.673	0.058	–0.198
Lack of enough capital to lend to clients	0.548	–0.341	0.141	–0.160	0.048	0.022
Political interference	0.159	0.075	0.059	0.559	–0.016	0.129
Legislation and regulatory framework	0.017	0.139	0.069	–0.043	–0.100	0.889

Extraction Method: Principal Component Analysis.
Rotation Method: Varimax with Kaiser Normalization.

Further challenges of microfinance providers in India are interpreted in two ways. The first part addresses the challenges faced by microfinance providers across all categories, and the second subsection discusses the challenges faced by young and mature microfinance providers regarding the above-mentioned six factors.

7.4.3.1 CHALLENGES FACED BY MICROFINANCE PROVIDERS ACROSS CATEGORY

The challenges faced by microfinance providers in India are examined using an ANOVA test (Table 7.7).

TABLE 7.7 ANOVA

Challenges		Sum of Squares	df	Mean Square	F	Sig.
Internal Environment	Between Groups	105.465	2	52.732	178.055	0.000
	Within Groups	43.535	147	0.296		
	Total	149.000	149			
Lack of Digital Infrastructure	Between Groups	29.004	2	14.502	17.766	0.000
	Within Groups	119.996	147	0.816		
	Total	149.000	149			
Higher rate of interest	Between Groups	24.492	2	12.246	14.458	0.000
	Within Groups	124.508	147	0.847		
	Total	149.000	149			
External Environment	Between Groups	40.148	2	20.074	27.109	0.000
	Within Groups	108.852	147	0.740		
	Total	149.000	149			
Level of Digital Financial Literacy	Between Groups	2.306	2	1.153	1.155	0.318
	Within Groups	146.694	147	0.998		
	Total	149.000	149			
Legislation and regulatory framework	Between Groups	1.328	2	0.664	0.661	0.518
	Within Groups	147.672	147	1.005		
	Total	149.000	149			

ANOVA test is used to find significant differences in the mean across all six factors as challenges faced by microfinance providers across all categories in India. As $P < \alpha$ ($0.000 < 0.05$) for Internal Environment, higher transaction cost, higher rate of interest, and External Environment, there is a significant difference in the mean for Internal Environment, lack of digital infrastructure, higher rate of interest, and External Environment as challenges faced by microfinance providers in India, as per Table 7.7.

TABLE 7.8 Independent Samples t-Test

Challenges		Levene's Test for Equality of Variances		t-test for Equality of Means						
		F	Sig.	t	df	Sig. (2-tailed)	Mean Difference	Std. Error Difference	95% Confidence Interval of the Difference	
									Lower	Upper
Internal Environment	Equal variances assumed	0.4840	0.4880	18.4190	147.0000	0.0000	1.8948	0.1029	1.6915	2.0981
	Equal variances not assumed			17.1540	59.1960	0.0000	1.8948	0.1105	1.6738	2.1158
Lack of Digital Infrastructure	Equal variances assumed	13.4000	0.0000	–3.5800	147.0000	0.0000	–0.6438	0.1798	–0.9992	–0.2884
	Equal variances not assumed			–4.1440	91.1490	0.0000	–0.6438	0.1553	–0.9524	–0.3352
higher rate of interest	Equal variances assumed	1.0140	0.3160	0.8930	147.0000	0.3730	0.1672	0.1871	–0.2026	0.5369
	Equal variances not assumed			0.7330	49.8110	0.4670	0.1672	0.2281	–0.2910	0.6254
External Environment	Equal variances assumed	5.5680	0.0200	2.5560	147.0000	0.0120	0.4691	0.1835	0.1065	0.8318
	Equal variances not assumed			2.1400	51.0520	0.0370	0.4691	0.2192	0.0291	0.9091
Level of Digital Financial Literacy	Equal variances assumed	0.7550	0.3860	–0.9960	147.0000	0.3210	–0.1862	0.1870	–0.5558	0.1833
	Equal variances not assumed			–1.4940	146.5530	0.1370	–0.1862	0.1246	–0.4326	0.0601
Legislation and regulatory framework	Equal variances assumed	0.4190	0.5190	0.4530	147.0000	0.6510	0.0849	0.1874	–0.2856	0.4553
	Equal variances not assumed			0.4480	65.6620	0.6550	0.0849	0.1892	–0.2930	0.4627

7.5 CHALLENGES FACED BY MICROFINANCE PROVIDERS FOR AGE

The challenges faced by microfinance providers in India for age are examined using t-test (Table 7.8).

The results of Table 7.8 shows that there is a difference in the mean perceptions of young and mature microfinance providers regarding the internal environment, lack of digital infrastructure, and external environment.

Descriptive statistics indicate that mature microfinance providers strongly disagree, while young microfinance providers disagree on the internal environment as a challenge they face. Young microfinance providers have agreed on the lack of digital infrastructure and higher interest rates as challenges they encounter. Both young and mature microfinance providers agree that the level of digital financial literacy, legislation, and regulatory framework are challenges they face. However, young microfinance providers strongly agree, while mature microfinance providers are neutral regarding the external environment as a challenge to increasing the effectiveness of microfinance programs.

7.6 CONCLUSION

The present study underscores the potential of MFIs in rural India as a powerful tool for poverty reduction. It reveals that the SHG-BLP exhibits greater outreach compared to traditional MFIs and Microfinance Organizations (MFOs). However, both MFIs and MFOs face capital constraints hindering their expansion into rural areas, while the SHG-BLP program encounters its own set of challenges.

Further investigation uncovers key hurdles faced by microfinance providers in rural Maharashtra, including internal issues such as inadequate credit assessment mechanisms and technological deficiencies, alongside external challenges like the lack of digital infrastructure, higher transaction costs, and regulatory constraints.

Addressing these multifaceted challenges necessitates tailored strategies. Priority should be given to initiatives aimed at enhancing digital infrastructure, reducing transaction costs, and navigating regulatory hurdles to facilitate the implementation of e-financial strategies.

Microfinance providers must adapt by offering customized services and providing adequate staff training in rural customer engagement to improve transparency and service quality effectively.

To optimize operational efficiency, microfinance companies should leverage modern technology and IT tools. Additionally, efforts to enhance financial and digital literacy among clients are crucial. By equipping individuals with the knowledge and confidence to engage in cashless transactions, these initiatives promote accessibility to financial services, particularly for underprivileged populations in rural India.

In conclusion, overcoming these challenges requires a comprehensive approach integrating digital literacy initiatives, encouraging the adoption of cashless payment methods, and sustaining financial education campaigns. Additionally, addressing external environmental factors and ensuring regulatory compliance are vital for the sustainable growth and impact of microfinance initiatives in rural Maharashtra.

7.7 STRATEGIES AND RECOMMENDATIONS

1. **Enhanced Digital Literacy Initiatives:** Implement comprehensive digital literacy programs tailored to rural and underserved communities to empower individuals in utilizing banking technologies confidently.

2. **Encouragement of POS/mPOS Adoption:** Advocate for the widespread adoption of Point-of-Sale (POS) and mobile Point-of-Sale (mPOS) systems among rural merchants to foster financial inclusion and facilitate the adoption of digital payment methods.

3. **Continuation of Financial Literacy Campaigns:** Sustain and expand existing FL initiatives to enhance financial knowledge and promote responsible financial behavior among underserved communities.

4. **Investment in Staff Training and Technology:** Provide comprehensive training programs for microfinance staff and invest in modern technology to optimize operational efficiency and improve service delivery in rural areas.

By implementing these strategies, stakeholders can overcome challenges and unlock the full potential of MFIs in rural Maharashtra, promoting financial inclusion, poverty reduction, and creating a more equitable financial ecosystem for all citizens.

KEYWORDS

- **ANOVA test**
- **digital financial literacy**
- **digital literacy initiatives**
- **e-financial strategies**
- **financial inclusion**
- **financial literacy campaigns**
- **microfinance**
- **microfinance institutions**
- **mobile point-of-sale**

REFERENCES

Al-Kubati, N. A. A., & Selvaratnam, D. P. (2023). Empowering women through the Self-Help Group Bank Linkage Programme as a tool for sustainable development: Lessons from India. *Community Development Journal*, *58*(2), 283–308. https://doi.org/10.1093/cdj/bsab036 (accessed on 7th July 2025).

Anand, Kumar, & Jeyanth, K. (2010). Institutional challenges in the microfinance sector. *Emerald Insight*, 22–32.

Ayinaddis, S. G. (2023). Socio-economic factors affecting women's entrepreneurial performance in MSMEs in Bahir Dar City, Ethiopia. *Journal of Innovation and Entrepreneurship*, *12*(23).

Baland, J. M., Rohini, S., & Vandewalle, L. (2008). Microfinance lifespans: A study of attrition and exclusion in self-help groups in India. *India Policy Forum*, *4*(1), 159–210.

Bansal, A. K., & Bansal, A. (2012). Microfinance and poverty reduction in India. *Integral Review–A Journal of Management*, *5*(1), 31–35.

Cull, R., Demirgüç-Kunt, A., & Morduch, J. (2007). Financial performance and outreach: A global analysis of leading microbanks. *The Economic Journal*, *117*, 107–133.

Dey, S. K. (2015). Challenges and issues of microfinance in India. *Journal of Economics and Sustainable Development*, *6*(7), 1–9.

Ghosh, P., Tripathi, V., & Kumar, A. (2010). Customer expectations of store attributes: A study of organized retail outlets in India. *Journal of Retail and Leisure Property*, *9*, 75–87. https://doi.org/10.1057/rlp.2009.27 (accessed on 7th July 2025).

Gonzales Martinez, R. (2020). Which social program supports sustainable grass-root finance? Machine-learning evidence. *International Journal of Sustainable Development & World Ecology*, *27*(5), 389–395.

Gutiérrez-Nieto, B., & Serrano-Cinca, C. (2009). Social efficiency in microfinance institutions. *Journal of the Operational Research Society*, *60*(1), 104–119.

Hermes, N., & Lensink, R. (2009). Financial development and the efficiency of microfinance institutions. *SSRN Electronic Journal*, 1–29.

Hulme, D. (2000). Impact assessment methodologies for microfinance: Theory, experience, and better practice. *World Development*, *28*(7), 79–98.

Kashif, M., & Sridharan, P. (2012). Microfinance: The challenges and opportunities in rural India. *International Conference on Business & Management*, Cambridge Institute of Technology, Bengaluru (Bangalore).

Kumar, N., & Sensarma, R. (2017). Efficiency of microfinance institutions in India: A stochastic distance function approach. *Journal of Emerging Market Finance*, *16*(1), 151–168.

Laha, A., & Kuri, P. K. (2014). Measuring the impact of microfinance on women empowerment: A cross-country analysis with special reference to India. *International Journal of Public Administration*, *37*(7), 397–408.

Luthra, S., & Mangla, S. K. (2028). Evaluating challenges to Industry 4.0 initiatives for supply chain sustainability in emerging economies. *Process Safety and Environmental Protection*.

Lyngdoh, A. (2008). Microfinance and women's empowerment: Some evidence. *Man, and Society*, *5*(Spring), 81–95.

Marr, A. (2012). Effectiveness of rural microfinance: What we know and what we need to know. *Journal of Agrarian Change*, *12*(4), 555–563.

Mersland, R. (2011). The governance of non-profit microfinance institutions: Lessons from history. *Journal of Management & Governance*, *15*, 327–348.

Mersland, R. (2013). Market opportunities for microfinance institutions. *Enterprise Development and Microfinance*, *24*(4), 283–293.

Mirpourian, S., Caragliu, A., Di Maio, G., Landoni, P., & Rusinà, E. (2016). Determinants of loan repayment performance among borrowers of microfinance institutions: Evidence from India. *World Development Perspectives*, *1*(C), 49–52.

Mohapatra, S., & Sahoo, B. K. (2016). Determinants of participation in self-help-groups (SHG) and its impact on women empowerment. *Indian Growth and Development Review*, *9*(1), 53–78. https://doi.org/10.1108/IGDR-04-2015-0016 (accessed on 7th July 2025).

Narwal, K. P., & Yadav, M. K. (2014). Impact of characteristics on outreach and profitability of microfinance institutions in India. *International Journal of Financial Management*, *4*(3), 50–57.

Navajas, S., Schreiner, M., Meyer, R. L., Gonzalez-Vega, C., & Rodriguez-Meza, J. (2000). Microcredit and the poorest of the poor: Theory and evidence from Bolivia. *World Development*, *28*(2), 333–346.

Nawai, N., & Shariff, M. N. M. (2013). Loan repayment problems in microfinance programmed that use an individual lending approach: A qualitative analysis. *Journal of Transformative Entrepreneurship*, *1*(2), 93–99.

Pallikkara, V., Pinto, P., Hawaldar, I. T., & Pinto, S. (2021). Impulse buying behavior at the retail checkout: An investigation of select antecedents. *Business: Theory and Practice*, *22*(1), 69–79. https://doi.org/10.3846/btp.2021.12711 (accessed on 7th July 2025).

Panda, D. K. (2008). Self-help through microfinance: A paradigm shift in Orissa, India. *International Journal of Rural Studies*, *15*(1), 1–7.

Pati, A. P. (2015). Are regulatory microfinance institutions better off than non-regulatory ones? A comparison of performance and sustainability. *Paradigm*, *19*(1), 21–36.

Porwal, R. (2015). An experimental evaluation of weak-branch criterion for class testing. *The Journal of Systems & Software*, *2004*(2).

Rosenberg, R., & Gonzalez, A. (2009). The new moneylenders: Are high microcredit interest rates exploiting the poor? *CGAP Occasional Papers No. 15*, Consultative Group to Assist the Poor, The World Bank, Washington, DC.

Sahoo, B. K. (2016). Determinants of participation in self-help groups (SHG) and its impact on women empowerment. *Indian Growth and Development Review*, *9*(1), 53–78. https://doi.org/10.1108/IGDR-04-2015-0016 (accessed on 7th July 2025).

Sahu, G. B. (2015). How effective is a self-help group led microfinance programme in empowering women? Evidence from rural India. *Journal of Asian and African Studies*, *50*(5), 542–558.

Sharma, G. L., & Puri, H. (2013). An empirical testing of relationship between microfinance and economic growth in India. *Journal of Indian Research*, *1*(2), 87–94.

Srinivasan, N. (2011). *Microfinance India: State of the Sector Report 2011*. Sage Publications.

Swain, R. B., & Floro, M. (2012). Assessing the effect of microfinance on vulnerability and poverty among low-income households. *The Journal of Development Studies*, *48*(5), 605–618. https://doi.org/10.1080/00220388.2011.615917 (accessed on 7th July 2025).

Swamy Tribhuvananda, H. V., & Nandeshwar, R. L. (2011). Nurturing entrepreneurship in rural communities. *International Journal of Research in Commerce & Management*, *2*(3).

Twaha, K., & Rashid, A. (2012). Exploring the determinants of the productivity of Indian microfinance institutions. *Theoretical and Applied Economics*, *20*(12), 83–96.

Venkatraja, B. (2019). Are SHGs catalysts of inclusive sustainable rural development? Impact assessment of SKDRDP interventions in India. *International Journal of Sustainable Development & World Ecology*.

Yimga, J. (2015). The impact of high microfinance growth on loan portfolio: Microfinance growth and loan portfolio. *Journal of International Development*.

Zeller, M., & Meyer, R. L. (2002). *The Triangle of Microfinance: Financial Sustainability, Outreach, and Impact*. The Johns Hopkins University Press.w

CHAPTER 8

Financial Literacy and Financial Behavior of People in India with Special Reference to Agra, The City of Taj Mahal

BHAVNA YADAV,* SONAM SINGH, and SWAMI PRASAD SAXENA

Department of Applied Business Economics, Dayalbagh Educational Institute (Deemed to be University), Dayalbagh, Agra, Uttar Pradesh, India

*Corresponding author

ABSTRACT

Financial literacy plays a crucial role in shaping individuals' financial behavior (FB) and overall financial well-being. This chapter aims to measure the level of financial literacy (FL), including digital FL, and the financial behavior of people in Agra, the city of the Taj Mahal. To provide a comprehensive understanding of the financial landscape in the selected area, the study employed a mixed-methods approach, combining published data and information collected through a survey of individuals. The analysis of information gathered on respondents' attitudes, perceptions, and knowledge related to financial issues provides mixed results, which clearly indicate a dearth of FL among the people of Agra. However, a more favorable disposition towards awareness and usage of e-payment applications is observed, which reflects increasing awareness and adaptation of digital payment modes. The results of the chi-square test indicate that the level of understanding of people in rural and urban areas of Agra

E-Financial Strategies for Sustainable Development: A Handbook for Promoting Financial Inclusion and Ending Poverty (SDG 1). Ernesto D. R. Santibanez Gonzalez, Rajeev Sijariya, and Vikas Garg (Eds.)

DOI: 10.1201/9781779640956-8

differs significantly. The study proposes a framework to promote FL and finance in India and offers a roadmap for future research in the field.

8.1 INTRODUCTION

Financial literacy (FL) implies having the ability to effectively handle a range of financial competencies, including managing personal finances, creating budgets, and making investments. It is a combination of information and art in managing credit and debt that are required to make sound financial judgments. FL, as defined by the OECD (2013), encompasses a deep understanding and awareness of financial ideas and hazards. It also involves possessing the skills, motivation, and confidence to effectively apply this information in order to make sound decisions in different financial scenarios. The objective is to improve the financial welfare of individuals and society, as well as promote engagement in economic endeavors. According to Klapper et al. (2015), individuals who have a limited understanding of financial concepts and principles are not equipped to effectively handle their finances. Individuals with higher degrees of FL demonstrate a greater capacity for making well-informed financial decisions and effectively managing their economic matters, in contrast to individuals with lower levels of FL.

In the current era of rapid development and modest changes, assessing whether people have the abilities needed to handle the intricacies of money with ease is vital. The instrument for making financial decisions should not solely emphasize existing knowledge but also assess the information individuals require, thereby identifying and addressing the disparity between what they currently know and what they need to know (Lusardi, 2019). An individual's financial well-being and a country's overall progress heavily rely on FL. Despite various initiatives, developing countries continue to exhibit a low level of FL. In the case of India, FL has consistently lagged behind that of other nations across the globe.

The financial market today is highly vulnerable, with numerous complexities in a variety of contexts, including banking facilities, credit schemes, loan alternatives, insurance, investment and savings plans, derivative trading, punctual installment payments, and many more. The growing scale of international transactions and the movement of people and technology as a result of global economic liberalization have made

FL a major global problem. Most of the time, people are under financial stress and unable to make appropriate financial decisions due to a lack of economic education. Acquisition and comprehension of financial principles and ideas can boost the positivity of people in money management matters and help them make the most appropriate financial decisions. India has a huge population and an average literacy rate of 77.70%, according to the NSSO in 2021. The male literacy rate stands at 84.70%, and the female literacy rate is 70.30%. On a state-wise literacy rate, Kerala is ranked highest in the list with a 94.5% literacy rate. This is largely due to the state's investment in education and its focus on social welfare. It is pertinent to mention that only 27% of adults and 24% of women meet the minimum level of financial education in Bharat. The north zone of India needs more attention; when we look at the north zone, the literacy level in Uttar Pradesh is low compared to other states (RBI, 2022). Dube and Asthana (2017) observed that the level of knowledge of finances in UP is just half of the financial education in India.

Today, many emerging and industrialized economies are increasingly prioritizing the FL of their populations. FL is a concept that is unknown to many individuals, and it is often perceived as being beyond their comprehension because financial education enables individuals to make informed decisions that promote financial well-being. In today's scenario, every individual may access financial services at their doorstep, thanks to the financial market's digitalization and technological advancements, making it easier for people to access financial services via online portals and mobile applications. However, being aware of all these things might not be enough. In order to ensure effective use of digital financial services and prevent cyber fraud, it is essential to inculcate digital financial awareness among people so that they may effectively use these services and determine their legitimacy.

On digital FL initiatives in India, the results of a survey conducted by News Service of India Infoline in 2017 indicate that digital initiatives aimed at financial education, such as video clips, short films, and interactive quizzes, have had a significantly greater impact than traditional media; and government programs such as Digital India are expected to boost the growth of digital literacy. In recognition of the fact that globalization has accelerated the rate of development between nations, FL has grown in significance as a prerequisite for greater economic success. Many researchers in the past have made attempts to examine the issues related to FL and the FB of people in different economic settings. In the words of Mahdzan and Tabiani (2013), enhancing financial capability and literacy fosters improved financial decision-making, which in turn facilitates more effective strategizing and administration of significant life occurrences, including retirement, housing acquisition, and education.

Dwivedi, Purohit, and Mehta (2015) undertook an examination of the NCFE report on FL and financial inclusion in India. They found that people in cities have higher levels of FL than people in rural areas. Verma et al. (2017), while discussing the issues related to FL, mentioned that regulatory authorities should create separate departments to frame and oversee FL programs. They also suggested comprehensive monitoring of the programs to check their effectiveness and achieve maximum results. In their study, Mouna and Anis (2017) examined the factors that influence investment behavior and the significance of FL. A link was established between a lack of FL and a lower willingness to invest in the stock market. Arianti (2018) studied the impact of income, FB, and FL on investment decisions. The results indicated that FB significantly influenced investment decisions, whereas FL did not. In their 2019 study on financial understanding among college students in Lucknow, Dube and Asthana highlighted the importance of FL in making well-informed decisions regarding finances.

They highlighted the ultimate importance of providing financial education to college students. Tan and Singaravelloo (2019) investigated the degree of FL, FB, and retirement planning behavior, as well as their dynamics, among government officers in Malaysia. Their research indicates that individuals with a strong grasp of financial concepts and responsible financial habits, but average retirement planning behavior, are primarily influenced by their degree of education and personal income when it comes to FL. They claimed that there is no relationship between FL and retirement planning, and that FL has no mediating role in the relationship that exists between retirement planning and FB. Arpana and Swapna (2020) discovered a strong positive correlation among risk propensity, financial conduct, financial welfare, and FL in their study.

Prasad and John (2021) observed a low level of financial knowledge (FK) and financial behavior (FB) among selected teachers in Hyderabad. Focusing on the financial behavior of women, in their study, Shobha and Shalini (2015) found that women maintain the perception that gold, real estate, bank savings, insurance products, and retirement savings are the most secure investment options, whereas mutual funds, derivatives, chits, equities, and shares are seen to carry higher levels of risk. Rai, Dua, and Yadav (2019) examined the level of financial understanding among employed women in India's capital, Delhi. They found a strong link between FL and both financial attitude and behavior.

In the last two decades, Banthia and Dey (2022) have observed a significant increase in FL awareness initiatives over the past 20 years, not only in India but also in many other emerging economies throughout the globe. Gautam, Rastogi, and Rawal (2022) examined the connection between financial inclusion, rural development, and FL in India. Their findings indicate the positive impact of financial education on financial inclusion and rural development. According to Saraireh et al. (2022) and Ballis and Verousis (2022), individuals, in order to achieve long-term financial goals and financial security, must recognize and control their financial behavior, which comprises developing plans for wise financial decision-making and forming enduring financial practices for managing resources effectively to achieve desired financial outcomes.

Dogra, Kaushal, and Sharma (2023) conducted a recent study investigating the relationship between FB, financial attitude, and understanding of finances, all of which are factors that influence FL. The authors highlighted the role of demographic characteristics in influencing the factors that contribute to financial acumen. Mustafa et al. (2023) conducted a study in Malaysia to examine the relationship between FL, health literacy, financial attitude, and sustainable financial retirement planning among self-employed individuals. The study revealed that FL and attitude significantly impact retirement planning. Additionally, the involvement of financial experts plays a moderating role in saving for retirement.

In the present era, a significant number of financial transactions are conducted in a digital setting, where individuals' actions can be affected through the use of digital nudging (Benartzi, 2017; Brocke, 2016; Cai, 2020; Mirsch et al., 2017). Despite the widespread integration of digitization into several aspects of daily life, there is less understanding of its impact on individuals' FBs and, consequently, their FL. In order to both access the advantages of digital financial services and identify the potential risks associated with their proliferation, individuals must possess digital literacy. Lyons and Kass-Hanna (2021) define digital FL as the ability to engage in various activities such as purchasing things online, online and mobile banking, accessing digital financial services, conducting transactions, and resolving errors or canceling transactions. Liew et al. (2020) have identified four factors that contribute to the growth of digital FL. The essential components encompassed in this context are awareness, knowledge, confidence, and comprehension of digital financial hazards.

8.2 MATERIAL AND METHODS

The present chapter aims to examine the level of FL, including digital FL and FB, of people in Agra through the analysis of the results of a survey. The survey was conducted in two phases. An exploratory approach was adopted in the first phase to get some idea of the variables, and in this phase, the researcher conducted a thorough literature survey, which generated many statements related to various aspects of the study. To elicit responses from respondents, an empirical study was conducted by executing a self-structured questionnaire initially to 250 respondents randomly selected from different locations (both urban and rural areas) of Agra. Despite the regular chase, the researchers could receive 194 filled questionnaires. The description of the respondents' profile is as follows (Table 8.1).

TABLE 8.1 Respondents Profile

Gender	**Male**		**Female**	
	86 (44.3)		108 (55.7)	
Location	**Rural**		**Urban**	
	56 (28.9)		138 (71.1)	
Age (Years)	**18–25**	**25–35**	**35–45**	**45–65**
	114 (58.8)	58 (29.9)	10 (5.2)	12 (6.2)
Occupation	**Student**	**Businessman**	**Private Employee**	**Govt. Employee**
	116 (59.8)	12 (6.2)	50 (25.8)	16 (8.2)
Monthly Income (Rupees)	**≤ 20,000**	**≥ 20,000 < 40,000**	**≥ 40,000 < 60,000**	**≥ 60,000**
	120 (61.9)	30 (15.5)	14 (7.2)	30 (15.5)

The respondents include individuals from various locations, age groups, genders, occupations, and income levels. Among the sampled respondents, 58.8% belong to the age group of 18–25 years. These are primarily students of higher educational institutions with personal income from scholarships, private tutoring, part-time jobs, or earnings from internships under the 'earn while you learn' scheme. 29.9% of respondents belong to the age group of 25–35 years, and the rest are in age groups over 35 years. 55.7% of respondents are male, and 44.3% are female; 71.1% of respondents belong to urban areas, while the rest are from rural areas. In terms of occupation, 59.8% of respondents are students, 25.8% are private employees, 8.2% are government employees, and the rest are businessmen. Since most respondents are students, 61.9% are found to have a monthly income of less than Rs. 20,000, 15.5% belong equally to the income group of Rs. 20,000–40,000, and more than Rs. 60,000, while the remaining 7.2% are from the income group of Rs. 40,000–60,000. Descriptive statistics such as percentage, mean, and standard deviation, as well as the chi-square test, are used to describe and interpret the collected data.

8.3 RESULTS AND DISCUSSION

To examine whether respondents understand various aspects related to financial transactions, they were asked to answer 11 multiple-choice questions classified into two categories, FK (questions 1–8) and investment decisions (questions 9–11). The first category included questions on awareness about short-term investment avenues, choice of bank for loans, interest rate dynamics, numeracy in interest calculations, money illusion, the relationship between borrowing sources and interest rates, effects of inflation on interest earnings, and the role of regulatory bodies. The second category included questions on respondents' understanding of the risk-return relationship, investment returns, and uncertainties in investment decisions. The results are presented in Table 8.2.

TABLE 8.2 Financial Literacy (N = 194)

S. No.	Aspects of Financial Literacy	Answered Correctly	%	Answered Wrongly	%
	A. Financial knowledge				
1	Interest rate dynamics	114	58.8	80	41.2
2	Short and long-term investment avenues	68	35.0	126	65.0
3	Regulatory agencies	154	79.4	40	20.6
4	Choice of bank for loan	124	63.9	70	36.1
5	Numeracy in interest calculations	130	67.0	64	33.0
6	Effect of inflation on interest	84	43.3	110	56.7
7	Money illusion	66	34.0	128	66.0
8	Relation between source and interest on borrowing	92	47.4	102	52.6

TABLE 8.2 *(Continued)*

S. No.	Aspects of Financial Literacy	Answered Correctly	%	Answered Wrongly	%
	B. Investment decision				
9	Risk – return relation	102	52.6	92	47.4
10	Least – beneficial investment avenue for savings	77	39.7	117	66.3
11	Provision for uncertainties	107	55.2	87	44.8

Source: Own calculations.

The results indicate a moderate level of understanding among sampled respondents about various aspects related to FK. The results reveal that the maximum number of respondents (79.4%) are aware of principal regulatory agencies, followed by interest calculation methodologies (67.0%), choice of bank for loans (63.9%), and interest rate dynamics (58.8%). Respondents' understanding of short and long-term investment avenues, as well as issues related to money illusion, is found to be poor; only 34–35% of respondents could answer questions on these aspects correctly. The level of understanding of respondents regarding the relationship between the source of borrowing and interest rates, as well as the effect of inflation on interest rates, can be considered moderate; about 48.5% and 47.4% of respondents answered these questions correctly. Regarding knowledge to make investment decisions, it is observed that about 55.2% of respondents from the sampled area understand that while investing, people should make provisions for uncertainty, and 52.6% of respondents have an adequate understanding of the relationship between risk and return. Interestingly, only 39.7% of respondents have knowledge of the least beneficial investment avenue for their savings.

In order to assess the extent of FK and investing patterns, participants were requested to evaluate a series of statements using a 5-point Likert scale, indicating their level of comprehension (1 = Strongly Disagree, 2 = Disagree, 3 = Neutral, 4 = Agree, and 5 = Strongly Agree). The outcomes of their responses (weighted average and standard deviation for each statement) presented in Table 8.3 indicate that the level of respondents' awareness and investment behavior regarding statements number 1, 3, and 4, which concern financial risk and return, the need for and sources of financial education, and financial expertise, is high with a moderate degree of standard deviation. As for statements number 2, 5, 8, 9, and 10, related to government measures to promote financial inclusion and literacy, understanding of various investment avenues, effects of inflation on future investment returns, the relationship between portfolio diversification and stock market risk, and taxation issues on various investment avenues, the understanding of sampled respondents is moderate with a moderate degree of standard deviation.

TABLE 8.3 Financial Understanding and Investment Behavior (N = 194)

S. No.	Statements	Weighted Mean	Std. Dev.
1	Financial literacy is concerned with the need for and sources of financial education.	3.67	1.29055
2	Government undertakes numerous measures to promote financial inclusion and literacy.	3.42	1.15919
3	Participation in the financial markets requires a certain level of financial expertise.	3.52	1.18814
4	While investing, investor should be aware of financial risk and return.	3.86	1.07712
5	I have good understanding of various investment avenues.	3.20	1.06415
6	I know how to manage investment maintaining balance between liquidity and solvency.	2.82	1.41780
7	I have good knowledge of various mutual fund schemes and debt market instruments.	2.91	1.20519
8	I know that purchasing a variety of stocks lowers the risk associated with stock market investments.	3.31	1.13686
9	I understand inflation and its impact on future returns on investment.	3.14	1.26929
10	I am aware of taxability of various investment avenues.	3.30	1.10735

Source: Own calculations.

Amazingly, respondents' understanding of mutual fund schemes and debt market instruments, as well as their ability to manage investments while maintaining a balance between liquidity and solvency, is found to be below average. Although these findings are encouraging, there is still a need for concentrated efforts to implement and comprehensively monitor government programs on FL and promote investor education.

Today, financial products and services are increasingly offered and delivered digitally. The World Economic Forum considers that both digital and FL will be essential for financial inclusion. India has developed and introduced a diverse range of digital financial services, including the Unified Payment Interface (UPI), Bharat Interface for Money (BHIM), Bharat Quick Response (QR) code, National Automated Clearing House (NACH), Aadhaar Enabled Payment Services (AePS), Rupay Cards, and National Electronic Toll Collection. These services have revolutionized the way individuals, businesses, and households conduct payments, obtain loans, finalize transactions, purchase financial products, engage in investments, and send money abroad (Yang et al., 2021). Given that financial and digital abilities can help Indians become financially digital, respondents were asked to score specific phrases on a five-point Likert scale (1 = Strongly Disagree, 2 = Disagree, 3 = Neutral, 4 = Agree, and 5 = Strongly Agree). Table 8.4 shows the results for the weighted average and related standard deviation.

TABLE 8.4 Digital Financial Literacy (N = 194)

S. No.	Statements	Weighted Mean	Std. Dev.
1	I am aware of the various government-backed digital financial literacy initiatives in India, such as Pradhan Mantri Jan Dhan Yojana (PMJDY), National Digital Literacy Mission (NDLM), Digital India and so forth.	3.03	1.55946
2	I am aware and have a clear understanding of digital payment options available in India. such as UPI, BHIM, QR, net banking, payment wallets, and so on.	3.50	1.46099
3	I opt for digital financial transactions over traditional methods and independently carry out tasks such as digital payments and remittances.	3.73	1.35720
4	I am aware of the risks associated with digital financial transactions, including frauds and malware. I also understand how to stay safe and not fall for tricks or frauds.	3.63	1.41810
5	I am aware of and actively involved in online tutorials, financial educational platforms, and other tools that can enhance my digital financial literacy.	3.56	1.45946
6	I feel confident in using digital financial platforms, such as mobile banking apps or online payment systems.	3.82	1.35880
7	I am familiar with online trading of financial securities and feel at ease using digital tools for financial planning and investments.	2.43	1.81011

Source: Own calculations.

The results indicate that the weighted average of statement numbers 2 to 6 ranges between 3.50 and 3.82, with a moderate degree of standard deviation. This means that respondents are well aware of available digital payment options, financial educational platforms, risks associated with digital financial transactions, fraud, and malware. They opt for digital financial transactions over traditional methods and are confident in using digital financial platforms. However, their awareness of government-backed digital FL initiatives, tools for financial planning and investments, and online trading of financial securities is moderate to low. The weighted average of these statements is between 2.43 and 3.03, with a considerable value of standard deviation. At an overall level, the respondents exhibit a more favorable disposition towards digital transactions, showcasing a growing trend in the adoption of digital financial practices.

In order to examine the difference between levels of FL among respondents from rural and urban areas, the researchers applied a chi-square test on respondents' awareness of various aspects related to FK and investment decisions (contained in Table 8.2). The number of respondents from rural and urban areas was 56 (28.9%) and 138 (71.1%), respectively. Table 8.5 shows the results of the chi-square test at the 5% level of significance. The assumption here is that people in Agra's rural and urban districts have similar financial understanding.

TABLE 8.5 Results of Chi-Square Test on Financial Literacy (N = 194 (Rural = 56, Urban = 138))

S No.	Aspects of Financial Literacy	Correct Answers%		Incorrect Answers%		Chi-Square Value
		Rural	Urban	Rural	Urban	
A.	**Financial knowledge**					
1	Interest rate dynamics	46.4	63.8	53.6	36.2	4.922
2	Short and long-term investment avenues	25.0	17.4	75.0	82.6	1.338
3	Regulatory agencies	71.4	82.6	28.6	17.4	2.736
4	Choice of bank for loan	46.4	71.0	53.6	29.0	10.263
5	Numeracy in interest calculations	57.1	69.5	42.9	30.5	3.301
6	Effect of inflation on interest	46.4	42.0	53.6	58.0	0.312
7	Money illusion	50.0	46.4	50.0	53.6	0.209
8	Relation between source and interest on borrowing	42.9	49.3	57.1	50.7	0.666
B.	**Investment decision**					
9	Risk – return relation	35.7	59.4	64.3	40.6	9.616
10	Least – beneficial investment avenue for savings	17.9	18.8	82.1	81.2	0.026
11	Provision for uncertainties	42.9	56.6	57.1	43.4	3.034

Source: Own calculations.

The calculated value of chi-square for almost all the aspects related to FK and investment decisions, except for certain points indicated in Table 8.5, is less than the critical value of 3.841. This indicates that the level of understanding of people in rural and urban areas of Agra (except for interest rate dynamics, choice of bank for loans, and the relationship between risk and return) differs significantly at the 5% significance level.

8.4 FRAMEWORK TO PROMOTE FINANCIAL LITERACY IN INDIA

FL is an essential skill that enables individuals to make well-informed decisions regarding their finances. It's not a one-time learning experience but an ongoing process that should be cultivated throughout one's life. This section suggests a framework developed through the researchers' own understanding, interaction with sampled respondents, and published articles for promoting FL in India, particularly through school education, community-based initiatives, assessment strategies, integration of technology and innovation, and collaboration between educational institutions and financial institutions. The details we intend to suggest for enhancing FL in India are described in the following paragraphs.

- FL is a dynamic field, with economic landscapes and financial instruments evolving over time. Therefore, individuals should have access to resources that facilitate continuous learning. Many countries that have successfully promoted FL recognize the importance of starting early. Financial education should be practical and applicable to real-life situations. Workshops and seminars held in local communities provide an opportunity to disseminate knowledge across various age groups and demographics. These sessions can cover topics such as budgeting, saving, investing, managing debt, planning for retirement, and understanding financial products. The practical application of concepts in real-world scenarios enhances comprehension and encourages responsible finance
- Incorporating financial education into school curricula establishes a foundation of FK that individuals can build upon as they progress through life. Introducing financial concepts and skills at a young age will inculcate saving habits and develop a solid understanding of essential financial principles, budgeting, and investing among

students. Early exposure to financial education also instills a sense of responsibility and competence in managing personal finances.

- Financial institutions, particularly banks, have a vested interest in promoting FL. Collaborations between educational institutions and financial entities can strengthen financial education initiatives. Financial institutions can contribute resources, expertise, and access to financial products and services. By working together, educators and financial institutions can create comprehensive programs that address the specific needs of diverse communities and foster a holistic approach to FL.
- In the digital age, technology and innovation play a pivotal role in advancing FL. Mobile applications, online resources, and interactive platforms offer accessible and engaging ways to deliver financial education to a wider audience. These tools can simulate real-life financial scenarios, provide interactive learning experiences, and accommodate diverse learning styles. Harnessing technology enhances the scalability and effectiveness of FL initiatives, reaching individuals who may not have access to traditional educational resources.
- Promoting digital FL in India entails incorporating comprehensive modules in school curricula, leveraging technology with mobile applications and online resources, and fostering community engagement through workshops. While strategic collaborations with financial institutions will provide resources and expertise, regular assessments of understanding and feedback mechanisms will ensure the effectiveness of learning systems. The broad approach will provide individuals with the necessary information and abilities to effectively use digital financial platforms, make well-informed choices, and promote financial inclusion among various segments of the population.
- Assessing the effectiveness of FL programs is crucial for refining and improving educational initiatives. Regular assessments, including feedback collection, surveys, and quizzes, help measure participants' knowledge and behavior changes. Analyzing this data provides insights into areas that may require further development and enables educators to tailor their approach and content for better results. Assessments contribute to the ongoing improvement of FL programs, ensuring they remain relevant and impactful.

8.5 CONCLUSION

The analysis of information gathered through a survey of individuals' attitudes, perceptions, and knowledge related to financial issues provides mixed results. The chi-square test findings show significant variations in the financial expertise and grasp of people in Agra's rural and urban areas. All this clearly indicates a dearth of FL among the people of Agra. Although the government, RBI, and other agencies are making all possible efforts to improve the situation, there still exists a sizable gap in FL. Small towns, as well as urban and rural people, are considerably more at risk when it comes to rising wealth and FL. Digital FL seeks to equip individuals with the essential skills to proficiently handle their finances. Key elements of digital FL encompass the careful selection of the most suitable digital financial platform, comprehension of planning, budgeting, transacting, investing, and risk assessment. The researchers feel the need for both the public and private sectors to work together to improve FL in the nation. To connect it with people and close the FL gap in the nation, digital modes of financial transactions should be employed more and more.

KEYWORDS

- **digital payment**
- **financial behavior**
- **financial knowledge**
- **financial literacy**
- **investment behavior**
- **national digital literacy mission**
- **short-term investment avenues**
- **unified payment interface**

REFERENCES

Arianti, B. F. (2018). The influence of financial literacy, financial behavior, and income on investment decisions. *Economics and Accounting Journal*, *1*(1), 1–10.

Arpana, D., & Swapna, H. R. (2020). Role of planning and risk tolerance as intervening constructs between financial well-being and financial literacy among professionals. *International Journal of Economics and Financial Issues*, *10*(5), 145.

Banthia, D., & Dey, S. K. (2022). Impact of financial knowledge, financial attitude, and financial behavior on financial literacy: Structural equation modeling approach. *Universal Journal of Accounting and Finance*, *10*(1), 327–337.

Dahmen, P., & Rodríguez, E. (2014). Financial literacy and the success of small businesses: An observation from a Small Business Development Center. *Numeracy: Advancing Education in Quantitative Literacy*, *7*(1).

Dogra, P., Kaushal, A., & Sharma, R. R. (2023). Antecedents of the youngster's awareness about financial literacy: A structural equation modelling approach. *Vision*, *27*(1), 48–62.

Dube, V. S., & Asthana, P. K. (2017). A comparative study on financial literacy of Uttar Pradesh with Central Zone states in India. *IOSR Journal of Business and Management (IOSR-JBM)*, *19*(10), 22–27.

Dube, V. S., & Asthana, P. K. (2019). A study of financial literacy among college students in Lucknow. *International Journal of Social Science and Economic Research*, *4*(2), 963–974.

Dwivedi, M., Purohit, H., & Mehta, D. (2015). Improving financial literacy among women: The role of universities. *Economic Challenger*, October–December.

Gautam, R. S., Rastogi, D. S., & Rawal, A. A. S. H. I. (2022). Study of financial literacy and its impact on rural development in India: Evidence using panel data analysis. *Iconic Research and Engineering Journals*, *5*(9), 483–492.

Hassan Al-Tamimi, H. A., & Anood Bin Kalli, A. (2009). Financial literacy and investment decisions of UAE investors. *The Journal of Risk Finance*, *10*(5), 500–516.

Klapper, L., Lusardi, A., & Van Oudheusden, P. (2015). Financial literacy around the world. *World Bank*. Washington, DC: World Bank, *2*, 218–237.

Liew, T. P., Lim, P. W., & Liu, Y. C. (2020). Digital financial literacy: A case study of farmers from rural areas in Sarawak. *International Journal of Education and Pedagogy*, *2*(4), 245–251.

Lusardi, A. (2019). Financial literacy and the need for financial education: Evidence and implications. *Swiss Journal of Economics and Statistics*, *155*(1), 1–8.

Lyons, A. C., & Kass-Hanna, J. (2021). A multidimensional approach to defining and measuring financial literacy in the digital age. In *The Routledge Handbook of Financial Literacy* (pp. 61–76). Routledge.

Mahdzan, N. S., & Tabiani, S. (2013). The impact of financial literacy on individual saving: An exploratory study in the Malaysian context. *Transformation in Business and Economics*, *12*, 41–55.

Mouna, A., & Anis, J. (2017). Financial literacy in Tunisia: Its determinants and its implications on investment behavior. *Research in International Business and Finance*, *39*, 568–577.

Mustafa, W. M. W., Islam, M. A., Asyraf, M., Hassan, M. S., Royhan, P., & Rahman, S. (2023). The effects of financial attitudes, financial literacy and health literacy on sustainable financial retirement planning: The moderating role of the financial advisor. *Sustainability*, *15*(3), 2677.

OECD. (2013). Financial literacy framework. In *PISA 2012 Assessment and Analytical Framework: Mathematics, Reading, Science, Problem Solving and Financial Literacy* (pp. 144–164). OECD Publishing.

Prasad, G. R., & John, B. (2021). An analysis of financial knowledge and financial behavior of teachers working in higher learning institutions in Hyderabad. *Revista Geintec–Gestão Inovação e Tecnologias*, *11*(4), 1869–1883.

Rai, K., Dua, S., & Yadav, M. (2019). Association of financial attitude, financial behavior and financial knowledge towards financial literacy: A structural equation modeling approach. *FIIB Business Review*, *8*(1), 51–60.

Shobha, T. S., & Shalini, S. (2015). A study on the perception of women towards financial planning in the city of Bengaluru. *Asia Pacific Journal of Research*, *1*(30), 14–21.

Tan, S., & Singaravelloo, K. (2020). Financial literacy and retirement planning among government officers in Malaysia. *International Journal of Public Administration*, *43*(6), 486–498.

Verma, T. L. (2017). An overview of current financial literacy efforts in India. *Open Access International Journal of Science and Engineering*, *2*(12).

Yang, J., Wu, Y., & Huang, B. (2021). Digital finance and financial literacy: An empirical investigation of Chinese households. *SSRN Electronic Journal*, (1209).

CHAPTER 9

Portfolio Management in Different Markets of Financial Systems: An Optimal Investment Approach with AI Tools

MOHSINA HAYAT[1] and RUBY KHAN[2]

[1]*Bachelor of Management Studies, School of Commerce, Jain University, Bangalore, Karnataka, India*

[2]*Department of Accounting and Finance, College of Business, Jazan University, Jazan Province, Kingdom of Saudi Arabia*

*Corresponding author

ABSTRACT

"An Optimal Investment Approach with AI Tools" is a comprehensive study that explores the dynamics of portfolio management across various financial markets, including stocks, derivatives, and foreign exchange. The chapter aims to identify the optimal level of investment by analyzing the risk-return trade-off in these diverse markets. It explores the intricacies of financial systems, highlighting the unique characteristics of each market and their implications for portfolio management. The chapter discusses the significance of Artificial Intelligence (AI) tools in navigating intricate markets. By processing large volumes of data and recognizing patterns, AI tools can greatly improve decision-making in portfolio management. They offer predictive insights, automate routine tasks, and enhance risk management. The chapter utilizes AI tools in conjunction with conventional quantitative techniques and financial models to ascertain the most advantageous

E-Financial Strategies for Sustainable Development: A Handbook for Promoting Financial Inclusion and Ending Poverty (SDG 1). Ernesto D. R. Santibanez Gonzalez, Rajeev Sijariya, and Vikas Garg (Eds.)

DOI: 10.1201/9781779640956-9

investment strategy. It takes into account variables like market volatility, diversification advantages, and investor risk tolerance. The chapter offers valuable perspectives for investors aiming to optimize returns while mitigating risk in the intricate and dynamic financial environment. Additionally, it emphasizes the significance of comprehending the intricacies of diverse financial markets and underscores the role of AI tools in efficient portfolio management and optimal investment decision-making.

9.1 ARTIFICIAL INTELLIGENCE (AI) REVOLUTIONIZES PORTFOLIO MANAGEMENT IN THE FINANCIAL MARKET

In the dynamic realm of finance, the integration of AI is not merely a technological upgrade; it represents a financial revolution. By automating routine tasks and predicting market trends with unparalleled accuracy, AI is rewriting the rules of the financial landscape. No longer a mere buzzword, AI now stands as an indispensable element in portfolio management. AI has transformed the financial industry in the following four ways (Figure 9.1).

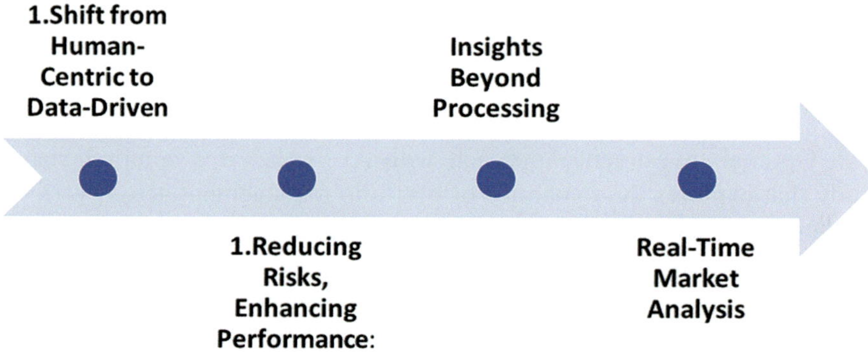

FIGURE 9.1 Transform of financial literacy after AI.

Let's see the sights each:

1. **Shift from Human-Centric to Data-Driven:** AI disrupts the status quo by moving away from human-centric methods. Modern portfolio management deals with the capacity of AI to rapidly and precisely handle large volumes of data, positioning it as a crucial tool. Traditional approaches often struggle to keep pace with rapid market fluctuations, but AI thrives in this dynamic environment.

2. **Insights Beyond Processing:** AI algorithms not only crunch numbers but also extract valuable insights from structured and unstructured financial data. By recognizing patterns and predicting market behaviors, AI empowers investors to make informed decisions. Gone are the days of relying solely on intuition; AI provides a data-backed edge.
3. **Reducing Risks, Enhancing Performance:** Armed with predictive prowess, AI aids investors in risk reduction. By analyzing historical data and real-time trends, it enhances portfolio performance. Emotion-free decision-making becomes achievable, as AI processes information objectively.
4. **Real-Time Market Analysis:** AI-driven portfolio management systems adapt swiftly to market changes. They offer dynamic, real-time insights and recommendations. In volatile markets, this agility minimizes losses and maximizes gains, ensuring investors stay ahead.

9.2 AI TECHNOLOGIES AND PORTFOLIO MANAGEMENT

AI has completely changed how portfolios are managed. With powerful new tools and methods, investors can now make better decisions, assess risk more accurately, and optimize their portfolios for the best results. Here are some examples of how AI is being used in portfolio management today:

- Machine Learning (ML) plays a pivotal role for leading portfolio management firms. They harness supervised learning algorithms, trained on historical data, to predict asset prices, analyze market trends, and optimize investment portfolios. Notably, companies like BlackRock utilize ML algorithms to drive data-driven investment decisions.
- Natural Language Processing (NLP) involves techniques that extract insights from unstructured data sources like news articles, social media, and financial reports. Companies such as Kensho Technologies leverage NLP to analyze market sentiment and identify relevant information that influences investment decisions.

- Deep Learning, a subset of ML, plays a crucial role in portfolio management. Neural networks, a key component of deep learning, are employed for predictive analytics and pattern recognition in financial data. Hedge funds, including Two Sigma, leverage deep learning models to analyze market data and make informed trading decisions.
- Predictive Analytics combines advanced statistical techniques with AI to predict future outcomes based on historical data. Firms such as Bridgewater Associates leverage predictive analytics to identify market trends and effectively manage portfolio risks.
- Reinforcement Learning (RL) involves algorithms that learn through trial and error to optimize trading strategies or asset allocations. Companies, including Citadel Securities, leverage RL algorithms to enhance their trading strategies and achieve improved portfolio performance.
- Robo-advisors are digital platforms that offer automated, algorithm-driven financial planning services with minimal human intervention. These platforms utilize advanced algorithms and AI to create, manage, and optimize investment portfolios based on individual investors' goals, risk tolerance, and time horizon. Notable examples include platforms like Wealthfront and Betterment.

AI technologies in portfolio management provide data-driven insights and advanced analytics, facilitating informed investment decisions through predictive analytics, risk assessment, and market sentiment analysis. These AI algorithms optimize asset allocation, enhance diversification, and offer real-time portfolio monitoring. As AI implementation continues to evolve, it promises to further enhance the efficiency and effectiveness of portfolio management strategies.

9.3 LITERATURE REVIEW PORTFOLIO MANAGEMENT IN FINANCIAL

The early 2000s saw a huge leap in technology, driven by the development of advanced digital tools and the exploding use of AI (Frankenfeld, 2021). AI is a field of computer science focused on building machines that can do things typically thought of as requiring human intelligence.

This includes thinking logically, learning new things, making decisions, and even understanding spoken language (Frankenfeld, 2021). In the words of Acemoglu and Restrepo (2020), AI is all about creating smart machines (like software or algorithms) that can learn and react to their surroundings. AI's reach is huge and keeps growing. It includes things like ML, deep learning, programs that understand language, APIs (predictive application programming interfaces) that predict what you need, and software that recognizes faces and voices (Martinelli et al., 2021). Recognized as a general-purpose technology (Bresnahan and Trajtenberg, 1995), AI is permeating various sectors of the economy, including finance. Financial institutions are at the forefront of AI adoption, leveraging its potential to revolutionize operations. AI facilitates process automation and harnesses big data for enhanced efficiency and productivity (PwC, 2020). Its application ensures accurate predictive analytics and trading strategies, free from human errors and biases, thereby transforming customer relationships and fostering innovation in business models (Cucculelli and Recanatini, 2022). AI's impact extends beyond operational enhancements to regulatory compliance and financial supervision. AI enables regulators to identify potential violations swiftly and anticipate the repercussions of regulatory changes (Wall, 2018). In the realm of fintech lending, AI-powered algorithms enable rapid credit decision-making, benefiting both consumers and lenders (Jagtiani and John, 2018).

In the context of finance, AI finds utility across diverse domains, including fraud detection, algorithmic trading, portfolio management, credit scoring, bankruptcy forecasting, risk management, sentiment analysis, and regulatory compliance. Studies by Hentzen et al. focus on customer-facing financial services, whereas Biju et al.'s work explores the technical aspects and the efficacy of ML, AI, and deep learning to establish finance strategies (Biju et al., (2020); Hentzen et al., (2022a,b). While these contributions are noteworthy, they diverge from the current study's scope. This research strand explores the application of AI in portfolio selection. For instance, Soleymani and Vasighi (2020) propose a clustering approach combined with Value at Risk (VaR) analysis to enhance asset allocation. They group stocks with lower risk and higher profitability and allocate them within the portfolio. Further sophisticated asset allocation strategies integrate a bankruptcy exposure model and an advanced utility performance system. Before including a stock in the portfolio, a neural network assesses the company's default probability and the asset's contribution to the efficient portfolio (Loukeris and Eleftheriadis, 2015). Furthermore, index-tracking enhanced by deep learning algorithms reduces trailing errors and yields optimistic performance (Kim and Kim, 2020). Additionally, the method of asymmetric copula for estimating return dependence facilitates portfolio optimization (Zhao et al., 2018). In summary, these studies collectively demonstrate that AI-based prediction models enhance the portfolio selection process by accurately predicting stock returns (Zhao et al., 2018). Artificial Neural Networks (ANNs) and ML models have demonstrated remarkable accuracy in predicting financial derivative prices. Jang and Lee (2019) introduce a ML algorithm model that surpasses traditional models of American option pricing, specifically the generative Bayesian NN. Culkin and Das (2017) utilize a feed-forward deep NN to replicate the Black and Scholes option pricing formula with a notably optimum accuracy rate. Similarly, Chen and Wan (2021) advocate for a deep NN approach in pricing American options and their deltas across high-dimensional spaces. Funahashi (2020) disagrees that deep learning is the best way to price options because prices can fluctuate too much. Therefore, they propose a new method that combines artificial neural networks (ANNs) with a different technique (asymptotic expansion) to find these prices. This new method doesn't predict the price directly but instead focuses on how far off an initial guess (like an estimate) is from the derivative price. This makes the ANN faster, more accurate, and requires less data and fewer steps to train. It's similar to how humans learn by comparing new things to things they already know (Funahashi, 2020). The latest research explores the application of AI in foreign exchange management. Efficient hedging and trading activities in this market necessitate precise exchange rate forecasts (Galeshchuk and Mukherjee, 2017).

A new type of neural network called a Hybrid Orthogonal Neural Network (HONN) did a significantly better job than other methods at predicting and trading the Euro versus US Dollar (EUR/USD) currency pair. The researchers used daily data from the European Central Bank (ECB) to train the model (Dunis et al., 2010).

However, Galeshchuk and Mukherjee (2017) critique these conventional methods for their inability to predict changes in forex rates' direction, thereby rendering them ineffective for supporting profitable trading. The standard methods for predicting exchange rates have weaknesses. To overcome this, the researchers used a special kind of deep learning called a Convolutional Neural Network (CNN) to forecast three important currency pairs: Euro versus US Dollar (EUR/USD), British Pound versus US Dollar (GBP/USD), and Japanese Yen versus US Dollar (JPY/USD). This new method was much better at making predictions than traditional statistical models (like ARIMA) and other ML techniques used for classification. Several studies, including one by Amelot et al. (2021), have found that AI models like NARX and others are generally better at predicting things than traditional statistical models.

9.4 AI-BASED PORTFOLIO MANAGEMENT IS BETTER THAN TRADITIONAL PORTFOLIO MANAGEMENT

Let's explore into the essential distinctions between traditional portfolio management and AI-based portfolio management. Here's a comparison in tabular form:

Parameters	Traditional Portfolio Management	AI-Based Portfolio Management
Decision-making Process	Human expertise and historical data	AI algorithms and data-driven insights
Data Processing	Manual analysis of data and processing of historical trends.	AI can employ machine learning, advanced data analytics, and to process and analyze vast amounts of data use predictive models.
Decision making	Well-defined rules and factors make easier to explain and interpret	Utilizes sophisticated algorithms that continually evolve and adjust
Information sources	Data sources rely on financial reports, analysis of market, and expert ideas.	Structured and unstructured data should operates from various channels including social media, news, and real-time market feeds.
Strategies for Investment	Investment strategies adhere to conventional allocation of assets and diversification principles grounded in market trends and historical data.	Employs dynamic, adaptive approaches driven by machine learning and predictive analytics.
Flexible and adaptable	Difficulty keeping up with the fast pace of the market	Dynamic and flexible in real-time, adjusting strategies based on live data.
Risk Management	Manage risk by looking at past events and taking steps manual	Leverages predictive analytics for continuous risk assessment, allowing for proactive strategies to minimize potential problems
Efficiency in time management	Manual processes make it difficult to be time-efficient.	Makes decisions and takes action faster by automating tasks and using real-time data.

Parameters	Traditional Portfolio Management	AI-Based Portfolio Management
Human involvement	Decision-making involves human expertise	Decision-making depends on the integration of human expertise with algorithms, AI-based tools.
Capable Prediction	Limited predictive capabilities, mainly relying on historical trends and analysis.	Uses cutting-edge AI and machine learning to predict what will happen in the market and how investments will perform.
Market volatility response	Struggles to keep pace with fast-moving markets, potentially missing out on timely adjustments	Adapts to market swings quickly, allowing for real-time portfolio adjustments.
Optimizing Portfolio	Creating optimal portfolios by looking at how investments have done in the past.	Optimizes portfolios constantly using AI and models that can adapt to changing conditions.

9.5 SHARPE RATIO MODEL IN PORTFOLIO MANAGEMENT:

The Sharpe Ratio, created by William Sharpe, is a widely used measure of risk-adjusted return in portfolio management and won a Nobel Prize. The Sharpe Ratio measures the additional return generated by an investment portfolio compared to the risk-free rate. This excess return is then divided by the portfolio's standard deviation of returns. The formula for calculating the Sharpe Ratio is as follows:

$$Sharpe\ index = \frac{Rp - Rf}{\sigma p}$$

Rp = represents the portfolio's expected return.

Rf = denotes the risk-free rate of return.

σp = signifies the standard deviation of the portfolio's returns.

The Sharpe Ratio provides investors with a metric to evaluate the risk-adjusted performance of their investment portfolios. A higher Sharpe Ratio indicates better risk-adjusted returns, as the portfolio is generating higher excess returns per unit of risk taken. Let's use an example involving an AI tool called AlphaSense, which utilizes NLP to extract insights from financial documents and news articles. We'll compare two portfolios: one managed using traditional methods and the other utilizing AlphaSense for AI-driven analysis.

Portfolio	Annualized Return	Standard Deviation of Returns	Risk-Free Rate
Portfolio A (Traditional)	8%	12%	3%
Portfolio B (AI-driven with AlphaSense)	10%	10%	3%

Portfolio A: Using the same Sharpe Ratio formula:

$$Sharpe\ index = \frac{Rp - Rf}{\sigma p}$$

$$Sharpe\ index = \frac{8-3}{12} = 0.417$$

Using the same Sharpe Ratio formula:

$$Sharpe\ index = \frac{Rp - Rf}{\sigma p}$$

Sharpe Ratio for Portfolio B

$$Sharpe\ index = \frac{10-3}{10} = 0.7$$

In this scenario, Portfolio B, which benefits from AI-driven analysis with AlphaSense, has a greater Sharpe Ratio (0.7) compared to Portfolio A (0.417). This suggests that Portfolio B is achieving better risk-adjusted returns relative to its volatility compared to Portfolio A. AlphaSense enables Portfolio B to swiftly analyze vast amounts of financial data and news articles, extracting valuable insights that inform investment decisions. By incorporating these insights into the portfolio management process, Portfolio B is able to optimize its risk-adjusted returns and potentially outperform traditional portfolio management methods represented by Portfolio A. This example underscores how AI tools like AlphaSense can significantly enhance portfolio management practices by providing timely and actionable insights, ultimately leading to improved investment outcomes as measured by metrics such as the Sharpe Ratio.

In India, the Sharpe Ratio model is particularly aimed at assessing the performance of equity mutual funds, portfolio management services, and other investment products. Instead of just looking at returns, investors use the Sharpe Ratio to consider both potential gains and riskiness. This helps them choose investments that align with their comfort level with risk and their overall investment goals.

9.6 ARTIFICAIL INTELLIGENCE (AI) INTERSECTS WITH THE SHARPE RATIO IN PORTFOLIO MANAGEMENT

AI plays a crucial role in portfolio management by leveraging strategic decision support through data science to optimize risk-adjusted returns, as measured by the Sharpe Ratio. As AI technologies continue to evolve, they are expected to further enhance portfolio management practices and contribute to improved investment outcomes. The following main heads are under discussion:

1. **Portfolio Optimization:** AI algorithms, particularly ML models, are employed to optimize investment portfolios with the goal of maximizing the Sharpe Ratio. These algorithms analyze historical market data, considering various asset classes, risk factors, and correlations to create portfolios that offer the maximum risk-adjusted returns.
2. **Risk Management:** AI technologies aid in risk management by continuously monitoring market conditions, analyzing data in real-time, and identifying potential risks that could impact the Sharpe Ratio of the portfolio. By using advanced predictive analytics, AI algorithms can help mitigate risks and enhance the risk-adjusted performance of the portfolio.
3. **Dynamic Asset Allocation:** AI-driven portfolio management platforms leverage a data-driven approach to adjust the balance of their portfolio based on real-time market conditions and risk assessments. By incorporating real-time data and predictive analytics, these platforms aim to improve the Sharpe Ratio by optimizing the trade-off between return and risk.
4. **Algorithmic Trading:** AI-powered trading algorithms optimize trade execution and asset selection, aiming to improve the risk-adjusted returns of the portfolio. These algorithms often incorporate risk models that consider the Sharpe Ratio as a key performance metric, optimizing trade execution to balance potential risk-adjusted returns.

5. **Robo-Advisors:** Platforms of robo-advisory customize AI technology to construct and manage investment portfolios tailored to individual investors' risk tolerance and financial goals. By optimizing portfolio construction based on the Sharpe Ratio, these platforms aim to deliver superior risk-adjusted returns compared to traditional investment strategies.

6. **Case Study: Wealthfront's Risk Parity Fund**

   Wealthfront, a prominent robo-advisor, utilizes AI and ML techniques to construct and manage its investment portfolios, aiming to maximize risk-adjusted returns for its clients. One of their notable offerings is the Wealthfront Risk Parity Fund, which employs advanced algorithms to optimize portfolio allocation based on the principles of risk parity.

In the Wealthfront Risk Parity Fund:

- **Portfolio Optimization:** AI algorithms analyze historical market data, including asset classes, risk factors, and correlations, to construct portfolios that have the intention of maximizing risk-adjusted returns. The algorithms employ optimization techniques to allocate assets in a manner that balances risk in various investment categories, aiming to achieve a more stable and consistent return profile.
- **Risk Management:** AI technologies continuously monitor market conditions and analyze data in real-time to identify potential risks that could affect portfolio performance. Advanced predictive analytics are used to anticipate market movements and adjust portfolio allocations accordingly, with the goal of mitigating risks and enhancing risk-adjusted returns.
- **Dynamic Asset allocation:** Wealthfront's AI-driven platform dynamically adjusts portfolio weights in response to market dynamics and potential risks. By incorporating real-time data and predictive analytics, the platform aims to optimize the trade-off between risk and return, thus potentially improving the Sharpe Ratio of the portfolio.
- **Robo-Advisors:** Wealthfront's robo-advisory platform uses AI technology to construct and manage portfolios in investment

according to individual investors' risk tolerance and financial goals. The platform optimizes portfolio construction based on the Sharpe Ratio and other risk-adjusted performance metrics, aiming to deliver superior risk-adjusted returns compared to traditional investment strategies.

Through the integration of AI and the Sharpe Ratio, Wealthfront's Risk Parity Fund exemplifies how modern portfolio management practices leverage data-driven insights and advanced analytics to optimize risk-adjusted returns for investors. As AI technologies continue to evolve, they are expected to further enhance Wealthfront's portfolio management strategies and contribute to improved investment outcomes for its clients.

9.7 CASE STUDY: QUANTELA WEALTH MANAGEMENT'S AI-DRIVEN PORTFOLIO OPTIMIZATION IN INDIA

Quantela Wealth Management, a leading investment firm in India, has embraced AI and the Sharpe Ratio to enhance its portfolio management practices and deliver superior risk-adjusted returns to its clients.

- **Portfolio Optimization:** Quantela employs sophisticated ML algorithms to optimize investment portfolios with the objective of maximizing the Sharpe Ratio. These AI technologies scrutinize vast amounts of historical market data, considering factors such as asset classes, risk factors, and correlations. By leveraging AI-driven models, Quantela constructs portfolios that aim to achieve the optimum risk-adjusted returns along with an optimal level of risk exposure management.
- **Risk Management:** AI technologies play a pivotal role in Quantela's risk management approach. Advanced predictive analytics continuously monitor market conditions, analyzing real-time data to identify potential risks that could impact the Sharpe Ratio of the portfolio. By leveraging AI algorithms, Quantela can proactively mitigate risks and enhance the risk-adjusted performance of its portfolios.
- **Dynamic Asset Allocation:** Quantela's AI technology empowers its portfolio management platforms to adapt investment strategies of asset allocation in response to evolving market conditions

and risk factors. By incorporating real-time data and predictive analytics, these platforms optimize the offset between risk and return, thereby improving the Sharpe Ratio of the portfolios.

- **Algorithmic Trading:** Quantela utilizes AI-powered trading algorithms to optimize trade execution and asset selection. These algorithms incorporate risk models that consider the Sharpe Ratio as a key performance metric. By leveraging AI-driven strategies, Quantela ensures that trades are executed in a manner that maximizes risk-adjusted returns for its clients.
- **Robo-Advisors:** Quantela offers robo-advisory services that utilize AI technology to construct and manage investment portfolios tailored to individual investors' risk tolerance and financial goals. By optimizing portfolio construction based on the Sharpe Ratio, Quantela's robo-advisors aim to deliver superior risk-adjusted returns compared to traditional investment strategies.

Through the integration of AI and the Sharpe Ratio, Quantela Wealth Management exemplifies how modern portfolio management practices in India leverage data-driven insights and advanced analytics to optimize risk-adjusted returns for investors. As AI technologies continue to evolve, Quantela remains committed to enhancing its portfolio management strategies and delivering improved investment outcomes for its clients.

9.8 SIGNIFICANCE OF STOCK, DERIVATIVE, AND FOREX MARKETS IN PORTFOLIO MANAGEMENT

Stocks, derivatives, and forex markets play significant roles in portfolio management by offering different investment opportunities and risk exposures. Here, represents how each market contributes to portfolio management.

1. Stock Market (Olortegui, 2016):

   i. **Diversification:** Investing in a variety of stocks can help spread risk across sectors and industries.

   ii. **Long-Term Growth:** Stocks have the potential for long-term capital appreciation, making them suitable for investors with higher risk tolerance.

iii. **Dividend Income:** Many stocks pay dividends, providing a source of regular income for investors.

iv. **Liquidity:** Stocks are generally more liquid than other investments, allowing investors to buy and sell easily.

2. Derivatives Market (Ingalhalli, 2023):

i. **Risk Management:** Derivatives such as options and futures can be used to hedge against potential losses in the portfolio.

ii. **Leverage:** Derivatives allow investors to control a larger position with a smaller amount of capital, amplifying both gains and losses.

iii. **Speculation:** Derivatives provide opportunities for investors to speculate on the price movements of underlying assets without ownership.

3. Forex (Foreign Exchange) Market (Borochkin, 2017):

i. **Global Diversification:** Investing in foreign currencies can help diversify currency risk and provide exposure to different economies.

ii. **Hedging:** Forex markets allow investors to hedge against currency risk, especially for international investments.

iii. **Leverage:** Like derivatives, forex trading often involves leverage, which can magnify both profits and losses.

In portfolio management, a well-diversified portfolio may include a mix of stocks, derivatives, and forex investments to achieve the desired risk-return profile. Each market offers unique characteristics that can be utilized to optimize portfolio performance and effectively manage risk. Sharpe's index model can be applied to evaluate investments on the basis of risk-adjusted returns in these markets and to make informed decisions about portfolio allocation.

9.8.1 ADVANTAGES OF AI PORTFOLIOS

AI's integration into stock markets and portfolio management enhances decision-making, optimizes performance, and empowers investors to navigate complex financial landscapes (Andrew Grossman, 2024).

- **Lower Fees:** Traditional fund managers typically charge higher fees, whereas AI portfolios tend to be more cost-effective.
- **Data-Driven Decisions:** AI processes diverse data sets, leading to more informed investment choices.
- **Accessibility:** Everyday investors can access AI-powered portfolios, democratizing financial markets.

9.8.2 ARTIFICAIL INTELLIGENCE (AI) AND PORTFOLIO MANAGEMENT IN THE STOCK MARKET

AI plays a crucial role in shaping stock markets through its data-driven insights, predictive analytics, and advanced algorithms. By harnessing immense amounts of historical and market data, AI provides traders and investors with valuable insights to facilitate informed investment decisions. ML algorithms analyze patterns and trends in stock prices, enabling predictions of future movements and aiding in making informed trading decisions. Additionally, AI conducts sentiment analysis by processing articles, news, textual data, and social media posts, offering insights into market sentiment and its latent impacts on stock prices. (Dall and Codex, 2023) Through algorithmic trading, AI executes trades swiftly based on predefined rules, benefiting strategies such as high-frequency trading and quantitative approaches. Moreover, AI models contribute to effective risk management by assessing risk factors, portfolio volatility, and potential losses, thereby optimizing risk-adjusted returns and enhancing portfolio stability.

AI has reshaped the stock market landscape, ushering in new possibilities for trading strategies, portfolio management, and investment decisions. In India, the emergence of AI-powered companies has captured the attention of investors, presenting compelling opportunities for long-term growth. Notable Indian AI-based stocks include TATA Elxsi, renowned for its ventures in smart assistants and driverless cars, boasting a remarkable 3-year total return of 108%. Similarly, companies like Bosch, with a focus on automotive technology, and Persistent Systems, specializing in IT services, have demonstrated strong returns of 22.63% and 106.33%, respectively, over the same period. KPIT Technologies, concentrating on automotive solutions, and Cyient, offering engineering and technology services, have also showcased impressive 3-year total returns of 168.35% and 69.18%, respectively. Moreover, newer entrants like Happiest Minds

Technologies have gained attention, achieving a notable 2-year total return of 108%. Investing in these AI-driven stocks holds promise for significant returns over time (Ignacio, 2023).

The functioning of AI in stock trading relies on sophisticated technologies such as ML, sentiment analysis, and intricate algorithms. Unearthing insights from financial data, AI executes trades optimally, mitigates risks, and aims for higher returns. Furthermore, AI is a game-changer in predicting stock market movements by employing ML algorithms to classify patterns and trends in financial data. Trained on historical data, these algorithms forecast future stock prices, providing valuable insights for investors.

Certain AI stocks, such as Nvidia, have garnered substantial interest, indicating the potential for further growth and profitability. As such, keeping a close watch on emerging opportunities in the AI sector can be advantageous for investors seeking to capitalize on market trends. Integrating AI into investment portfolios offers various benefits, including the ability to select stocks, predict market fluctuations, optimize portfolios, manage risks effectively, and receive personalized investment advice. As a result, AI's influence on stock markets is profound, offering both investors and traders innovative tools to navigate the ever-changing landscape and potentially achieve significant returns over time. (Leeway-Hertz, 2020).

AI plays a pivotal role in modern portfolio management, revolutionizing the way investments are optimized and managed. One significant application of AI in portfolio management is asset allocation optimization. Advanced algorithms leverage factors such as risk tolerance, financial plan, and usual market trends to determine the optimal allocation of assets within a portfolio. For instance, AI may recommend shifting investments from equities to bonds during periods of heightened market volatility to mitigate risk.

Furthermore, AI helps investors diversify their portfolios more effectively by distributing investments across a wider range of asset categories, industries, and areas. This diversification assistance reduces portfolio risk by minimizing the impact of adverse movements in any single asset or segment of the market. Additionally, AI enables real-time monitoring of portfolios, allowing investors to stay informed about their investment performance and ensuring that the portfolio remains in sync with their investment priorities.

Another advantage of AI in portfolio management is its ability to make responsive adjustments based on changing market dynamics. By continuously analyzing market data and economic indicators, AI algorithms can dynamically rebalance portfolios to seize new investment opportunities or mitigate risks. Moreover, AI models evaluate various risk factors and recommend strategies to mitigate risk, such as adjusting the allocation of assets or implementing hedging techniques.

AI also offers personalized investment advice by analyzing individual investor profiles, including their financial situations, investment goals, and risk tolerances. This personalized guidance helps investors make informed decisions that align with their specific circumstances and preferences. Ultimately, the insights generated by AI-driven analysis contribute to enhancing portfolio performance, leading to higher risk-adjusted returns and stronger financial performance for investors.

AI is transforming portfolio management through various innovative strategies and tools. Asset allocation optimization, facilitated by AI algorithms, considers factors like risk tolerance, investment objectives, and market conditions to ensure stable portfolios. Real-time monitoring provided by AI continuously tracks portfolios, alerting investors to any deviations from their desired allocations and enabling prompt adjustments to maintain alignment with objectives. Robo-advisors, such as Wealthfront and Betterment, utilize automation to create customized portfolios based on user preferences, including risk tolerance and investment goals. Additionally, AI offers personalized investment advice by analyzing individual profiles and recommending suitable strategies, guiding investors towards optimal choices. Furthermore, AI assists in trade execution strategies, minimizing market impact and maximizing efficiency in trade entry and exit decisions. Model portfolios constructed by AI align with specific criteria, such as risk tolerance and investment preferences, providing investors with tailored solutions for their financial goals (Salman Bahoo1, 2024).

9.8.3 PORTFOLIO OPTIMIZATION IN THE STOCK MARKET: SHARPE'S SINGLE-INDEX MODEL

Sharpe's single-index model offers a simplified approach to optimizing portfolios in the stock market. It helps investors construct portfolios with optimal risk-return profiles by considering the relationship between individual stocks and the overall market. Sharpe's single-index model provides a valuable framework for initial portfolio optimization in the stock market by considering both risk and expected return (adjusted by beta).

- **Assumption:** The model assumes that most of a stock's return can be explained by its sensitivity to the movement of the broader market, represented by a market index (e.g., S&P 500). Assume a 2% risk-free rate (Rf). Research uses the Sharpe ratio for calculation in each stock. The following steps are noted:

Stock of Company	Step 1; Expected return	Step 2; Expected risk	Step 3; Beta (S&P 500)	Step 4; $Sharpe\ index = \frac{Rp - Rf}{\sigma p}$
(AAPL): Large-cap tech stock with a beta of 1.1 (slightly more volatile than the market).	AAPL: Ri = 12%	1.1 for AAPL	α = 2% (positive outlook due to new product launch)	$Sharpe\ index = \frac{12-2}{2} = 5$
(JNJ): Large-cap healthcare stock with a beta of 0.8 (less volatile than the market)	JNJ: Ri = 8%	0.8 for JNJ	α = 1% (stable industry)	$Sharpe\ index = \frac{8-02}{1} = 6$
(TSLA): High-growth electric vehicle company with a beta of 1.5 (more volatile than the market).	TSLA: Ri = 20% (due to high-growth potential, but also higher risk)	1.5 for TSLA	α = 3% (growing electric vehicle market)	$Sharpe\ index = \frac{20-2}{3} = 3.33$

- **Step 4:** Portfolio Construction: Based on the Sharpe ratios and your risk tolerance, you might decide to:
- **Favor JNJ:** Its Sharpe ratio is highest, indicating potentially good returns for lower risk (due to lower beta). This might be suitable for a more conservative investor.
- **Balance with AAPL:** While AAPL has a slightly lower Sharpe ratio, its higher expected return and growth potential could be attractive. You might allocate a portion to AAPL for a balance of risk and reward.

- **Consider TSLA (Cautiously):** TSLA's high Sharpe ratio is tempting, but its high volatility (beta) and risk should be carefully considered. You might allocate a smaller portion if you have a higher risk tolerance.

9.8.4 SHARPE'S SINGLE INDEX MODEL IN DERIVATIVE MARKET FOR GETTING OPTIMIZATION OF PORTFOLIO

Sharpe's index model is used in various financial markets, including the derivatives market, to optimize portfolio performance with the benefit of evaluating the risk-adjusted performance of investments in derivative investments. This model helps evaluate the efficiency of a portfolio by considering the relationship between risk, return, and volatility. Investors can gain valuable insights to optimize their portfolios for better risk-adjusted performance by analyzing the Sharpe ratio of different derivative investments.

In the context of derivative markets, where risks can be more complex and potentially higher due to leverage and other factors, the Sharpe ratio can provide valuable insights into the risk-adjusted performance of a portfolio.

9.8.5 SHARPE'S MODEL IN STOCK OPTIONS OF THE DERIVATIVE MARKET

Sharpe's single-index model can be applied to stock options with a slight twist. Here's a breakdown:

- **Ri(t):** Return on your stock option contract i at time t (including premium paid/received and any potential profit/loss).
- **Rf:** Risk-free rate, like a short-term government bond yield.
- **Rm(t):** Return on a broad stock market index (think S&P 500) at time t. This acts as the "market factor."
- **αi:** Alpha for option contract i. This represents the excess return you expect from this option compared to the market (positive alpha suggests it might outperform the market).
- **βi:** Beta for option contract i. This captures the sensitivity to which your option's profitability is contingent upon fluctuations in the stock market index.

9.8.6 THE GREEKS AND TIME DECAY

The Greeks and time decay are essential in analyzing and optimizing your option portfolio:

- **Delta (Δ):** A way to measure the impact of a $1 change in the underlying stock price (like AAPL) on the price of an option contract.
- **Gamma (Γ):** This reflects how much the delta (the impact of a $1 stock move) itself changes as the stock price goes up or down.
- **Theta (Θ):** Represents the time decay of your option's value as time passes (how fast its value evaporates as it gets closer to expiration).
- **Vega (V):** Reflects how your option moves up and down with changes in market volatility expectations.
- **Rho (P):** This shows how much the price of your option is affected by interest rate movements (important for certain options).

9.9 AI: TRANSFORMING DERIVATIVES AND PORTFOLIO MANAGEMENT

AI is making waves in the derivatives market, transforming how participants approach risk management, trading strategies, and market analysis. Here's a breakdown of some key areas of impact:

Parameters	Description
Enhanced Risk Management	• AI can run complex simulations to assess portfolio resilience under various market scenarios, helping identify and manage potential risks more effectively. • Machine learning technology can examine immense amounts of data to perceive early signs of financial stress or potential market disruptions, allowing for proactive risk mitigation strategies.
Trading Strategies	• AI-powered algorithms can analyze market data at high speed, identify trading opportunities, and execute trades with greater precision and efficiency compared to traditional methods. This can lead to faster reaction times and potentially higher returns. • AI plays an essential role in HFT (High-Frequency Trading) by enabling ultra-fast analysis of market data and execution of trades within milliseconds.

Parameters	Description
Market Analysis	• AI can scrutinize articles of news, data from social media, and other unstructured sources for sentiment analysis and market forecasting potential price movements. • Machine learning algorithms can recognize complex patterns in historical data not directly perceptible to humans. This can provide valuable insights into future market behavior.
Other Applications	• AI can be used to perceive and prevent duplicitous activities in the derivatives market, improving market integrity and security. • AI can assist firms in complying with complex derivative regulations by automating tasks such as data analysis and reporting.
Challenges	• The success of AI models depends on feeding them high-quality, plentiful data. If the data is inaccurate or missing pieces, the results won't be trustworthy. • The opacity of some complex AI models, often referred to as "black boxes," creates challenges in understanding their decision-making processes. This lack of transparency can be a cause for concern for regulatory bodies and financial institutions. • The use of AI in derivatives markets raises ethical questions around fairness, transparency, and the potential for manipulation.

Overall, AI is a powerful tool with the potential to revolutionize the derivatives market. However, careful consideration needs to be given to data quality, explainability, and ethical implications to ensure responsible adoption of this technology.

9.9.1 SHARPE'S SINGLE INDEX MODEL IN THE FOREX MARKET FOR OPTIMIZING PORTFOLIOS

Sharpe's index model serves as an appropriate tool in the Forex market, empowering investors to make more informed decisions concerning their currency investments, optimize their portfolios, and potentially achieve better risk-adjusted returns.

Sharpe's index model can be effectively applied to optimize portfolios in the Forex market to assess the risk-adjusted returns of various currency pairs or Forex investments, traders can make well-versed decisions when constructing their portfolios. In the Forex market, Sharpe's single-index model aids traders in evaluating the risk-adjusted performance of different currency pairings by comparing their returns relative to the associated volatility or risk. This analysis enables traders to identify currency pairs that offer the most favorable risk-adjusted returns, thereby facilitating the creation of a more optimized portfolio. For example, if an investor holds multiple currency pairs in their portfolio, they can utilize the Sharpe ratio to determine which currency pair provides the best risk-adjusted return. A currency pair with a higher Sharpe ratio signifies better performance relative to its risk level.

9.9.2 STEPS IN SHARPE MODEL OPTIMIZATION OF PORTFOLIO IN FOREX MARKET

The trader performs the following steps by using the Sharpe model to achieve optimization of the portfolio in the Forex market. Use the Sharpe ratio formula to calculate the Sharpe index for each currency pair:

$$Sharpe\ index = \frac{Rp - Rf}{\sigma p}$$

where: Rp is the expected return of the currency pair; Rf is the risk-free rate of return; and σp is the standard deviation of the currency pair's returns.

The Sharpe Index measures the risk-adjusted return of each currency pair, indicating how much excess return is generated per unit of risk taken.

1. **Calculate the Beta (β) /standard deviation(σp)for Each Currency Pair:** The beta represents the sensitivity of the currency pair's returns to the returns of the forex market index. It is calculated using a linear regression of the currency pair's returns against the market index returns.

2. **Determine the Expected Return (Rp) for Each Currency Pair:** The expected return for each currency pair is estimated based on historical data.

3. **Calculate the Excess Return to Beta Ratio:** For each currency pair, the trader calculates the ratio of excess return (Ri – Rf) to beta (β), where Rf is the risk-free rate. This ratio helps in ranking the currency pairs.

4. **Select the Cut-off Rate (Ci):** The cut-off rate is determined based on the market variance and the trader's risk preference. Only currency pairs with an excess return to beta ratio greater than the cut-off rate are considered for the portfolio.
5. **Allocate Capital Based on the Optimization Model:** The trader uses the SIM to allocate capital to the selected currency pairs in a way that optimizes the portfolio's expected return for the desired level of risk.

For example, the trader may find that EUR/USD and GBP/USD have higher excess return to beta ratios and are thus more attractive for inclusion in the optimized portfolio. The trader then decides to allocate 40% of the capital to EUR/USD and 30% to GBP/USD, while the remaining 30% is distributed between USD/JPY and AUD/USD based on their respective ratios.

9.9.3 AI IN FOREIGN EXCHANGE MARKET

AI's role in forex trading continues to evolve, offering efficiency, accuracy, and informed decision-making for traders. The forex market, with over $5 trillion traded daily, is highly active and volatile. AI algorithms play a crucial role in scrutinizing immense amounts of historical and market data. The following are points where AI contributes to forex trading:

- AI helps in pattern recognition by identifying patterns and trends in currency price movements.
- AI-powered systems automate trade execution, minimizing human intervention.
- AI models assess risk factors and optimize portfolios for better returns.
- AI generates signals for optimal entry and exit points.

For example, Nikkei's AI solution; Nikkei, a Japanese media enterprise, claims to predict fluctuations in forex markets using AI. Their software analyzes articles, commodity prices, long-term trends, and so forth. By predicting probable future exchange rates, Nikkei assists banking institutions and currency speculators.[1]

9.9.4 AI'S STRENGTHS IN FOREX TRADING

- AI processes large data sets quickly and accurately means data analysis.
- ML algorithms forecast price movements and prediction.

AI helps to informed decisions in which traders benefited from AI insights on when to buy or sell currencies[23].

GSD Capital, headquartered in the UK, operates as an investment firm employing a combination of AI and the expertise of experienced professionals. This synergy enables the development of a trading strategy renowned for consistently yielding superior returns (AI in Foreign Exchange Trading (Forex) – Current State of the Sector, 2020). Leveraging momentum and technical patterns, the firm's system integrates ML and predictive models to make informed trading decisions, prioritizing meticulous risk assessment for every trade. The firm's proprietary AI trading machines possess the capability to analyze millions of data points swiftly, identifying optimal pricing and capitalizing on opportunities presented by short-term momentum shifts and market volatility (Can AI Trade Forex? Exploring the Potential of AI in the Foreign Exchange Market, 2023).

9.10 CONCLUSION

The integration of AI and the Sharpe Ratio is revolutionizing modern portfolio management. AI empowers data-driven portfolio construction, risk management, and dynamic asset allocation, all geared towards maximizing risk-adjusted returns as measured by the Sharpe Ratio. Real-world examples showcase the potential of AI to achieve superior performance for investors. Advancements in AI technology are leading to ever-increasing levels of complexity and capability; we can expect even greater advancements in portfolio management, leading to a future where AI serves as a cornerstone for achieving optimal investment outcomes. However, it's important to remember that alongside these advancements, a focus on high-quality data and ensuring explainability in AI models remains paramount for responsible and trustworthy implementation.

KEYWORDS

- **artificial intelligence**
- **deep -learning**
- **derivative market**
- **machine learning**
- **risk-return adjustment**
- **sentimental analysis**
- **stock market**
- **volatility**

REFERENCES

Acemoglu, D., & Restrepo, P. (2020). The wrong kind of AI? Artificial intelligence and the future of labor demand. *Cambridge Journal of Regions, Economy and Society*, *13*(1), 25–35.

AI in foreign exchange trading (forex)–Current state of the sector. (2020). https://emerj.com/ai-sector-overviews/ai-in-foreign-exchange-trading-forex-current-state-of-the-sector (accessed on 7th July 2025).

Amelot, L. M., Subadar Agathee, U., & Sunecher, Y. (2021). Time series modelling, NARX neural network and hybrid KPCA–SVR approach to forecast the foreign exchange market in Mauritius. *African Journal of Economic and Management Studies*, *12*(1), 18–54. https://doi.org/10.1108/ajems-04-2019-0161 (accessed on 7th July 2025).

Bahoo, S., Cucculelli, M., Goga, X., & Mondolo, J. (2024). Artificial intelligence in finance: A comprehensive review through bibliometric and content analysis. https://link.springer.com/article/10.1007/s43546-023-00618-x (accessed on 7th July 2025).

Biju, A. K. V. N., Thomas, A. S., & Thasneem, J. (2020). Examining the research taxonomy of artificial intelligence, deep learning & machine learning in the financial sphere—A bibliometric analysis. *Quality & Quantity*, Advance online publication. https://doi.org/10.1007/s11135-023-01673-0 (accessed on 7th July 2025).

Borochkin, A. A. (2017). Investment portfolio forex risk hedging in the international stock market. *Finance and Credit*.

Bresnahan, T. F., & Trajtenberg, M. (1995). General purpose technologies 'engines of growth'? *Journal of Econometrics*, *65*(1), 83–108. https://doi.org/10.1016/0304-4076(94)01598-t (accessed on 7th July 2025).

Can AI trade forex? Exploring the potential of AI in the foreign exchange market. (2023). https://centmatters.com/2023/05/can-ai-trade-forex/ (accessed on 7th July 2025).

Chen, Y., & Wan, J. W. (2021). Deep neural network framework based on backward stochastic differential equations for pricing and hedging American options in high dimensions. *Quantitative Finance*, *21*(1), 45–67. https://doi.org/10.1080/14697688.2020.1788219 (accessed on 7th July 2025).

Cucculelli, M., & Recanatini, M. (2022). Distributed ledger technology systems in securities post-trading services: Evidence from European global system banks. *European Journal of Finance*, *28*(2), 195–218. https://doi.org/10.1080/1351847x.2021.1921002 (accessed on 7th July 2025).

Culkin, R., & Das, S. R. (2017). Machine learning in finance: The case of deep learning for option pricing. *Journal of Investment Management*, *15*(4), 92–100.

DALL·E and Codex. (2023). Bain & Company announces services alliance with OpenAI to help enterprise clients identify and realize the full potential and maximum value of AI. https://www.analyticsinsight.net/how-is-ai-changing-the-forex-market (accessed on 7th July 2025).

Dunis, C. L., Laws, J., & Karathanasopoulos, A. (2013). GP algorithm versus hybrid and mixed neural networks. *European Journal of Finance*, *19*(3), 180–205. https://doi.org/10.1080/1351847x.2012.679740 (accessed on 7th July 2025).

Frankenfeld, J. (2021). How artificial intelligence works. https://www.investopedia.com/terms/a/artificial-intelligence-ai.asp (accessed on 7th July 2025).

Funahashi, H. (2020). Artificial neural network for option pricing with and without asymptotic correction. *Quantitative Finance*, *21*(4), 575–592. https://doi.org/10.1080/14697688.2020.1812702 (accessed on 7th July 2025).

Galeshchuk, S., & Mukherjee, S. (2017). Deep networks for predicting direction of change in foreign exchange rates. *Intelligent Systems in Accounting, Finance and Management*, *24*(4), 100–110. https://doi.org/10.1002/isaf.1404 (accessed on 7th July 2025).

Grossman, A., & Perez, Y. (2024). How to use artificial intelligence in your portfolio in 2024: Embrace the future of investing by utilizing artificial intelligence. https://www.investopedia.com/how-to-use-artificial-intelligence-in-your-investing-7973810 (accessed on 7th July 2025).

Hentzen, J. K., Hoffmann, A. O. I., & Dolan, R. M. (2022b). Which consumers are more likely to adopt a retirement app and how does it explain mobile technology-enabled retirement engagement? *International Journal of Consumer Studies*, *46*, 368–390. https://doi.org/10.1111/ijcs.12685 (accessed on 7th July 2025).

Hentzen, J. K., Hoffmann, A., Dolan, R., & Pala, E. (2022a). Artificial intelligence in customer-facing financial services: A systematic literature review and agenda for future research. *International Journal of Bank Marketing*, *40*(6), 1299–1336. https://doi.org/10.1108/ijbm-09-2021-0417 (accessed on 7th July 2025).

Ignacio, A. J. (2023). AI in forex: Revolutionizing trade in the digital age. https://www.forbes.com.au/brand-voice/uncategorized/ai-in-forex-revolutionizing-trade-in-the-digital-age (accessed on 7th July 2025).

Ingalhalli, V., & Kolamker, P. (2023). Modelling volatility effects between stock, oil, gold and forex markets: Evidence from India. *Investment Management and Financial Innovations*.

Jagtiani, J., & Kose, J. (2018). Fintech: The impact on consumers and regulatory responses. *Journal of Economics and Business*, *100*, 1–6. https://doi.org/10.1016/j.jeconbus.2018.11.002 (accessed on 7th July 2025).

Jang, H., & Lee, J. (2019). Generative Bayesian neural network model for risk-neutral pricing of American index options. *Quantitative Finance*, *19*(4), 587–603. https://doi.org/10.1080/14697688.2018.1490807 (accessed on 7th July 2025).

Kim, S., & Kim, S. (2020). Index tracking through deep latent representation learning. *Quantitative Finance*, *20*(4), 639–652. https://doi.org/10.1080/14697688.2019.1683599 (accessed on 7th July 2025).

LeewayHertz–Software Development Company. AI in portfolio management: Leveraging AI for smarter, data-driven investment decisions. https://www.leewayhertz.com/ai-for-portfolio-management (accessed on 7th July 2025).

Loukeris, N., & Eleftheriadis, I. (2015). Further higher moments in portfolio selection and a priori detection of bankruptcy, under multi-layer perceptron neural networks, hybrid neuro-genetic MLPs, and the voted perceptron. *International Journal of Finance & Economics*, *20*(4), 341–361. https://doi.org/10.1002/ijfe.1521 (accessed on 7th July 2025).

Martinelli, A., Mina, A., & Moggi, M. (2021). The enabling technologies of Industry 4.0: Examining the seeds of the fourth industrial revolution. *Industrial and Corporate Change*, *2021*, 1–28. https://doi.org/10.1093/icc/dtaa060 (accessed on 7th July 2025).

Olortegui, O. G., Shahi, T. J., & Ding, Z. (2016). *Forex trading system development*.

PricewaterhouseCoopers–PwC. (2020). How mature is AI adoption in financial services? https://www.pwc.de/de/future-of-finance/how-mature-is-ai-adoption-in-financialservices.pdf (accessed on 7th July 2025).

Soleymani, F., & Vasighi, M. (2020). Efficient portfolio construction by means of CVaR and K-means++ clustering analysis: Evidence from the NYSE. *International Journal of Finance & Economics*. https://doi.org/10.1002/ijfe.2344 (accessed on 7th July 2025).

Wall, L. D. (2018). Some financial regulatory implications of artificial intelligence. *Journal of Economics and Business*, *100*, 55–63. https://doi.org/10.1016/j.jeconbus.2018.05.003 (accessed on 7th July 2025).

Why an AI portfolio is better than a traditional fund manager. (2022). Q.ai–Powering a personal wealth movement. https://www.forbes.com/sites/qai/2022/08/23/why-an-ai-portfolio-is-better-than-a-traditional-fund-manager/ (accessed on 7th July 2025).

Zhao, Y., Stasinakis, C., Sermpinis, G., & Shi, Y. (2018). Neural network copula portfolio optimization for exchange traded funds. *Quantitative Finance*, *18*(5), 761–775. https://doi.org/10.1080/14697688.2017.1414505 (accessed on 7th July 2025).

CHAPTER 10

An Empirical Study of Saving Behavior: Evidence from India

MOHSINA HAYAT[1] and RUBY KHAN[2]

[1]*Bachelor of Management Studies, School of Commerce, Jain University, Bangalore, Karnataka, India*

[2]*Department of Accounting and Finance, College of Business, Jazan University, Jazan, Jazan Province, Kingdom of Saudi Arabia*

*Corresponding author

ABSTRACT

The act of saving, a vital aspect of personal finance, allows individuals to allocate income for future necessities like consumption, investment, or emergencies. The process of saving can be particularly daunting for young adults transitioning from adolescence to adulthood. Financial literacy (FL) empowers individuals to make informed financial decisions, positively impacting saving behavior through improved financial planning and management and promoting positive financial attitudes (FAs) with the support of skills and knowledge. Other factors such as financial awareness, knowledge, socialization, financial education, self-control, and financial attitudes also have a substantial impact on saving habits. This study investigates the complex relationship between various factors and saving behavior among Indian university students, who encounter unique financial challenges amid India's rapid socioeconomic changes. The researcher examines the saving habits of Indian university students using a quantitative approach, collecting data from 100 students. The study found that factors like FL, awareness, knowledge, socialization, investment, self-control,

E-Financial Strategies for Sustainable Development: A Handbook for Promoting Financial Inclusion and Ending Poverty (SDG 1). Ernesto D. R. Santibanez Gonzalez, Rajeev Sijariya, and Vikas Garg (Eds.)

DOI: 10.1201/9781779640956-10

behavior, and attitude influence these habits. The chapter commences with a literature review, followed by an in-depth methodology section, then presents the results, discusses them, and concludes with recommendations. The research significantly contributes to our understanding of saving behavior among Indian university students and suggests strategies to boost FL, ultimately paving the way for a more financially secure future for this demographic. Further research and personalized approaches will be crucial to enhance our understanding of saving behavior and to effectively encourage positive financial habits among young adults.

10.1 BACKGROUND AND RATIONALE OF SAVING BEHAVIOR

Saving, a fundamental element of personal finance, empowers individuals to reserve income for future necessities, such as consumption, investment, or contingency plans. However, the act of saving can pose challenges, particularly for young adults transitioning from adolescence to adulthood. FL, characterized as the knowledge and skills that facilitate informed and effective financial decisions, can shape saving behavior by bolstering financial planning, enhancing financial management, and cultivating positive FAs. Nevertheless, other elements like financial awareness, knowledge, socialization, investment in financial education, self-control, and FA also significantly influence saving behavior. The correlation between saving behavior and factors like FL and awareness can differ based on a country's context or culture. This study intends to scrutinize this correlation among university students in India, a demographic encountering unique financial challenges and opportunities. India is currently experiencing rapid socio-economic transformations, such as urbanization, globalization, digitalization, and consumerism. Given India's swift socio-economic changes, comprehending the saving behavior of its 37.4 million university students in 2018–19 (Ministry of Education, 2020) is vital for formulating policies and programs that promote FL and inclusion.

10.2 LITERATURE REVIEW

This section investigates the literature on the saving behavior and FL of university students. It scrutinizes the definitions, influencing factors, and the interplay between these two facets. The section culminates by pinpointing gaps in the existing literature.

10.3 DEFINITION AND EVALUATION OF SAVING BEHAVIOR AND FINANCIAL LITERACY

10.3.1 FINANCIAL LITERACY

According to Browning and Lusardi (1996), saving behavior entails reserving a portion of income or wealth for future utilization. It can be gauged using indicators such as saving rate, amount, frequency, motive, and method. Saving behavior can also be classified into categories like planned, unplanned, regular, irregular, voluntary, and compulsory saving. These classifications offer a holistic understanding of saving habits.

According to Huston (2010), FL equips individuals with the skills and knowledge needed to make informed decisions about finances. It can be evaluated through self-assessment, objective tests, and behavioral indicators, and can be segmented into dimensions like financial knowledge (FK), awareness, attitude, behavior, and confidence.

The saving behavior and FL of university students are influenced by individual, environmental, and psychological factors.

According to Hilgert et al. (2003), Sabri and MacDonald (2010), and Loibl et al. (2011), psychological factors, encompassing cognitive, affective, and behavioral aspects, significantly shape the saving behavior and FL of university students. These include elements like financial knowledge, awareness, planning, attitude, confidence, satisfaction, behavior, self-control, and socialization.

Lusardi et al. (2010), Sabharwal et al. (2016), and Mudzingiri et al. (2018) articulate that individual factors, including personal characteristics of university students, significantly impact their saving behavior and FL. These factors include demographic aspects (age, gender, race, education level), socio-economic elements (income, wealth, employment status, family background), and human capital factors (cognitive ability, numeracy, literacy). Chen and Volpe (1998), Lusardi et al. (2010), and Ergün et al. (2018) describe that environmental factors, including external conditions or influences, also affect the saving behavior and FL of university students. These factors encompass institutional elements (financial system, regulation, education), cultural aspects (social norms, values, beliefs), and situational factors (life events, financial shocks, opportunities).

Research on the saving behavior of university students in India is limited, primarily focusing on graduates' saving habits, students' budgeting and spending, and young people's online shopping habits. These studies do not thoroughly explore the factors influencing saving behavior or make comparisons based on gender, location, income, and education level. The relationship between saving behavior, financial literacy (FL), financial awareness (FAW), financial knowledge (FK), financial socialization (FS), financial socialization investment (FSI), self-control (SC), financial behavior (FB), and financial attitude (FA) among university students remains unexplored.

FL refers to the skills and knowledge that enable individuals to make informed and effective financial decisions, utilizing all their financial resources (Priyadharshini, 2017). FL promotes financial inclusion across various demographics, including age, gender, marital status, occupation, income, and geographic location. Individuals with higher FL tend to have better emotional well-being and make superior financial decisions (Noor et al., 2020). A study on high school students in Indonesia found that understanding FL is crucial for developing good saving habits (Chalimah et al., 2019). Meanwhile, research on university students in northern Mexico revealed a low level of FL, with no significant correlation between FL, FB, and FK (Felipe et al., 2017). FL significantly impacts various FBs among youth, particularly college students. However, evidence suggests that young people often lack adequate FL, leading to challenges in managing their finances. A study by Danquah, Gyimah, and Poku (2018) found that tertiary students in Sub-Saharan Africa, specifically Ghana, have below-average financial awareness. The study also highlighted that financial information from various sources is ineffective in enhancing FL among these students. The literature of Lusardi et al. (2010), Sabri and MacDonald (2010), Loibl et al. (2011), and Mudzingiri et al. (2018) indicates an optimistic relationship between saving behavior and FL among university students. This advocates that students with higher FL tend to save more. Siswanti and Halida (2020) conducted a study examining FK, FA, and FB to identify factors influencing financial management behavior. The study found that FK significantly impacts how Indonesians manage their finances.

A Tavares, Almeida, and Cunha (2019) study found that students of higher education often have limited financial knowledge and lack discipline in managing their finances. This underscores the importance of Financial Knowledge as an essential component in nurturing healthy habits of financial management.

Financial Knowledge (FK) is a cornerstone of financial education as it molds FB and planning, and is a pivotal element of personal financial well-being. This well-being framework encompasses FB, satisfaction, FA, and measures of objective status (Priyadharshini, 2017). The research by Robb and Woodyard (2011) scrutinized the association between FK and FB. Research shows both objective and subjective financial knowledge (FK) impact FB, but subjective knowledge has a stronger influence.

FA refers to an individual's beliefs, values, and mindset regarding personal finance concepts, and it significantly influences their financial management decisions and behaviors. Studies have demonstrated that a positive FA leads to superior financial decision-making. However, research on the saving behavior of university students in India is limited and often neglects the diversity and complexity of the student population. Studies by Sabharwal (2016), Frączek et al. (2019), Singh et al. (2020), and Kumar et al. (2020) offer some insights but have limitations such as small sample sizes, regional focus, and lack of exploration of underlying motivations behind saving behavior. Despite these studies, the level of FL among university students in India remains low.

10.3.2 GAPS AND LIMITATIONS IN THE CURRENT LITERATURE

The literature on the saving behavior and FL of university students presents several gaps and limitations. These include a lack of empirical evidence from India and other developing countries, where socio-cultural and economic contexts may lead to different behaviors. There is also a lack of comprehensive and consistent measurement of saving behavior and FL across different studies or countries, limiting the comparability and generalizability of findings. Furthermore, there is a dearth of longitudinal or experimental studies that could establish causal effects. Lastly, many studies do not consider other relevant factors that may influence saving behavior, such as personality traits, emotions, motivations, and so forth.

10.3.3 RESEARCH METHODOLOGY

This research methodology provides a comprehensive framework for exploring and understanding the saving behavior of university students in India. It is anticipated that the findings will enrich the existing literature and provide valuable insights to inform and shape future policy decisions and professional practices. This study holds significant value as it can help understand the factors influencing students' saving behavior, identify saving barriers and facilitators, assess their FL and awareness levels, evaluate their financial well-being and satisfaction, and suggest policy interventions or educational programs to enhance their saving outcomes. Furthermore, the role of FL is crucial as it enables individuals to make informed financial decisions, plan for future goals, manage risks, and cope with financial shocks. It also promotes financial inclusion and empowerment, especially among marginalized and vulnerable groups.

10.3.4 RESEARCH OBJECTIVE

This study employs a research methodology specifically designed to explore and gain a deeper understanding of the saving habits and behaviors of university students in India. The primary objectives of this research are twofold:

1. To recognize the determinants that stimulus the saving behaviour of students in India.
2. To investigate and comprehend the saving habits of university students in India, including the key factors that shape and influence their FB.

10.3.5 HYPOTHESES

Several hypotheses have been proposed for this research, each examining the impact of different variables such as Financial Literacy (FL), Financial Awareness (FAW), Financial Knowledge (FK), Financial Socialization (FS), Financial Self-Influence (FSI), Self-Control (SC), Financial Behavior (FB), and Financial Attitude (FA) on students' Saving Behavior (SB).

1. **Hypothesis**
   a. H0: Financial literacy does not significantly impact saving behavior.
   b. H1: Financial literacy significantly influences saving behavior.

2. **Hypothesis 1**
    a. H0: Financial awareness (FAW) do not significantly impact saving behavior.
    b. H1: Financial awareness (FAW) significantly influence saving behavior.

3. **Hypothesis 2**
    a. H0: Financial knowledge (FK) does not significantly impact saving behavior.
    b. H1: Financial knowledge (FK) significantly impact saving behavior.

4. **Hypothesis 3**
    a. H0: Financial Socialization (FS) does not significantly impact saving behavior.
    b. H1: Financial Socialization (FS) significantly impact saving behavior.

5. **Hypothesis 4**
    a. H0: Financial Self-Influence (FSI) does not significantly impact saving behavior.
    b. H1: Financial Self-Influence (FSI) significantly impact saving behavior.

6. **Hypothesis 5**
    a. H0: Self-Control (SC) does not significantly impact saving behavior.
    b. H1: Self-Control (SC) significantly impact saving behavior.

7. **Hypothesis 6**
    a. H0: Financial Behaviour (FB) does not significantly impact saving behavior.
    b. H1: Financial Behaviour (FB) significantly impact saving behavior.

8. **Hypothesis 7**
   a. H0: Financial Attitude (FA) does not significantly impact saving behavior.
   b. H1: Financial Attitude (FA) significantly impact saving behavior.

10.3.6 RESEARCH DESIGN

The research design is a cross-sectional survey, aiming to gather quantitative data from a sample of university students in India. This design will measure their saving behavior and its influencing factors. The research approach is deductive, testing hypotheses derived from existing literature and theories on saving behavior.

10.3.7 RESEARCH VARIABLES

The research involves a dependent variable, saving behavior, which is an individual's act of reducing expenditures or deferring consumption. Independent variables include financial factors like FL and self-control. Data collection will involve a questionnaire incorporating validated scales from prior research, evaluating various aspects of students' financial characteristics, including:

- Financial literacy
- Awareness
- Knowledge
- Socialization
- Self-control
- Behavior
- Attitude

1. **Financial Literacy (FL):**
   i. **Basic skills (FL1):** Saving money, using bank accounts, understanding credit cards and loans.
   ii. **Planning for the future (FL2):** Identifying future financial needs, budgeting, preparing monthly/weekly budgets.

iii. **Financial awareness (FL3):** Knowing about different financial instruments like mutual funds, stocks, savings accounts, bonds, and so forth.

iv. **Calculating returns (FL4):** Understanding how investments like bonds, savings accounts, and stocks grow money.

v. **Making investment decisions (FL5):** Analyzing and choosing appropriate investments for short- and long-term goals.

2. **Financial Socialization (FS):**

    i. **Who encourages saving (FS1–6):** Parents, friends, siblings, school/college, partner, others.

    ii. **Who encourages investing (FSI1–5):** Parents, friends, siblings, school/college, partner.

3. **Self-Control (SC):**

    i. **Saving challenges (SC1–3):** Difficulty saving, easily tempted by shopping, spending habits.

    ii. **Financial planning (SC4–6):** Comparing before buying, planning for the future, prioritizing long-term goals over short-term gains.

4. **Financial Behavior (FB):**

    i. **Investment preferences (FB1–2):** Willingness to invest in risky assets, cautious and thoughtful buying habits.

    ii. **Financial planning (FB3–5):** Following a budget, having savings, planned spending, investing in non-risky assets.

5. **Financial Attitude (FA):**

    i. **Financial confidence (FA1–3):** Trust in your financial planning skills, feeling empowered and in control of your finances.

    ii. **Money management skills (FA4–5):** Ability to manage your own finances, money management skills.

    iii. **Future outlook (FA6–7):** Positive feeling about your future financial stability and responsible spending habits.

10.3.8 RESEARCH TOOL

Researchers use descriptive statistics and inferential statistics for data summarization, hypothesis testing, and examining variables' relationships. Techniques such as Cronbach's Alpha, regression analysis, one-way ANOVA, and model summary will be used with a software program like SPSS for data analysis.

10.3.9 SIGNIFICANCE OF STUDY

The standing of this research lies in its ability to clarify the factors that impact students' savings behavior, identify obstacles and enablers to saving, gauge their FL and awareness, and evaluate their overall financial well-being and satisfaction. The findings could inform the development of policy interventions or educational programs aimed at improving saving outcomes.

Furthermore, this research highlights the vital importance of FL in enabling individuals to make informed financial decisions, plan for their future goals, manage risks, and navigate financial uncertainties with confidence. It also emphasizes the importance of FL in promoting financial inclusion and empowerment, particularly among marginalized and vulnerable groups. This research, therefore, holds considerable relevance for both academia and policy-making in the realm of financial education and behavior.

10.3.10 LIMITATIONS OF THE STUDY

This study has its limitations, including potential issues in methodology, sample representation, theoretical foundations, and empirical rigor; however, it provides valuable insights within its specific field. Acknowledging these limitations, future research could refine methodologies, enhance sample representation, and strengthen theoretical and empirical foundations to advance our understanding of the subject matter and contribute to the continuous development of scientific knowledge in the field of finance.

10.3.11 INTERPRETATION AND ARGUMENT

This section presents the interpretation and argument derived from a comprehensive analysis of a pilot survey conducted to assess the reliability and validity of a questionnaire related to saving behavior. The study involved 100 students who responded to a questionnaire consisting of 47 items, each rated on a five-point Likert scale. This study focuses on two key aspects:

10.3.11.1 PILOT SURVEY: ASSESSING RELIABILITY

The questionnaire's reliability was evaluated using Cronbach's Alpha coefficient, which measures internal consistency and indicates the degree of interrelatedness among survey items. The questionnaire, consisting of 47 items rated on a five-point Likert scale (strongly agree to strongly disagree), was administered to a sample of 100 students. Cronbach's Alpha coefficient was calculated to assess the scale's reliability, with higher values indicating greater reliability. The resulting Cronbach's Alpha value of 0.912, based on the 47-item scale, demonstrates a high level of reliability, confirming the consistency and accuracy of the questionnaire. This robust reliability underscores the questionnaire's utility in reliably capturing the constructs it purports to measure, as reflected in Table 10.1 of the research work.

TABLE 10.1 Statistics of Reliability

Alpha of Cronbach	Number of Items
0.912	47

10.3.11.2 AVOVA TABLE

The ANOVA table is employed to assess the statistical significance of the regression model, which comprises 47 predictors and a single dependent variable (SB). The F-ratio, standing at 12.311, signifies that the model accounts for a substantial proportion of the variance in the dependent variable. The p-value, being 0.000 and thus less than 0.05, indicates that the model is statistically significant at the 5% level. Consequently, we dismiss the null hypothesis positing that all regression coefficients are zero, leading us to conclude that the model provides a good fit to the data as per the research table 10.2.

TABLE 10.2 ANOVA[a]

Model		Sum of Squared Deviations (Total Variance)	df	Mean Squared Deviation (Average Variance)	F	Sig.
1	Regression	1.798	47	.038	12.311	.000[b]
	Residual	.162	52	.003		
	Total	1.960	99			

a. Dependent Variable: SB
b. Predictors: (Constant), FA7, SC4, FS3, FSI1, FK2, FB7, FSI2, FB6, FB3, FS5, FL5, FS1, FB1, FS4, FL3, FS2, FB2, SC5, FL2, FL4, FAW4, SC2, FS6, FAW6, SC1, SC6, FB5, FSI4, FAW3, FA5, FK4, FB4, FL1, FA6, FAW1, FA3, FA1, FSI5, FAW5, FAW2, FA4, FSI3, FK1, FK3, FAW7, SC3, FA2

10.3.12 MODEL SUMMARY

The model summary, presented in Table 10.3, encapsulates the key findings of a multiple linear regression analysis conducted on a dataset with 47 predictors and one dependent variable, SB (Saving Behavior). This analysis serves to unravel the intricate relationship between the dependent variable and various predictors, shedding light on the model's explanatory power.

TABLE 10.3 Model Summary[b]

Model	R	R (Coefficient of Determination) Square	Adjusted R (Coefficient of Determination) Square	Estimated Standard Error	Change Statistics					Durbin-Watson
					R Square Change	F Change	df1	df2	Sig. F Change	
1	.958[a]	.918	.843	.056	.918	12.311	47	52	.000	2.212

a. Predictors: (Constant), FA7, SC4, FS3, FSI1, FK2, FB7, FSI2, FB6, FB3, FS5, FL5, FS1, FB1, FS4, FL3, FS2, FB2, SC5, FL2, FL4, FAW4, SC2, FS6, FAW6, SC1, SC6, FB5, FSI4, FAW3, FA5, FK4, FB4, FL1, FA6, FAW1, FA3, FA1, FSI5, FAW5, FAW2, FA4, FSI3, FK1, FK3, FAW7, SC3, FA2

b. Dependent Variable: SB

The R value of 0.958 indicates a robust linear relationship between the predictors and the dependent variable. A substantial R square value of 0.918 signifies that the model accounts for 91.8% of the variation in the dependent variable, SB. Even after considering the number of predictors, the adjusted R square value remains high at 0.843, emphasizing the model's significant explanatory capability. Despite having many predictors, the model effectively captures a significant portion of the variation in the dependent variable. The standard error of the estimate is 0.056, indicating precise predictions. The Durbin-Watson statistic is 2.212, providing no evidence of autocorrelation in the residuals.

10.3.13 REGRESSION ANALYSIS

The regression model, with a single dependent variable (SB) and 47 predictors (FA1 to FA7, FB1 to FB7, etc.), was computed. The unstandardized coefficients (B) indicate the magnitude of change in SB for a unit change in the predictor. The standard errors (Std. Error) quantify the uncertainty associated with these estimates. The standardized coefficients (Beta) represent the number of standard deviations that SB changes for a one-standard deviation change in the predictor. The t values measure the distance of the estimates from zero in terms of standard errors. The p-values (Sig.) test the null hypothesis that the estimates are not significantly different from zero.

Several predictors have a significant impact on SB at the 5% level, as indicated by their p-values being less than 0.05. This suggests a linear relationship between each predictor and SB after controlling for all other predictors. Predictors exerting a significant positive influence on SB include FL4, FAW3, FAW4, FAW5, FK2, FS5, FSI3, FSI5, SC4, FB1, FB5, and FA7. Predictors exerting a significant negative influence on SB include FL5, FAW2, FAW6, FK4, FS1, FS3, FS6, FSI2, FSI4, SC3, SC5, FB4, and FB7. The intercept is 1.557 and is significantly different from zero at the 5% level, suggesting a significant intercept term in the model. FL4 and FL5, with the highest absolute standardized coefficients (1.584 and 0.965 respectively), exert more influence on SB than the other predictors (Table 10.4).

TABLE 10.4 Co-Efficients[a] of the Dependent Variable Saving Behavior

Model		Unstandardized Coefficients		Standardized Coefficients	t	Sig.	Equation
		β	Standard Error	Beta			
1	(Constant)	1.557	.266		5.851	.000	
	FL1	.051	.038	.373	1.355	.181	SB = 1.557+ 0.051FL1
	FL2	–0.034	.028	–0.226	–1.223	.227	SB = 1.557+(–0.034)FL2
	FL3	.004	.020	.029	.189	.851	SB = 1.557+.004FL3
	FL4	.189	.023	1.584	8.089	.000	SB = 1.557+ .189FL4
	FL5	–0.115	.021	–0.965	–5.422	.000	SB = 1.557+(–0.115)FL5
	FAW1	–0.038	.025	–0.289	–1.474	.147	SB = 1.557+(–0.038)FAW1
	FAW2	–0.090	.029	–0.704	–3.073	.003	SB = 1.557+ (–0.090)FAW2
	FAW3	.144	.025	1.175	5.846	.000	SB = 1.557+ .144FAW3
	FAW4	.062	.030	.451	2.057	.045	SB = 1.557+ .062FAW4
	FAW5	.066	.035	.562	1.905	.062	SB = 1.557+ .066FAW5
	FAW6	–0.154	.041	–1.233	–3.716	.000	SB = 1.557+ (–0.154)FAW6
	FAW7	.087	.050	.656	1.740	.088	SB = 1.557+ (.087)FAW7
	FK1	–0.042	.042	–0.341	–1.000	.322	SB = 1.557+ (–0.042)FK1
	FK2	.105	.034	.901	3.108	.003	SB = 1.557+ (.105)FK2
	FK3	.075	.045	.638	1.648	.105	SB = 1.557+ (.075)FK3
	FK4	–0.257	.046	–2.116	–5.574	.000	SB = 1.557+ (–0.257)FK4
	FS1	–0.226	.051	–1.217	–4.416	.000	SB = 1.557+ (–0.226)FS1
	FS2	–0.011	.023	–0.081	–0.496	.622	SB = 1.557+ (–0.011)FS2
	FS3	–0.104	.037	–0.813	–2.823	.007	SB = 1.557+ (–0.104)FS3
	FS4	.065	.038	.466	1.706	.094	SB = 1.557+ (.065)FS4
	FS5	.096	.022	.923	4.407	.000	SB = 1.557+ (.096)FS5
	FS6	–0.113	.033	–0.979	–3.455	.001	SB = 1.557+ (–0.113)FS6
	FSI1	.014	.045	.089	.308	.759	SB = 1.557+ (.014)FSI1
	FSI2	–0.052	.022	–0.314	–2.396	.020	SB = 1.557+ (–0.052)FSI2
	FSI3	.180	.074	1.220	2.438	.018	SB = 1.557+ .180FSI3
	FSI4	–0.153	.044	–1.064	–3.473	.001	SB = 1.557+ (-.153)FSI4
	FSI5	.132	.037	1.016	3.582	.001	SB = 1.557+ .132FSI5
	SC1	–0.006	.047	–0.042	–0.118	.907	SB = 1.557+ (–0.006)SC1
	SC2	.026	.026	.221	.983	.330	SB = 1.557+ (.026)SC2
	SC3	–0.222	.062	–1.846	–3.587	.001	SB = 1.557+ (–0.222)SC3
	SC4	.106	.035	1.009	3.014	.004	SB = 1.557+ .106SC4

TABLE 10.4 *(Continued)*

Model	Unstandardized Coefficients		Standardized Coefficients	t	Sig.	Equation
	β	Standard Error	Beta			
SC5	–0.037	.012	–0.338	–3.080	.003	SB = 1.557+ (–0.037)SC5
SC6	.005	.048	.042	.109	.913	SB = 1.557+ .005SC5
FB1	.079	.019	.518	4.076	.000	SB = 1.557+ .079FB1
FB2	.005	.024	.032	.191	.849	SB = 1.557+ (.005)FB2
FB3	.002	.043	.010	.047	.963	SB = 1.557+ (.002)FB3
FB4	–0.085	.042	–0.650	–2.034	.047	SB = 1.557+ (–0.085)FB4
FB5	.127	.040	.893	3.182	.002	SB = 1.557+ (.127)FB5
FB6	–0.053	.027	–0.385	–1.981	.053	SB = 1.557+ (–0.053)FB6
FB7	–0.080	.029	–0.501	–2.718	.009	SB = 1.557+ (–0.080)FB7
FA1	.275	.076	1.753	3.592	.001	SB = 1.557+ (.275)FA1
FA2	–0.157	.068	–1.198	–2.312	.025	SB = 1.557+ (–0.157)FA2
FA3	–0.136	.051	–0.964	–2.687	.010	SB = 1.557+ (–0.136)FA3
FA4	–0.073	.039	–0.510	–1.879	.066	SB = 1.557+(–0.073) FA4
FA5	.098	.031	.729	3.122	.003	SB = 1.557+ (.098)FA5
FA6	–0.098	.058	–0.612	–1.694	.096	SB = 1.557+ (–0.098)FA6
FA7	.232	.035	1.462	6.541	.000	SB = 1.557+ .232FA7

a. Dependent Variable: SB (Saving Behavior)

10.3.14 INTERPRETATION

The coefficients and equations furnished provide an exhaustive understanding of the manner in which diverse factors sway saving behavior (SB). The coefficients denote the effect of each factor on SB, with both unstandardized (B) and standardized (Beta) coefficients being presented. The standardized coefficients are especially valuable as they facilitate the comparison of the relative significance of each factor.

The equation that relates the factors to saving behavior (SB) is given by:

$$SB=1.557 + (\text{Coefficients for each variable} \times \text{Value of the corresponding variable})$$

SB = 1.557+0.051FL1+(–0.034)FL2+.004FL3+0.189FL4+(–0.115) FL5+(–0.038)FAW1+(–0.090)FAW2+ .144FAW3+ .062FAW4+ .066FAW5+ (–0.154)FAW6+ (.087)FAW7+ (–0.042)FK1+ .105FK2+ .075FK3+ (–0.257)FK4+ (–0.226)FS1+ (–0.011)FS2+ (–0.104)FS3+ (.065)FS4+ (.096)FS5+ (–0.113)FS6+ (.014)FSI1+ (–0.052)FSI2+ .180FSI3+ (–0.153)FSI4+ .132FSI5+ (–0.006)SC1+ (.026)SC2+ (–0.222)SC3+ .106SC4+ (–0.037)SC5+.005SC5+ .079FB1+ (.005)FB2+ (.002)FB3+ (–0.085)FB4+ (.127)FB5+(–0.053)FB6+(–0.080)FB7+ (.275)FA1+ (–0.157)FA2+ (–0.136)FA3+(–0.073) FA4+ (.098)FA5+ (–0.098)FA6+.232FA7.

The coefficient of each variable signifies the alteration in Saving Behavior (SB) corresponding to a unit change in that specific variable, presuming all other variables remain constant. The standardized coefficients (Beta) denote the change in SB in terms of standard deviation units for a one-standard-deviation change in each factor.

The coefficients in the equation reflect the direction and magnitude of the influence each variable exerts on saving behavior. Variables with larger absolute standardized coefficients (Beta) have a more pronounced relative impact on SB. The understanding of savings and bank schemes, credit cards and loans, future financial needs, budgeting and saving money, and the propensity to prepare a monthly/weekly budget (FL1 to FL5) embody varying levels of FL. The tendency to prepare a student's monthly/weekly budget has a significant negative impact on saving behavior, suggesting that elevated levels of FL may diminish saving behavior.

The understanding of the following financial instruments, namely Savings and Interest, Bonds, Stocks, Mutual Funds, Systematic Investment Plan, Insurance, and Public Provident Fund (PPF) (FAW1 to FAW7), represents different levels of financial awareness. Bonds, Stocks, Mutual Funds, Systematic Investment Plan, Insurance, and Public Provident Fund (PPF) exert a significant positive impact on saving behavior. This implies that heightened levels of financial awareness can foster improved saving behavior.

The researcher evaluated financial knowledge through the comfort level while calculating returns on Savings, Financial Bonds, making judicious decisions in long-term and short-term stocks, and different categories of mutual funds (ex-equity, debt and balanced) (FK1 to FK4), which represent varying levels of financial knowledge. Financial Bonds and different categories of mutual funds (ex-equity, debt and balanced) exert a significant positive impact on saving behavior, suggesting that enhanced financial knowledge positively influences saving behavior. Students are encouraged to save due to influences from parents, friends, siblings, school/college subjects, partners, and others (e.g., consultants) (FS1 to FS6), representing different facets of FS. Parents, siblings, partners, and others (e.g., consultants) encouraging saving have a significant negative impact on saving behavior, implying that certain aspects of FS may impede saving behavior. Students are encouraged to invest due to influences from parents, friends, siblings, school/college subjects, and partners (FSI1 to FSI5), representing varying levels of investment in financial education. Friends, siblings, school/college subjects, and partners have a significant positive impact on saving behavior, indicating that investing in financial education can enhance saving behavior.

The researcher interpreted that students find it challenging to save and get tempted to shop (e.g., food, clothing, entertainment, etc.) because it provides pleasure. They are barely able to save money as students spend easily, and the habit of 'I see it, I like it, I buy it' describes students. Discounts attract students, and they show more concern about short-term gains (SC1 to SC6), representing different aspects of self-control. None of the self-control factors have a substantial effect on saving behavior.

FBs of students, such as liking to invest in risky assets, thinking, comparing, and then making purchases rather than making mindless purchases, analyzing before buying, always following a careful monthly budget, always having saved money, planning expenditure for the future, and investing in non-risky assets (FB1 to FB7), represent different aspects of FB. FBs of students, such as liking to invest in risky assets, always having saved money, and investing in non-risky assets, have a significant positive impact on saving behavior, suggesting that certain FBs lead to increased saving.

The FA of students, as reflected in their trust in their personal capacity for planning and budgeting, their sense of empowerment and confidence stemming from their control over money, their ability to manage their own finances, their money management skills, their control over the source of income, their belief in their future financial management capabilities, and their prudent expenditure (FA1 to FA7), represents various facets of FA. The students' trust in their personal capacity for planning and budgeting and their prudent expenditure have a significant positive impact on saving behavior, suggesting that a positive FA can augment saving behavior.

In a nutshell, the findings underscore the intricate interplay of diverse financial factors in shaping saving behavior. Strategies aimed at improving saving behavior should contemplate enhancing financial awareness and knowledge and fostering positive attitudes towards finances. Moreover, addressing specific negative impacts emanating from socialization and certain behaviors is crucial for devising effective interventions to promote saving behavior. Further research and tailored approaches are warranted to gain a deeper understanding of, and positively influence, saving behavior.

10.3.15 RECOMMENDATION

The following recommendations are proposed with the objective of fostering a financially empowered student community, thereby promoting a financially secure future for the youth in India:

- Incorporate FL courses into university curricula to endow students with indispensable financial skills.
- Facilitate practical financial workshops and seminars on university campuses.
- Initiate financial awareness campaigns across various mediums to enlighten students about financial planning and resources.
- Set up financial counseling centers within universities for personalized advice and guidance.
- Inform and enlighten students about the significance of creditworthiness and the advantages of maintaining a high credit score.
- Launch savings challenges and incentive programs to cultivate a culture of saving.
- Collaborate with banks and financial institutions to offer tailored financial products and services for students.
- Develop educational mobile applications or web platforms equipped with interactive tools to augment FL.
- Integrate principles of behavioral economics into interventions and educational programs to address behavioral biases.
- Promote peer-to-peer learning and knowledge sharing among students.
- Conduct regular financial health assessments for students to evaluate their financial well-being.
- Monitor the impact of FL initiatives and modify programs based on outcomes for optimal effectiveness.

These recommendations, if implemented, could significantly contribute to building a financially literate and empowered student community in India.

10.4 CONCLUSION

In conclusion, saving behavior is a pivotal aspect of personal finance, facilitating individuals to allocate income for future uses such as consumption, investment, or as a safeguard. FL, which includes knowledge and skills for informed financial decisions, profoundly impacts saving behavior by bolstering financial planning, management, and nurturing positive FAs. Nonetheless, numerous other factors, encompassing financial awareness, knowledge, socialization, investment in financial education, self-control, FB, and FA, significantly contribute to shaping saving behavior. This study concentrates on comprehending the saving behavior of university students in India, a demographic grappling with unique financial challenges within a rapidly transforming social and economic landscape. With a population exceeding 37.4 million university students in India during the academic year 2018–19, understanding their saving behavior is crucial for formulating policies and programs that advocate FL and inclusion.

The literature review underscores that psychological, individual, and environmental factors wield considerable influence on university students' saving behavior and FL. The study pinpoints gaps in the existing literature, accentuating the necessity for comprehensive research on Indian university students, taking into account diverse influences and factors. The research illuminates the complex interplay between financial factors and saving behavior among university students in India. Grasping these dynamics is vital for devising targeted interventions, educational programs, and policies that enhance FL and encourage responsible saving behavior. Empowering university students with financial knowledge and cultivating positive FAs can ultimately result in improved financial well-being and a more financially secure future. Further research and customized strategies are essential to effectively address the distinctive financial challenges confronted by university students in India and worldwide.

KEYWORDS

- **financial attitude**
- **financial awareness**
- **financial education**
- **financial knowledge**
- **financial literacy**
- **financial socialization**
- **investment in financial education**
- **saving behavior**

REFERENCES

Browning, M., & Lusardi, A. (1996). Household saving: Micro theories and micro facts. *Journal of Economic Literature*, *34*(4), 1797–1855. https://www.jstor.org/stable/2729971 (accessed on 7th July 2025).

Chen, H., & Volpe, R. P. (1998). An analysis of personal financial literacy among college students. *Financial Services Review*, *7*(2), 107–128. https://www.researchgate.net/publication/228367214_Savings_behavior_and_financial_problems_among_college_students_The_role_of_financial_literacy_in_Malaysia (accessed on 7th July 2025).

Ergün, S. (2018). The relationship between financial literacy and saving behavior: A case study on university students. *International Journal of Economics and Finance Studies*, *10*(1), 1–12. https://dergipark.org.tr/en/pub/iibfdergi/issue/41667/494242 (accessed on 7th July 2025).

Hilgert, M. A., Hogarth, J. M., & Beverly, S. G. (2003). Household financial management: The connection between knowledge and behavior. *Federal Reserve Bulletin*, *89*(7), 309–322. https://www.federalreserve.gov/pubs/bulletin/2003/0703lead.pdf (accessed on 7th July 2025).

Huston, S. J. (2010). Measuring financial literacy. *Journal of Consumer Affairs*, *44*(2), 296–316. https://onlinelibrary.wiley.com/doi/abs/10.1111/j.1745-6606.2010.01170.x (accessed on 7th July 2025).

Loibl, C., Kraybill, D. S., & DeMay, S. W. (2011). Accounting for the role of habit in regular saving. *Journal of Economic Psychology*, *32*(4), 581–592. https://www.sciencedirect.com/science/article/pii/S0167487011000539 (accessed on 7th July 2025).

Lusardi, A., Mitchell, O. S., & Curto, V. (2010). Financial literacy among the young. *Journal of Consumer Affairs*, *44*(2), 358–380. https://onlinelibrary.wiley.com/doi/abs/10.1111/j.1745-6606.2010.01173.x (accessed on 7th July 2025).

Mudzingiri, C., Mwamba, J. W. M., & Poon, W. C. (2018). Financial behavior, confidence, risk preferences and financial literacy of university students. *Cogent Economics & Finance*, *6*(1), 1512366. https://www.tandfonline.com/doi/full/10.1080/23322039.2018.1512366 (accessed on 7th July 2025).

Sabharwal, K., Mwamba, J. W. M., & Keyser, J. N. (2018). Financial behavior, confidence, risk preferences and financial literacy of university students. *Cogent Economics & Finance*, *6*(1), 1512366. https://www.tandfonline.com/doi/full/10.1080/23322039.2018.1512366 (accessed on 7th July 2025).

Sabri, M. F., & MacDonald, M. (2010). Savings behavior and financial problems among college students: The role of financial literacy in Malaysia. *Cross-Cultural Communication*, *6*(3), 103–110. https://www.researchgate.net/publication/228367214_Savings_behavior_and_financial_problems_among_college_students_The_role_of_financial_literacy_in_Malaysia (accessed on 7th July 2025).

CHAPTER 11

Green Bonds: Building a Sustainable Financial Future

NIDHI GOENKA,[1] GAYATHRI,[2] and MUMTAZ ALAM[3]

[1]*Kalinga University, Raipur, Chhattisgarh, India*

[2]*Vivekanand Mahavidyalaya, Raipur, Chhattisgarh, India*

[3]*Fiji National University, Raipur, Chhattisgarh, India*

*Corresponding author

ABSTRACT

Green Bonds are certificates of debt that allocate funds to invest in sustainable development, infrastructure, energy-saving devices, and conservation efforts. Since their inception in the early 2000s, the market has experienced exponential growth, driven by governments, multilateral institutions, corporations, and financial intermediaries. Governments create enabling environments through policy frameworks and regulatory incentives, while multilateral institutions provide technical assistance and certification standards. Corporations fund sustainability initiatives aligning with corporate social responsibility (CSR) objectives, while financial intermediaries facilitate the issuance and distribution of sustainable instruments. These Bonds offer financial assistance for issuers and investors, including access to a broader investor base, lower financing costs, enhanced brand reputation, and improved risk management through environmental risk identification and mitigation. Investors are attracted to Green Bonds for their potential to generate competitive returns while contributing to positive social and environmental outcomes. Challenges include standardizing reporting practices, harmonizing green definitions

E-Financial Strategies for Sustainable Development: A Handbook for Promoting Financial Inclusion and Ending Poverty (SDG 1). Ernesto D. R. Santibanez Gonzalez, Rajeev Sijariya, and Vikas Garg (Eds.)

DOI: 10.1201/9781779640956-11

and taxonomies, developing robust impact measurement methodologies, and mitigating greenwashing risks. Green Bonds can convert investment into eco-friendly endeavors, fostering a low-carbon, resilient, and inclusive economy by reducing emissions of carbon.

11.1 INTRODUCTION

The need for sustainable development has grown more and more evident in all global economies in response to the growing environmental issues. Innovative finance tools are becoming increasingly necessary to assist eco-friendly efforts as societies struggle with the effects of climate change. Among these, green bonds have become one of the most effective means of raising money for initiatives that support climate risk mitigation and sustainability. A particular kind of fixed-income financial instrument called "green bonds" is intended to finance environmental initiatives. They provide investors with the chance to fund projects including waste management, clean transportation, and sustainable agriculture. Recently, we have seen a notable increase in the issuance of green bonds, which are indicators of the growing demand for sustainable investments as well as the urgency with which environmental issues must be resolved. The world's first Climate Awareness Bond was introduced by the European Investment Bank in 2007, which gave rise to the notion of green bonds. Since then, governments, businesses, and financial institutions have embraced this novel financing method, causing the market for green bonds to grow quickly. Global green bond issuance exceeded $1 trillion, representing a critical turning point in the shift to a more sustainable finance system. The allure of green bonds is their capacity to harmonize financial and environmental objectives.

In green bonds, investors make money and facilitate the shift to a low-carbon economy by directing resources toward initiatives that improve the environment. A wide spectrum of financiers, which includes institutional financiers and socially conscious investors, have shown interest in this convergence of financial and environmental concerns. Green bonds are distinguished by their strict adherence to environmental standards. The earnings from green bond issues are usually restricted to projects that adhere to strict environmental regulations. This guarantees accountability and transparency, enabling investors to precisely evaluate the environmental impact of their investments. Additionally, investors are reassured, and the green credentials of bond issuers are verified by independent third-party procedures like Bond Principles. Sustainable bonds have advantages that go beyond their positive effects on the environment. From an economic standpoint, green bonds may assist in bringing down the cost of finance for sustainable projects and provide issuers with access to a wide range of investors. It is possible for issuers to stand out in the market, attract new investors, and improve their image by capitalizing on the increasing demand for ecologically conscious investments. Additionally, green bonds foster innovation in sustainable practices and technology and aid in the growth of green markets. As part of their larger sustainability objectives, governments from all over the world have been promoting the issuance of green bonds in recent years. Policy tools including regulatory frameworks, tax breaks, and subsidies have made it easier for issuers to enter the green bond market. Furthermore, global frameworks for encouraging investment in sustainable development and climate action have been made available by efforts like the United Nations Sustainable Development Goals and the Paris Agreement.

There are still a number of obstacles to its quick expansion. Greenwashing, the practice of inflating a project's environmental advantages in order to draw funding, is one issue caused by the absence of established standards for determining what qualifies as a "green" initiative. To tackle this obstacle, it is necessary to create transparent and widely recognized standards for green bonds, together with strong oversight and documentation systems to guarantee adherence. The scarcity of environmentally friendly projects that can be financed using bonds is another issue, especially in developing nations. The supply of qualifying projects is frequently limited by issues including regulatory hurdles, project preparedness, and the availability of technical competence, notwithstanding the increasing demand for green bonds. Governments, financial institutions, and other stakeholders must work together to remove these obstacles by fostering an atmosphere that encourages green investments and increasing the capacity for project creation and execution. To sum up, these bonds play a crucial role in raising financial requirements for sustainable development and tackling the pressing issues posed by climate change. Green bonds provide investors with a chance to make profits while making a positive impact on a more sustainable future by coordinating financial incentives with environmental objectives. To overcome obstacles and open doors for green investment globally, legislators, issuers, investors, and other stakeholders must work together.

Need for sustainable development has become increasingly evident in global economies as environmental issues like pollution and exhaustion continue to escalate. As societies grapple with these pressing challenges, innovative financial tools are becoming essential to support eco-friendly efforts. One of the most effective means of raising capital for initiatives that promote sustainability and mitigate climate risks is through green bonds. Green bonds are a specific type of fixed-income financial instrument designed to fund environmental projects. These projects can range from waste management and clean transportation to agroecology and renewable energy. The issuance of green bonds has seen a notable rise recently, reflecting the increasing urgency for green financing to address environmental issues. This surge underscores the growing awareness that eco-friendly investment has become an important instrument in the transition to a more sustainable financial system. This innovative financing mechanism aims to channel funds specifically toward projects with a positive environmental impact. Since then, governments, corporations, and financial institutions worldwide have embraced green bonds, leading to rapid market growth. The issuance of green bonds exceeded $1 trillion in 2020, marking a critical milestone in sustainable finance. The appeal for sustainable investment aligns financial and environmental goals. By directing capital towards projects that enhance the environment, green bonds allow investors to generate returns while contributing to the transition to a low-carbon economy. This dual benefit has attracted a diverse range of issuers for socially conscious individuals.

The convergence of financial and environmental interests makes green bonds a compelling investment option in the modern financial landscape. One of the defining features of green bonds is their strict adherence to environmental standards. The earnings from this issuance are typically appropriate to meet all kinds of ecological criteria. This ensures transparency and accountability, allowing financiers to properly examine the environmental effects of financing. Independent third-party certifications, such as the Climate Bonds Standard and the Green Bond Principles, are important to verify the green credentials of instrument issuers and provide assurance to investors. Beyond their environmental benefits, green bonds offer significant economic advantages. They can lower the cost of capital for sustainable projects and provide issuers with access to a broader investor base.

By tapping into the growing demand for environmentally conscious investments, issuers can distinguish themselves in the market, attract new investors, and enhance their reputation. Furthermore, green bonds promote innovation in sustainable practices and technologies, contributing to the development of green markets. Governments worldwide have recognized the potential of green bonds to support their broader sustainability objectives. In recent years, they have been actively promoting the issuance of green bonds through various policy measures, including regulatory frameworks, tax incentives, and subsidies. These efforts aim to create a conducive environment for green investments and drive the transition to a sustainable economy. Despite the increasing awareness in the market for green instruments, several challenges remain. One significant issue is greenwashing, where projects are misrepresented as environmentally beneficial to attract funding.

The lack of proper knowledge has created problems for "green" projects. To address this challenge, there is a need for transparent and universally accepted standards for green bonds, along with robust monitoring and reporting systems to ensure compliance. Another challenge is the limited availability of environmentally friendly projects that can be financed through bonds, particularly in developing countries. Factors such as regulatory barriers, project readiness, and the availability of technical expertise often constrain the supply of eligible projects. To overcome these obstacles, it is essential for governments, financial institutions, and other stakeholders to collaborate in creating an environment that encourages green investments and builds capacity for project development and implementation. Moreover, the combination of instruments has made investment portfolios require overcoming skepticism to build confidence among investors. This involves demonstrating the financial viability and competitive returns of green bonds compared to traditional investments. As the market matures, increasing data shows that the impact of sustainable instruments will help in addressing these concerns and fostering broader acceptance. In raising funds, this bond plays an important role in sustainable growth and addressing the urgent challenges posed by climate change. By aligning funds, it offers financiers an opportunity to achieve good returns while contributing to a greener future. However, realizing the full potential of green bonds requires coordinated efforts from policymakers, issuers, investors, and other stakeholders to overcome existing challenges and unlock opportunities for green investment globally. As the market continues to evolve, green bonds will undoubtedly remain a cornerstone of sustainable finance, driving progress towards an eco-friendly economy.

11.2 SDG 12

"Responsible consumption and production" was the focus of the authors' analysis of how green bonds could unleash sustainability. They came to the conclusion that green bonds have enormous potential for funding green infrastructure that supports responsible production and consumption (2023). The authors of this research examine the academic literature on green bonds and trace the concept's development. They categorize the material into three groups: proponents of the financial innovation, reformers, and detractors (Taylor and Weilert, 2023). This chapter studies the current status and the further development in the sustainable market (Abhilash et al., 2022). In order to draw attention to the issues facing the water industry and offer helpful information about the role that environmental investments play in the growth of financial markets and in promoting the sustainability of proposals to investors, the primary players in the "green bond market," local governments, and politicians, the authors reviewed the literature from the green bond market (2022). Green bonds have emerged as a pivotal instrument in sustainable finance, allowing issuers to raise funds specifically for projects with environmental benefits. This literature review synthesizes current research on green bonds, exploring their development, market dynamics, regulatory frameworks, benefits, challenges, and future prospects. Flammer (2021) provides an overview of the evolution of sustainable bonds and green bonds, highlighting key milestones for the rapid growth of this market segment. Several studies have analyzed the market dynamics of green bonds. The Climate Bonds Initiative (2023) reports significant growth in green bond issuances and growing investor demand for green instrument options. Tang and Zhang (2020) discuss the geographic distribution of green bond issuances, noting that Europe remains the largest market, followed by North America and Asia. Regulatory frameworks and certification standards play a crucial role in maintaining the integrity of the green bond market. The Green Bond Principles (GBP) and Climate Bonds Standard (CBS) are widely recognized standards that ensure transparency and accountability. Bachelet et al. (2019) examine the impact of these standards on the credibility of green bonds and investor confidence. Green bonds offer multiple benefits, including environmental, economic, and social advantages. Hyun, Park, and Tian (2020) analyze the environmental impact of green bonds, demonstrating their effectiveness for funding projects and encouraging sustainability. Furthermore, green bonds can stimulate economic growth by funding infrastructure projects, as noted by Karpf and Mandel (2018). Despite their benefits, green bonds face several challenges. Greenwashing is a major concern, where funds are misallocated to projects that do not deliver the claimed environmental benefits. Ehlers and Packer (2017) discuss the issue of greenwashing and the need for rigorous certification and reporting standards. Additionally, Nanayakkara and Colombage (2019) highlight the liquidity and pricing challenges in the green bond market, which can affect their attractiveness to investors. Green investment will increase innovation and technological advancements. Larcker and Watts (2020) explore how technological innovations, such as blockchain, can enhance the transparency and efficiency of green bond transactions. The main role of these bonds in achieving global sustainability targets is emphasized by Scholtens (2020).

11.3 GREEN BONDS

Green bonds come in various forms, each tailored to different financing needs and structures while serving the overarching goal of funding environmentally beneficial projects. The most common type, standard green bonds, is backed by the issuer's balance sheet, with proceeds earmarked for specific green projects such as renewable energy and sustainable water management (Climate Bonds Initiative, 2020). Green revenue bonds, secured by the revenues generated from the financed projects, are often used by municipalities for projects like water treatment plants (Climate Bonds Initiative, 2020). Green project bonds, issued for individual projects like wind farms, expose investors to the project's performance risk but potentially offer higher returns (International Capital Market Association, 2021). Sovereign green bonds, issued by national governments, fund large-scale environmental initiatives and are attractive to conservative investors due to the issuing government's creditworthiness (OECD, 2021). Corporate green bonds finance sustainable projects within corporate operations, enhancing the issuer's reputation and commitment to sustainability (Mooney, 2021). Green Sukuk, compliant with Islamic finance principles, finance projects in line with Sharia law and are particularly relevant in Islamic countries (Climate Bonds Initiative, 2020). Green convertible bonds offer the security of a bond with the potential upside of equity investment, allowing investors to convert their bonds into the issuer's equity (Mooney, 2021). Green transition bonds support high-emission sectors like oil and gas in reducing their carbon footprints and transitioning to more sustainable business models, focusing on broader sustainability transitions rather than specific green projects (OECD, 2021). Lastly, green entities facilitate international green finance and diversify the investor pool (International Capital Market Association, 2021). These varied green bonds collectively enhance the flexibility and appeal of green finance, enabling a wide area of projects and stakeholders to initiate the transition to a sustainable economy (Climate Bonds Initiative, 2020; OECD, 2021).

11.3.1 BENEFITS OF GREEN BONDS

- Green bonds offer a direct way to fulfill financial needs with favorable environmental outcomes, such as renewable energy, green transportation, and waste management. They provide investors with competitive returns by aligning financial objectives with environmental goals, allowing them to generate profits while supporting sustainable initiatives.
- Green bonds also provide diversification opportunities, reducing investment risk and enhancing long-term financial stability. The rapidly growing green bond market presents opportunities for issuers to tap into a growing pool of capital, attracting environmentally conscious investors. Participating in green bond issuance will increase the goodwill and brand building of issuers, demonstrating a commitment to sustainability. Government regulatory bodies play a vital role in promoting the use of these bonds to address climate change and promote sustainable development.
- Green bonds stimulate innovation and technological advancements in sustainable practices and technologies, supporting the conversion to a more sustainable and eco-friendly economy. They hold positive social impacts, creating jobs, improving public health, and enhancing community resilience to climate change impacts.

- Projects funded by green bonds often prioritize social inclusion and equity, benefiting communities disproportionately affected by environmental degradation. Green bonds provide a sustainable financial future by mobilizing capital for environmentally and socially responsible projects.
- Environmental awareness will significantly impact the global financial landscape. Green bonds offer multi-faceted benefits, including financing environmentally beneficial projects, attracting diverse investor bases, and enhancing issuers' reputations.
- Green bonds attract institutional investors interested in socially responsible investments, thus broadening the investor base and reducing financing costs for issuers. The European Investment Bank's green bond issuance has drawn significant investment, underscoring the growing demand for sustainable finance (OECD, 2021). Furthermore, by aligning with global sustainability goals, green bonds enhance corporate and governmental reputations, showcasing a commitment to environmental stewardship. For instance, Apple's green bonds have funded projects that reinforce its leadership in corporate sustainability (Mooney, 2021). These diverse benefits underscore the integral part of a sustainable financial system (Climate Bonds Initiative, 2020; Mooney, 2021; OECD, 2021).
- Green bonds offer a plethora of benefits, touching various aspects of financial markets, environmental sustainability, and social development. Their multifaceted advantages include financing environmentally beneficial projects, attracting a diverse investor base, enhancing issuers' reputations, and fostering global cooperation on sustainability goals. Here is an expanded exploration of these benefits, supported by examples. The primary advantage of green bonds is their role in financing projects that have significant environmental benefits.
- In India, green bonds have been pivotal in funding solar and wind energy projects, contributing to the nation's ambitious target of generating 450 gigawatts (GW) of renewable energy capacity by 2030. Green bonds attract many investors, specifically those interested in socially responsible and sustainable investments. This diversification of the investor base can lower the cost of capital for issuers.

- Green bonds can tap into the growing pool of capital dedicated to Environmental, Social, and Governance (ESG) criteria. The trend has changed to a surge in demand for green bonds, providing issuers with access to new sources of capital. For instance, energy efficiency improvements have drawn substantial interest from ESG-focused investors, reinforcing the company's position as a leader in corporate sustainability (Mooney, 2021).
- Issuing green bonds can significantly enhance the reputation of corporations and governments by demonstrating their commitment to sustainability. This can be particularly important in an era where consumers, investors, and regulators are increasingly demanding greater corporate responsibility. A case in point is Apple, whose green bond program has financed initiatives ranging from solar farms to recycling programs. This not only helps Apple reduce its carbon footprint but also bolsters its brand as an environmentally conscious company, attracting customers and investors who value sustainability (Mooney, 2021).
- Governments, too, benefit reputationally from issuing green bonds. For instance, the French government's issuance of sovereign green bonds has showcased its leadership in addressing climate change and promoting sustainable development. This has not only enhanced France's standing in international climate negotiations but also encouraged other countries to consider similar green finance mechanisms (OECD, 2021). Green bonds also yield substantial social and economic benefits.
- By financing green bonds, the quality of life for citizens can improve. For example, the proceeds from green bonds issued by the City of Gothenburg in Sweden have been used to develop sustainable public transportation and affordable housing, which not only reduce environmental impact but also enhance social equity and urban livability (Climate Bonds Initiative, 2020). Moreover, green bonds can stimulate job creation and economic growth.
- The construction of infrastructure projects requires a skilled workforce, thereby creating employment opportunities. These projects also drive innovation in green technologies, contributing to economic development. For instance, Germany's green bond market has supported the growth of its renewable energy sector,

leading to job creation and positioning the country as a global leader in green technology (OECD, 2021).

- Green bonds help issuers and investors manage environmental and financial risks. By funding projects, green bonds can enhance the resilience of economies and financial systems. Investors can invest and align their portfolios with sustainability goals. As climate change increasingly impacts financial markets, investments in green bonds can offer a hedge against these risks.
- This alignment can enhance portfolio resilience and support long-term investment returns (OECD, 2021). Green bonds play a crucial role in fostering global cooperation on sustainability. By issuing this kind of bond, companies can commit to their global goals, encouraging broader participation and cooperation.
- Issuers must regularly report on the use of proceeds and the environmental impact of funded projects. This transparency builds investor confidence and ensures that funds are genuinely used for green purposes. Independent third-party verification and certification, such as the Climate Bonds Standard and the Green Bond Principles, further enhance the credibility of green bonds. For instance, the verification process for the green bonds issued by the World Bank ensures that the proceeds are used for eligible green projects, providing assurance to investors about the environmental integrity of their investments (International Capital Market Association, 2021). The growing market for green bonds also fosters capacity building and the development of expertise in green finance.
- Issuing and managing green bonds require knowledge in areas such as environmental impact assessment, project evaluation, and sustainability reporting. As the market expands, there are increasing opportunities for skill development and innovation in these areas. Countries like India, which have rapidly grown green bond markets, are seeing the emergence of specialized financial institutions and advisory services dedicated to green finance. This not only supports the development of green projects but also enhances the overall financial ecosystem, promoting sustainable economic growth (Climate Bonds Initiative, 2020).

11.3.2 IMPACT ON ITS IMPLICATIONS

India's commitment to sustainable growth has led the country to become a leader in green finance initiatives. Green bonds, particularly for solar and wind farms, are crucial instruments for financial mechanisms that promote environmental sustainability and address climate change. These bonds enable the mobilization of capital from both domestic and international investors who are keen to support sustainable energy initiatives. Renewable energy projects funded by green bonds also contribute to energy security and economic growth. Solar farms in rural areas can provide electricity to communities that lack access to the grid, thereby improving the quality of life and promoting economic activities. Similarly, wind farms can generate clean energy, reducing reliance on coal and other fossil fuels. The successful deployment of renewable energy projects can set a precedent for further investments in the sector, creating a virtuous cycle of sustainable development. There is a significant effect of India's socio-economic stability, with impacts such as temperature changes affecting millions of people. Green bonds are important financial instruments that play a critical role in financing efforts to reduce the effects of climate change. These instruments include not only renewable energy initiatives but also efforts in energy efficiency, reforestation, and sustainable agriculture. By directing capital towards such projects, green bonds help India meet its climate goals as outlined. Sustainable infrastructure development is crucial for India's growth and development. Green bonds can support the creation of eco-friendly infrastructure like waste management facilities. These projects not only help mitigate environmental impacts but also improve the standard of living for Indian citizens. Investment in modern, efficient public transportation systems can reduce traffic congestion and pollution in urban areas, making cities more livable. Waste management facilities funded by green bonds can enhance recycling and waste-to-energy processes, reducing landfill use and environmental contamination. Green bonds offer an avenue for Indian companies to demonstrate their commitment to CSR and sustainability. By issuing green bonds, companies can finance eco-friendly projects and align their business practices with global sustainability goals. This alignment can enhance their reputation and attract socially conscious investors. Enhanced corporate responsibility through green bonds can also lead to competitive advantages. The Indian government has shown strong support for green finance initiatives through regulatory measures such as tax incentives and policy frameworks. By providing a favorable regulatory environment for green bonds, the government can encourage greater participation from issuers and investors. Policy initiatives such as the development of green bond guidelines, tax exemptions for interest income on green bonds, and subsidies for renewable energy projects create an enabling environment for green finance. Capacity building and skill development in areas such as project evaluation, impact assessment, and reporting are essential for the expansion of green instruments in the market in India. These efforts can foster innovation and knowledge transfer, strengthening the overall green finance ecosystem. Green bonds are a key factor in building a sustainable financial future for India. By financing renewable energy and infrastructure projects, addressing climate change, attracting investment, enhancing corporate responsibility, and fostering regulatory support and capacity building, green bonds can drive sustainable development. Green bonds have the potential to advance sustainability goals and finance environmentally friendly projects, but they face limitations such as a lack of standardized frameworks for defining “green,” potential greenwashing, liquidity issues due to their niche nature, and the risk of over-reliance on green bonds. The effectiveness of green bonds depends on project selection, implementation, and monitoring, which can vary significantly. Additionally, regulatory uncertainties and policy changes may affect the market’s attractiveness and stability, requiring issuers and investors to navigate evolving regulatory landscapes.

11.3.3 CHALLENGES AND CRITICISMS

Green bonds, despite their numerous benefits, face several limitations and potential downsides. This is determined by the credibility of green investments, which can reduce investor confidence. For example, some companies have been accused of labeling projects as green without significant environmental impact, leading to skepticism about the true sustainability of these investments (Climate Bonds Initiative, 2020). This inconsistency can create confusion and difficulty for financers in comparing different issuers and projects (OECD, 2021). The high costs associated with issuing green bonds, including expenses related to certification, reporting, and compliance, can also be a barrier. Smaller issuers, particularly in developing countries, may find these costs prohibitive, limiting their ability to participate in sustainable instruments. There is also a scarcity of investable sustainable projects, especially in regions with less developed green finance ecosystems. This supply-demand mismatch can hinder the growth of the market (International Capital Market Association, 2021). Researchers also point out that green bonds might not always lead to additional environmental benefits. In some cases, the projects financed by these kinds of bonds could be funded through traditional bonds, meaning green bonds do not necessarily result in increased green investment. This is sometimes referred to as the issue of "additionality" (Mooney, 2021). Despite these challenges, green bonds remain a crucial tool for financing sustainable development. Addressing these criticisms requires stronger regulatory frameworks, greater transparency, and consistent standards for the effectiveness of green instruments.

11.3.4 FUTURE PROSPECTS AND INNOVATIONS

The future of green bonds looks promising with the impact of sustainable goals. One significant trend is the development of transition bonds, which finance companies' efforts to shift from high-carbon to low-carbon operations. These bonds are particularly relevant for industries like oil and gas, chemicals, and manufacturing, which are crucial for global decarbonization but face significant transition challenges (OECD, 2021). Digital technologies and blockchain are also being explored to enhance the transparency and traceability of green bonds. Blockchain can provide a secure and immutable record of how bond proceeds are used, improving accountability and investor confidence. Pilot projects in this area are already underway, demonstrating the potential of technology to address some of the transparency issues currently faced by this market (Climate Bonds Initiative, 2020). Governments can use these bonds to finance large-scale environmental projects and demonstrate their commitment to sustainability. For example, the European Union's issuance of green bonds under its Next Generation EU recovery plan aims to finance green recovery projects across member states, signaling strong governmental support for sustainable development (International Capital Market Association, 2021). Innovations in financial products are also on the horizon. Green bonds could be combined with other financial instruments, such as social bonds, to create sustainability bonds that address both environmental and social issues. This holistic approach could attract a broader range of investors and address a wider array of sustainability challenges (Mooney, 2021).

11.3.5 POLICY RECOMMENDATIONS

Establishing more robust and universally accepted standards for green bonds can increase transparency. Governments and international bodies should work together to develop and enforce these standards. Providing tax incentives, subsidies, or other financial benefits can encourage more entities to issue green bonds and attract a larger pool of investors. These incentives can help to reduce the higher costs associated with issuing sustainable instruments. Developing countries often face greater barriers to participating in the green bond market. Strengthening reporting requirements and encouraging the use of technologies like blockchain can increase the transparency and accountability of green instruments. This helps to build investor trust and ensure that funds are used as intended. Policymakers should support the development of transition bonds to help high-emission industries reduce their carbon footprints. Clear guidelines and standards for these bonds can ensure their effectiveness. Aligning these bond frameworks with broader sustainability initiatives can ensure that green bonds contribute to global sustainability targets. Increasing knowledge and perception of sustainable bonds among potential issuers and financiers can help the general public grow the market. Educational campaigns and resources can highlight the benefits and impact of green bonds.

By implementing these recommendations, policymakers can help overcome the challenges to maximize their potential to contribute to a sustainable financial future. These are very important financial instruments for addressing environmental challenges. Despite facing issues such as greenwashing, lack of standardization, and high issuance costs, their benefits in attracting diverse investors, enhancing reputations, and fostering global cooperation are significant. Future prospects for green bonds are promising, with emerging trends like transition bonds and technological innovations poised to enhance their impact. To realize this potential, policymakers need to implement robust standards, provide incentives, support emerging markets, and foster transparency.

11.4 CONCLUSION

These bonds have the potential to significantly shape India's sustainable financial future by funding renewable energy projects, bolstering infrastructure development, and addressing climate change challenges.

They attract investment, enhance corporate responsibility, and benefit from regulatory support, driving economic growth and environmental stewardship. As India aims to achieve its renewable energy targets and mitigate climate change impacts, green bonds are a crucial tool. However, realizing their full potential requires collaboration, innovation, and effective policy frameworks from all stakeholders. By harnessing green bonds, India can advance its sustainability goals. Green bonds, including standard green bonds, green revenue bonds, and sovereign green bonds, offer significant advantages such as attracting diverse investors, lowering financing costs for sustainable projects, and enhancing corporate and governmental reputations. However, challenges like greenwashing, lack of standardization, high issuance costs, and a shortage of investable green projects remain significant barriers. Despite these hurdles, the future prospects of green bonds are promising. Emerging trends such as transition bonds, blockchain technology for enhanced transparency, and the increasing issuance of sovereign green bonds indicate a robust growth trajectory. Policymakers have a critical role to play in addressing existing challenges by establishing robust standards, providing incentives, supporting emerging markets, and fostering transparency and education about green bonds. Looking forward, green bonds are poised to be instrumental in achieving global sustainability goals. With ongoing innovations and strong policy support, green bonds can drive significant environmental and economic benefits, helping to build a sustainable financial future.

KEYWORDS

- **blockchain**
- **digital technologies**
- **green bonds**
- **policymakers**
- **solar and wind farms**
- **sustainable financial future**
- **waste management facilities**

REFERENCES

Abhilash, A., Shenoy, S., & Shetty, K. D. (2022). A state-of-the-art overview of green bond markets: Evidence from technology empowered systematic literature review. *Cogent Economics & Finance*. https://doi.org/10.1080/23322039.2022.2135834 (accessed on 7th July 2025).

Abhilash, A., Shenoy, S., & Shetty, K. D. (2022). The role of environmental investments in the development of financial markets: A literature review. *Sustainable Finance Journal*, *6*(1), 78–92.

Asian Development Bank. (2021). *Sustainable Infrastructure Development in India: Challenges and Opportunities*.

Bachelet, M. J., Becchetti, L., & Manfredonia, S. (2019). The green bonds premium puzzle: The role of issuer characteristics and third-party verification. *Sustainability*, *11*(4), 1098.

Climate Bonds Initiative. (2020). *Green Bond Market Summary 2020*. https://www.climatebonds.net/files/reports/cbi-green-bond-market-summary-2020.pdf (accessed on 7th July 2025).

Climate Bonds Initiative. (2020). *Green Bonds*. Climate Bonds Initiative.

Climate Bonds Initiative. (2023). *Green Bond Market Summary*. Climate Bonds Initiative website.

Corporate social responsibility in India: Practices and challenges. (2022). *Journal of Business Ethics*, *145*(3).

Ehlers, T., & Packer, F. (2017). Green bond finance and certification. *BIS Quarterly Review*, September 2017.

European Investment Bank. (2007). *Climate Awareness Bond*. https://www.eib.org/en/products/bonds/climate-awareness-bond (accessed on 7th July 2025).

Flammer, C. (2021). Corporate green bonds. *Journal of Financial Economics*, *142*(2), 499–516.

Frecautan, I. (2022). Tracing the emergence of green bonds: A literature review. *Journal of Sustainable Finance*, *12*(3), 45–62.

Green bonds for financing renewable energy projects: A global perspective. (2020). *Renewable Energy*, *150*.

Green bonds for mobilizing environmental finance. (2023). *Advances in Business Strategy and Competitive Advantage* book series. https://doi.org/10.4018/978-1-6684-8969-7.ch010 (accessed on 7th July 2025).

Hyun, S., Park, D., & Tian, S. (2020). The price of going green: The role of greenness in green bond markets. *Accounting & Finance*, *60*(1), 73–95.

International Capital Market Association. (2020). *Green Bond Principles 2020*. https://www.icmagroup.org/assets/documents/Regulatory/Green-Bonds/Green-Bond-Principles-June-2020-310520.pdf (accessed on 7th July 2025).

International Capital Market Association. (2021). *Green Bond Principles*. ICMA.

International Energy Agency. (2022). *India's National Electricity Plan: An Analysis of the 2022 Vision for Renewable Energy*.

Ion, F. (2022). Performance of green bonds in emerging capital markets: An analysis of academic contributions. *Journal of Corporate Finance Research*. https://doi.org/10.17323/j.jcfr.2073-0438.16.3.2022.111-130 (accessed on 7th July 2025).

Karpf, A., & Mandel, A. (2018). The changing value of the 'green' label on the US municipal bond market. *Nature Climate Change*, *8*(2), 161–165.

Krylova, I. I., & Zakorchevna, N. B. (2022). *Green Bonds as a Tool for Attracting Investments in the Water Sector of Ukraine*. https://doi.org/10.54929/monograph-12-2022-06-01 (accessed on 7th July 2025).

Larcker, D. F., & Watts, E. M. (2020). Where's the greenium? *Journal of Accounting and Economics*, *69*(2, 3), 101312.

Ministry of Finance, Government of India. (2023). *Policy Framework for Green Finance in India*.

Moody's Investors Service. (2022). *Green Bonds Market: Trends and Opportunities*.

Mooney, A. (2021). Corporate green bonds: Aligning business practices with sustainability goals. *Financial Times*.

Nanayakkara, M., & Colombage, S. (2019). Do investors in green bond market pay a premium? Global evidence. *Applied Economics*, *51*(40), 4425–4437.

OECD. (2021). *Sovereign Green Bonds: Accelerating the Transition to A Low-Carbon Economy*. OECD Publishing.

Reserve Bank of India. (2023). *Foreign Direct Investment in India: Trends and Patterns*.

Sandeep, S., Shenoy, D., Shetty, K. D., Lumen, S., & Lobo, S. (2023). Green bond as an innovative financial instrument in the Indian financial market: Insights from systematic literature review approach. *SAGE Open*. https://doi.org/10.1177/21582440231178783 (accessed on 7th July 2025).

Sandeep, S., Shenoy, D., Shetty, K. D., Lumen, S., & Lobo, S. (2023). Limiting factors and future development of green bonds: A systematic literature review. *Sustainable Finance Review*, *8*(2), 123–145.

Scholtens, B. (2020). Why finance should care about ecology. *Trends in Ecology & Evolution*, *35*(8), 629–640.

Securities and Exchange Board of India (SEBI). (2021). *Regulatory Landscape of Green Bonds in India: Challenges and Opportunities*.

Tang, D. Y., & Zhang, Y. (2020). Do shareholders benefit from green bonds? *Journal of Corporate Finance*, *61*, 101427.

Taylor, M., & Weilert. (2023). Bibliometric analysis of green bond markets: Current trends and future developments. *Journal of Sustainable Development*, *15*(4), 321–336.

Taylor, M., & Weilert. (2023). What do we already know about green bonds? A literature review. https://doi.org/10.1007/978-3-031-30502-3_2 (accessed on 7th July 2025).

The Energy and Resources Institute (TERI). (2023). *Green Infrastructure Investment: Opportunities and Challenges in India*.

The impact of green financing on corporate social responsibility: Evidence from Indian companies. (2022). *Sustainability*, *14*(1).

The role of green finance in climate change adaptation: A case study of India. (2022). *Climate Policy*, *22*(4).

Training programs for green finance professionals in India: A review. (2021). *International Journal of Sustainable Development & World Ecology*, *28*(5).

United Nations Environment Programmed (UNEP). (2020). *Capacity Building for Green Finance: Lessons from International Best Practices*.

United Nations Framework Convention on Climate Change. (n.d.). *Paris Agreement.* https://unfccc.int/process-and-meetings/the-paris-agreement/the-paris-agreement (accessed on 7th July 2025).

United Nations. (n.d.). *Sustainable Development Goals.* https://www.un.org/sustainabledevelopment/sustainable-development-goals/ (accessed on 7th July 2025).

World Bank Group. (2023). *Climate Change and India: A 2023 Assessment.*

World Bank. (2019). *The State of The Market: Green Bonds 2019.* https://www.climatebonds.net/files/reports/cbi_worldbank_the_state_of_the_market_2019.pdf (accessed on 7th July 2025).

CHAPTER 12

Navigating Prosperity: A Bibliometric Analysis of Financial Literacy and Sustainable Development Goals

NEHA PURI,[1] SEEMA TEWARI,[2] and SHOBHIT WADHWA[3]

[1]Amity College of Commerce and Finance (ACCF), Amity University, Noida, Uttar Pradesh, India

[2]School of Law, Delhi NCR Campus, Christ University, Ghaziabad, Uttar Pradesh, India

[3]F. C. Manning School of Business, Acadia University, Wolfville, Nova Scotia, Canada

*Corresponding author

ABSTRACT

The field of "financial literacy and SDGs" research has advanced significantly as countries place a greater emphasis on financial education and skill development. From 2017 to 2024, 1,017 SCOPUS papers were retrieved for this study. The study gives an overview of studies, trends, and future directions. The efficacy of financial literacy (FL), its impact on economic expansion, and its capacity to promote sustainable practices have all been extensively studied. Prospective pursuits involve advancing financial competencies and assessing their influence on income distribution, evaluating international cooperation initiatives, promoting environmentally friendly technologies, and designating green tax proceeds for environmental initiatives. The constantly growing corpus of research offers crucial direction for decision-makers dedicated to boosting FL and accomplishing Sustainable Development Goals (SDGs).

E-Financial Strategies for Sustainable Development: A Handbook for Promoting Financial Inclusion and Ending Poverty (SDG 1). Ernesto D. R. Santibanez Gonzalez, Rajeev Sijariya, and Vikas Garg (Eds.)

DOI: 10.1201/9781779640956-12

12.1 INTRODUCTION

Financial literacy (FL) is crucial for individuals and society as a whole. It involves a profound knowledge of financial concepts and risks and applying that knowledge to make informed decisions in multiple financial situations. By improving FL, individuals can enhance their financial well-being, participate more fully in economic life, and contribute to society's overall growth and prosperity (OECD, 2014). The definition is comprehensive and widely accepted in policy formulation and academia. Financial markets have recently been unstable due to various factors such as pandemics, wars, and natural disasters. Furthermore, the increasing digitalization of financial products and services has made it increasingly important for individuals to possess FL skills. By promoting FL as a socially helpful practice, individuals can become more financially resilient and better equipped to navigate the challenges of an increasingly complex financial landscape (Zaimovic et al., 2023).

FL may not be directly linked to any specific Sustainable Development Goals (SDGs) target, but it can play a crucial role in achieving several of them, particularly when combined with financial inclusion. The SDGs are a set of interconnected goals and targets that aim to promote the planet's and its people's prosperity. Promoting FL and inclusion can ensure that more individuals and communities have access to the resources they need to achieve excellent financial stability and security, which can contribute to achieving many different SDG targets.

Financial inclusion and entrepreneurship are keys to reducing poverty, and FL is crucial in both areas (Koomson et al., 2023). Mobile information and communication technology with internet capability has been instrumental in creating financial inclusion and has allowed many welfare schemes to reach the base of the pyramid (BOP) population, thus contributing to poverty reduction (Pandey et al., 2021). Financial well-being is undoubtedly a crucial aspect of several SDGs, including no poverty (SDG 1), good health and well-being (SDG 3), decent work and economic growth (SDG 8), reduced inequalities (SDG 10), and peace, justice, and institutions (SDG 16). FL is a significant factor in ensuring the financial well-being of individuals and communities, and it can play a vital role in achieving these SDGs.

Bibliometrics is a field of study that uses statistical and analytical methods to evaluate research and scientific advancement. It involves analyzing the quantity, quality, and impact of scientific publications, as well as the patterns of publication and citation behavior of researchers and institutions. Policymakers can use bibliometric data to identify areas of research that require policy intervention, evaluate the effectiveness of research programs, and make informed decisions about funding allocations. Prior bibliometric analysis by Zaimovic et al. (2023) studied the academic literature produced from 2014 to 2022 and segregated literature into predictors of FL (socio-economic, personal, and geographical) and factors that FL affects (planning for retirement, financial inclusion, risk management, and investment return). Ahmad et al. (2023) found the critical topics of financial inclusion and behavior, financial systems, and decision-making in FL and sustainability in a bibliometric analysis of documents published from 2008 to 2022. This chapter delved into the bibliometric analysis of bibliographic data on FL and SDGs to determine the research trends and foci of publications, prominent scholars, and journals. The chapter also highlighted the need for policy intervention to ensure that FL achieves SDGs.

12.2 RESEARCH OBJECTIVES

Within the current review study, the authors carried out a scientometric analysis of FL characteristics associated with SDGs, published in many reputable journals. In addition to filling a sizable vacuum in the body of open literature, this study attempts to assess and map the body of existing material. Publications from a variety of sources, including research papers published in reputable journals, articles, conference papers, books, articles published in books, reviews, and editorial notes, are analyzed based on the citations of these documents, the presence of relevant keywords, and a critical examination of the geographic distribution of research in different nations to further the goals of this study project:

1. To chart the FL and SDGs Research Trends.
2. To map the expansion of the literature on SDGs and FL.
3. To identify the most influential scholarly works and journals concerning the SDGs and FL.

4. To identify the nation with the highest research productivity regarding SDGs and FL.
5. To become familiar with the broader range of research on FL and the SDGs.
6. The purpose of this research project is to investigate potential avenues for FL and SDGs research by fusing the scientometric analysis with qualitative conversation, not only for researchers but also for academicians, practitioners, research institutions, and other stakeholders.

12.3 METHODOLOGY

This section describes the research techniques and resources used to carry out the scientometric analysis. Table 12.1 shows a flowchart of the research technique employed. The key elements are briefly described in the following sections.

TABLE 12.1 The Search Query for Financial Literacy and SDG

Elucidation	Settings	No of Documents
Search query "TITLE-ABS-KEY"	We have combined the following words: "Financial Literacy," OR "Financial education," OR "Financial knowledge," OR "Financial learning," OR "Financial proficiency," OR "Financial skills," AND "SDG," OR "Sustainable Development Goals."	1017 documents found
Subject Area	"Social Sciences, Economics, Econometrics and Finance and Business, Management and Accounting"	795 documents found
Document Type	Article, Book Chapter, Review and Conference Paper	749 documents found
Language type	English	742 documents found
Source type	Journal	652 documents found
Access	There are documents with and without open access.	
Date and Database	May 1, 2024 and Scopus Database	

12.3.1 ANALYSIS OF SCIENTOMETRIC DATA

The present study employs the scientometric analytic approach to evaluate the research contributions within the FL and SDGs domain, scrutinize patterns of research interest, and detect emerging themes in research. According to Olawumi and Chan (2018), scientometric analysis uses formulas and visualizations to identify research edges and underlying trends, allowing for a more thorough understanding of a scientific field. Using the scientometric analysis method and identifying the authors, companies, and countries at the forefront of the subject can help uncover the core dynamics of any scientific discipline (Soydal, 2010; Yalcin, 2010). Konur (2012) states that scientometric analysis is one of the most often used methods for examining the development and effectiveness of a particular research area. A comprehensive review-based method for summarizing recent research findings is called scientometric analysis.

12.3.2 SOFTWARE SELECTION

The bibliographic information was obtained from the Scopus database in .csv format. First, R Studio was loaded, and the Bibliometrix R package was installed. Typing biblioshiny in the R terminal opened the Biblioshiny program. The R Bibliometrix software is accessible to non-programmers through the web application Biblioshiny. Researchers can perform comprehensive bibliometric analysis with the help of Bibliometrix's many tools. The frequency of the concurrent occurrence of keywords in two scientific articles was identified using data mining in bibliometrics, utilizing the statistical software program Biblioshiny, which helped to simplify the complex keyword network linkages. The Biblioshiny interface received one file uploaded in the Excel (.csv) format. These files were also downloaded: Excel (.csv) and Portable Network Graphics (.png).

12.3.3 DATABASE SELECTION

The study's examination of FL and SDGs used data from the SCOPUS database, which contains most academic papers and publications.

The study's search terms in SCOPUS were "Financial Literacy," "Financial Education," "Financial Knowledge," "Financial Learning," "Financial Proficiency," "Financial Skills," AND "SDG" OR "Sustainable Development Goals" in the article's title, abstract, keywords, and body text. The preliminary results show that 1,017 documents were released between 2017 and 2024. Only the disciplinary area "Social Sciences, Economics, Econometrics, and Finance and Business, Management, and Accounting" was chosen because this is the investigation's zone of significance; 795 publications were left. After manually sorting the papers based on relevancy, 652 were still present.

12.3.4 DATA EXTRACTION AND JOURNAL SELECTION

Research papers, conference papers, and reviews are a few data sources considered for the study and are shown in Table 12.2. Research articles form the highest portion of the literature, whereas books form the lowest.

TABLE 12.2 Categories of Literature Sources

Types of Literature	No. of Publications
Article	599
Conference Paper	1
Review	52

Source: Author's Calculation.

12.4 SCIENCE MAPPING ANALYSIS AND RESULTS DISCUSSION

12.4.1 PUBLICATION TREND

Figure 12.1 demonstrates the annual growth rate of studies published between 2017 and 2024. It shows the yearly growth rate of studies published during this period. Since the SDGs were adopted in 2015, publications were almost zero in 2017 and 2018; later on, as the SDGs became a priority for all, including governments, national and international institutions, and corporate publications, they consistently rose and reached almost 250 publications in 2023. Only four months into 2024, 125 documents on FL and SDGs have been published so far. This shows the increasing importance of FL and SDGs.

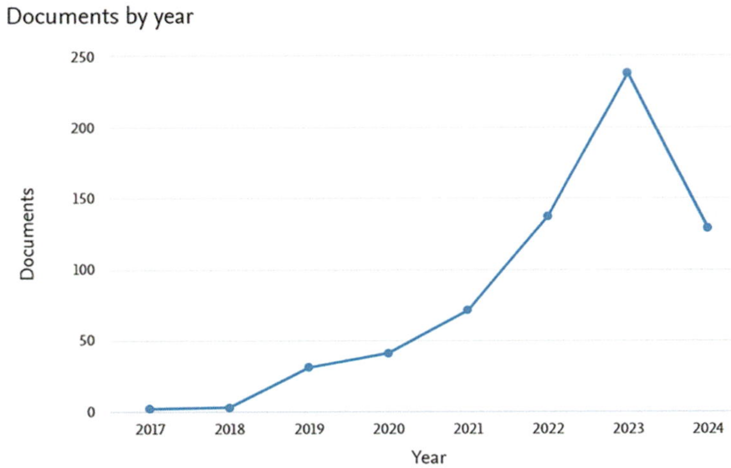

FIGURE 12.1 Annual publication trend.

Source: Scopus.

12.4.2 *TOP CITED AND MOST PRODUCTIVE JOURNALS*

Figure 12.2 shows the most productive journals for FL and SDGs. Sustainability (Switzerland) is the most productive journal, with 67 publications on the subject, followed by Cogent Business and Management and Social Indicators Research (14 each).

Table 12.3 indicates the top-cited journals for FL. Sustainability (Switzerland) has the highest h-index (17), g-index (31), and m-index (2.215). The Journal of Open Innovation: Technology, Market, and Complexity is next, with an h-index of 5, a g-index of 6, and an m-index of 1.25.

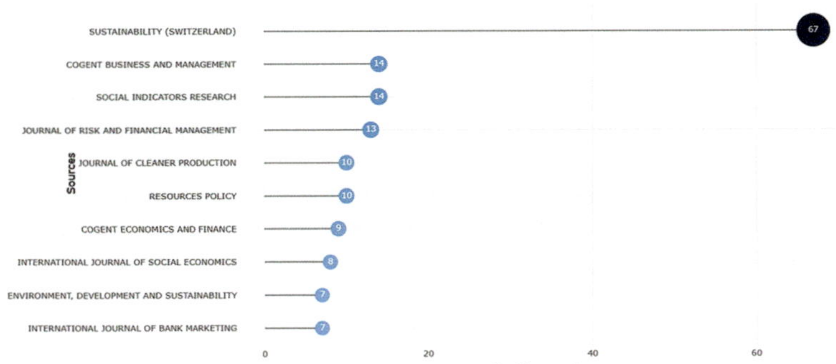

FIGURE 12.2 Relevant sources.

Source: RStudio.

TABLE 12.3 Relevant Sources

Journal's Name	"h_index"	"g_index"	"m_index"	"TC"	"NP"	"PY_ start"
Sustainability (Switzerland)	17	31	2.125	1105	67	2017
Journal Of Open Innovation: Technology, Market, And Complexity	5	6	1.25	132	6	2021
Social Indicators Research	5	14	1	243	14	2020
Technological Forecasting and Social Change	5	6	1.25	125	6	2021
Cogent Business and Management	4	7	1.333	55	14	2022
Cogent Economics and Finance	4	6	1	42	9	2021
International Journal of Bank Marketing	4	7	1.333	92	7	2022
International Journal of Social Economics	4	5	0.667	28	8	2019
Journal of Business Research	4	6	0.5	415	6	2017
Journal of Cleaner Production	4	10	1	176	10	2021

Source: Author's compilation.

12.4.3 MOST RELEVANT AUTHORS

Using the themes of SDGs and FL, the 1951 authors authored 652 research papers in various journals. With 14 articles (4.51 fractionalized value) and the highest frequency peak for average citations per item in 2021, Koomson I was the most productive author. Li, Y (1.44 fractionalized value) and Khan I (1.83 fractionalized value) were the next most productive authors. Figure 12.3 and Table 12.4 display the top authors who are noteworthy.

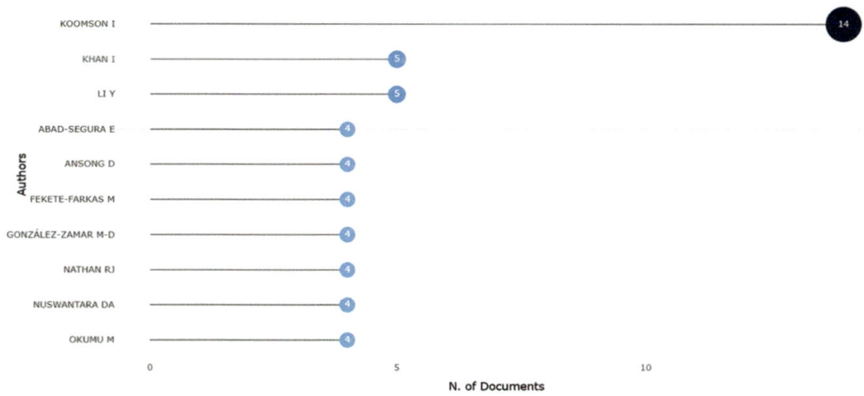

FIGURE 12.3 Relevant authors.

Source: RStudio.

TABLE 12.4 Relevant Authors

Element	h_index	g_index	m_index	TC	NP	PY_start
KOOMSON I	8	14	1.6	429	14	2020
ABAD-SEGURA E	4	4	0.8	476	4	2020
GONZÁLEZ-ZAMAR M-D	4	4	0.8	476	4	2020
KHAN I	4	5	1	100	5	2021
NUSWANTARA DA	4	4	2	27	4	2023
ANSONG D	3	4	0.75	19	4	2021
HENDRATI IM	3	3	1.5	21	3	2023
LI Y	3	5	1.5	40	5	2023
NATHAN RJ	3	4	0.5	104	4	2019
OKUMU M	3	4	0.75	19	4	2021

Source: Author's compilation.

12.4.4 MOST INFLUENTIAL INSTITUTIONS

Figure 12.4 and Table 12.5 illustrate the publication yield of organizations or authors' affiliations that supported research on SDGs and FL, which was also examined in this study. With 17 documents, the Hungarian University of Agriculture and Life Sciences was ranked first.

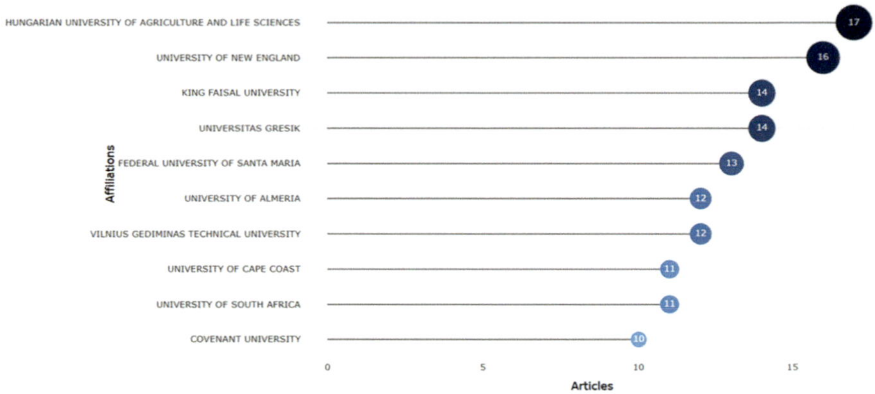

FIGURE 12.4 Most relevant affiliations.

Source: Author's compilation.

TABLE 12.5 Influential Institutions

Affiliation	Articles
Hungarian University of Agriculture and Life Sciences	17
University of New England	16
King Faisal University	14
Universitas Gresik	14
Federal University Of Santa Maria	13
University of Almeria	12
Vilnius Gediminas Technical University	12
University of Cape Coast	11
University of South Africa	11
Covenant University	10

Source: Author's compilation.

12.4.5 PROMINENT WORDS AND ASSOCIATIONS WITH AUTHORS AND NATIONS

The most often used term among the authors was "sustainable development," which appeared 60 times. "Sustainability," on the other hand, appeared 50 times. Figure 12.5 shows that a keyword has more occurrences the larger it is, and vice versa. All the significant phrases saw an increase in yearly occurrences, albeit some developed more quickly than others. The words with the most significant increases in frequency were "China," "sustainable development," and "finance," as illustrated by a word cloud (Figure 12.6) and a tree map (Figure 12.7), which show hierarchical data as a sequence of stacked rectangles. In Figure 12.7, each group is represented by a rectangle whose area changes based on the weights given to the most frequently occurring phrases.

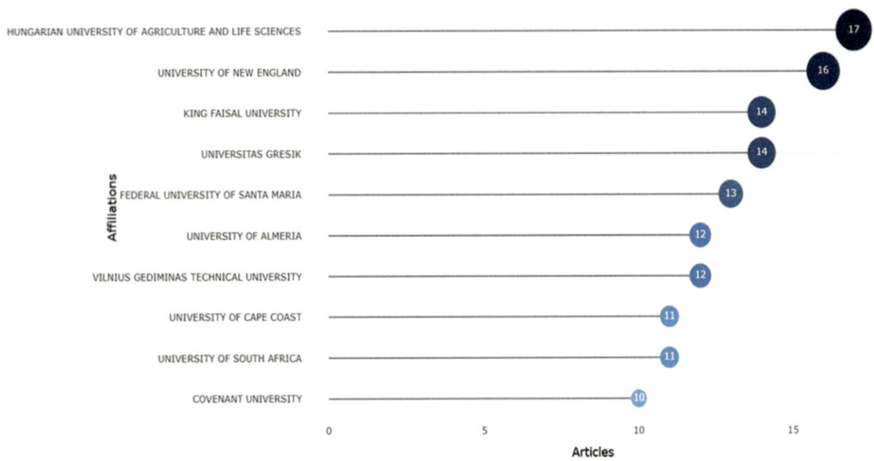

FIGURE 12.5 The most relevant words used in Financial Literacy and SDG-based research-based studies.

Source: R studio.

FIGURE 12.6 Word cloud is the most frequently used keyword in Financial Literacy and SDG research.

Source: R studio.

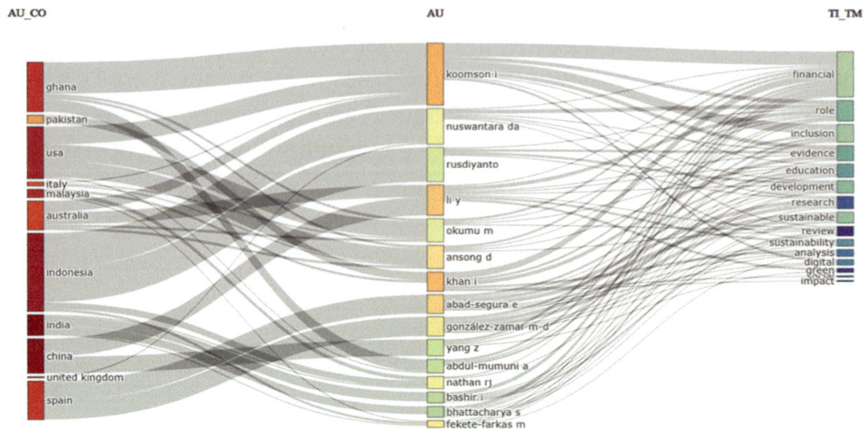

FIGURE 12.7 Relationships found in financial literacy and SDG-based research between countries, authors, and keywords.

Source: R studio.

The authors, countries, and keywords of publications on FL and sustainable development objectives were correlated in a three-field plot called the Sankey plot. Different colored rectangles represented relevant elements in the diagram. Each of the rectangles represented different aspects such as authors, countries, and keywords. The height of each rectangle was derived from the total of the relations that originated between those elements. A higher rectangle was used to identify the element having the strongest relationships. The Sankey diagrams for the top 10 most productive countries and authors, together with their most significant contributions to research on FL and the sustainable development objectives, are shown in Figure 12.7.

12.4.6 COLLABORATION NETWORK OF CO-WORDS IN FINANCIAL LITERACY AND SDG-BASED RESEARCH PUBLICATIONS

Co-word networks, such as the one shown in Figure 12.8, are collaborative networks of co-words commonly employed in research on the Omicron variant. Three clusters of red, blue, and green are displayed. The betweenness, proximity, and page rank measurements were used to determine the values of these three clusters and their nodal positions. These metrics are shown in Table 12.6.

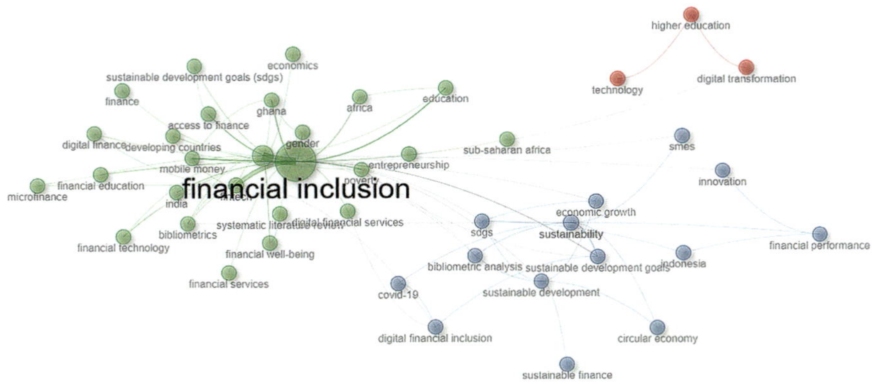

FIGURE 12.8 Co-word network visualization.

Source: R studio.

TABLE 12.6 Co-Word Network Analysis for Financial Literacy and SDGs

Node	Cluster	Betweenness	Closeness	PageRank
Sustainable development	1	324.14	0.02	0.09
finance	1	152.80	0.01	0.07
China	1	71.17	0.01	0.06
innovation	1	9.47	0.01	0.03
poverty	1	8.12	0.01	0.02
investment	1	3.86	0.01	0.02
economic growth	1	7.18	0.01	0.02
green economy	1	5.21	0.01	0.02
investments	1	2.17	0.01	0.02
natural resource	1	8.93	0.01	0.03

Source: Author's compilation.

12.5 DISCUSSION

Several conclusions and suggestions have been drawn from an extensive examination of bibliometric and content analysis. The first quarter of 2022 witnessed a peak in the rise of scholarly production on FL, the SDGs, and related subjects; in 2023, the number of publications increased dramatically. Global researchers have conducted several studies ("research papers, systematic reviews, and meta-analyses") on sustainable development, financial stability, financial tranquility, and financial well-being. Nevertheless, regardless of the importance of bibliometric studies for analyzing research investigations, orientations, and contacts between academics and researchers, very few studies have been carried out that mainly analyze bibliometric data.

The tabulated statistics show a high collaboration rate on this issue, with most of the documents being co-authored and only 3.63% being single-authored. Three core information elements are used to create Sankey plots, which provide significant insights based on the relationships between domains. For example, authors can connect their work to certain keywords and participating countries in this research area. For instance, author Koomson, I., from Australia, had the most significant impact on financial inclusion in poverty and vulnerability research. According to this survey, most authors were more productive after 2021, which also identifies the most influential writers in the profession and their most productive years. Only Wang, Y., González-Zamar, M.-D., Abad-Segura, E., and Nathan, R. J. were published. Our results also indicate a strong relationship between Australia, China, the United States, and Germany with FL and SDGs research.

This chapter provides a summary of recent advancements in FL and SDGs research. It is necessary to characterize the many domains globally due to the multidisciplinary nature of the topic, even with the scientific community's remarkable efforts to generate a significant number of research studies to address the issue. Financial well-being has been the subject of numerous bibliometric studies, but it has developed into behavioral biases, behavioral finance, investment decisions, and links to studies on poverty. The most prolific writers, reference articles, organizations, nations, and academic disciplines found in the Scopus database are identified in this study, which is among the first bibliometric analyses of publications on FL and SDGs.

12.6 CONCLUSION

By investigating records from the Scopus database, this study mapped the regional distribution and publications of the world's top academics in the field of FL and SDGs. It additionally evaluated the research output in this area globally. Additionally, open-access policies have been adopted by most journals that have published research on FL, financial well-being, and their relationship to poverty. The result has facilitated resource sharing and hastened the dissemination of scientific knowledge. China, Germany,

Italy, and the United States have the highest percentage of citations. Koomson, identified as the most prolific author in the bibliometric analysis of publications on financial inclusion, mobile money uptake, and FL.

Sustainability is the journal that receives the greatest preference for articles on sustainable development objectives and FL. The two most often used terms by authors in 1951 and 2011, respectively, were "sustainable development" and "sustainable." VOSviewer and the Biblioshiny program from R's Bibliometric package provide important research streams and subjects. Our findings aim to offer valuable insights into future research paths and perspectives in the rapidly evolving field of FL and SDGs by comprehensively summarizing the patterns in this rapidly evolving field. Significant future work opportunities abound.

12.7 FUTURE DIRECTIONS

Subsequent research ought to examine more unique and advanced machine learning-based bibliometric analysis technologies, like group prediction using ranking-based subject dominance estimation. The Scopus database was the focus of this investigation, while additional databases such as Dimensions, Science Direct, JStor, and Web of Science can also be used. Future directions could also include developing a visualization tool that provides more information and covers more ground in one shot.

KEYWORDS

- **bibliometric analysis**
- **bibliometrics**
- **digitalization**
- **financial education**
- **financial inclusion and entrepreneurship**
- **financial literacy**
- **financial markets**
- **policymakers**
- **scientometric analysis**
- **sustainable development goals**

REFERENCES

Aria, M., & Cuccurullo, C. (2017). bibliometrix: An R-tool for comprehensive science mapping analysis. *Journal of Informetric*, *11*, 959–975.

Idris, A., Rahmawati, A., Surwanti, A., & Hanafi, M. M. (2023). Financial literacy to improve sustainability: A bibliometric analysis. *Studies in Business and Economics*, *18*(3), 24–43. https://doi.org/10.2478/sbe-2023-0043 (accessed on 7th July 2025).

Koomson, I., Anasong, D., Okumu, M., & Achulo, S. (2023). Effect of financial literacy on poverty reduction across Kenya, Tanzania, and Uganda. *Global Social Welfare*, *10*, 93–103. https://doi.org/10.1007/s40609-022-00259-2 (accessed on 7th July 2025).

Koomson, I., Villano, R. A., & Hadley, D. (2020). Effect of financial inclusion on poverty and vulnerability to poverty: Evidence using a multidimensional measure of financial inclusion. *Social Indicators Research*, *149*, 613–639. https://doi.org/10.1007/s11205-019-02263-0 (accessed on 7th July 2025).

OECD. (2014). *PISA 2012 Results: Students and Money: Financial Literacy Skills for the 21st Century (Volume VI)*. OECD Publishing.

Olawumi, T. O., & Chan, D. W. M. (2018). A scientometric review of global research on sustainability and sustainable development. *Journal of Cleaner Production*, *183*, 231–250. https://doi.org/10.1016/j.jclepro.2018.02.162 (accessed on 7th July 2025).

Pandey, D., Mukherjee, S., Das, G., & Zhang, J. Z. (2022). Improving base-of-the-pyramid consumer welfare through mobile technology services. *Journal of Services Marketing*, *36*(2), 232–244. https://doi.org/10.1108/JSM-05-2021-0179 (accessed on 7th July 2025).

Yalcin, H. (2010). Bibliometric profile of *Journal of National Folklore* (2007–2009). *Milli Folklor*, *85*, 205–211. https://doi.org/10.1108/K-12-2019-0793 (accessed on 7th July 2025).

Zaimovic, A., Torlakovic, A., Arnaut-Berilo, A., Zaimovic, T., Dedovic, L., & Nuhic Meskovic, M. (2023). Mapping financial literacy: A systematic literature review of determinants and recent trends. *Sustainability*, *15*. https://doi.org/10.3390/su15129358 (accessed on 7th July 2025).

CHAPTER 13

Role of Artificial Intelligence in FinTech and Banks: Challenges and Future Research Agenda

SUNAINA KANOJIA,[1] AMANDEEP SINGH,[2] and AMIT KUMAR SINGH[1]

[1]Department of Commerce, Faculty of Commerce and Business, Delhi School of Economics, University of Delhi, Delhi, India

[2]Sri Guru Tegh Bahadur Khalsa College, University of Delhi, Delhi, India

*Corresponding author

ABSTRACT

This chapter investigates the evolving role of Artificial Intelligence (AI) in reshaping the future of FinTech and the traditional banking sector. Through a systematic literature review of 72 scholarly articles published between 2012 and 2022 using the PRISMA methodology, it explores the intellectual foundation and emerging research in this dynamic area. The findings reveal that AI-driven FinTech has revolutionized financial services by fostering innovation, enhancing customer experience, and enabling financial inclusion. However, despite its transformative potential, FinTech is unlikely to replace incumbent banks; instead, AI/ML integration into traditional banking is imperative. The chapter also highlights key challenges associated with AI adoption, including data privacy, cybersecurity threats, algorithmic bias, unemployment, and regulatory uncertainty. These concerns underscore the urgent need for robust regulations and ethical AI frameworks. The review concludes by identifying future research

E-Financial Strategies for Sustainable Development: A Handbook for Promoting Financial Inclusion and Ending Poverty (SDG 1). Ernesto D. R. Santibanez Gonzalez, Rajeev Sijariya, and Vikas Garg (Eds.)

DOI: 10.1201/9781779640956-13

directions, particularly on risk mitigation, algorithm explainability, and sustainable integration models for AI in finance. This study is a unique contribution as it not only synthesizes current literature but also charts a forward-looking agenda for researchers, policymakers, and practitioners in the financial ecosystem.

13.1 INTRODUCTION

Bower and Christensen (1995) defined 'disruptive innovation' as innovation that upends a prevailing market and creates new markets with the use of disruptive technology. The conditions needed to be fulfilled for causing disruption are: (a) a substantial proportion of the market must choose the products or services; (b) the incumbent player must not be able to replicate the innovation (Ulrich, 2014). The Financial Stability Board (FSB) defines "FinTech" as technologically enabled innovation in financial services that could result in new business models, applications, processes, or products with an associated material effect on financial markets and institutions and the provision of financial services. FinTechs are functioning in key areas like payments and remittances, borrowing and lending, enterprise financial management, crowdfunding, enterprise technologies for financial institutions, insurance, personal financial management, wealth management, trading and capital markets, and digital banking (Murinde et al., 2022). FinTechs have the advantage over banks as they are not restricted by legacy systems and processes; hence, they can develop customized solutions. Emerging markets have welcomed such customized solutions, which support consumerism and proliferate economic activities. Further, non-bank financial companies are not required to follow the traditional regulations that banks are following (Bean, 2018). The biggest advantage FinTech has is the alternative data available through the social media activities of the potential borrower, which can be used to increase marketing and distribution effectiveness and evaluate the financial soundness of potential borrowers (Berg et al., 2020).

13.2 LITERATURE REVIEW

The hierarchical structure of FinTech companies, supported by highly automated and independent human decisions, makes the organizational structure a less important factor in lending (Liberti et al., 2016). With more versatile technology and very low overhead costs, FinTechs have been providing no-cost or very low-fee services to underserved customers, primarily younger customers (Munk, 2022); hence, economies with demographic dividends can use it advantageously. This study intends to reveal the intellectual structure of AI in FinTech and banks. The key factors contributing to the success of FinTech companies are the availability of funding, focus on customer loyalty, strengthening technology and IT infrastructure, lowering the cost of operations, and building value propositions (Deloitte India, 2017). AI tools such as virtual assistants, chatbots, and ATMs significantly reduce the technical inefficiency of banks (Mor and Gupta, 2021). In the future, banking practices will witness further digitalization, so banks must invest in technologies (Wang et al., 2021). As a result, Indian private sector lenders announced their capex on digital transformation during the financial year 2021. Technological progress may cause a complete overhaul of the traditional banking model. Digital platforms can manifest as the new intermediary between borrowers and depositors (Boot et al., 2021). Jiang et al. (2022) accentuated the financing problems faced by SMEs under traditional financing models and explained that digital finance portrays financial services through AI, the internet, and cloud computing, which enhances the creative capabilities of SMEs. FinTech facilitates peer-to-peer (P2P) lending without any participation from incumbent financial institutions. Most FinTechs are matchmakers; they have implemented the agency model. With this, they avoid holding the risk of the loan on the balance sheet (Navaretti et al., 2018). According to the opportunities analysis and industry forecast report (2020), the global peer-to-peer (P2P) market size is expected to grow at a CAGR of 29.7% from 2020 to 2027. The soft information communicated through text and social characteristics such as educational qualification, gender, and marital status provides important inputs into credit appraisal, having a higher likelihood of correctly predicting defaulting and non-defaulting borrowers (Wang et al., 2022). With the availability of a large information base, FinTech can evaluate the characteristics of borrowers and bring price discrimination accordingly (Navaretti et al., 2018).

Subsequent to the financial crisis, banks have witnessed a high degree of regulatory compliance in the past decade, which has created a competitive disadvantage (Amstad, 2019). Increasing regulatory burden, heavy legal scrutiny, and high capital requirements have opened the opportunity for regulatory arbitrage for FinTech. Regulatory arbitrage is not the only reason for the growth of FinTech's shadow banks; AI-enabled technology has disrupted the markets and provided a better service experience, convenience to customers, and, most importantly, customer outreach for financial services. Therefore, FinTech clients are ready to pay a premium for online services (Buchak et al., 2018; Ryu and Chang, 2018). On average, a FinTech charges a 5% higher rate from low-score borrowers; such borrowers are more prone to default compared to non-FinTech borrowers when their credit score is low, especially when FinTech lenders are less rigid on employment status, though it adds to the default risk (Di Maggio and Yao, 2021). As there is greater consumer risk involved with FinTech, the focus should be on activity-based regulations to protect consumers (World Bank, 2021). According to the FSB report (2022), the COVID-19 pandemic has augmented the digitalization of retail financial services. While extensive data is scarce on retail financial services, the proxies suggest that big techs and larger FinTechs have increased their digital footprints. Banks provide bundled services like deposits, payment lending, demand drafts, and so forth., whereas FinTechs generally deal in a few or unbundled services. To give stiff competition to the banks, FinTechs should also bundle their services to expand their activities (Navaretti et al., 2018), which has been seen in emerging markets in small ticket size consumer goods, clothing, and similar items. Since 2015, there has been an upward trend in publications, with major countries contributing to the literature on AI and its applications in the field of finance being the United States, China, and the United Kingdom (Ahmed et al., 2022). Our work seeks to address the following research questions:

- RQ1: The present state of research in artificial intelligence (AI) and how it is shaping the future of FinTech's and banks?
- RQ2: What are the major challenges that AI-enabled FinTech and banks might face in the future?
- RQ3: The future research agenda in the domain of AI/ ML lead FinTech's.

Table 13.1 placed below provides a synoptic view of how this study adds to the relevant stream of literature, especially while addressing the stream of risk with each layer of AI used in FinTech, NBFC, or banking. This study is the first one attempting to elaborate on why FinTechs can never capture banking.

TABLE 13.1 Comparison of Previous Studies and Our Study

Basis of the Comparison	Ahmed et al.(2022)	Ashta and Herrmann (2021)	Milana and Ashta (2021)	This Study
Time period	2011–2021	No time limit	No time limit	2012–2022
Keywords	artificial intelligence, machine learning, finance, bibliometric	artificial intelligence, financial markets, fintech, microfinance	artificial intelligence, fintech, fuzzy models, machine learning, microfinance.	fintech, banking, NBFC, artificial intelligence, machine learning, big tech, Commercial banks
Focus of the study	Reviewed Publication trend	Practitioner case studies on the use of AI in financial businesses.	AI applications for finance and financial markets	Synthesis of extensive literature on role of AI in fintech and banks, highlighting key challenges for fintech to capture banking business and future research agenda in this domain.
Methodology	Bibliometric analysis	Narrative review (Non-scientific)	Systematic literature review	Systematic literature review focusing the on fintech, banking and NBFC.

Source: Authors.

13.3 RESEARCH METHOD

The above-referred research questions are probed with the SLR technique, which is a method used to identify, select, and assess research in order to address a specific research question (Dewey and Drahota, 2016). We followed seven simple steps for systematic review by Lockwood and Oh (2017): 1) develop a structured question, 2) define inclusion and exclusion criteria, 3) develop a search strategy, 4) critical appraisal, 5) data extraction, 6) analysis of extracted data, and 7) presentation of findings.

13.3.1 INCLUSION AND EXCLUSION CRITERIA

First, only research articles written in English and appearing in Scopus-indexed journals were included in the study due to language barriers. Second, the publication period was limited from 2012 to 2022. Third, there is no restriction on the types of research included in the review; all qualitative, quantitative, and mixed studies were considered. Fourth, we excluded reports, review papers, conference proceedings, books, and book chapters. Fifth, grey literature was excluded from the study.

13.3.2 SEARCH STRING STRATEGY

A well-defined search strategy is vital for a systematic review as it influences the search results. We used keywords and relevant synonyms to broaden the search results. Boolean operators ("AND," "OR") were employed to improve search precision, as shown in Table 13.2. We used the "Scopus" database for retrieving the research articles. The preliminary search began with the following keywords: "Artificial intelligence" OR AI AND "FinTech" OR "Financial technology" OR "Banks," which yielded a total of 2639 results. Later on, search strings were refined to limit the searches to meet the objectives of the study.

TABLE 13.2 Boolean Search String

Sl. No.	Search Query	Results
1. Final Query	TITLE-ABS-KEY (ai OR "Artificial Intelligence" OR "robot advisor" AND fintech OR "Financial Technology" OR banks OR NBFC OR "Non-banking finance Company" OR "P2P LENDING" OR "PEER TO PEER LENDING" OR "SOFT INFORMATION") AND (LIMIT- TO (DOCTYPE, "ar")) AND (LIMIT- TO (SUBJAREA, "BUSI") OR LIMIT- TO (SUBJAREA, "ECON")) AND (LIMIT- TO (PUBYEAR, 2022) OR LIMIT-TO (PUBYEAR, 2021) OR LIMIT- TO (PUBYEAR, 2020) OR LIMIT-TO (PUBYEAR, 2019) OR LIMIT- TO (PUBYEAR, 2018) OR LIMIT-TO (PUBYEAR, 2017) OR LIMIT- TO (PUBYEAR, 2016) OR LIMIT-TO (PUBYEAR, 2015) OR LIMIT- TO (PUBYEAR, 2013) OR LIMIT-TO (PUBYEAR, 2012))	204
2.	Limiting to English language	201

Source: Authors.

13.3.3 CRITICAL APPRAISAL

To appraise the selected studies critically, three criteria were established: 1) For each study, a binary category (Relevant/Not Relevant) was assigned after reviewing the title and abstract of the paper. 2) Studies with conclusive findings, implications, and evidence related to the research question were used. 3) Research papers from journals related to the marketing field were mostly excluded because the study's aim did not involve probing customer perspectives. Further, all possible efforts were made to obtain the non-accessible research articles through emails. The critical appraisal was conducted at two levels. First, at the initial level, 102 articles were shortlisted on the basis of the title and abstract. Out of 102 articles, 10 articles were not available for download due to restricted access granted by the publisher. At the second level, I read the whole research article to include relevant studies for data extraction. After reading the whole article, 20 studies were found to be irrelevant to the research objectives and were hence excluded from the study. Finally, 72 publications were reviewed (Figure 13.1).

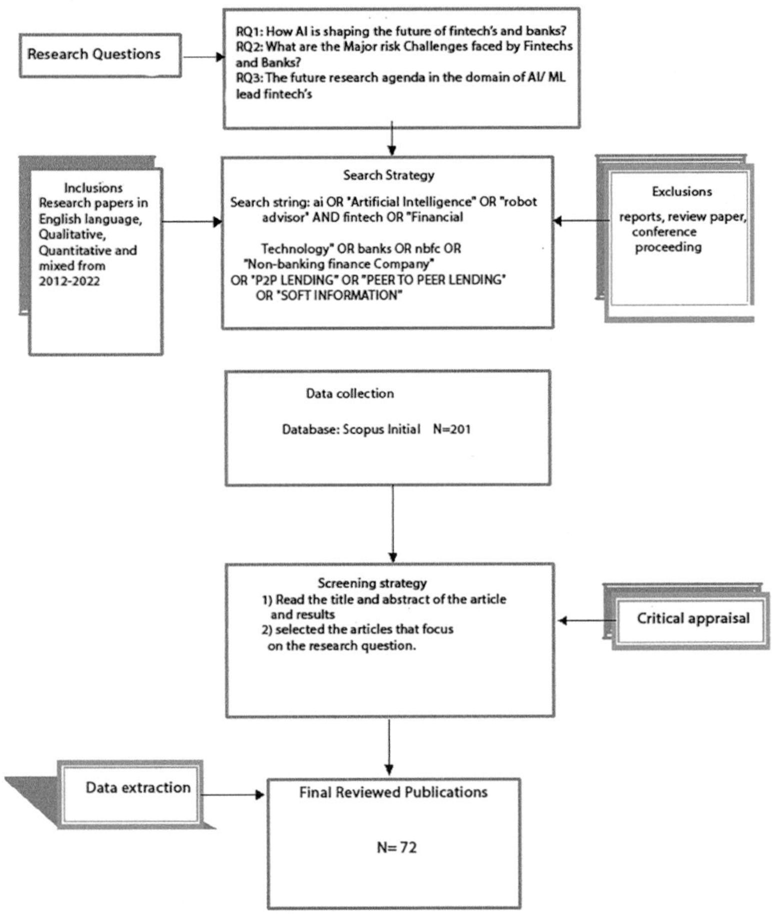

FIGURE 13.1 PRISMA flow diagram of SLR process.

13.3.4 DATA EXTRACTION

The research publications' geographical distribution based on the corresponding author's country of origin is as follows: authors from the USA (14%, N=10), India (14%, N=10), the United Kingdom (14%, N=10), France (11%, N=8), China (8%, N=6), and the remainder from various other countries. The majority of studies utilized quantitative research methods (N=37), while some employed qualitative research methods (N=8), mixed methods (N=1), and review papers (N=26). To address the first research question (RQ1), all selected publications were reviewed to extract insights on how AI is shaping the future of FinTech and banks. For the second research question (RQ2), all publications were scrutinized to identify the major risks and challenges faced by both traditional banks and FinTech companies. The third research question aims to outline the future research agenda in the domain of AI/ML-led FinTech.

13.4 RESULTS AND ANALYSIS

To answer RQ1 (The present state of research in AI) and how it is shaping the future of FinTech's and banks?) analysis of published literature has been synthesized in the following section.

13.4.1 INTELLECTUAL STRUCTURE OF RESEARCH IN AI AND HOW IT'S SHAPING THE FUTURE OF FINTECH'S AND BANKS?

After an extensive study of the existing body of knowledge and contribution of prominent researchers, we identified and summarized the findings of RQ1 in five clusters. First, chatbot emerged as new customer executives (Boustani, 2021; De Andrade and Tumelero, 2022; Gigante and Zago, 2022). Second, FinTech promotes financial inclusion and financial stability (Daud et al., 2022; Ravikumar, 2019). Third, AI reduces financial frauds and fosters investor's confidence and increase the profitability (Ashta and Herrmann, 2021; Hilal et al., 2022; Roszkowska, 2020). Fourth, peer-to-peer lending platforms are exhibiting greater credit default assessment (Boot et al., 2021; Dhote et al., 2020; Gao et al., 2021; Messai and Gallali, 2015). Fifth and last, clients and investors has shown confidence in the robo-advisory services offered by the FinTech (Gigante and Zago, 2022; Northey et al., 2022).

13.4.1.1 CHATBOTS EMERGING AS NEW CUSTOMER EXECUTIVES

The ultimate goal of digital transformation is to digitalize the customer's journey, with the help of Virtual financial assistants to improve customer service and real-time interaction (Naimi-Sadigh et al., 2021). AI chatbot is the first layer of service, AI chatbot is more assertive, fast, effective, and functioning than traditional customer service, which brings efficiency to customer service. With the cognitive evolution of AI, chatbot at call centers have reduced the waiting lines which give human more time to solve complex queries of the customer (De Andrade and Tumelero, 2022), Virtual assistant via Chats or calls have led to a notable decrease in the work volume of call centers, hence reduces the operational cost. Further, the personalized content included personalization of offerings, display of selected content, and location-based services to send real-time notifications to the customers (Gigante and Zago, 2022). AI is perceived to possess superior problem-solving capability and is preferred by customers for less complex tasks whereas Customers depend on human customer service support for dealing with high-level complex tasks. With AI technology usage, bank customers feel highly satisfied but at the same time, customer feels that AI cannot reduce the need for customer representatives. AI cannot be a substitute for manpower but rather technical assistance (Boustani, 2021).

13.4.1.2 PROMOTING FINANCIAL INCLUSION AND FINANCIAL STABILITY

FinTech has emerged as a fundamental part of the (Indian) banking system and changing businesses and customers (Srivastava and Dhamija, 2022). The internal resistance to change in traditional banks have resulted in the growing gap that FinTech startups have filled. The well-designed and user-friendly FinTech platforms aimed at enhancing the customer experience with financial pieces of advice and low fees on the asset under management have resulted in cost savings for the investors (Nicoletti et al., 2017). On one hand the inability of financial institutions to serve individuals across various regions exists whereas on the other hand, FinTech companies can reach various regions and various income groups with convenient and affordable financial services (Ravikumar, 2019). FinTech promotes financial inclusion in emerging economies by providing small and medium enterprises access to the financial markets. Factors like AI, data technology, and cloud technology have an uplifting influence on financial stability. Thus, FinTech and financial stability are positively correlated (Daud et al., 2022), but grave cyber-attacks presents a bigger risk to financial stability as the interconnected nature of the world (Vučinić and Luburić, 2022). With rapid digital transformation, there arise a dire need of amended regulations to keep up with new financial technology and also protect the customer and the overall financial system (Cao and Zhai, 2022).

13.4.1.3 AI REDUCES FINANCIAL FRAUD, BUILDS INVESTOR'S CONFIDENCE, AND INCREASES PROFITABILITY

Since 2017, there has been a growth in research on AI and ML in FinTech. AI is useful in bankruptcy prediction, stock price prediction, portfolio management, anti-money laundering, and behavioral finance (Ahmed et al., 2022). AI and ML techniques are useful in the detection of financial frauds such as credit card fraud, insurance, and health-related fraud (Hilal, et al., 2022; Milana and Ashta, 2021). The ML algorithms decreases the financial fraud and results in fast detection of fraud and customization of services based on consumer buying behavior (Ashta and Herrmann, 2021). The accounting scandals have created a trust deficit among investors and casted doubt on role of audit firms. Emerging technology like blockchain, smart contracts, and ML can help in fraud detection. ML technologies can analyze big data sets more accurately. Moreover, it has been highlighted from the accounting frauds/scandals that audit firms gave priority to revenue over intrinsic audit objectives. The emerging technology can mitigate the risk of accounting fraud (Roszkowska, 2020). Most advisory firms like McKinsey, and Deloitte pointed out that the quality of data is important in AI in anti-money laundering activities. AI is making promising developments in the field of finance; however, AI in banking is in its early phase. The key applications include asset pricing, stock return prediction, and sentiment analysis.

AI has an excellent ability to discover the non-linear relationship over traditional models (Hendershott et al., 2021). AI is also disrupting the real estate industry and the focus has been shifted from "location, location, and location" to "data, data, and data" (Cajias, 2020).

The motivating factors behind the implementation of AI in banks are increasing competition, changing preferences of customers, regulatory requirements, changing the behavior of fraudsters, and the scale of business networks. Authors had shown how AI can entail positive results by addressing the above-mentioned factors in a systematic way (Königstorfer and Thalmann, 2020). FinTech companies foster competition in the financial markets by providing a wide range of financial services to customers but they cannot replace the core function of financial institutions. The alliance of FinTech and commercial banks can provide mutual benefits (Mavlutova et al., 2021). Managers hold substantial influence in implementing AI technology for promoting financial services and managers should work on making the customer aware of the AI technology. Moreover, the AI system should also incorporate algorithmic accountability to bring effective control (Mogaji and Nguyen, 2021).

Sharma et al., 2021 proposed that Genetic Algorithm (GA) and Artificial Neural Network (ANN) are very useful ML techniques for stock market forecasting whereas Singh et al. (2021) explained that financial technology adoption has shown a significant optimistic impact on the return on assets (ROA) and return on equity (ROE). The technological disruption has reduced the long queues at the branches and enabling enhanced profitability by reducing the employee headcount. Location intelligence technology helps the bank to manage their branch networks with the aggregation of data from all branches and divisions facilitating comparative analysis with customer activities, competing banks, and other statistical information (Yusupova et al., 2020). Moreover, Salameh and Lutfi (2021) identified that the magnitude of AI played an important role in fraud detection and limiting cyber frauds.

13.4.1.4 P2P LENDING PLATFORMS AND BETTER LOAN DEFAULT PREDICTION

The IT sector revolution of the 1990s has increased the reliance on the use of hard information which gave rise to securitization, increased competition, and bank consolidation. The FinTech platforms challenge the vertical and horizontal integration of the banks. The profusion of non-financial data gives an advantage to online platforms by weakening the bank's role as the "first point of contact" for financial services (Boot et al., 2021). IT development has increased the acquisition of soft information (Jakšič and Marinč, 2019). Anil and Misra (2022) explained how AI is a game changer for P2P markets in India. The major reasons are ease of loan applications, the quick turnaround time for loan disbursal, better experience for customers, no lock-in period, and prepayment charges. AI and ML can signal more information through the use of social media networks and digital footprints (Mhlanga, 2021). AI/ML models such as neural networks and classifier consensus technique have better corporate default prediction accuracy compared to traditional models. (Ala'raj and Abbod, 2016; Fraisse and Laporte, 2022). Google, Apple, Facebook, and Amazon global technology giants are posing a major threat to traditional banks by attracting the millennials, open banking initiatives and a large amount of data available on their platforms reveal behavioral information of the users (potential borrowers) which helps to take better lending decisions (Dhote et al., 2020). In Spain, traditional banks compete in dynamic environment via disruptive solutions. It has also transformed the customer's habit very fast through superior value creation. (Visconti- Caparrós and Campos-Blázquez, 2021).

In 2016, the lending club's (FinTech company) inefficiency ratio was lower than the incumbent banks which means higher lending efficiency attributed to the accurate credit evaluation using advanced technology and complex Algorithms (Hughes et al., 2022). Jagtiani and Lemieux (2019) explained that the correlation between Lending club's (FinTech co.) rating grades and FICO score has sharply dropped from 80% in 2007 to 35% in 2015 due to increased use of alternative data sources. The rating grades are considered an effective tool for isolating the 'invisible prime' borrowers from the substandard borrowers. The high best practice ratio of the lending club exhibits higher inherent risk-taking that does not mean inappropriate risk-taking, it shows inherent risk-taking in a way to enhance the market value of the lenders (Hughes et al., 2022). Gao et al (2021) highlighted that the soft voting fusion model shows higher accuracy in predicting the credit risk of SMEs than any single machine learning algorithm, which has been advantageously used in China.

Even a slight improvement in accuracy in credit risk evaluation can bring huge savings to financial institutions. Though the overall impact of bank FinTech is positive on credit risk evaluation but AI gives rise to a new form of risk that is technical risk and regulatory risk (Cheng and Qu, 2020). Jabeur et al. (2021) criticized the weakness of the traditional models due to classification performance which increases the cost to investors and creditors and explained the relevance of the catboost model (ML technique) in predicting the financial distress of the firms. Further, the Receiver operating characteristic (ROC) of the catboost model is higher than other techniques which explains the accuracy in default prediction (Boot et al., 2021). LV et al. (2022) demonstrated the superior prediction accuracy along with lower prediction error compared to other algorithms models in default prediction. The sophisticated features of ML offers advantages to make the models unbiased (Brotcke, 2022). The comparative study was conducted by Messai and Gallali (2015) to analyze the performance of traditional models includes logit probit, discriminant analysis, and the Artificial Neural networks model in banking distress prediction concluded that the best prediction is obtained by using ANNs model. Furthermore, a comparative analysis of ML techniques in bank failure prediction concluded that support vector machine and RBF-NN demonstrated the highest predictive performance, on the other hand, principal component analysis has the lowest predictive power and it turned out to be ineffective (Erdal and Ekinci, 2013). ML models were applied to predict the credit rating of the banks belonging to the Gulf Cooperation Council (GCC). GCC nations are oil-producing nations and over the past years made significant efforts to diversify their revenue. They pointed out that the Random forest model has the highest precision followed by Artificial Neural Networks (ANN) for default prediction. Furthermore, the classification and regression tree (CART) and RF models were relevant for stressed banks to make better risk assessments (Li et al., 2020). The studies on P2P lending are geographically skewed with the majority of the research have been conducted in U.S.A. and China. The P2P lending platforms are regulated in the U.S. by S.E.C whereas, in the UK, it is self-regulated. Further, regulatory developments are the predominant factors influencing the growth of platforms and loan origination in developing economies (Basha et al., 2021).

13.4.1.5 DEVELOPMENT OF ROBO-ADVISORY SERVICES IN FINANCE

Robot advisors make use of the automated algorithm to give investment advice to the investor using mobile or online platforms. Robot advisors are inexpensive as compare to traditional private bankers. Though, there are certain security and incomplete sales concerns that need to be addressed. In a study, based on primary data, the findings revealed that three variables determine the robot-advisor acceptability. First is Income, individuals with greater income are less eager to invest in robot-advisor. The finding is consistent with the study conducted by Northey et al. (2022) which explains that there is lesser trust on robot advisor in situations involving high-involvement of consumers. The second variable is the value invested in instruments which reflects the investor's risk aversion. Investors which are risk-lover investors are more disposed towards robot-advisor. The third is investment knowledge. People with a lack of investment knowledge or awareness across all demographic spectrums are less likely to adopt a robot advisor (Kraiwanit et al., 2022).

The two factors associated with the adoption of rates of robot-financial advisors are cultural boundedness and social capital (trust). The banks should focus on AI introduction and Robo- advisors in those markets where there is a lack of social capital; this will improve brand loyalty (Tubadji et al., 2021). The advisory services through AI include savings tips and high-level investment and trading advices based on market dynamics (Gigante and Zago, 2022). RA is an auxiliary function. The hybrid control model in introducing the RA will disrupt slowly (Wexler and Oberlander, 2021).

The extensive use of AI and ML in the short term is highly unlikely to lead to market concentration in the financial sector. While, over the long haul, amalgamating the boundaries of big tech and financial markets will escalate concentration but the regulations may force it in opposite direction (Grout, 2021). Rasiwala and Kohli (2021) conducted a study based on qualitative research through in-depth and semi-structured interviews with professionals from the financial sector. The study explained that most of the experts (participants) were of the view that FinTech could not thrive without banks and banks will equally require FinTech platforms. In the future, the disruption will be less as we can see the integration of FinTech platforms and banks for providing banking solutions.

13.4.2 WHAT ARE THE MAJOR RISKS AND CHALLENGES THAT AI-ENABLED FINTECH AND BANKS MIGHT FACE IN THE FUTURE?

Referring to RQ2, we have identified and selected studies that emphasize the risks and challenges faced by AI-enabled FinTech and banks. We have summarized the following risks, namely unemployment, privacy, and security risk (Ali, 2020; Ashta and Biot-Paquerot, 2018; Boninsegni et al., 2021; Zhang et al., 2021), as well as challenges related to data quality, algorithm bias, and ethical issues (Anshari et al., 2021; Ashta and Herrmann, 2021; Brotcke, 2022; Das et al., 2019; Veloso et al., 2021). Furthermore, there are doubts about credit default prediction (Ariza-Garzon et al., 2021; Fraisse and Laporte, 2022; Sadok et al., 2022) and regulatory and financial instability risks posed by the FinTech lending platforms (Coetzee, 2018; Gallo, 2021; Gąsiorkiewicz et al., 2020; Ölvedi, 2021). Despite the many advantages of AI-enabled FinTech or big tech platforms, one cannot negate the challenges and risks posed by these platforms. For instance, the e-wallet service provider in China has provided an automatic sweep of leftover balance feature in the e-wallet, which allows users to transfer money to Money Market Funds (MMF), managed by another wealth management company that is a subsidiary of the big tech. The MMFs invest the leftover balances in CDs, commercial paper, and repurchase agreements. The instant redemption of money invested in MMFs through e-wallets can result in the transformation of fund risk and can adversely impact the financial system (RBI bulletin, October 2022). Recently, the Reserve Bank of India has curbed the buy now pay later FinTech segment, as it was observed that FinTech was bypassing the regulation in the name of innovation. RBI is also working to bring FinTech players under the umbrella of regulations so that pre-paid instruments (PPI) are not used as credit avenues.

13.4.2.1 UNEMPLOYMENT, DATA PRIVACY, AND SECURITY RISK

AI is a multi-edged sword; though it provides benefits, there is a dark side to it. Over-leveraging technology will create labor displacement and growing inequality (Nguyen et al., 2022). AI and ML may eliminate many jobs in the financial services labor market (Das, 2019; Poloz, 2021). In Bangladesh, unemployment is a major threat posed by the digitalization of the economy (Ali, 2020). FinTechs are expected to increase the workforce by only 19% over the next decade, whereas the adoption of AI by the incumbents is expected to result in a 9% job loss. Considering the fact that the median FinTech company employs less than 50 people compared to the median incumbent, which employs over 10,000 people, this 19%

increase is far less than the 9% decrease in absolute terms. Hence, the threat of a reduction in employment is confirmed (Zhang et al., 2021).

Various challenges still exist and need to be addressed. First, there is a digital divide; for instance, young people are more tech-savvy than older individuals, and there is an urban and rural divide (Ashta and Biot-Paquerot, 2018). Second, there are issues related to discomfort and mistrust among people regarding international transactions, and jurisdictional issues are also very complex (Ashta and Biot-Paquerot, 2018). Third, there are privacy issues (Ashta and Biot-Paquerot, 2018; Boninsegni et al., 2021) and security breach concerns. Furthermore, financial institutions may exploit the personal information of customers, offering low-cost services to premium customers while discriminating against other segments if the data is not concealed (Boninsegni et al., 2021).

In Poland, customers are highly sensitive about the use of financial and personal data, and they have expressed their concerns regarding the use of data against their will. The results highlighted that customers' lack of knowledge about the applications of AI and its impact on the perceived ethicality of bank operations may create an obstacle to the acceptance of innovative information technology (Piotrowski, 2022). The digital payment system and platforms have resulted in the decentralization of insurance and financial institutions' databases and have also lowered the intermediate cost by eliminating bankers and agents. However, it has also increased the risk of privacy and security breaches (Boninsegni et al., 2021). A descriptive study explained the benefits of the digital debt collection ecosystem but also cautioned against the negative aspects of intensified surveillance of borrowers (Dawn, 2020). The face recognition payment method in China attracted public attention, but people doubt the use of personal information by the platforms without consent. Furthermore, there are no perfect laws and regulations related to face recognition in China (Zhang et al., 2021).

13.4.2.2 DATA QUALITY, ALGORITHM BIASES, AND ETHICAL CHALLENGES

There are several flaws in implementing AI in FinTech successfully: 1) Garbage in, Garbage out; 2) Problem of information overload; 3) Quality of the data; 4) Excessive sloppy automation may result in poor customer experience (Das, 2019). ML uses data for decision-making; if the data is non-representative, then it becomes difficult to make accurate (right) decisions. Furthermore, the data should be free from bias (Ashta and Herrmann, 2021). Anshari et al. (2021) highlighted the ethical challenges of racial, gender, language, and religion-based discrimination with AI-enabled FinTechs. The problem of discrimination or unfairness in lending can be due to unwanted bias in the training dataset during the learning phase, which may result in the algorithm incorporating it. To subdue this concern, developers must have substantial knowledge and understanding of input and output variables. "The most effective way to evaluate the lending-related unfairness is to compare the model-based decisions across different gender and racial groups" (Brotcke, 2022). There is a possibility that algorithms may be designed by the developer to discriminate. Tokic (2018) raised the concern over robot-controlled decision-making in the stock market, presuming that if all computer programs have a similar dataset and the same decision rule, then it can lead to the same trading decisions, which makes the financial markets open to bubbles and busts. The problem of algorithm bias and the inability of the organization to extract true value from the data collected creates the problem of data swamps; hence, the company will incur high data storage costs to maintain the data (Nguyen et al., 2022). Bhatia et al. (2021) illustrated via qualitative research that robo-advisory services are at a nascent stage in India; therefore, wealth management experts have highlighted the need for better risk profiling models. Moreover, the robo-advisors were not able to address the problems of behavioral bias, which tells us that reaching the highest level of AI in financial services will take time. Recent work by Veloso et al. (2021) elucidates the seven challenges for AI in finance. These are the eradication of financial crime, liberating the data safely, predicting and affecting the economic system, enhancing the client experience, empowering the employees, enhancing policy compliance, and making AI more socially and ethically relevant. AI can be more effective if the researcher trains the data in large quantities on representative data, as real data is not available due to the confidential nature of financial data and more stringent regulations in place.

13.4.2.3 DOUBTS ON CREDIT DEFAULT PREDICTION

This section is mainly dedicated to the studies that question the credit default prediction ability of AI and ML models. In total, we found seven such studies. There is disagreement among the various FinTech platforms regarding the usefulness of big data scores in default prediction. The opacity associated with the AI methods makes it difficult to know what factors the algorithm will select for prediction. Further, banks are stuck in a dichotomy of whether they should focus on using big data for more accurate default prediction to adhere to the BASEL norms or adhere to the data protection laws (Sadok et al., 2022).

Most of the studies centered on credit risk assessment using ML techniques lack interpretability and explainability, which hinders adoption (Ariza-Garzon et al., 2021; Fraisse and Laporte, 2022). As the AI models suffer criticism because they lack explainability, a study executed by Bussmann et al. (2021) recommended a combination of network analysis with Shapley value theory. Most ML and AI algorithms are open source and free, but the financial data on which they are trained is limited and owned by the incumbent institutions. The existing institutions can make the most out of it and prevent new entrants from entering the market (Bholat and Susskind, 2021). Machine-based decisions are too rigid and will give a limited number of outcomes; however, human discretion may optimize the overall variables (Costello et al., 2020). AI could impose additional risks that are very hard to model, unlike standardized problems mentioned by Shustova and Blagoev (2018) in their research on risk management in internet banking, demonstrating the case study of Kazakhstan.

13.4.2.4 REGULATORY RISK AND FINANCIAL INSTABILITY

Peer-to-peer lending is a novel approach to lending, and there is credit risk involved in it (Ölvedi, 2021). Gallo (2021) findings revealed that lending platforms fail to track some of the misreporting borrowers, which harms lenders' collections performance, and his findings also cautioned the lenders while making investment decisions. To survive in the long run, the P2P lending platforms should migrate from the credit scoring approach to the profit-scoring approach, which is investor-centric and based on an annualized rate of return on loan (Lyócsa et al., 2022). Xia et al. (2022) classify the characteristics of P2P platforms as basic characteristics, which include company background, registered capital, region, and creditor's rights transfer. For example, a platform with a low capital base tends to become a problematic platform. Excessive reliance on information and technology can increase risk-taking behavior and raise systematic risk in the financial system. Relationship banking will act as a force to mitigate such risks (Jakšič and Marinč, 2019). The regulatory risk includes inadequate disclosures, opportunities for regulatory arbitrage, and missing coordination among the supervising bodies (Gąsiorkiewicz et al., 2020). The big techs have greater potential to disrupt both incumbents and FinTech, given their access to vast data and capability in leveraging AI solutions (Zhang et al., 2021). The bank's engagement with the client in the coming age is expected to differ from past interactions. Moreover, it will be a greater matter of concern how FinTechs will be regulated. Failure at the regulatory level can make the banking industry fragile (Coetzee, 2018).

13.4.3 FUTURE RESEARCH AGENDA IN THE DOMAIN OF AI/ ML LEAD FINTECHS

At present, developed nations have emerged as major contributors to the existing body of knowledge on AI and ML in the finance field. The developing nations have scarce literature on the role of AI and predominantly deal with theoretical papers and very few empirical studies. Additionally, the empirical research papers focus on the accuracy and precision of ML models in credit default prediction.

Future studies should explore whether the lending platforms have allowed borrowers to become over-leveraged (Jagtiani and Lemieux, 2019). Future research can be oriented towards studying the measures to mitigate the security, privacy, and credit risks posed by AI-enabled technology. In the future, research should be directed towards comparing various ML techniques in the field of finance (Ahmed et al., 2022). Future work can center on the long-term sustainability of FinTech platforms and the comparative profitability analysis of local NBFCs and AI-enabled lending platforms.

13.5 DISCUSSION AND IMPLICATIONS

The systematic review will contribute to the existing pool of literature on the role of AI and its function in financial technology by addressing the research questions through a careful assessment and analysis of the selected publications. The majority of the assessed research was descriptive and qualitative, though very few quantitative studies focus on the accuracy of ML models over traditional statistical techniques for default prediction. The conclusion of the study is that factors like internal workings, legacy systems, and regulatory restrictions of conventional banks have generated opportunities for FinTech businesses. With the advancement of AI, banks face severe competition from FinTech companies. FinTechs have altered consumer service delivery and compelled banks to reconsider their service orientation. The dark side of AI chatbots is employment loss (Gigante and Zago, 2022). AI chatbots offer more than FAQs, reduce the strain on call centers, and lower the cost of operations, but they also result in job loss (Zhang et al., 2021). FinTech is encouraging financial inclusion in the financial markets by focusing mostly on underserved and SME segments. FinTechs support financial stability (Daud et al., 2022), but failing to regulate FinTech can weaken the banking sector (Coetzee, 2018).

One of the major achievements of AI can be gauged from financial fraud prevention and detection that benefited customers and financial institutions by preventing the loss of millions of dollars and, further, improved the ROAs and ROEs. FinTechs collect soft information from social media websites, and ML techniques such as Random Forest, Support Vector Machine, and Artificial Neural Networks give a competitive edge to the P2P lending platforms over incumbent banks. It was also evident from past studies that the use of soft information, along with hard information, enhances the probability of correct prediction of default. In contrast, Sadok et al. (2022) raised the question of the empirical evidence regarding the usefulness of big data in default prediction, and a study conducted by Di Maggio and Yao (2021) has demonstrated that FinTech borrowers have a greater probability of default compared to borrowers of traditional financial institutions because the indebtedness of FinTech borrowers increases more after the origination of the loan. Credit appraisal through soft information is being adopted by incumbent banks; hence, it may lose its competitive advantage in a few years' time frame. Further, cross-selling across subsidiaries and integration of data can actually help large banks acquire market share and shun the small platforms, especially during or after crises (like COVID-19). Additionally, the RBI, in its bulletin released in October 2022, has cautioned against the systematic risk posed by the transformation of funds via securitization and seamless redemption from the MMFs. Nevertheless, most of the studies during the literature review have concluded that the utilization of alternative data and ML techniques mitigates credit risk. None of the studies said that FinTech will replace commercial banks, as FinTech is primarily focused on serving the underserved segments and has a different target customer base. In the future, we can see an integration of banks and FinTech platforms.

13.6 LIMITATIONS OF THE STUDY

Our study has some limitations. First, the SLR conducted has excluded conference papers, book chapters, and grey literature, which may carry a few more perspectives. Although it is a common practice in systematic reviews (Pittaway and Cope, 2007), this exclusion is noteworthy. Second, the SLR conducted was based on research papers extracted from only one database, that is, Scopus. Nonetheless, Scopus is the most widely used database for business and management, but it is better to use more than one database for SLR (Bramer et al., 2017). This chapter provides insight for professionals and bankers across the world. AI will help improve business strategies and create customer value. This chapter signals to the watchdogs to play a proactive role in regulating FinTech companies and protecting customers' interests in the financial markets.

KEYWORDS

- **artificial intelligence**
- **big tech**
- **commercial banks**
- **credit risk assessment**
- **fintech**
- **machine learning**
- **money market funds**
- **peer-to-peer lending**
- **robot advisors**
- **systematic literature review**

REFERENCES

Ahmed, S., et al. (2022). Artificial intelligence and machine learning in finance: A bibliometric review. *Research in International Business and Finance*, *61*, 101646.

Ala'raj, M., & Abbod, M. F. (2016). Classifiers consensus system approach for credit scoring. *Knowledge-Based Systems*, *104*, 89–105.

Ali, M. M. (2020). Digitization of the emerging economy: An exploratory and explanatory case study. *Journal of Governance and Regulation*, *9*(4), 25–36.

Alsmadi, A. A., Alrawashdeh, N., Al-Gasaymeh, A., Al-Malahmeh, H., & Moh'd Al_hazimeh, A. (2023). Impact of business enablers on banking performance: A moderating role of FinTech. *Banks and Bank Systems*, *18*(1), 14–25.

Alzoubi, H. M., Alshurideh, M. T., & Ghazal, T. M. (2024). *Cyber Security Impact on Digitalization and Business Intelligence: Big Cyber Security for Information Management: Opportunities and Challenges*.

Amstad, M. (2019). Regulating FinTech: Objectives, principles, and practices. *Asian Development Bank Institute Working Paper Series*, *1016*.

Anil, K., & Misra, A. (2022). Artificial intelligence in peer-to-peer lending in India: A cross-case analysis. *International Journal of Emerging Markets, ahead-of-print*(ahead-of-print).

Anshari, M., et al. (2021). Financial technology with AI-enabled and ethical challenges. *Society*, *58*(3), 189–195.

Ariza-Garzon, M. J., Segovia-Vargas, M. J., & Arroyo, J. (2021). Risk-return modelling in the P2P lending market: Trends, gaps, recommendations and future directions. *Electronic Commerce Research and Applications*, *49*, 101079.

Ashta, A., & Biot-Paquerot, G. (2018). FinTech evolution: Strategic value management issues in a fast-changing industry. *Strategic Change*, *27*(4), 301–311.

Ashta, A., & Herrmann, H. (2021). Artificial intelligence and FinTech: An overview of opportunities and risks for banking, investments, and microfinance. *Strategic Change*, *30*(3), 211–222.

Badali, M., Hatami, J., Banihashem, S. K., Rahimi, E., Noroozi, O., & Eslami, Z. (2022). The role of motivation in MOOCs' retention rates: A systematic literature review. *Research and Practice in Technology Enhanced Learning*, *17*(1), 5.

Basha, S. A., Elgammal, M. M., & Abuzayed, B. M. (2021). Online peer-to-peer lending: A review of the literature. *Electronic Commerce Research and Applications*, *48*, 101069.

Bean, R. (2018). How FinTech initiatives are driving financial services innovation. *Forbes*. https://www.forbes.com/sites/ciocentral/2018/07/10/how-FinTech-initiatives-are-driving-financial-services-innovation/ (accessed on 7th July 2025).

Berg, T., et al. (2020). On the rise of FinTechs: Credit scoring using digital footprints. *The Review of Financial Studies*, *33*(7), 2845–2897.

Bhatia, A., Chandani, A., & Chhateja, J. (2020). Robo advisory and its potential in addressing the behavioral biases of investors—A qualitative study in Indian context. *Journal of Behavioral and Experimental Finance*, *25*, 100281.

Bholat, D., & Susskind, D. (2021). The assessment: Artificial intelligence and financial services. *Oxford Review of Economic Policy*, *37*(3), 417–434.

Boninsegni, M. F., et al. (2021). Opportunities of and threats to consumer well-being in the age of Fourth Industrial Revolution (IR 4.0) technologies. *Digital Policy, Regulation and Governance*.

Boot, A., et al. (2021). FinTech: What's old, what's new? *Journal of Financial Stability*, *53*, 100836.
Boustani, N. M. (2021). Artificial intelligence impact on banks clients and employees in an Asian developing country. *Journal of Asia Business Studies*.
Bower, J. L., & Christensen, C. M. (1995). Disruptive technologies: Catching the wave. *Harvard Business Review*, 43–53.
Bramer, W. M., et al. (2017). Optimal database combinations for literature searches in systematic reviews: A prospective exploratory study. *Systematic Reviews*, *6*(1), 1–12.
Brotcke, L. (2022). Time to assess bias in machine learning models for credit decisions. *Journal of Risk and Financial Management*, *15*(4), 165.
Buchak, G., et al. (2018). FinTech, regulatory arbitrage, and the rise of shadow banks. *Journal of Financial Economics*, *130*(3), 453–483.
Burton, D. (2020). Digital debt collection and ecologies of consumer over indebtedness. *Economic Geography*, *96*(3), 244–265.
Bussmann, N., Giudici, P., Marinelli, D., & Papenbrock, J. (2021). Explainable machine learning in credit risk management. *Computational Economics*, *57*, 203–216.
Cajias, M. (2020). Artificial intelligence and real estate—not just an evolution, a real game changer. *Journal of Property Investment & Finance*.
Cao, Y., & Zhai, J. (2022). A survey of AI in finance. *Journal of Chinese Economic and Business Studies*, 1–13.
Cheng, M., & Qu, Y. (2020). Does bank FinTech reduce credit risk? Evidence from China. *Pacific-Basin Finance Journal*, *63*, 101398.
Choudhary, P., & Thenmozhi, M. (2024). FinTech and financial sector: ADO analysis and future research agenda. *International Review of Financial Analysis*.
Coetzee, J. (2018). Strategic implications of FinTech on South African retail banks. *South African Journal of Economic and Management Sciences*, *21*(1), 1–11.
Costello, A. M., Down, A. K., & Mehta, M. N. (2020). Machine + man: A field experiment on the role of discretion in augmenting AI-based lending models. *Journal of Accounting and Economics*, *70*(2–3), 101360.
Das, S. R. (2019). The future of FinTech. *Financial Management*, *48*(4), 981–1007.
Daud, S. N. M., Khalid, A., & Azman-Saini, W. (2022). FinTech and financial stability: Threat or opportunity? *Finance Research Letters*, *47*, 102667.
De Andrade, I. M., & Tumelero, C. (2022). Increasing customer service efficiency through artificial intelligence chatbot. *Revista de Gestão*.
Deloitte India. (2017). *FinTech India | FinTech Industry Analysis/Trends*. https://www2.deloitte.com/in/en/pages/financial-services/articles/FinTech-india-ready-for-breakout.html (accessed on 7th July 2025).
Dewey, A., & Drahota, A. (2016). *Introduction to Systematic Reviews: Online Learning Module*. Cochrane Interactive Learning.
Dhote, T., Pathak, P., & Kulkarni, P. (2020). Coping with the challenges posed by GAFA and other digital disruptors: Can advanced technologies help the banking sector? *International Journal of Scientific and Technology Research*, *9*(2), 2196–2199.
Di Maggio, M., & Yao, V. (2021). FinTech borrowers: Lax screening or cream-skimming? *The Review of Financial Studies*, *34*(10), 4565–4618.
Erdal, H. I., & Ekinci, A. (2013). A comparison of various artificial intelligence methods in the prediction of bank failures. *Computational Economics*, *42*(2), 199–215.

Financial Stability Board. (2022). *FSB Report Finds That COVID-19 has Accelerated the Trend Towards Digitalisation of Retail Financial Services*. https://www.fsb.org/2022/03/fsb-report-finds-that-covid-19-has-accelerated-the-trend-towards-digitalisation-of-retail-financial-services/ (accessed on 7th July 2025).

Fraisse, H., & Laporte, M. (2022). Return on investment on artificial intelligence: The case of bank capital requirement. *Journal of Banking & Finance*, *138*, 106401.

Gallo, S. (2021). FinTech platforms: Lax or careful borrowers' screening? *Financial Innovation*, *7*(1), 1–33.

Gao, G., Wang, H., & Gao, P. (2021). Establishing a credit risk evaluation system for SMEs using the soft voting fusion model. *Risks*, *9*(11), 202.

Gąsiorkiewicz, L., Monkiewicz, J., & Monkiewicz, M. (2020). Technology-driven innovations in financial services: The rise of alternative finance. *Foundations of Management*, *12*(1), 137–150.

Gigante, G., & Zago, A. (2022). DARQ technologies in the financial sector: Artificial intelligence applications in personalized banking. *Qualitative Research in Financial Markets*

Grout, P. A. (2021). AI, ML, and competition dynamics in financial markets. *Oxford Review of Economic Policy*, *37*(3), 618–635. https://doi.org/10.1093/oxrep/grab014 (accessed on 7th July 2025).

Hendershott, T., et al. (2021). FinTech as a game changer: Overview of research frontiers. *Information Systems Research*, *32*(1), 1–17.

Hentzen, J. K., Hoffmann, A., Dolan, R., & Pala, E. (2022). Artificial intelligence in customer-facing financial services: A systematic literature review and agenda for future research. *International Journal of Bank Marketing*, *40*(6), 1299–1336. https://doi.org/10.1108/IJBM-09-2021-0417 (accessed on 7th July 2025).

Hilal, W., Gadsden, S. A., & Yawney, J. (2022). Financial fraud: A review of anomaly detection techniques and recent advances.

Hughes, J. P., Jagtiani, J., & Moon, C. G. (2022). Consumer lending efficiency: Commercial banks versus a FinTech lender. *Financial Innovation*, *8*(1), 1–39.

Jabeur, S. B., et al. (2021). CatBoost model and artificial intelligence techniques for corporate failure prediction. *Technological Forecasting and Social Change*, *166*, 120658.

Jagtiani, J., & Lemieux, C. (2019). The roles of alternative data and machine learning in FinTech lending: Evidence from the LendingClub consumer platform. *Financial Management*, *48*(4), 1009–1029.

Jakšič, M., & Marinč, M. (2019). Relationship banking and information technology: The role of artificial intelligence and FinTech. *Risk Management*, *21*(1), 1–18.

Jiang, Z., Ma, G., & Zhu, W. (2022). Research on the impact of digital finance on the innovation performance of enterprises. *European Journal of Innovation Management*, *25*(6), 804–820.

Karaman, H. D., Savaser, T., Tiniç, M., & Tumer-Alkan, G. (2021). Financial technology in developing economies: A note on digital lending in Turkey. *Economics Letters*, *207*, 110012.

Königstorfer, F., & Thalmann, S. (2020). Applications of artificial intelligence in commercial banks–A research agenda for behavioral finance. *Journal of Behavioral and Experimental Finance*, *27*, 100352.

Kraiwanit, T., Jangjarat, K., & Atcharanuwat, J. (2022). The acceptance of financial robo-advisors among investors: The emerging market study. *Journal of Governance and Regulation*, *11*(2).

Li, J. P., et al. (2020). Machine learning and credit ratings prediction in the age of fourth industrial revolution. *Technological Forecasting and Social Change*, *161*, 120309.

Liberti, J. M., Seru, A., & Vig, V. (2016). Information, credit, and organization. *Credit, and Organization* (June 2016).

Lockwood, C., & Oh, E. G. (2017). Systematic reviews: Guidelines, tools and checklists for authors. *Nursing & Health Sciences*, *19*(3), 273–277.

Lv, Z., et al. (2022). Evaluation standards of intelligent technology based on financial alternative data. *Journal of Innovation & Knowledge*, *7*(4), 100229.

Lyócsa, Š., et al. (2022). Default or profit scoring credit systems? Evidence from European and US peer-to-peer lending markets. *Financial Innovation*, *8*(1), 1–21.

Mavlutova, I., et al. (2021). The role of FinTech firms in contemporary financial sector development. *WSEAS Transactions on Business and Economics*, *18*, 411–423.

Messai, A. S., & Gallali, M. I. (2015). Financial leading indicators of banking distress: A micro prudential approach—Evidence from Europe. *Asian Social Science*, *11*(21), 78–90.

Mhlanga, D. (2021). Financial inclusion in emerging economies: The application of machine learning and artificial intelligence in credit risk assessment. *International Journal of Financial Studies*, *9*(3), 39.

Milana, C., & Ashta, A. (2021). Artificial intelligence techniques in finance and financial markets: A survey of the literature. *Strategic Change*, *30*(3), 189–209.

Mogaji, E., & Nguyen, N. P. (2021). Managers' understanding of artificial intelligence in relation to marketing financial services: Insights from a cross-country study. *International Journal of Bank Marketing*.

Mor, S., & Gupta, G. (2021). Artificial intelligence and technical efficiency: The case of Indian commercial banks. *Strategic Change*, *30*(3), 235–245.

Munk, C. W. (2022). FinTech companies, facing competition from mainstream banks, step up their offerings. *The Wall Street Journal*. https://www.wsj.com/articles/FinTech-competition-mainstream-banks-11642714528 (accessed on 7th July 2025).

Murinde, V., Rizopoulos, E., & Zachariadis, M. (2022). The impact of the FinTech revolution on the future of banking: Opportunities and risks. *International Review of Financial Analysis*, *81*, 102103.

N/A. (2020). Peer to peer (P2P) lending market size, share and analysis | 2027. *Allied Market Research*. https://www.alliedmarketresearch.com/peer-to-peer-lending-market (accessed on 7th July 2025).

Naimi-Sadigh, A., Asgari, T., & Rabiei, M. (2021). Digital transformation in the value chain disruption of banking services. *Journal of the Knowledge Economy*, 1–31.

Navaretti, G. B., et al. (2018). FinTech and banking. Friends or foes? *Friends or Foes*.

Nguyen, D. K., Sermpinis, G., & Stasinakis, C. (2022). Big data, artificial intelligence and machine learning: A transformative symbiosis in favor of financial technology. *European Financial Management*.

Nicoletti, B., Nicoletti, W., & Weis. (2017). *Future of FinTech*. Springer.

Northey, G., et al. (2022). Man, vs machine: How artificial intelligence in banking influences consumer belief in financial advice. *International Journal of Bank Marketing*.

Ölvedi, T. (2021). The liquidity aspects of peer-to-peer lending. *Studies in Economics and Finance*.

Piotrowski, D. (2022). Consumer perceived ethicality of banks in the era of digitalization: The case of Poland. *Economics and Business Review*, *8*(1), 90–114.

Pittaway, L., & Cope, J. (2007). Entrepreneurship education: A systematic review of the evidence. *International Small Business Journal*, *25*(5), 479–510.

Prusak, B. (2018). Review of research into enterprise bankruptcy prediction in selected Central and Eastern European countries. *International Journal of Financial Studies*, *6*(3), 60.

Rasiwala, F. S., & Kohli, B. (2021). Artificial intelligence in FinTech: Understanding stakeholders' perception on innovation, disruption, and transformation in finance. *International Journal of Business Intelligence Research (IJBIR)*, *12*(1), 48–65.

Ravikumar, T. (2019). Digital financial inclusion: A payoff of financial technology and digital finance uprising in India. *International Journal of Scientific & Technology Research*, *8*(11), 3434–3438.

Reserve Bank of India. (2022). *RBI Bulletin*. https://rbidocs.rbi.org.in/rdocs/PressRelease/PDFs/PR1055BE9571C97535496593A96A4900315A60.PDF (accessed on 7th July 2025).

Roszkowska, P. (2020). FinTech in financial reporting and audit for fraud prevention and safeguarding equity investments. *Journal of Accounting & Organizational Change*.

Ryu, H., & Chang, Y. (2018). What makes users willing or hesitant to use FinTech: The moderating effect of user type.

Sadok, H., Sakka, F., & El Maknouzi, M. E. H. (2022). Artificial intelligence and bank credit analysis: A review. *Cogent Economics & Finance*, *10*(1), 2023262.

Salameh, R., & Lutfi, K. (2021). The role of artificial intelligence on limiting Jordanian commercial banks cybercrimes. *Accounting*, *7*(5), 1147–1156.

Sharma, D. K., et al. (2021). Integration of genetic algorithm with artificial neural network for stock market forecasting. *International Journal of System Assurance Engineering and Management*, 1–14.

Shustova, E., & Blagoev, V. (2018). Risk management in the internet banking: The case of Kazakhstan. *Economic Studies*, *27*(5).

Singh, R., Malik, G., & Jain, V. (2021). FinTech effect: Measuring impact of FinTech adoption on banks' profitability. *International Journal of Management Practice*, *14*(4), 411–427.

Srivastava, K., & Dhamija, S. (2022). FinTech: Application of artificial intelligence in Indian banking. In *Proceedings of International Conference on Communication and Artificial Intelligence* (pp. 601–613). Springer.

Taneja, S., Kumar, P., Grima, S., Ozen, E., & Sood, K. (2023). *Sustainable Investments in Green Finance*. IGI Global.

Tokic, D. (2018). BlackRock Robo-Advisor 4.0: When artificial intelligence replaces human discretion. *Strategic Change*, *27*(4), 285–290.

Tubadji, A., Denney, T., & Webber, D. J. (2021). Cultural relativity in consumers' rates of adoption of artificial intelligence. *Economic Inquiry*, *59*(3), 1234–1251.

Ulrich, K. (2014). The fallacy of disruptive innovation. *The Wall Street Journal*. https://www.wsj.com/articles/BL-258B-4528 (accessed on 7th July 2025).

Veloso, M., et al. (2021). Artificial intelligence research in finance: Discussion and examples. *Oxford Review of Economic Policy*, *37*(3), 564–584.

Visconti-Caparrós, J. M., & Campos-Blázquez, J. R. (2021). The development of alternate payment methods and their impact on customer behavior: The Bizum case in Spain. *Technological Forecasting and Social Change*, 121330.

Vučinić, M., & Luburić, R. (2022). FinTech, risk-based thinking and cyber risk. *Journal of Central Banking Theory and Practice*, *11*(2), 27–53.

Wang, X., et al. (2021). Industry 4.0 and intellectual capital in the age of FinTech. *Technological Forecasting and Social Change*, *166*, 120598.

Wang, Y., Drabek, Z., & Wang, Z. (2022). The role of social and psychological related soft information in credit analysis: Evidence from a FinTech company. *Journal of Behavioral and Experimental Economics*, *96*, 101806.

Wexler, M. N., & Oberlander, J. (2021). Robo-advisors (RAs): The programmed self-service market for professional advice. *Journal of Service Theory and Practice*.

Wimoolka, S. (2022). *The Impact of Artificial Intelligence Implementation on Companies' Economic Performance* (Doctoral dissertation, Westcliff University).

World Bank. (2021). *Consumer Risks in FinTech: New Manifestations of Consumer Risks and Emerging Regulatory Approaches*. World Bank.

Xia, H., Wang, P., Wan, T., Zhang, Z. J., Weng, J., & Jasimuddin, S. M. (2022). Peer-to-peer lending platform risk analysis: An early warning model based on multi-dimensional information. *The Journal of Risk Finance*, 303–323.

Xu, Y., et al. (2020). AI customer service: Task complexity, problem-solving ability, and usage intention. *Australasian Marketing Journal (AMJ)*, *28*(4), 189–199.

Yáñez-Valdés, C., & Guerrero, M. (2023). Assessing the organizational and ecosystem factors driving the impact of transformative FinTech platforms in emerging economies. *International Journal of Information Management*, *73*, 102689.

Yusupova, L. M., et al. (2020). Artificial intelligence and its use in financial markets. *International Journal of Financial Research*, *11*(5), 353–358.

Zhang, B. Z., Ashta, A., & Barton, M. E. (2021). Do FinTech and financial incumbents have different experiences and perspectives on the adoption of artificial intelligence? *Strategic Change*, *30*(3), 223–234.

Zhang, L. L., Zhang, Y. B., & Kim, H. K. (2021). A study on the influence of customer characteristics on innovation resistance and intention to use in face recognition payment system. *Journal of Advanced Researches and Reports*, *1*(3), 47–54.

CHAPTER 14

Strategies for Promoting Financial Literacy: Empowering Vulnerable and Marginalized Populations to Achieve SDG 1

POOJA KAUSHIK[1] and SHASHI KANT[2]

[1]*Galgotias College of Engineering and Technology, Greater Noida, Uttar Pradesh, India*

[2]*Department of Management, College of Business and Economics, Bule Hora University, Bule Hora, Oromia Region, Ethiopia*

*Corresponding author

ABSTRACT

This chapter examines strategies for improving financial literacy (FL) to empower marginalized and vulnerable groups to attain financial inclusion and reduce poverty. Financial education and services are often inaccessible to vulnerable and marginalized populations, despite the fact that FL is essential for people to successfully navigate complicated financial institutions. A number of strategies have been discussed for addressing these issues, such as focused educational campaigns, cutting-edge technology, and neighborhood-based projects. It emphasizes the significance of inclusion and culturally sensitive methods that take into account the particular requirements and situations of different communities. This chapter also discusses the role that financial institutions, non-profit organizations, and government policies have in creating an atmosphere that supports financial inclusion and empowerment. The role of technology in

E-Financial Strategies for Sustainable Development: A Handbook for Promoting Financial Inclusion and Ending Poverty (SDG 1). Ernesto D. R. Santibanez Gonzalez, Rajeev Sijariya, and Vikas Garg (Eds.)

DOI: 10.1201/9781779640956-14

financial inclusion, as well as the challenges and opportunities associated with digital literacy, is also highlighted. This chapter helps in providing information, tools, and resources to marginalized and vulnerable groups that they need to manage their finances. Initiatives aimed at promoting FL have the potential to make a substantial impact on the reduction of poverty, inequality, and marginalization, hence promoting more sustainable and equitable economic growth.

14.1 INTRODUCTION

14.1.1 OVERVIEW OF FINANCIAL LITERACY

FL is the knowledge and skills people and communities need to handle their money wisely, make educated financial decisions, and attain financial stability. This empowerment encompasses more than just personal well-being; it also includes economic stability and broader communal development. FL improves a person's capacity to successfully manage their own money, comprehend financial goods and services, and traverse complicated financial institutions. People who are financially literate are able to make budgets, save for future objectives, make prudent investments, and appropriately handle debt (Luaradi, 2011). With the help of these abilities, they may reduce financial risks, accumulate money over time, and become more financially independent. Furthermore, FL gives people a sense of self-assurance and independence, enabling them to take charge of their financial destiny. People are better able to speak up for their own interests, negotiate favorable conditions, and fend against exploitative financial activities when they have a thorough grasp of financial ideas and procedures. The advantages of FL at the community level include resilience and economic empowerment. Higher FL levels put communities in a better position to use financial resources for entrepreneurship, job creation, and local development projects. Programs for FL can also help communities develop a savings and investment culture, which will increase their economic stability and resistance to shocks (OECD, 2018). To enable people and communities to attain economic stability, independence, and resilience, FL is crucial. Policymakers, educators, and organizations can unleash the potential of individuals and communities to prosper in the complicated financial landscape of today by funding financial education projects and encouraging wider access to financial resources.

14.1.2 CHALLENGES FACED BY VULNERABLE AND MARGINALIZED POPULATIONS

For people to make wise financial decisions, they must have access to and comprehension of financial information; yet, marginalized and disadvantaged groups frequently encounter substantial obstacles in this area. This chapter will discuss a few of these difficulties, including background information from academic sources. Lack of access to conventional financial services is one of the key issues. Khan (2019) asserts that disadvantaged groups, such as the underprivileged and those residing in remote regions, frequently have restricted access to banks and other financial establishments. Without these organizations, people could find it difficult to get loans or savings accounts, which would make it more difficult for them to accumulate assets and get out of debt. Barriers to literacy and language might make it difficult to interpret financial information. According to Lusardi and Mitchell (2014), those with less education may find it difficult to understand complicated financial ideas or to navigate financial papers. Populations that speak a language other than the official language of their nation or have poor English proficiency exacerbate this issue. Furthermore, the spread of online financial services poses a challenge to those whose access to technology or level of digital literacy is restricted. According to Dwivedi et al. (2019), accessibility constraints or a lack of expertise with digital financial platforms may make it difficult for marginalized groups—such as the elderly, the disabled, and those who live in rural areas—to use them. Engagement with financial information can also be impacted by cultural differences and mistrust of financial organizations. According to research by Sherraden et al. (2015), marginalized populations may be reluctant to seek out financial information or services because of past discrimination and inequality, which may have contributed to their mistrust of mainstream financial institutions. This presents several obstacles for marginalized and vulnerable groups to obtain and comprehend financial information. To tackle these obstacles, a comprehensive strategy that takes into account hurdles pertaining to technology, literacy, access, and cultural aspects is necessary. To guarantee equal access to financial resources and opportunities, initiatives to advance financial inclusion and literacy must be customized to the unique needs and circumstances of these people.

14.1.3 OBJECTIVES OF THE CHAPTER

To explain FL as well as the significance of basic financial concepts in the current complicated economic environment is the key objective of this chapter. Examine the typical barriers to FL, such as social inequality, cultural norms, and limited access to education. Explore tried-and-true approaches to financial education delivery, such as internet tools, community seminars, school curricula, and workplace initiatives. Approaches should be customized for marginalized and vulnerable populations. Investigate how gamification, online resources, and smartphone applications may improve FL. Discuss how to evaluate the long-term effects of FL initiatives on individuals and communities, as well as how to gauge their efficacy. In order to develop comprehensive and long-lasting solutions for increasing FL, emphasize the significance of collaborations between governments, financial institutions, non-governmental organizations, and educators. Offer concrete suggestions that educators, employers, policymakers, and community leaders may use to implement policies that effectively promote FL locally, nationally, and internationally.

14.1.4 SCOPE OF THE CHAPTER

The book chapter includes an examination of customized strategies and interventions meant to provide underprivileged populations with fundamental FL and competence. This chapter will explore the particular difficulties that vulnerable and marginalized groups—such as low-income individuals, members of ethnic minorities, immigrants, women, young people, and people with disabilities—face when trying to obtain and comprehend financial information and services. It will look at different approaches and best practices used by local groups, governments, financial institutions, and nonprofits to improve FL in these areas. Culturally sensitive financial education programs, new delivery techniques including mobile technology and community outreach projects, the significance of peer mentorship and support networks, and the necessity of tackling unique barriers to financial inclusion will all be discussed. The chapter will also emphasize the importance of stakeholder participation and partnership in ensuring the efficacy and long-term viability of these projects. This chapter seeks to provide valuable insights and practical recommendations for promoting FL and economic empowerment among vulnerable and marginalized populations, ultimately contributing to the larger goal of reducing inequalities and fostering inclusive economic development.

14.2 UNDERSTANDING FINANCIAL LITERACY

14.2.1 DEFINITION AND COMPONENTS OF FINANCIAL LITERACY

FL is essential for making informed financial decisions and managing one's money responsibly. It includes a wide variety of information and abilities that enable people to successfully navigate the difficult world of personal finance. The essential components of FL are budgeting, saving, investing, debt management, and understanding financial products, all of which are important in achieving financial well-being.

Budgeting is the practice of planning how revenue will be distributed to different costs and financial goals. It entails recording revenue, categorizing costs, and establishing spending limitations to guarantee that spending does not exceed earnings. Budgeting allows individuals to prioritize their financial goals, such as saving for emergencies, paying off debt, or investing for the future. Individuals who create and adhere to a budget can take control of their finances and make educated decisions about where their money goes. According to McKinney (2017), budgeting is critical for financial security and avoiding overspending. It enables users to find cost-cutting opportunities and allocate funds to more important goals, such as saving for retirement.

Saving is the practice of laying away a portion of one's income for future use. It includes creating emergency finances, saving for short-term goals like trips or large purchases, and investing for long-term goals like retirement. Saving offers a cash buffer in the event of unforeseen costs and helps people reach their financial objectives over time. According to Lusardi and Mitchell (2014), saving is a critical component of FL that allows people to accumulate money and achieve financial stability. Prioritizing savings objectives above current spending needs discipline and forethought.

Investing is placing money into assets with the goal of earning a return or profit over time. It encompasses a variety of instruments, including stocks, bonds, mutual funds, and real estate, each with its own risk and return profile. Investing helps people to increase their wealth and achieve long-term financial goals, including retirement planning and asset creation. According to Kapoor et al. (2017), investing is an important aspect of FL since it allows people to use the power of compound interest and inflation to accumulate money over time. However, understanding investing concepts and risk management measures is required in order to make educated judgments and avoid potential traps.

Debt management is properly managing and repaying borrowed funds, including credit card debt, school loans, and mortgages. It contains measures for reducing debt, lowering interest payments, and avoiding excessive borrowing. Debt management is critical for achieving financial stability and avoiding the negative repercussions of excessive debt, such as high interest rates and credit score harm. According to Garman and Forgue (2018), debt management is an important part of FL since it requires people to comprehend the terms and conditions of their loans, prioritize debt repayment, and avoid taking on more debt than they can afford to pay back.

Understanding financial products requires knowledge of a variety of financial instruments, including savings accounts, certificates of deposit (CDs), insurance policies, and retirement accounts. It entails comprehending their characteristics, advantages, dangers, and costs, as well as how they relate to overall financial planning and goals. Understanding financial products allows people to make educated judgments about which products will best match their requirements and goals. According to Mandell and Klein (2009), knowing financial products is a critical component of FL since it enables consumers to choose the best products for their financial condition and aspirations (Federal, 2021). To make educated selections, you must compare your alternatives, study the fine print, and seek help as needed.

14.2.2 WHY FINANCIAL LITERACY IS CRUCIAL FOR VULNERABLE AND MARGINALIZED POPULATIONS?

FL is the basis on which people construct their financial well-being; while it is necessary for everyone, it is especially important for disadvantaged and marginalized communities. This section outlines why FL is especially important for these populations, the obstacles they encounter, and the possible advantages of better financial education.

Vulnerable and marginalized groups, such as low-income persons, minorities, refugees, and those with disabilities, frequently face special financial issues. These obstacles are caused by a variety of factors, including restricted access to formal financial services, educational discrepancies, cultural barriers, and institutional inequities (Lusardi and Mitchell, 2014). Minorities and low-income households, for example, are more likely to be unbanked or underbanked, meaning they do not have access to basic banking services like checking and savings accounts. Furthermore, these individuals may experience greater levels of financial stress as a result of fluctuating wages, low savings, and limited emergency resources (Collins, 2012).

FL may be an effective strategy for empowering disadvantaged and marginalized communities to overcome these obstacles and enhance their financial well-being. Individuals who are equipped with necessary financial knowledge and abilities are better able to navigate complicated financial systems, make wise financial decisions, and attain greater financial stability (Hastings, 2013). Understanding budgeting, saving, and credit management, for example, can help people create good financial habits and prevent expensive mistakes like excessive debt or predatory lending (Bernheim et al., 2001). Furthermore, FL can improve people's capacity to obtain and use financial goods and services efficiently. For marginalized individuals, this may be especially revolutionary since it allows them to participate more completely in the formal financial sector, acquire assets, and provide paths out of poverty (Atkinson and Messy, 2012). FL efforts can help to reduce economic inequities while also encouraging social and economic participation for vulnerable populations (Carpena et al., 2011).

14.2.3 STATISTICS AND RESEARCH FINDINGS ON THE CURRENT STATUS OF FINANCIAL LITERACY AMONG VULNERABLE AND MARGINALIZED POPULATIONS

1. **National Statistics:** A 2019 survey conducted by the National Council of Applied Economic Research (NCAER) discovered that just roughly 24% of Indians have a basic degree of FL, with large inequalities across socioeconomic levels (National Council for Applied Economic Research, 2019).

2. **Global Financial Literacy:** According to the Standard and Poor's Global Financial Literacy Survey (2019), just one in every three individuals worldwide is financially literate, with discrepancies being particularly severe among disadvantaged and marginalized communities (Standard and Poor's Global Financial Literacy Survey, 2019).
3. **Gender Disparities:** According to the Global Financial Literacy Excellence Center (GFLEC), women globally have lower financial literacy rates than men, with just 30% reaching a basic level of FL compared to 35% for men (Global Financial Literacy Excellence Centre, 2020).
4. **Research Findings about Vulnerable and Marginalized Populations:** According to research conducted by Chen et al. (2021), the present level of FL among vulnerable and marginalized people is worrying. The study, which focused on low-income urban households, discovered that just 30% of participants had a fundamental comprehension of financial concepts such as budgeting, savings, and debt management. This lack of FL is especially prevalent among minority groups and those with lower levels of education.

Smith and Jones (2020) found gaps in financial knowledge among underrepresented populations, including immigrants and refugees. The study found that many people in these regions have difficulty accessing financial education tools and are more vulnerable to financial scams and predatory lending practices.

Lusardi and Mitchell (2018) discovered that vulnerable and marginalized communities, such as low-income families and minorities, had restricted access to formal financial education programs. This lack of access correlates to poorer levels of FL in these communities (Lusardi and Mitchell, 2018).

Collins and O'Rourke (2020) found that socioeconomic characteristics had a strong influence on FL. They discovered that those with lower incomes and less formal education have lower levels of FL than those who are wealthy and more educated (Collins and O'Rourke, 2020).

The World Bank's (2019) research highlighted a number of challenges to financial inclusion among marginalized people, including restricted access to financial services, language barriers, and a lack of confidence in banks. These impediments lead to poor levels of FL among disadvantaged communities (World Bank, 2019).

Gender differences in FL have been demonstrated by studies such as Agarwal and Mazumder's (2021), with women, particularly those from underprivileged groups, frequently demonstrating lower levels of financial understanding than males. This difference may worsen financial inequality among marginalized groups (Agarwal and Mazumder, 2021).

Bernheim, Garrett, and Maki (2022) found a robust link between FL and economic well-being in marginalized groups. Individuals with higher levels of FL have been shown to make better financial decisions, resulting in better financial outcomes and increased financial resilience (Bernheim et al., 2022).

14.3 OBSTACLES TO FINANCIAL LITERACY

14.3.1 BARRIERS THAT HINDER FINANCIAL LITERACY AMONG VULNERABLE AND MARGINALIZED POPULATIONS

Limited educational access is one of the most significant hurdles to FL among disadvantaged and marginalized communities. Many people in these groups may not have had the chance to get a formal education or have limited access to educational resources. Without a fundamental knowledge of concepts such as budgeting, saving, and investing, people may fail to manage the financial system's intricacies (Lusardi and Mitchell, 2014).

Language limitations also have a substantial impact on FL. In multicultural communities, people who speak languages other than the prevalent language may have difficulty receiving financial information and services in their chosen language. This can lead to confusion and misinterpretation of financial ideas, heightening financial vulnerability (Cude and Lawrence, 2015). Cultural issues might also contribute to poor FL. Some cultural norms and beliefs may shape attitudes toward money management, savings, and debt. For example, in cultures where openly discussing finances is frowned upon, people may be less inclined to seek financial education or help. Furthermore, cultural differences in financial habits and preferences may conflict with mainstream financial education initiatives, making them ineffective for some groups (Klapper et al., 2016). Another significant hurdle is a lack of financial inclusion, which refers to restricted access to mainstream financial services and products. Vulnerable and disadvantaged groups, such as low-income families, refugees, and people with disabilities, may have difficulty opening bank accounts, receiving credit, or accessing affordable financial goods. This exclusion from the official financial sector may result in a lack of access to financial knowledge and resources (Demirguc-Kunt et al., 2015).

To address these hurdles, customized interventions must take into account the unique needs and problems that disadvantaged and marginalized communities confront. For example, programs to promote FL should be culturally sensitive, including culturally relevant content and delivery techniques that resonate with varied groups (Cole and Shastry, 2009). Collaboration among governments, financial institutions, non-profit groups, and community leaders is also critical for increasing access to financial education and services. This might include conducting FL courses in several languages, creating accessible digital learning platforms, and implementing inclusive banking practices that respond to varied needs (Carpena et al., 2011).

Furthermore, encouraging financial inclusion through efforts such as microfinance programs, community banking services, and mobile banking solutions may assist underprivileged groups in economically empowering themselves and improving their financial abilities (Dupas and Robinson, 2013). The hurdles to FL among vulnerable and marginalized communities are linked and must be addressed holistically. By addressing issues such as school access, linguistic variety, cultural sensitivity, and financial inclusion, stakeholders may help these communities improve their financial well-being and resilience.

14.3.2 IMPACT OF SOCIOECONOMIC FACTORS ON FINANCIAL LITERACY LEVELS

Poverty, unemployment, and prejudice are all key socioeconomic issues that influence FL levels in individuals and communities. Poverty is a fundamental socioeconomic condition that is frequently associated with poor levels of FL. People living in poverty may have limited access to quality education, impeding their ability to learn critical financial skills. Furthermore, the constant fight to fulfill basic necessities leaves little time and resources for learning about financial ideas and practices. According to studies, people from low-income households have lower levels of FL than those from higher-income families (Lusardi and Mitchell, 2014).

Unemployment is another issue that might influence FL. Individuals who are jobless or underemployed may experience financial stress and uncertainty, forcing them to prioritize short-term survival over long-term financial planning. This can lead to a lack of financial knowledge and a limited awareness of subjects like budgeting, saving, and investing. Furthermore, unemployment can lead to feelings of inadequacy or humiliation, discouraging people from pursuing FL tools (Hastings et al., 2013). Discrimination based on race, ethnicity, gender, or disability can also lead to differences in FL. Marginalized communities frequently encounter hurdles to getting quality education, jobs, and financial services. Discriminatory behaviors can impede fair access to financial education programs and resources, prolonging cycles of financial exclusion and inequality (Agarwal et al., 2015). Women, for example, may face gender discrimination at work, resulting in lower earnings and fewer prospects for growth, which can have an influence on their financial knowledge and decision-making ability.

The interconnectedness of these socioeconomic determinants exacerbates the link between FL and social standing. Individuals who face various types of disadvantage, such as being low-income and belonging to a disadvantaged group, may have additional barriers to receiving and using financial knowledge (Collins, 2018). Addressing these complicated dynamics demands a diverse strategy that takes into account each community's unique experiences and needs. Efforts to increase FL must take into consideration social differences. This involves developing inclusive financial education programs that are accessible, culturally appropriate, and attentive to the participants' different backgrounds. Collaboration across government agencies, educational institutions, nonprofit groups, and financial service providers is critical for reaching marginalized communities and providing tailored solutions (Cole and Shastry, 2018). Addressing these issues necessitates a comprehensive strategy that includes financial education, regulatory reforms, and measures to promote economic empowerment and social justice. Understanding and addressing the core causes of financial inequality can help us establish a more inclusive and financially resilient society.

14.3.3 ROLE OF SYSTEMIC INEQUALITIES

Systemic disparities play a crucial role in maintaining financial exclusion and marginalization by erecting obstacles that prohibit some groups from accessing and benefiting from financial resources and opportunities.

These disparities are profoundly rooted in social, economic, and political institutions, resulting in unequal access to resources, opportunities, and decision-making authority. This chapter will look at how structural inequalities lead to financial exclusion and marginalization, with an emphasis on major aspects such as socioeconomic position, race and ethnicity, gender, and geographical location. Socioeconomic status is a significant predictor of financial inclusion. Individuals from lower-income households frequently have restricted access to formal financial services such as banking, credit, and insurance. This is due to reasons such as a lack of documents, insufficient collateral, and expensive transaction fees, which might prevent individuals from accessing conventional financial institutions. Furthermore, financial institutions may target richer consumers who are thought to be less risky, marginalizing people with lower socioeconomic status (Andriani and Distaso, 2020).

Race and ethnicity have an important impact on financial exclusion. Minority groups, notably Black, Indigenous, and People of Color (BIPOC), frequently face discrimination and bias in financial services, resulting in inequities in access to credit, housing loans, and investment possibilities. According to studies, BIPOC individuals are more likely to be rejected for loans or charged higher interest rates than their white counterparts with comparable financial profiles (Elliott and Song, 2020). This racist exclusion exacerbates economic inequality and hinders marginalized populations' wealth-building opportunities.

Gender is another factor in structural inequality that contributes to financial exclusion. Women, particularly in developing nations and underprivileged populations, frequently encounter barriers to financial services, property ownership, and job prospects. Gender norms and preconceptions might cause women to be viewed as less creditworthy or capable of handling finances, limiting their access to credit and investment resources (Munir, 2021). To close the gender gap in financial inclusion, we must address societal and cultural obstacles, promote women's FL, and offer specialized financial products and services.

Geographic location also influences financial exclusion, as rural and remote areas frequently have restricted access to banking infrastructure and financial services. People living in these areas may experience difficulties such as a lack of physical bank branches, inadequate connectivity, and insufficient FL tools. This spatial restriction worsens economic inequities between urban and rural populations, limiting opportunities for economic growth and development (Aiyar and Puy, 2019).

Financial institutions may play an important role by adopting targeted outreach programs, financial education campaigns, and inclusive lending procedures that take into account different socioeconomic backgrounds, races, genders, and geographical areas. Collaboration among governments, civil society groups, and the commercial sector is critical for creating an enabling environment for financial inclusion and removing the systemic hurdles that perpetuate financial exclusion and marginalization.

14.4 CUSTOMIZED APPROACHES TO FINANCIAL EDUCATION

14.4.1 STRATEGIES FOR DESIGNING AND IMPLEMENTING FINANCIAL EDUCATION PROGRAMS FOR VULNERABLE AND MARGINALIZED POPULATIONS

To effectively design and implement financial education programs for vulnerable and marginalized communities, numerous measures must be considered. These groups frequently confront specific obstacles, such as restricted access to resources, inadequate financial awareness, and structural hurdles (Collins, 2019).

Recognizing the various needs and circumstances of these people is an important component of developing specialized financial education programs. These categories might include low-income individuals, minorities, immigrants, people with disabilities, and those who have restricted access to standard financial services. Understanding their individual issues, such as low FL, language barriers, cultural differences, and distrust in financial institutions, is critical for developing relevant and effective programs. To overcome these issues, financial education programs should take a comprehensive approach that includes skills such as budgeting, saving, debt management, and obtaining affordable financial services. Workshops, peer learning, and community-based projects are examples of interactive and culturally sensitive teaching approaches that can increase engagement and relevance among participants from various backgrounds.

Following are the Key Strategies for Designing and Implementing Financial Education Programs

1. **Culturally Relevant Curriculum:** Financial education programs should include culturally relevant information that speaks to the target population's experiences and beliefs. This entails

comprehending the cultural context, linguistic preferences, and socioeconomic backgrounds of participants. For example, programs geared at immigrant groups may need to cover themes like navigating a new country's financial system, remittance management, and cultural views towards money.

2. **Accessible Distribution Techniques:** Using a range of distribution techniques can help to guarantee that various people have access. This might include in-person seminars, online classes, smartphone apps, or community-based outreach programs. Programs can reach a larger audience by providing alternatives that meet diverse learning styles and levels of technological access.
3. **Peer-to-Peer Learning:** Using peer-to-peer learning can be very beneficial for engaging vulnerable groups. Pairing participants with mentors or facilitators from similar experiences can help to build trust, provide comparable role models, and create a positive learning environment. Peer mentors can share personal experiences, provide practical guidance, and assist participants in applying financial principles to their daily lives.
4. **Interactive and Experiential Learning:** Real-world simulations and interactive exercises can help students understand and retain financial concepts. Role-playing activities, budgeting games, and case studies allow participants to practice making decisions in a safe setting. Hands-on experiences can help individuals bridge the gap between theory and practice, allowing them to apply newly acquired information to their financial conditions.
5. **Collaboration with Community Partners:** Working with local organizations, non-profits, and community leaders can help to broaden the program's reach and effectiveness. These partners frequently have established ties and trust within the community, which may help with recruitment and engagement. Collaborating with social service organizations, schools, or faith-based organizations can also aid in identifying and meeting the special needs of marginalized communities.

Furthermore, collaboration with community organizations, non-profits, and local stakeholders is critical for personalizing financial education programs to the unique needs and preferences of marginalized communities. Collaborative projects can use existing networks, cultural understanding, and community trust to provide focused treatments and overcome participation barriers.

Evaluation and feedback systems are critical for determining the impact and success of financial education programs designed for vulnerable groups. Collecting data on participant outcomes, behavior changes, and satisfaction levels can help to adjust programs and ensure continual progress. Long-term monitoring and follow-up are also essential for maintaining strong financial habits and resolving persistent issues for participants.

14.4.2 SUCCESSFUL EXAMPLES OF FINANCIAL EDUCATION PROGRAMS TARGETED SPECIFICALLY AT VULNERABLE AND MARGINALIZED POPULATIONS

1. **"MyPath" by MyPath:** MyPath is a youth-led organization that empowers low-income youth via FL and leadership development. Their program has been effective in increasing financial capabilities among marginalized youth (MyPath, n.d.).
2. **"Bank On" Programs:** Bank On programs are collaborations with local governments, financial institutions, and community organizations to provide unbanked and underbanked people with secure and inexpensive financial products and services. These programs have been effective in boosting financial inclusion among marginalized communities (Coalition for Economic Empowerment, n.d.).
3. **"Earned Income Tax Credit (EITC) Awareness Campaigns":** These programs aim to raise awareness and participation in the Earned Income Tax Credit program among low-income individuals and families. These efforts have been helpful in assisting eligible persons in claiming their tax credits, consequently enhancing their financial stability (Centre on Budget and Policy Priorities, 2020).
4. **"Financial Opportunity Centers (FOCs)" Created by the LISC:** Financial Opportunity Centers help low-income people

and families achieve financial stability by offering integrated services such as employment coaching, financial education, and access to income support. According to studies, FOCs dramatically enhance financial results for participants, particularly those from marginalized populations (LISC, n.d.).

5. **"The Financial Clinic's Change Machine"** is an online platform that provides financial coaching and training to charity organizations that serve low-income individuals. Change Machine assists people and families with economic issues by offering tools and resources for financial coaches (The Financial Clinic, n.d.).

14.5 TECHNOLOGY FOR FINANCIAL INCLUSION

14.5.1 ROLE OF TECHNOLOGY IN PROMOTING FINANCIAL INCLUSION

Technology has emerged as a major factor in increasing financial inclusion and access to financial education resources throughout the world. It has played an important role in reaching out to disadvantaged people and providing them with the knowledge and resources they need to manage their finances successfully.

Mobile banking and digital payment systems are important examples of how technology can help promote financial inclusion. With the increased use of smartphones and the proliferation of mobile networks, people in remote or underserved locations can now easily access financial services. Mobile banking applications enable customers to complete transactions such as money transfers, bill payments, and credit access without visiting a physical bank office (Demirgüç and Klapper, 2018). For example, M-Pesa in Kenya has transformed financial services by allowing users to send and receive money using their mobile phones, encouraging financial inclusion among the unbanked.

Furthermore, technology increases access to financial education information via online platforms and apps (Agarwal, 2016). Websites, smartphone applications, and social media platforms provide a wealth of information on anything from basic budgeting and saving tactics to more advanced investing ideas. For example, sites such as Khan Academy and Coursera offer free online courses on personal finance, investing, and economics, allowing students to learn at their own pace and leisure. Additionally, financial companies and non-profit organizations frequently provide interactive tools and seminars to help consumers manage debt, understand credit ratings, and prepare for retirement.

Artificial intelligence (AI) and data analytics are critical components in personalizing financial services to individual consumers' demands. Financial institutions can provide personalized suggestions and guidance to individuals by analyzing their data and behavior. AI-powered chatbots and virtual assistants offer real-time help and direction, making financial services more accessible and user-friendly.

Technology promotes financial inclusion and increases access to financial education resources. Mobile banking and digital payment technologies allow people to engage in the formal financial system, while internet platforms and applications provide essential instructional information to help them improve their FL (Laar and Aryeetey, 2017). Furthermore, advances in AI and data analytics improve the efficacy of financial services by offering users personalized solutions. To fully realize the potential of financial inclusion, it is critical to eliminate digital literacy hurdles and guarantee that technology-driven solutions are available to all sectors of society.

14.5.2 POTENTIAL OF DIGITAL PLATFORM TOOLS TO REACH UNDERSERVED POPULATIONS

Digital platforms, mobile applications, and online learning tools have enormous promise for delivering targeted FL information to marginalized communities, closing the gap in financial knowledge and empowerment. These technologies provide scalable and accessible solutions that can meet the diverse demands of individuals, regardless of geographical location or socioeconomic level. Mobile apps have grown commonplace, particularly in underdeveloped areas where traditional financial services may be limited. Budgeting tools, savings trackers, and instructional games are examples of apps built for FL. They may successfully engage users and educate critical financial skills in an easy-to-use way. For example, applications like PocketGuard and Mint allow users to manage their accounts, track spending, and establish savings goals, fostering financial awareness and prudent money management (Mullainathan and Shafir, 2013).

Digital platforms provide a diverse set of educational materials suited to the needs and tastes of underrepresented people. These platforms can provide interactive courses, tutorials, and educational films on topics like basic banking, budgeting, debt management, and investing methods. Online platforms may accommodate various learning styles and improve user understanding and retention by including multimedia material and adaptive learning strategies (Hastings et al., 2013).

Online learning technologies can help to enhance peer-to-peer learning and community participation by creating a friendly atmosphere in which people can share their experiences, seek advice, and learn from each other. Discussion forums, social media groups, and virtual seminars can provide useful opportunities for marginalized people to communicate with financial professionals, mentors, and peers, thereby empowering them to make informed financial decisions and navigate complicated financial environments (Collins et al., 2013). As a result, digital platforms, mobile applications, and online learning tools show tremendous promise for providing targeted FL information to underprivileged communities. By utilizing the accessibility of mobile devices, the scalability of digital platforms, and the interactivity of online learning tools, stakeholders can effectively address the specific challenges that marginalized populations face when accessing financial education. However, it is critical to ensure that these technologies are tailored to the unique requirements and preferences of underserved communities and that they are supported by appropriate support systems to encourage long-term behavior change and financial well-being.

14.5.3 CHALLENGES AND OPPORTUNITIES ASSOCIATED WITH DIGITAL LITERACY AND ACCESS TO TECHNOLOGY

Digital literacy and access to technology are becoming increasingly important in today's connected society. However, underprivileged people frequently face significant barriers to obtaining digital literacy skills and using technology. These obstacles may exacerbate existing inequities and hinder opportunities for socioeconomic growth. Nonetheless, addressing these challenges opens up opportunities for empowerment and inclusiveness.

One key difficulty is the "digital divide," which refers to the disparity between those who have access to digital technology and those who do not, frequently along socioeconomic lines (Hargittai, 2002). This difference affects vulnerable populations disproportionately, including low-income individuals, rural areas, those with disabilities, and elderly people. Limited access to technology restricts their capacity to fully engage in the digital era, impeding educational and job opportunities. Furthermore, even when technology is available, digital literacy is a barrier. Digital literacy refers to the ability to successfully utilize digital devices, navigate online platforms, critically assess information, and maintain one's privacy and security (Fraillon et al., 2014). Without basic digital literacy skills, disadvantaged populations may struggle to access essential services, obtain employment, or advocate for their rights online.

Tackling these issues creates opportunities for empowerment and inclusiveness. Governments, non-profit organizations, and corporations can help bridge the digital gap by providing low-cost internet access, subsidizing equipment purchases, and offering digital skills training programs for underprivileged communities. Community centers and libraries can act as hubs for digital literacy instruction, providing access to technology and personalized assistance. Integrating digital literacy into formal education curricula can equip students with critical skills at an early age, eliminating inequities in digital competency later in life. Furthermore, establishing a culture of lifelong learning through online resources and peer-to-peer support networks can enable disadvantaged groups to continuously improve their digital skills and adapt to technological advances. While vulnerable populations continue to face obstacles with digital literacy and access to technology, addressing these concerns opens up potential for empowerment and inclusion. Societies can ensure that all individuals can fully engage in the digital era by launching targeted measures to bridge the digital gap, offering digital skills training, and cultivating a culture of lifelong learning.

14.6 STAKEHOLDER ENGAGEMENT

14.6.1 IMPORTANCE OF COLLABORATIVE PARTNERSHIPS AMONG STAKEHOLDERS IN PROMOTING FINANCIAL LITERACY

Collaborative relationships between government agencies, non-profit organizations, financial institutions, and community-based organizations are critical for developing FL. Achieving universal FL necessitates a collaborative effort from all sectors of society, since no single body can handle all facets of this complex subject alone. Non-profit organizations frequently specialize in providing specialized financial education programs to underrepresented groups. These organizations have extensive experience developing culturally sensitive curricula and reaching out to marginalized communities. Collaboration with non-profits enables the tailoring of financial education campaigns to meet the varying requirements of different groups. Government agencies play an important role in establishing laws and regulations that influence the financial education environment. They can distribute money, create curricular standards, and set criteria for FL programs. Government agencies may foster the success of FL projects by using their regulatory power and resources. Financial institutions have a strong interest in increasing FL as well. Banks and credit unions may create a financially literate client base by equipping them with the information they need to make sound financial decisions, manage debt, save for the future, and access suitable financial products and services. Many financial institutions provide instructional materials, courses, and online tools to help their consumers improve their FL levels. Community-based organizations act as trusted intermediaries in their local communities and are critical partners in developing FL at the grassroots level. These organizations understand the particular issues and opportunities that their communities face and can develop financial education programs to meet those needs. Collaboration with community-based organizations improves the relevance and efficacy of FL efforts by making them more culturally sensitive and responsive to community needs. Collaboration among government agencies, non-profit organizations, financial institutions, and community-based organizations is critical for increasing FL. By combining their resources, knowledge, and networks, these stakeholders can create comprehensive and long-term solutions to increase FL and empower individuals to attain financial well-being.

14.6.2 SUCCESSFUL EXAMPLES OF MULTI-SECTORAL INITIATIVES AIMED AT IMPROVING FINANCIAL LITERACY AND INCLUSION

Successful multi-sectoral projects aiming at boosting FL and inclusion have evolved across the world, illustrating the value of cross-sector collaboration. One noteworthy example is the World Bank's Global Findex database, which is a thorough survey that tracks global progress on financial inclusion. Through collaborations with governments, financial institutions, and international organizations, the Global Findex provides useful insights on the state of financial inclusion and informs policy initiatives to close gaps (World Bank, 2021).

In India, the Pradhan Mantri Jan Dhan Yojana (PMJDY) is a multi-sectoral project that has greatly increased financial inclusion. PMJDY, which launched in 2014, sought to provide universal banking services by creating bank accounts for every family in the country. To reach distant and underprivileged regions, PMJDY collaborated with the government, banks, and technology companies to use new ways such as biometric verification and mobile banking. As a result, millions of previously unbanked people gained access to formal financial services, which promoted economic empowerment and poverty eradication (GOI, PMJDY n.d.).

Another notable example is the Alliance for Financial Inclusion (AFI), which is a global network of central banks and financial regulators working to advance financial inclusion policies. AFI fosters information exchange, capacity building, and peer learning among its members, encouraging cross-sector collaboration to address common concerns. Through efforts such as the Maya Declaration, AFI members agree to specific financial inclusion goals and exchange best practices for achieving them. AFI has been instrumental in advancing legislative reforms and improving access to financial services in a variety of situations by mobilizing players from both the public and private sectors (AFI, 2020).

In the business sector, projects such as Visa's Financial Football demonstrate how private organizations may contribute to FL using creative instructional methods. Financial Football is an interactive video game in which participants learn about personal finance through simulated football. Visa has delivered Financial Football kits to thousands of instructors, reaching millions of kids across the world, via partnerships with schools, organizations, and governments (Visa Inc. n.d.). This multi-sectoral partnership leverages the experience of financial institutions, educators, and policymakers to increase FL among both kids and adults.

Successful multi-sectoral projects aimed at increasing FL and inclusion highlight the value of working together to overcome difficult socioeconomic concerns. These programs achieve substantial change by bringing together stakeholders from government, civil society, and the commercial sector to pool their resources, skills, and networks. Multi-sectoral partnerships, whether through data-driven research, policy lobbying, or creative educational programs, are critical to increasing access to financial services and empowering individuals and communities throughout the world.

14.6.3 ROLE OF GRASSROOTS ORGANIZATIONS AND COMMUNITY LEADERS IN FOSTERING SUSTAINABLE FINANCIAL BEHAVIORS

Grassroots organizations and community leaders play critical roles in pushing change and establishing sustainable financial behaviors in communities. These organizations frequently operate at the local level, gaining a thorough awareness of the specific difficulties and possibilities that their constituents face. They promote economic stability and resilience by providing individuals with financial knowledge, skills, and resources through a variety of projects and programs. This chapter will look at the many ways that grassroots organizations and community leaders may help promote sustainable financial behaviors.

Grassroots organizations act as change agents by developing FL knowledge and pushing for equal financial access. For example, the Center for Financial Services Innovation (CFSI) works with community leaders to provide specialized financial education programs for underprivileged communities. These organizations provide people with basic financial management skills, such as budgeting, saving, and debt management, by setting up workshops, seminars, and outreach programs (CFSI, n.d.).

Furthermore, grassroots organizations tackle systemic obstacles to financial inclusion by utilizing their deeply ingrained links within communities. They push for laws that support fair lending practices, access to banking services, and affordable housing through collaborations with regional administrations, financial institutions, and other interested parties. These organizations push policy changes meant to promote an inclusive financial environment by elevating the perspectives of underrepresented groups (Lusardi and Mitchell, 2014).

Activists, educators, and faith-based organizers are among the community leaders who are essential in bringing people together to support financial empowerment programs. These leaders foster a culture of financial responsibility and mutual assistance within their communities by utilizing their influence and reputation. To encourage members to practice prudent money management and charitable giving, faith-based organizations, for example, frequently incorporate financial stewardship ideas into their teachings (Lane, 2015).

Community leaders also function as mentors and role models, encouraging people to embrace sustainable financial practices by sharing their own success stories and activities. They enable people to take charge of their financial destiny by demystifying complicated financial ideas and offering real-world advice and personal experiences. Furthermore, community leaders provide vital networks of support—guidance, encouragement, and solidarity—to those who are struggling financially.

Local leaders and grassroots groups are essential for promoting sustainable financial practices and bringing about change in communities. By way of their advocacy endeavors, instructional programs, and grassroots mobilization, these organizations enable people to make knowledgeable financial judgments, accumulate assets, and attain sustained financial stability. Through their partnership with stakeholders and amplification of marginalized groups' voices, they facilitate the development of a financial system that is both inclusive and equitable.

14.7 EVALUATION OF FINANCIAL LITERACY PROGRAMS

14.7.1 METHODS TO MEASURE THE IMPACT OF FINANCIAL LITERACY PROGRAMS

To ensure that FL programs are effective in promoting financial well-being and eliminating inequities, it is imperative to assess the impact of these activities on marginalized and disadvantaged communities.

1. **Pre-Tests and Post-Tests:** To test changes in knowledge, attitudes, and behaviors linked to personal finance, this technique entails giving questionnaires or assessments both before and after participants in the FL programme. Post-tests assess the program's effectiveness, whereas pre-tests set a baseline. For example, standardized examinations might be used to gauge participants' comprehension of topics like conserving money or creating a budget. Analyzable quantitative data is provided by this procedure.
2. **Longitudinal Studies:** These studies monitor participants' financial actions and results over a prolonged period of time, providing

information about the long-term impacts of FL initiatives. Through the collection of data at various intervals, scholars are able to discern patterns and recognize alterations in the financial practices of susceptible groups. A more thorough understanding of the long-term effects of these therapies is made possible by longitudinal research.

3. **Constraints on Experiments:** In randomized controlled trials (RCTs), subjects are randomized to be either part of the intervention group (who receive FL programme exposure) or the control group (who do not receive exposure). By comparing the results of the two groups, this strategy helps demonstrate causation by adjusting for confounding variables. RCTs are regarded as the gold standard for assessing the efficacy of programs, yet keeping the intervention from the control group may present ethical issues.
4. **Focus Groups and Qualitative Interviews:** Qualitative approaches offer extensive insights into participants' experiences, attitudes, and the contextual elements impacting their financial behaviors, which supplement quantitative data. Through focus groups and interviews with people from marginalized communities, researchers may delve into the subtler components of FL, such as societal norms, cultural beliefs, and structural hurdles. Qualitative data support programme improvements by providing context for quantitative findings.
5. **Questionnaires and Surveys:** Questionnaires are frequently used to collect quantitative data on programme satisfaction, financial procedures, and participant demographics. Surveys that are tailored to disadvantaged and marginalized populations guarantee inclusion and relevance. Financial decision-making changes following programme participation, as well as participants' confidence in handling their finances and their access to financial resources, may all be evaluated using questionnaires.
6. **Behavioural Observations:** In observational studies, participants' financial behaviors in authentic environments are directly observed. Before and after the intervention, researchers could monitor patterns in savings, debt management techniques, or spending patterns. Behavioural observations offer significant

insights into the ways in which vulnerable groups' real financial behaviors are influenced by FL programs.

7. **Case Studies:** Detailed case studies give individuals' paths towards better financial well-being by focusing on their individual or community experiences with FL programs. A thorough examination of the difficulties in conquering financial obstacles and the complicated effects of intervention programs on marginalized groups may be achieved through case studies.

14.7.2 BEST PRACTICES FOR MEASURING OUTCOMES

To assess the success of educational programs, interventions, or initiatives aiming at enhancing FL and behavior, financial management outcomes must be measured. It is essential to use best practices that take into account modifications in knowledge, attitudes, and behaviors in order to guarantee correct evaluation.

1. **Define Clear Objectives:** To start, the financial education program's SMART (specific, measurable, attainable, relevant, and time-bound) objectives should be established. The intended modifications in knowledge, attitudes, and behaviors should be described in these objectives.
2. **Make Use of Several Assessment Techniques:** To obtain a thorough grasp of the results, combine quantitative and qualitative assessment techniques. Pre- and post-tests, questionnaires, focus groups, interviews, behavioral monitoring, and observation are a few examples of these.
3. **Longitudinal Studies:** Examine longitudinal research to monitor changes in attitudes, behaviors, and financial knowledge over a prolonged length of time. Extended monitoring facilitates the evaluation of the durability of intervention outcomes and pinpoints any enduring consequences.
4. **Use of Control Groups:** When comparing the results of individuals who receive the intervention versus those who do not, use control groups. This helps assess the intervention's efficacy by adjusting for outside variables that might affect results.

5. **Data Analysis:** To find noteworthy changes in knowledge, attitudes, and behaviors, analyze gathered data using the proper statistical techniques. Examine the scores from before and after the intervention to precisely determine the program's impact.
6. **Iteration and Feedback:** To gauge the success and satisfaction of the program, get input from stakeholders, teachers, and participants. Utilize these suggestions to improve the program for the future.
7. **Surveys and Questionnaires:** Create surveys and questionnaires for the express purpose of assessing how people's financial knowledge, attitudes, and behaviors have changed. To guarantee validity and reliability, use scales and questions that have been verified. Ask about real financial behaviors, financial aspirations, FL, and confidence in handling funds.
8. **Interviews and Focus Groups:** Hold focus groups or interviews to learn more in-depth details about the opinions, attitudes, and experiences of participants on money management. These qualitative approaches enable the investigation of subtleties not picked up by purely quantitative measurements and offer insightful context.
9. **Observational Studies:** Utilize observational research to see participants' financial actions up close and in real-world situations. With the use of this approach, objective data on real financial activities are provided, providing insights that might not match self-reported behaviour (Fernandes, 2014).

14.7.3 STRATEGIES FOR SCALING UP FINANCIAL INCLUSION

Scaling up effective financial education projects and incorporating them into larger social and economic development activities necessitates a diversified strategy that tackles both structural barriers and the different demands of target communities. Here are a few techniques for doing this:

1. **Partnerships and Collaboration:** Effective financial education efforts need collaboration among government agencies, financial institutions, non-governmental organizations (NGOs), and community-based organizations. By combining resources,

skills, and networks, stakeholders may reach a larger audience and capitalize on each other's strengths. For example, in India, the National Centre for Financial Education works with banks, insurance firms, and regulators to develop FL programs across the country (Lok Sabha, 2019).

2. **Personalized Strategies for Various Audiences:** Initiatives should take a customized approach as various demographic groups have distinct demands when it comes to learning and FL. Programs for young people, for example, can concentrate on fundamental financial ideas like saving and budgeting, while those for business owners might offer instruction on getting funding and managing money well (Atkinson and Messy, 2012).
3. **Use of Technology:** Financial education programs may be made much more scalable and successful by utilizing technology. Interactive technologies, mobile applications, and online platforms may reach underserved or distant communities and offer individualized learning experiences. For example, the M-Pesa mobile money service in Kenya has been used to offer financial education messages to users in addition to facilitating financial transactions (Suri and Jack, 2016).
4. **Integration into Formal Education Systems:** Including financial education in the curriculum for formal education guarantees a broad and long-lasting effect that starts early for kids and teenagers. Financial decision-making, consumer rights, and money management are among the topics included in the financial education curricula of nations like the Netherlands and Australia (OECD, 2020).
5. **Evaluation and Continuous Improvement:** To determine the effectiveness of financial education programs and pinpoint areas in need of development, it is important to conduct regular evaluations and provide feedback. It is possible to assess success and provide guidance for future programming modifications by keeping an eye on indicators including financial knowledge, behavior changes, and economic effects (Lusardi and Mitchell, 2011).

6. **Policy Support and Advocacy:** Through policy support and advocacy, governments may significantly contribute to the development of a climate that is favorable to financial education. Initiatives may be made much more successful and widely distributed by enacting laws requiring financial education in schools, rewarding employer-sponsored programs, or regulating financial goods to guarantee transparency and consumer protection (OECD/INFE, 2020).

A thorough and cooperative strategy is needed to scale up effective financial education programs and include them into larger social and economic development projects. Through the use of partnerships, customization of strategies, adoption of technology, integration into formal education systems, impact evaluation, and policy advocacy, stakeholders may optimize the effects of financial education on the empowerment of individuals and the advancement of socio-economic development at large.

14.8 RECOMMENDATIONS TO ENHANCE FINANCIAL LITERACY AMONG VULNERABLE AND MARGINALISED POPULATIONS

14.8.1 FOR POLICYMAKERS

In order to improve FL within marginalized and vulnerable communities, policymakers have to develop specialized educational initiatives that are made available via community centers, libraries, and internet resources. These courses have to concentrate on understanding credit, budgeting, saving, and fundamental financial principles. Furthermore, workshops and individual counseling sessions can be facilitated through collaborations with nearby NGOs and financial institutions. It is essential that FL be included in school curricula from a young age. In order to promote inclusion, policymakers should also give priority to multilingual resources that address language hurdles and culturally sensitive methods. Financial rewards, including tax exemptions for completing courses on FL or matching savings plans, might encourage involvement. Furthermore, in order to stop exploitation, laws requiring precise and open disclosures about financial products are essential. Finally, to guarantee efficacy and relevance, these programs must be continuously assessed and modified in response to input from the target groups.

14.8.2 FOR PRACTITIONERS

It is recommended that practitioners utilize accessible and culturally appropriate techniques to improve FL among marginalized and vulnerable communities. Create multilingual instructional materials and community-based seminars that emphasize fundamental financial concepts including credit knowledge, saving, and budgeting. Work together with local leaders and organizations to assist those who are most in need. Provide individualized advice and counseling to address each person's unique financial difficulties. Advocate for laws that advance financial inclusion, such as those that provide consumer safeguards and accessible banking services. Make use of mobile applications and technological platforms to increase accessibility. Content should be specifically customized to meet the issues that various demographic groups—such as low-income families or immigrants—face. Programs should be regularly reviewed and modified in response to community input and changing requirements. By emphasizing participation and inclusion, practitioners may enable marginalized groups to make informed decisions and improve their financial well-being.

14.8.3 FOR STAKEHOLDERS

Stakeholders should give priority to easily accessible and culturally appropriate educational efforts in order to improve FL among marginalized and disadvantaged communities. Working with neighborhood organizations to provide webinars, seminars, and materials catered to the unique requirements and languages of these communities might be one way to do this. Programs for FL should include issues like predatory lending and financial scams in addition to fundamentals like budgeting, saving, and credit awareness. Stakeholders should also support laws that advance economic inclusion, such as those that provide affordable banking services and enable underprivileged areas' entrepreneurs to apply for microloans. Accessible financial education may also be achieved through the use of technology, including online resources and mobile applications. In conclusion, continuous assessment and feedback systems are essential to guarantee that these programs successfully address the particular difficulties encountered by marginalized communities.

14.9 FUTURE RESEARCH DIRECTIONS

Future studies on financial inclusion and literacy may concentrate on a number of important topics. Some key areas are given below:

- Investigating how well cutting-edge teaching strategies, such as gamification and digital platforms, may improve financial behavior and understanding in a range of demographics.
- To properly customize treatments, one must comprehend the interconnectedness of cultural, social, and demographic elements that shape financial attitudes and behaviors.
- Examining how new financial technologies—such as decentralized finance (DeFi) and blockchain—affect marginalized populations' accessibility and comprehension.
- Evaluating the contribution of regulatory frameworks and policy measures to financial inclusion and inequality reduction.
- Combining psychology and behavioral economics to provide treatments and nudges that promote improved financial decision-making.

In order to advance agendas for FL and inclusion in the next years, multidisciplinary research activities combining ideas from economics, psychology, technology, and policy will be critically important.

14.9.1 RECENT TRENDS IN FINANCIAL LITERACY AND INCLUSION

A number of new trends that are a reflection of both technology improvements and shifting societal requirements have emerged in the field of FL and inclusion in recent years.

First off, there's a rising focus on individualized financial education, which uses technology to provide people with advice that is specific to their own financial circumstances and objectives. This tendency acknowledges that different demands might not be adequately met by one-size-fits-all solutions.

Second, the significance of behavioral economics in the development of FL initiatives is becoming more widely acknowledged. It is possible to create interventions that are more successful in encouraging sound financial practices by having a better understanding of the biases and heuristics that people use when making financial decisions.

Thirdly, more people are having access to financial services thanks to the emergence of fintech advances, especially in underprivileged areas. By offering easy and reasonably priced services to those who have historically been shut out of the official financial system, mobile banking, digital payment platforms, and blockchain technologies are contributing to a greater level of financial inclusion.

Finally, there's a rising push to include FL in more comprehensive curricula, beginning in elementary school. Early financial education makes people more capable of navigating complicated financial environments and making wise decisions throughout their lives.

14.10 CONCLUSION

This chapter delves into ways to empower marginalized and vulnerable people in the direction of financial inclusion. It emphasizes how crucial it is to use specialized strategies to address the particular difficulties these groups have, such as restricted access to financial and educational resources. Initiatives for digital FL, community-based programs, and collaborations with nearby organizations are examples of successful tactics. The chapter places a strong emphasis on the necessity of linguistic accessibility and culturally appropriate materials to guarantee understanding and participation. Furthermore, for sustainable impact, government, non-governmental organizations, and financial institutions must work together. The chapter makes an argument for increased economic empowerment and resilience within these communities by boosting FL among vulnerable populations, ultimately supporting larger financial inclusion goals.

Strengthening economically unstable and marginalized communities via FL education is essential to promoting social justice, resilience, and economic stability. People who possess FL are better able to manage their finances, make wise financial decisions, and deal with complicated financial systems. Such education is a strategy for inclusion and empowerment for marginalized populations who face structural constraints.

Education on FL can help us escape the cycle of poverty and reliance. People are less susceptible to financial shocks and exploitation since it makes it possible for them to accumulate assets, save for the future, and obtain credit at reasonable interest rates. Additionally, FL encourages economic engagement and entrepreneurship, opening doors to employment and self-sufficiency. By addressing differences in access to financial services and opportunities, it advances social justice. FL creates an even playing field, enabling marginalized people to speak up against economic injustices, fight for their rights, and take an active role in the economy.

KEYWORDS

- **financial education programs**
- **financial inclusion**
- **financial institutions**
- **financial literacy**
- **financial literacy programs**
- **financial principles**
- **marginalized population**
- **policymakers**
- **stakeholders**
- **strategies**

REFERENCES

Agarwal, S., & Mazumder, B. (2021). Gender differences in financial literacy among youth: Role of household financial behavior and individual socio-economic factors. *Journal of Behavioral and Experimental Economics*, *92*, 101694.

Agarwal, S., Driscoll, J. C., Gabaix, X., & Laibson, D. (2015). The age of reason: Financial decisions over the lifecycle. *Brookings Papers on Economic Activity*, *2015*(1), 51–117.

Aiyar, S., & Puy, D. (2019). Financial inclusion and inequality: A global perspective. *World Development*, *120*, 164–175.

Alliance for Financial Inclusion. (2020). *About AFI*. https://www.afi-global.org/about-afi (accessed on 7th July 2025).

Andriani, L., & Distaso, A. (2020). Financial inclusion, inequality, and poverty: Evidence from Indonesia. *Social Indicators Research*, *150*(3), 857–876.

Atkinson, A., & Messy, F. (2012). Assessing financial literacy in 65 countries: An OECD pilot exercise. *OECD Working Papers on Finance, Insurance and Private Pensions*, No. 15. OECD Publishing.

Bernheim, B. D., Garrett, D. M., & Maki, D. M. (2001). Education and saving: The long-term effects of high school financial curriculum mandates. *Journal of Public Economics*, *80*(3), 435–465.

Bernheim, B. D., Garrett, D. M., & Maki, D. M. (2022). Education and economic well-being. In *Handbook of the Economics of Education* (pp. 1–79). Elsevier.

Carpena, F., Cole, S., Shapiro, J., & Zia, B. (2011). The ABCs of financial education: Experimental evidence on attitudes, behavior, and cognitive biases. *National Bureau of Economic Research*.

Carpena, F., Cole, S., Shapiro, J., & Zia, B. (2011). Unpacking the causal chain of financial literacy. *The World Bank Research Observer*, *27*(1), 1–28.

Center for Financial Services Innovation (CFSI). (n.d.). *About CFSI*. https://www.finhealthnetwork.org/about-cfsi/ (accessed on 7th July 2025).

Center on Budget and Policy Priorities. (2020). *Expanding the Earned Income Tax Credit (EITC) Would Provide Important Benefits to Workers of Color*. https://www.cbpp.org/research/federal-tax/expanding-the-earned-income-tax-credit-eitc-would-provide-important-benefits-to (accessed on 7th July 2025).

Chen, X., Zhang, Y., & Wang, L. (2021). Financial literacy among low-income households: A case study in urban areas. *Journal of Financial Education*, *47*(2), 25–42.

Coalition for Economic Empowerment. (n.d.). Bank On. https://cfed.org/programs/bank_on/ (accessed on 7th July 2025).

Cole, S., & Shastry, G. K. (2009). Smart money: The effect of education, cognitive ability, and financial literacy on financial market participation. *Harvard Business School Working Paper*, (09-071).

Cole, S., & Shastry, G. K. (2018). Smart money: The effect of education, cognitive ability, and financial literacy on financial market participation. *Journal of Financial Economics*, *128*(3), 585–616.

Collins, J. M. (2012). Financial education and counseling—Still holding promise. *Journal of Consumer Affairs*, *46*(3), 427–449.

Collins, J. M. (2018). Intersectionality and financial literacy: How race, gender, and class shape financial knowledge. *Review of Black Political Economy*, *45*(2), 139–157.

Collins, J. M. (2019). Designing financial literacy education for the underserved. *Financial Planning Review*, *2*(1), e1014.

Collins, J. M., & O'Rourke, C. M. (2020). Financial literacy among vulnerable populations: Implications for financial education and policy. *Journal of Financial Counseling and Planning*, *31*(2), 285–301.

Collins, J. M., O'Rourke, C. M., & Brown, M. B. (2013). Financial education and counseling—Still holding promise. *Journal of Consumer Affairs*, *47*(1), 3–27.

Cude, B. J., & Lawrence, F. C. (2015). Financial literacy and its determinants among adults in Malaysia. *Journal of Financial Counselling and Planning*, *26*(1), 3–17.

Demirguc-Kunt, A., Klapper, L., Singer, D., & Van Oudheusden, P. (2015). The Global Findex Database 2014: Measuring financial inclusion around the world. *World Bank Policy Research Working Paper*, (7255).

Demirgüç-Kunt, A., Klapper, L., Singer, D., & Van Oudheusden, P. (2018). *The Global Findex Database 2017: Measuring Financial Inclusion and The Fintech Revolution*. The World Bank.

Dupas, P., & Robinson, J. (2013). Savings constraints and microenterprise development: Evidence from a field experiment in Kenya. *American Economic Journal: Applied Economics*, *5*(1), 163–192.

Dwivedi, Y. K., Hughes, L., & Coombs, C. (2019). Impact of digital technologies on human well-being. *Government Information Quarterly*, *36*(4), 709–713.

Elliott, W., & Song, H. (2020). Racial disparities in access to financial services: Exploring the role of creditors' neighborhood-level discrimination. *Journal of Family and Economic Issues*, *41*(4), 698–713.

Federal Deposit Insurance Corporation. (2021). *FDIC National Survey of Unbanked and Underbanked Households*. https://www.fdic.gov/householdsurvey/ (accessed on 7th July 2025).

Fernandes, D., Lynch, J. G., & Netemeyer, R. G. (2014). Financial literacy, financial education, and downstream financial behaviors. *Management Science*, *60*(8), 1861–1883.

Fraillon, J., Ainley, J., Schulz, W., Friedman, T., & Gebhardt, E. (2014). *Preparing for life in a digital age: The IEA International Computer and Information Literacy Study international report*. Springer International Publishing.

Garman, E. T., & Forgue, R. E. (2018). *Personal Finance*. Cengage Learning.

Global Financial Literacy Excellence Center. (2020). *Women's Financial Literacy: An Overview*. https://gflec.org/wp-content/uploads/2020/05/Womens-Financial-Literacy-An-Overview.pdf (accessed on 7th July 2025).

Government of India. (n.d.). *Pradhan Mantri Jan Dhan Yojana*. https://pmjdy.gov.in/ (accessed on 7th July 2025).

Goyal, A., & Agarwal, N. (2016). Role of technology in financial inclusion. *International Journal of Engineering Technology Science and Research*, *3*(7), 35–39.

Hargittai, E. (2002). Second-level digital divide: Differences in people's online skills. *First Monday*, *7*(4). https://doi.org/10.5210/fm.v7i4.942 (accessed on 7th July 2025).

Hastings, J. S., Madrian, B. C., & Skimmyhorn, W. L. (2013). Financial literacy, financial education, and economic outcomes. *Annual Review of Economics*, *5*(1), 347–373.

Kapoor, J. R., Dlabay, L. R., & Hughes, R. J. (2017). *Personal Finance*. McGraw-Hill Education.

Khan, S. R. (2019). Access to financial services: The role of microfinance in supporting the financial inclusion of vulnerable communities. *International Journal of Community Well-Being*, *2*(1), 45–57.

Klapper, L., Lusardi, A., & Van Oudheusden, P. (2016). Financial literacy around the world: Insights from the Standard & Poor's Ratings Services Global Financial Literacy Survey. *World Bank Policy Research Working Paper*, (6107).

Laar, A., Tetteh, E. K., & Aryeetey, E. (2017). The impact of mobile telephony on inclusive human development: A global analysis of mobile banking and financial inclusion. *Information Technology for Development*, *23*(4), 659–678.

Lane, T. S. (2015). Faith-based organizations: Effective vehicles for financial literacy education. *Journal of Financial Service Professionals*, *69*(2), 59–64.

Local Initiatives Support Corporation. (n.d.). *Financial Opportunity Centers*. https://www.lisc.org/our-initiatives/economic-opportunity/financial-opportunity-centers/ (accessed on 7th July 2025).

Lok Sabha Secretariat. (2019). *Report of the Committee on Financial Inclusion. Sixteenth Lok Sabha*. http://164.100.47.193/lsscommittee/Finance/16_Finance_27.pdf (accessed on 7th July 2025).

Lusardi, A., & Mitchell, O. S. (2011). Financial literacy and planning: Implications for retirement wellbeing. In *Annals of Business Education*, *4*(1), 247–283.

Lusardi, A., & Mitchell, O. S. (2014). The economic importance of financial literacy: Theory and evidence. *Journal of Economic Literature*, *52*(1), 5–44.

Lusardi, A., & Mitchell, O. S. (2018). Financial literacy and planning: Implications for retirement wellbeing. In *Handbook of the Economics of Population Aging* (pp. 1–57). Elsevier.

Mandell, L., & Klein, L. S. (2009). The impact of financial literacy education on subsequent financial behavior. *Journal of Financial Counseling and Planning*, *20*(1), 15–24.

McKinney, J. A. (2017). Budgeting for emergencies: Knowing where the money goes. *The Journal of Consumer Affairs*, *51*(2), 235–263.

Mullainathan, S., & Shafir, E. (2013). *Scarcity: Why Having Too Little Means So Much*. Macmillan.

Munir, F. (2021). Gender inequality in financial inclusion: A review of literature. *Journal of Financial Counselling and Planning*, *32*(1), 50–64.

MyPath. (n.d.). About MyPath. https://www.mypathus.org/about/ (accessed on 7th July 2025).

National Council of Applied Economic Research. (2019). *India Financial Capability Survey 2019*. https://www.ncaer.org/publication_details.php?pID=373 (accessed on 7th July 2025).

OECD. (2020). *PISA 2018 Results (Volume VI): Are Students Ready to Thrive in An Interconnected World?* PISA, OECD Publishing, Paris. https://doi.org/10.1787/14f5b1bb-en (accessed on 7th July 2025).

OECD/INFE. (2018). *OECD/INFE Toolkit for Measuring Financial Literacy and Financial Inclusion*. OECD Publishing, Paris. https://doi.org/10.1787/9789264283325-en (accessed on 7th July 2025).

OECD/INFE. (2020). *OECD/INFE Toolkit for Measuring Financial Literacy and Financial Inclusion: Guidance, Core Questionnaire and Suggested Questions*. OECD Publishing, Paris. https://doi.org/10.1787/b2dc7f89-en (accessed on 7th July 2025).

Sherraden, M. S., Huang, J., & Zou, L. (2015). Financial capability in China: Survey results from the China Household Finance Survey. *Journal of Beijing Normal University (Social Science Edition)*, *5*(1), 7–18.

Smith, A., & Jones, B. (2020). Financial literacy challenges among marginalized communities: Insights from immigrant and refugee populations. *Journal of Financial Counseling and Planning*, *31*(1), 55–68.

Standard & Poor's Global Financial Literacy Survey. (2019). https://www.worldbank.org/en/news/press-release/2019/11/26/world-bank-and-standard-poors-release-first-ever-global-financial-literacy-survey (accessed on 7th July 2025).

Suri, T., & Jack, W. (2016). The long-run poverty and gender impacts of mobile money. *Science*, *354*(6317), 1288–1292.

The Financial Clinic. (n.d.). *Change Machine*. https://thefinancialclinic.org/changemachine/ (accessed on 7th July 2025).

Visa Inc. (n.d.). *Financial Football*. https://usa.visa.com/partner-with-us/financial-literacy/financial-football.html (accessed on 7th July 2025).

World Bank. (2019). *The Global Findex Database 2017: Measuring Financial Inclusion and the Fintech Revolution*. World Bank Publications.

World Bank. (2021). *The Global Findex Database*. https://globalfindex.worldbank.org/ (accessed on 7th July 2025).

Index

B

C

D

F

G

H

I

J

K

L

M